Machine Learning with Spark

Second Edition

Develop intelligent machine learning systems with Spark 2.x

Rajdeep Dua
Manpreet Singh Ghotra
Nick Pentreath

BIRMINGHAM - MUMBAI

Machine Learning with Spark
Second Edition

First published: February 2015
Second edition: April 2017

Production reference: 1270417

Published by Packt Publishing Ltd.
Livery Place
35 Livery Street
Birmingham
B3 2PB, UK.
ISBN 978-1-78588-993-6

www.packtpub.com

Credits

About the Authors

Rajdeep Dua has over 16 years of experience in the Cloud and Big Data space. He worked in the advocacy team for Google's big data tools, BigQuery. He worked on the Greenplum big data platform at VMware in the developer evangelist team. He also worked closely with a team on porting Spark to run on VMware's public and private cloud as a feature set. He has taught Spark and Big Data at some of the most prestigious tech schools in India: IIIT Hyderabad, ISB, IIIT Delhi, and College of Engineering Pune.

Currently, he leads the developer relations team at Salesforce India. He also works with the data pipeline team at Salesforce, which uses Hadoop and Spark to expose big data processing tools for developers.

He has published Big Data and Spark tutorials at `http://www.clouddatalab.com`. He has also presented BigQuery and Google App Engine at the W3C conference in Hyderabad (`http://wwwconference.org/proceedings/www2011/schedule/www2011_Program.pdf`). He led the developer relations teams at Google, VMware, and Microsoft, and he has spoken at hundreds of other conferences on the cloud. Some of the other references to his work can be seen at `http://yourstory.com/2012/06/vmware-hires-rajdeep-dua-to-lead-the-developer-relations-in-india/` and `http://dl.acm.org/citation.cfm?id=2624641`.

His contributions to the open source community are related to Docker, Kubernetes, Android, OpenStack, and cloudfoundry.

You can connect with him on LinkedIn at `https://www.linkedin.com/in/rajdeepd`.

Manpreet Singh Ghotra has more than 12 years of experience in software development for both enterprise and big data software. He is currently working on developing a machine learning platform using Apache Spark at Salesforce. He has worked on a sentiment analyzer using the Apache stack and machine learning.

He was part of the machine learning group at one of the largest online retailers in the world, working on transit time calculations using Apache Mahout and the R Recommendation system using Apache Mahout.

With a master's and postgraduate degree in machine learning, he has contributed to and worked for the machine learning community.

His GitHub profile is `https://github.com/badlogicmanpreet` and you can find him on LinkedIn at `https://in.linkedin.com/in/msghotra`.

Nick Pentreath has a background in financial markets, machine learning, and software development. He has worked at Goldman Sachs Group, Inc., as a research scientist at the online ad targeting start-up, Cognitive Match Limited, London, and led the data science and analytics team at Mxit, Africa's largest social network.
He is a cofounder of Graphflow, a big data and machine learning company focused on user-centric recommendations and customer intelligence. He is passionate about combining commercial focus with machine learning and cutting-edge technology to build intelligent systems that learn from data to add value to the bottom line.
Nick is a member of the Apache Spark Project Management Committee.

About the Reviewer

Brian O'Neill is the principal architect at Monetate, Inc. Monetate's personalization platform leverages Spark and machine learning algorithms to process millions of events per second, leveraging real-time context and analytics to create personalized brand experiences at scale. Brian is a perennial Datastax Cassandra MVP and has also won InfoWorld's Technology Leadership award. Previously, he was CTO for Health Market Science (HMS), now a LexisNexis company. He is a graduate of Brown University and holds patents in artificial intelligence and data management.

Prior to this publication, Brian authored a book on distributed computing, *Storm Blueprints: Patterns for Distributed Real-time Computation,* and contributed to *Learning Cassandra for Administrators.*

All the thanks in the world to my wife, Lisa, and my sons, Collin and Owen, for their understanding, patience, and support. They know all my shortcomings and love me anyway. Together always and forever, I love you more than you know and more than I will ever be able to express.

www.PacktPub.com

For support files and downloads related to your book, please visit www.PacktPub.com.

Did you know that Packt offers eBook versions of every book published, with PDF and ePub files available? You can upgrade to the eBook version at www.PacktPub.com and as a print book customer, you are entitled to a discount on the eBook copy. Get in touch with us at service@packtpub.com for more details.

At www.PacktPub.com, you can also read a collection of free technical articles, sign up for a range of free newsletters and receive exclusive discounts and offers on Packt books and eBooks.

https://www.packtpub.com/mapt

Get the most in-demand software skills with Mapt. Mapt gives you full access to all Packt books and video courses, as well as industry-leading tools to help you plan your personal development and advance your career.

Why subscribe?

- Fully searchable across every book published by Packt
- Copy and paste, print, and bookmark content
- On demand and accessible via a web browser

Customer Feedback

Thanks for purchasing this Packt book. At Packt, quality is at the heart of our editorial process. To help us improve, please leave us an honest review on this book's Amazon page at `https://goo.gl/5LgUpI`.

If you'd like to join our team of regular reviewers, you can e-mail us at `customerreviews@packtpub.com`. We award our regular reviewers with free eBooks and videos in exchange for their valuable feedback. Help us be relentless in improving our products!

Table of Contents

Preface   1

Chapter 1: Getting Up and Running with Spark   9

    Installing and setting up Spark locally   11

    Spark clusters   12

    The Spark programming model   13

        SparkContext and SparkConf   14

        SparkSession   15

        The Spark shell   15

        Resilient Distributed Datasets   18

            Creating RDDs   19

            Spark operations   19

            Caching RDDs   22

        Broadcast variables and accumulators   23

    SchemaRDD   25

    Spark data frame   25

    The first step to a Spark program in Scala   26

    The first step to a Spark program in Java   29

    The first step to a Spark program in Python   33

    The first step to a Spark program in R   35

        SparkR DataFrames   35

    Getting Spark running on Amazon EC2   37

        Launching an EC2 Spark cluster   38

    Configuring and running Spark on Amazon Elastic Map Reduce   43

    UI in Spark   47

    Supported machine learning algorithms by Spark   49

    Benefits of using Spark ML as compared to existing libraries   55

    Spark Cluster on Google Compute Engine - DataProc   57

        Hadoop and Spark Versions   57

        Creating a Cluster   58

        Submitting a Job   61

    Summary   64

Chapter 2: Math for Machine Learning   65

    Linear algebra   67

        Setting up the Scala environment in Intellij   67

Setting up the Scala environment on the Command Line   69
Fields   69
    Real numbers   70
    Complex numbers   70
    Vectors   71
    Vector spaces   71
    Vector types   72
    Vectors in Breeze   72
    Vectors in Spark   73
    Vector operations   74
    Hyperplanes   78
    Vectors in machine learning   78
Matrix   79
    Types of matrices   79
    Matrix in Spark   80
    Distributed matrix in Spark   82
    Matrix operations   84
    Determinant   87
    Eigenvalues and eigenvectors   87
    Singular value decomposition   88
    Matrices in machine learning   90
Functions   91
    Function types   92
    Functional composition   94
    Hypothesis   95
Gradient descent   96
Prior, likelihood, and posterior   97
Calculus   98
    Differential calculus   98
    Lagranges multipliers   99
Plotting   100
Summary   102
Chapter 3: Designing a Machine Learning System   103
What is Machine Learning?   104
Introducing MovieStream   105
Business use cases for a machine learning system   106
    Personalization   106
    Targeted marketing and customer segmentation   107
    Predictive modeling and analytics   108
Types of machine learning models   108
The components of a data-driven machine learning system   109
    Data ingestion and storage   109
    Data cleansing and transformation   110

Model training and testing loop   112
Model deployment and integration   112
Model monitoring and feedback   113
Batch versus real time   114
Data Pipeline in Apache Spark   115
An architecture for a machine learning system   116
Spark MLlib   117
Performance improvements in Spark ML over Spark MLlib   117
Comparing algorithms supported by MLlib   119
Classification   119
Clustering   120
Regression   120
MLlib supported methods and developer APIs   120
Spark Integration   122
MLlib vision   122
MLlib versions compared   123
Spark 1.6 to 2.0   123
Summary   123

Chapter 4: Obtaining, Processing, and Preparing Data with Spark   125
Accessing publicly available datasets   126
The MovieLens 100k dataset   127
Exploring and visualizing your data   129
Exploring the user dataset   131
Count by occupation   137
Movie dataset   141
Exploring the rating dataset   145
Rating count bar chart   147
Distribution of number ratings   149
Processing and transforming your data   152
Filling in bad or missing data   153
Extracting useful features from your data   155
Numerical features   156
Categorical features   156
Derived features   158
Transforming timestamps into categorical features   159
Extract time of Day   159
Extract time of day   160
Text features   161
Simple text feature extraction   162
Sparse Vectors from Titles   165

Normalizing features	167
Using ML for feature normalization	168
Using packages for feature extraction	169
TFID	169
IDF	170
Word2Vector	171
Skip-gram model	171
Standard scalar	173
Summary	174
Chapter 5: Building a Recommendation Engine with Spark	**175**
Types of recommendation models	176
Content-based filtering	177
Collaborative filtering	177
Matrix factorization	179
Explicit matrix factorization	180
Implicit Matrix Factorization	183
Basic model for Matrix Factorization	184
Alternating least squares	185
Extracting the right features from your data	190
Extracting features from the MovieLens 100k dataset	190
Training the recommendation model	192
Training a model on the MovieLens 100k dataset	192
Training a model using Implicit feedback data	195
Using the recommendation model	196
ALS Model recommendations	197
User recommendations	198
Generating movie recommendations from the MovieLens 100k dataset	199
Inspecting the recommendations	200
Item recommendations	202
Generating similar movies for the MovieLens 100k dataset	202
Inspecting the similar items	207
Evaluating the performance of recommendation models	208
ALS Model Evaluation	208
Mean Squared Error	210
Mean Average Precision at K	212
Using MLlib's built-in evaluation functions	217
RMSE and MSE	217
MAP	218
FP-Growth algorithm	219
FP-Growth Basic Sample	219
FP-Growth Applied to Movie Lens Data	222
Summary	224

Chapter 6: Building a Classification Model with Spark   225

Types of classification models   227
  Linear models   228
    Logistic regression   230
    Multinomial logistic regression   231
    Visualizing the StumbleUpon dataset   232
    Extracting features from the Kaggle/StumbleUpon evergreen classification dataset   233
    StumbleUponExecutor   235
    Linear support vector machines   239
  The naive Bayes model   241
  Decision trees   244
  Ensembles of trees   247
    Random Forests   247
    Gradient-Boosted Trees   249
    Multilayer perceptron classifier   251
Extracting the right features from your data   253
Training classification models   254
  Training a classification model on the Kaggle/StumbleUpon evergreen classification dataset   254
Using classification models   256
  Generating predictions for the Kaggle/StumbleUpon evergreen classification dataset   256
  Evaluating the performance of classification models   257
  Accuracy and prediction error   257
  Precision and recall   259
  ROC curve and AUC   260
Improving model performance and tuning parameters   263
  Feature standardization   263
Additional features   267
  Using the correct form of data   270
  Tuning model parameters   271
    Linear models   272
      Iterations   273
      Step size   274
      Regularization   274
    Decision trees   276
      Tuning tree depth and impurity   277
    The naive Bayes model   278
  Cross-validation   279
Summary   282

Chapter 7: Building a Regression Model with Spark   283

Types of regression models	284
Least squares regression	285
Decision trees for regression	286
Evaluating the performance of regression models	287
Mean Squared Error and Root Mean Squared Error	287
Mean Absolute Error	288
Root Mean Squared Log Error	288
The R-squared coefficient	289
Extracting the right features from your data	289
Extracting features from the bike sharing dataset	289
Training and using regression models	294
BikeSharingExecutor	294
Training a regression model on the bike sharing dataset	296
Linear regression	296
Generalized linear regression	298
Decision tree regression	302
Ensembles of trees	306
Random forest regression	306
Gradient boosted tree regression	309
Improving model performance and tuning parameters	313
Transforming the target variable	313
Impact of training on log-transformed targets	317
Tuning model parameters	320
Creating training and testing sets to evaluate parameters	321
Splitting data for Decision tree	321
The impact of parameter settings for linear models	321
Iterations	322
Step size	323
L2 regularization	325
L1 regularization	325
Intercept	326
The impact of parameter settings for the decision tree	328
Tree depth	329
Maximum bins	330
The impact of parameter settings for the Gradient Boosted Trees	332
Iterations	332
MaxBins	333
Summary	335
Chapter 8: Building a Clustering Model with Spark	337
Types of clustering models	338
k-means clustering	338
Initialization methods	344
Mixture models	345

Hierarchical clustering	345
Extracting the right features from your data	346
Extracting features from the MovieLens dataset	346
K-means - training a clustering model	350
Training a clustering model on the MovieLens dataset	351
K-means - interpreting cluster predictions on the MovieLens dataset	353
Interpreting the movie clusters	353
Interpreting the movie clusters	355
K-means - evaluating the performance of clustering models	359
Internal evaluation metrics	359
External evaluation metrics	360
Computing performance metrics on the MovieLens dataset	360
Effect of iterations on WSSSE	361
Bisecting KMeans	364
Bisecting K-means - training a clustering model	365
WSSSE and iterations	372
Gaussian Mixture Model	375
Clustering using GMM	376
Plotting the user and item data with GMM clustering	378
GMM - effect of iterations on cluster boundaries	379
Summary	381
Chapter 9: Dimensionality Reduction with Spark	383
Types of dimensionality reduction	384
Principal components analysis	384
Singular value decomposition	385
Relationship with matrix factorization	386
Clustering as dimensionality reduction	386
Extracting the right features from your data	387
Extracting features from the LFW dataset	387
Exploring the face data	388
Visualizing the face data	390
Extracting facial images as vectors	391
Loading images	392
Converting to grayscale and resizing the images	392
Extracting feature vectors	395
Normalization	396
Training a dimensionality reduction model	398
Running PCA on the LFW dataset	398
Visualizing the Eigenfaces	399
Interpreting the Eigenfaces	401
Using a dimensionality reduction model	402

Projecting data using PCA on the LFW dataset	402
The relationship between PCA and SVD	403
Evaluating dimensionality reduction models	405
Evaluating k for SVD on the LFW dataset	406
Singular values	406
Summary	409
Chapter 10: Advanced Text Processing with Spark	411
What's so special about text data?	411
Extracting the right features from your data	412
Term weighting schemes	412
Feature hashing	413
Extracting the tf-idf features from the 20 Newsgroups dataset	415
Exploring the 20 Newsgroups data	417
Applying basic tokenization	419
Improving our tokenization	420
Removing stop words	422
Excluding terms based on frequency	425
A note about stemming	427
Feature Hashing	428
Building a tf-idf model	428
Analyzing the tf-idf weightings	431
Using a tf-idf model	432
Document similarity with the 20 Newsgroups dataset and tf-idf features	432
Training a text classifier on the 20 Newsgroups dataset using tf-idf	435
Evaluating the impact of text processing	438
Comparing raw features with processed tf-idf features on the 20 Newsgroups dataset	438
Text classification with Spark 2.0	438
Word2Vec models	441
Word2Vec with Spark MLlib on the 20 Newsgroups dataset	442
Word2Vec with Spark ML on the 20 Newsgroups dataset	443
Summary	445
Chapter 11: Real-Time Machine Learning with Spark Streaming	447
Online learning	448
Stream processing	449
An introduction to Spark Streaming	449
Input sources	450
Transformations	450
Keeping track of state	451
General transformations	451
Actions	452

Window operators	452
Caching and fault tolerance with Spark Streaming	453
Creating a basic streaming application	454
The producer application	455
Creating a basic streaming application	458
Streaming analytics	461
Stateful streaming	463
Online learning with Spark Streaming	**465**
Streaming regression	465
A simple streaming regression program	466
Creating a streaming data producer	467
Creating a streaming regression model	469
Streaming K-means	472
Online model evaluation	**472**
Comparing model performance with Spark Streaming	473
Structured Streaming	**477**
Summary	**477**
Chapter 12: Pipeline APIs for Spark ML	**479**
Introduction to pipelines	**479**
DataFrames	480
Pipeline components	480
Transformers	480
Estimators	480
How pipelines work	**483**
Machine learning pipeline with an example	**488**
StumbleUponExecutor	490
Summary	**500**
Index	**501**

Preface

In recent years, the volume of data being collected, stored, and analyzed has exploded, in particular in relation to activity on the Web and mobile devices, as well as data from the physical world collected via sensor networks. While large-scale data storage, processing, analysis, and modeling were previously the domain of the largest institutions, such as Google, Yahoo!, Facebook, Twitter, and Salesforce, increasingly, many organizations are being faced with the challenge of how to handle a massive amount of data.

When faced with this quantity of data and the common requirement to utilize it in real time, human-powered systems quickly become infeasible. This has led to a rise in so-called big data and machine learning systems that learn from this data to make automated decisions.

In answer to the challenge of dealing with ever larger-scale data without any prohibitive cost, new open source technologies emerged at companies such as Google, Yahoo!, Amazon, and Facebook, which aimed at making it easier to handle massive data volumes by distributing data storage and computation across a cluster of computers.

The most widespread of these is Apache Hadoop, which made it significantly easier and cheaper to both store large amounts of data (via the Hadoop Distributed File System, or HDFS) and run computations on this data (via Hadoop MapReduce, a framework to perform computation tasks in parallel across many nodes in a computer cluster).

However, MapReduce has some important shortcomings, including high overheads to launch each job and reliance on storing intermediate data and results of the computation to disk, both of which make Hadoop relatively ill-suited for use cases of an iterative or low-latency nature. Apache Spark is a new framework for distributed computing that is designed from the ground up to be optimized for low-latency tasks and to store intermediate data and results in memory, thus addressing some of the major drawbacks of the Hadoop framework. Spark provides a clean, functional, and easy-to-understand API to write applications, and is fully compatible with the Hadoop ecosystem.

Furthermore, Spark provides native APIs in Scala, Java, Python, and R. The Scala and Python APIs allow all the benefits of the Scala or Python language, respectively, to be used directly in Spark applications, including using the relevant interpreter for real-time, interactive exploration. Spark itself now provides a toolkit (Spark MLlib in 1.6 and Spark ML in 2.0) of distributed machine learning and data mining models that is under heavy development and already contains high-quality, scalable, and efficient algorithms for many common machine learning tasks, some of which we will delve into in this book.

Applying machine learning techniques to massive datasets is challenging, primarily because most well-known machine learning algorithms are not designed for parallel architectures. In many cases, designing such algorithms is not an easy task. The nature of machine learning models is generally iterative, hence the strong appeal of Spark for this use case. While there are many competing frameworks for parallel computing, Spark is one of the few that combines speed, scalability, in-memory processing, and fault tolerance with ease of programming and a flexible, expressive, and powerful API design.

Throughout this book, we will focus on real-world applications of machine learning technology. While we may briefly delve into some theoretical aspects of machine learning algorithms and required maths for machine learning, the book will generally take a practical, applied approach with a focus on using examples and code to illustrate how to effectively use the features of Spark and MLlib, as well as other well-known and freely available packages for machine learning and data analysis, to create a useful machine learning system.

What this book covers

Chapter 1, *Getting Up and Running with Spark*, shows how to install and set up a local development environment for the Spark framework, as well as how to create a Spark cluster in the cloud using Amazon EC2. The Spark programming model and API will be introduced and a simple Spark application will be created using Scala, Java, and Python.

Chapter 2, *Math for Machine Learning*, provides a mathematical introduction to machine learning. Understanding math and many of its techniques is important to get a good hold on the inner workings of the algorithms and to get the best results.

Chapter 3, *Designing a Machine Learning System*, presents an example of a real-world use case for a machine learning system. We will design a high-level architecture for an intelligent system in Spark based on this illustrative use case.

Chapter 4, *Obtaining, Processing, and Preparing Data with Spark*, details how to go about obtaining data for use in a machine learning system, in particular from various freely and publicly available sources. We will learn how to process, clean, and transform the raw data into features that may be used in machine learning models, using available tools, libraries, and Spark's functionality.

Chapter 5, *Building a Recommendation Engine with Spark*, deals with creating a recommendation model based on the collaborative filtering approach. This model will be used to recommend items to a given user, as well as create lists of items that are similar to a given item. Standard metrics to evaluate the performance of a recommendation model will be covered here.

Chapter 6, *Building a Classification Model with Spark*, details how to create a model for binary classification, as well as how to utilize standard performance-evaluation metrics for classification tasks.

Chapter 7, *Building a Regression Model with Spark*, shows how to create a model for regression, extending the classification model created in Chapter 6, *Building a Classification Model with Spark*. Evaluation metrics for the performance of regression models will be detailed here.

Chapter 8, *Building a Clustering Model with Spark*, explores how to create a clustering model and how to use related evaluation methodologies. You will learn how to analyze and visualize the clusters that are generated.

Chapter 9, *Dimensionality Reduction with Spark*, takes us through methods to extract the underlying structure from, and reduce the dimensionality of, our data. You will learn some common dimensionality-reduction techniques and how to apply and analyze them. You will also see how to use the resulting data representation as an input to another machine learning model.

Chapter 10, *Advanced Text Processing with Spark*, introduces approaches to deal with large-scale text data, including techniques for feature extraction from text and dealing with the very high-dimensional features typical in text data.

Chapter 11, *Real-Time Machine Learning with Spark Streaming*, provides an overview of Spark Streaming and how it fits in with the online and incremental learning approaches to apply machine learning on data streams.

Chapter 12, *Pipeline APIs for Spark ML*, provides a uniform set of APIs that are built on top of Data Frames and help the user to create and tune machine learning pipelines.

What you need for this book

Throughout this book, we assume that you have some basic experience with programming in Scala or Python and have some basic knowledge of machine learning, statistics, and data analysis.

Who this book is for

This book is aimed at entry-level to intermediate data scientists, data analysts, software engineers, and practitioners involved in machine learning or data mining with an interest in large-scale machine learning approaches, but who are not necessarily familiar with Spark. You may have some experience of statistics or machine learning software (perhaps including MATLAB, scikit-learn, Mahout, R, Weka, and so on) or distributed systems (including some exposure to Hadoop).

Conventions

In this book, you will find a number of text styles that distinguish between different kinds of information. Here are some examples of these styles and an explanation of their meaning.

Code words in text, database table names, folder names, filenames, file extensions, pathnames, dummy URLs, user input, and Twitter handles are shown as follows: "Spark places user scripts to run Spark in the bin directory."

A block of code is set as follows:

```
val conf = new SparkConf()
.setAppName("Test Spark App")
.setMaster("local[4]")
val sc = new SparkContext(conf)
```

Any command-line input or output is written as follows:

```
>tar xfvz spark-2.1.0-bin-hadoop2.7.tgz
>cd spark-2.1.0-bin-hadoop2.7
```

New terms and **important words** are shown in bold. Words that you see on the screen, for example, in menus or dialog boxes, appear in the text like this: "These can be obtained from the AWS homepage by clicking **Account** | **Security Credentials** | **Access Credentials**."

Warnings or important notes appear in a box like this.

Tips and tricks appear like this.

Reader feedback

Feedback from our readers is always welcome. Let us know what you think about this book-what you liked or disliked. Reader feedback is important for us as it helps us develop titles that you will really get the most out of. To send us general feedback, simply e-mail `feedback@packtpub.com`, and mention the book's title in the subject of your message. If there is a topic that you have expertise in and you are interested in either writing or contributing to a book, see our author guide at `www.packtpub.com/authors`.

Customer support

Now that you are the proud owner of a Packt book, we have a number of things to help you to get the most from your purchase.

Downloading the example code

You can download the example code files for this book from your account at `http://www.packtpub.com`. If you purchased this book elsewhere, you can visit `http://www.packtpub.com/support` and register to have the files e-mailed directly to you.

You can download the code files by following these steps:

1. Log in or register to our website using your e-mail address and password.
2. Hover the mouse pointer on the **SUPPORT** tab at the top.
3. Click on **Code Downloads & Errata**.
4. Enter the name of the book in the **Search** box.
5. Select the book for which you're looking to download the code files.
6. Choose from the drop-down menu where you purchased this book from.
7. Click on **Code Download**.

Once the file is downloaded, please make sure that you unzip or extract the folder using the latest version of:

- WinRAR / 7-Zip for Windows
- Zipeg / iZip / UnRarX for Mac
- 7-Zip / PeaZip for Linux

The code bundle for the book is also hosted on GitHub at `https://github.com/PacktPubl ishing/Machine-Learning-with-Spark-Second-Edition`. We also have other code bundles from our rich catalog of books and videos available at `https://github.com/Packt Publishing/`. Check them out!

Downloading the color images of this book

We also provide you with a PDF file that has color images of the screenshots/diagrams used in this book. The color images will help you better understand the changes in the output. You can download this file from `https://www.packtpub.com/sites/default/files/downloads/MachineLearningwithSpark SecondEdition_ColorImages.pdf`.

Errata

Although we have taken every care to ensure the accuracy of our content, mistakes do happen. If you find a mistake in one of our books-maybe a mistake in the text or the code-we would be grateful if you could report this to us. By doing so, you can save other readers from frustration and help us improve subsequent versions of this book. If you find any errata, please report them by visiting `http://www.packtpub.com/submit-errata`, selecting your book, clicking on the **Errata Submission Form** link, and entering the details of your errata. Once your errata are verified, your submission will be accepted and the errata will be uploaded to our website or added to any list of existing errata under the Errata section of that title.

To view the previously submitted errata, go to `https://www.packtpub.com/books/conten t/support`and enter the name of the book in the search field. The required information will appear under the **Errata** section.

Piracy

Piracy of copyrighted material on the Internet is an ongoing problem across all media. At Packt, we take the protection of our copyright and licenses very seriously. If you come across any illegal copies of our works in any form on the Internet, please provide us with the location address or website name immediately so that we can pursue a remedy.

Please contact us at `copyright@packtpub.com` with a link to the suspected pirated material.

We appreciate your help in protecting our authors and our ability to bring you valuable content.

Questions

If you have a problem with any aspect of this book, you can contact us at `questions@packtpub.com`, and we will do our best to address the problem.

1
Getting Up and Running with Spark

Apache Spark is a framework for distributed computing; this framework aims to make it simpler to write programs that run in parallel across many nodes in a cluster of computers or virtual machines. It tries to abstract the tasks of resource scheduling, job submission, execution, tracking, and communication between nodes as well as the low-level operations that are inherent in parallel data processing. It also provides a higher level API to work with distributed data. In this way, it is similar to other distributed processing frameworks such as Apache Hadoop; however, the underlying architecture is somewhat different.

Spark began as a research project at the AMP lab in University of California, Berkeley (`https://amplab.cs.berkeley.edu/projects/spark-lightning-fast-cluster-computing/`). The university was focused on the use case of distributed machine learning algorithms. Hence, it is designed from the ground up for high performance in applications of an iterative nature, where the same data is accessed multiple times. This performance is achieved primarily through caching datasets in memory combined with low latency and overhead to launch parallel computation tasks. Together with other features such as fault tolerance, flexible distributed-memory data structures, and a powerful functional API, Spark has proved to be broadly useful for a wide range of large-scale data processing tasks, over and above machine learning and iterative analytics.

For more information, you can visit:

- `http://spark.apache.org/community.html`
- `http://spark.apache.org/community.html#history`

Performance wise, Spark is much faster than Hadoop for related workloads. Refer to the following graph:

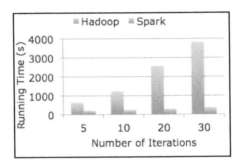

Source: https://amplab.cs.berkeley.edu/wp-content/uploads/2011/11/spark-lr.png

Spark runs in four modes:

- The standalone local mode, where all Spark processes are run within the same **Java Virtual Machine (JVM)** process
- The standalone cluster mode, using Spark's own built-in, job-scheduling framework
- Using **Mesos**, a popular open source cluster-computing framework
- Using YARN (commonly referred to as NextGen MapReduce), Hadoop

In this chapter, we will do the following:

- Download the Spark binaries and set up a development environment that runs in Spark's standalone local mode. This environment will be used throughout the book to run the example code.
- Explore Spark's programming model and API using Spark's interactive console.
- Write our first Spark program in Scala, Java, R, and Python.
- Set up a Spark cluster using Amazon's **Elastic Cloud Compute (EC2)** platform, which can be used for large-sized data and heavier computational requirements, rather than running in the local mode.
- Set up a Spark Cluster using Amazon Elastic Map Reduce

If you have previous experience in setting up Spark and are familiar with the basics of writing a Spark program, feel free to skip this chapter.

Installing and setting up Spark locally

Spark can be run using the built-in standalone cluster scheduler in the local mode. This means that all the Spark processes are run within the same JVM-effectively, a single, multithreaded instance of Spark. The local mode is very used for prototyping, development, debugging, and testing. However, this mode can also be useful in real-world scenarios to perform parallel computation across multiple cores on a single computer.

As Spark's local mode is fully compatible with the cluster mode; programs written and tested locally can be run on a cluster with just a few additional steps.

The first step in setting up Spark locally is to download the latest version `http://spark.apache.org/downloads.html`, which contains links to download various versions of Spark as well as to obtain the latest source code via GitHub.

 The documents/docs available at `http://spark.apache.org/docs/latest/` are a comprehensive resource to learn more about Spark. We highly recommend that you explore it!

Spark needs to be built against a specific version of Hadoop in order to access **Hadoop Distributed File System (HDFS)** as well as standard and custom Hadoop input sources Cloudera's Hadoop Distribution, MapR's Hadoop distribution, and Hadoop 2 (YARN). Unless you wish to build Spark against a specific Hadoop version, we recommend that you download the prebuilt Hadoop 2.7 package from an Apache mirror from `http://d3kbcqa49mib13.cloudfront.net/spark-2.0.2-bin-hadoop2.7.tgz`.

Spark requires the Scala programming language (version 2.10.x or 2.11.x at the time of writing this book) in order to run. Fortunately, the prebuilt binary package comes with the Scala runtime packages included, so you don't need to install Scala separately in order to get started. However, you will need to have a **Java Runtime Environment (JRE)** or **Java Development Kit (JDK)**.

 Refer to the software and hardware list in this book's code bundle for installation instructions. R 3.1+ is needed.

Once you have downloaded the Spark binary package, unpack the contents of the package and change it to the newly created directory by running the following commands:

```
$ tar xfvz spark-2.0.0-bin-hadoop2.7.tgz
$ cd spark-2.0.0-bin-hadoop2.7
```

Spark places user scripts to run Spark in the `bin` directory. You can test whether everything is working correctly by running one of the example programs included in Spark. Run the following command:

```
$ bin/run-example SparkPi 100
```

This will run the example in Spark's local standalone mode. In this mode, all the Spark processes are run within the same JVM, and Spark uses multiple threads for parallel processing. By default, the preceding example uses a number of threads equal to the number of cores available on your system. Once the program is executed, you should see something similar to the following lines toward the end of the output:

```
. . .
16/11/24 14:41:58 INFO Executor: Finished task 99.0 in stage 0.0
    (TID 99). 872 bytes result sent to driver
16/11/24 14:41:58 INFO TaskSetManager: Finished task 99.0 in stage
    0.0 (TID 99) in 59 ms on localhost (100/100)
16/11/24 14:41:58 INFO DAGScheduler: ResultStage 0 (reduce at
    SparkPi.scala:38) finished in 1.988 s
16/11/24 14:41:58 INFO TaskSchedulerImpl: Removed TaskSet 0.0,
    whose tasks have all completed, from pool
16/11/24 14:41:58 INFO DAGScheduler: Job 0 finished: reduce at
    SparkPi.scala:38, took 2.235920 s
Pi is roughly 3.1409527140952713
```

The preceding command calls class `org.apache.spark.examples.SparkPi` class.

This class takes parameter in the `local[N]` form, where `N` is the number of threads to use. For example, to use only two threads, run the following command `instead:N` is the number of threads to use. Giving `local[*]` will use all of the cores on the local machine-- that is a common usage.

To use only two threads, run the following command instead:

```
$ ./bin/spark-submit  --class org.apache.spark.examples.SparkPi
    --master local[2] ./examples/jars/spark-examples_2.11-2.0.0.jar 100
```

Spark clusters

A Spark cluster is made up of two types of processes: a driver program and multiple executors. In the local mode, all these processes are run within the same JVM. In a cluster, these processes are usually run on separate nodes.

For example, a typical cluster that runs in Spark's standalone mode (that is, using Spark's built-in cluster management modules) will have the following:

- A master node that runs the Spark standalone master process as well as the driver program
- A number of worker nodes, each running an executor process

While we will be using Spark's local standalone mode throughout this book to illustrate concepts and examples, the same Spark code that we write can be run on a Spark cluster. In the preceding example, if we run the code on a Spark standalone cluster, we could simply pass in the URL for the master node, as follows:

```
$ MASTER=spark://IP:PORT --class org.apache.spark.examples.SparkPi
  ./examples/jars/spark-examples_2.11-2.0.0.jar 100
```

Here, IP is the IP address and PORT is the port of the Spark master. This tells Spark to run the program on the cluster where the Spark master process is running.

A full treatment of Spark's cluster management and deployment is beyond the scope of this book. However, we will briefly teach you how to set up and use an Amazon EC2 cluster later in this chapter.

For an overview of the Spark cluster-application deployment, take a look at the following links:

- http://spark.apache.org/docs/latest/cluster-overview.html
- http://spark.apache.org/docs/latest/submitting-applications.html

The Spark programming model

Before we delve into a high-level overview of Spark's design, we will introduce the SparkContext object as well as the Spark shell, which we will use to interactively explore the basics of the Spark programming model.

While this section provides a brief overview and examples of using Spark, we recommend that you read the following documentation to get a detailed understanding:

Refer to the following URLs:

- For the Spark Quick Start refer to,
  `http://spark.apache.org/docs/latest/quick-start`
- For the Spark Programming guide, which covers Scala, Java, Python and R--, refer to, `http://spark.apache.org/docs/latest/programming-guide.html`

SparkContext and SparkConf

The starting point of writing any Spark program is `SparkContext` (or `JavaSparkContext` in Java). `SparkContext` is initialized with an instance of a `SparkConf` object, which contains various Spark cluster-configuration settings (for example, the URL of the master node).

It is a main entry point for Spark functionality. A `SparkContext` is a connection to a Spark cluster. It can be used to create RDDs, accumulators, and broadcast variables on the cluster.

Only one `SparkContext` is active per JVM. You must call `stop()`, which is the active `SparkContext`, before creating a new one.

Once initialized, we will use the various methods found in the `SparkContext` object to create and manipulate distributed datasets and shared variables. The Spark shell (in both Scala and Python, which is unfortunately not supported in Java) takes care of this context initialization for us, but the following lines of code show an example of creating a context running in the local mode in Scala:

```
val conf = new SparkConf()
.setAppName("Test Spark App")
.setMaster("local[4]")
val sc = new SparkContext(conf)
```

This creates a context running in the local mode with four threads, with the name of the application set to `Test Spark App`. If we wish to use the default configuration values, we could also call the following simple constructor for our `SparkContext` object, which works in the exact same way:

```
val sc = new SparkContext("local[4]", "Test Spark App")
```

Downloading the example code

You can download the example code files for all Packt books you have purchased from your account at http://www.packtpub.com. If you purchased this book from any other source, you can visithttp://www.pack tpub.com/supportand register to have the files e-mailed directly to you.

SparkSession

SparkSession allows programming with the DataFrame and Dataset APIs. It is a single point of entry for these APIs.

First, we need to create an instance of the SparkConf class and use it to create the SparkSession instance. Consider the following example:

```
val spConfig = (new SparkConf).setMaster("local").setAppName("SparkApp")
  val spark = SparkSession
    .builder()
    .appName("SparkUserData").config(spConfig)
    .getOrCreate()
```

Next we can use spark object to create a DataFrame:

```
val user_df = spark.read.format("com.databricks.spark.csv")
    .option("delimiter", "|").schema(customSchema)
    .load("/home/ubuntu/work/ml-resources/spark-ml/data/ml-100k/u.user")
val first = user_df.first()
```

The Spark shell

Spark supports writing programs interactively using the Scala, Python, or R **REPL** (that is, the **Read-Eval-Print-Loop**, or interactive shell). The shell provides instant feedback as we enter code, as this code is immediately evaluated. In the Scala shell, the return result and type is also displayed after a piece of code is run.

To use the Spark shell with Scala, simply run ./bin/spark-shell from the Spark base directory. This will launch the Scala shell and initialize SparkContext, which is available to us as the Scala value, sc. With Spark 2.0, a SparkSession instance in the form of Spark variable is available in the console as well.

Your console output should look similar to the following:

```
$ ~/work/spark-2.0.0-bin-hadoop2.7/bin/spark-shell
Using Spark's default log4j profile: org/apache/spark/log4j-
    defaults.properties
Setting default log level to "WARN".
To adjust logging level use sc.setLogLevel(newLevel).
16/08/06 22:14:25 WARN NativeCodeLoader: Unable to load native-
    hadoop library for your platform... using builtin-java classes
    where applicable
16/08/06 22:14:25 WARN Utils: Your hostname, ubuntu resolves to a
    loopback address: 127.0.1.1; using 192.168.22.180 instead (on
    interface eth1)
16/08/06 22:14:25 WARN Utils: Set SPARK_LOCAL_IP if you need to
    bind to another address
16/08/06 22:14:26 WARN Utils: Service 'SparkUI' could not bind on
    port 4040. Attempting port 4041.
16/08/06 22:14:27 WARN SparkContext: Use an existing SparkContext,
    some configuration may not take effect.
Spark context Web UI available at http://192.168.22.180:4041
Spark context available as 'sc' (master = local[*], app id = local-
    1470546866779).
Spark session available as 'spark'.
Welcome to
      ____              __
     / __/__  ___ _____/ /__
    _\ \/ _ \/ _ `/ __/  '_/
   /___/ .__/\_,_/_/ /_/\_\   version 2.0.0
      /_/

Using Scala version 2.11.8 (Java HotSpot(TM) 64-Bit Server VM,
    Java 1.7.0_60)
Type in expressions to have them evaluated.
Type :help for more information.

scala>
```

To use the Python shell with Spark, simply run the `./bin/pyspark` command. Like the Scala shell, the Python `SparkContext` object should be available as the Python variable, `sc`. Your output should be similar to this:

```
~/work/spark-2.0.0-bin-hadoop2.7/bin/pyspark
Python 2.7.6 (default, Jun 22 2015, 17:58:13)
[GCC 4.8.2] on linux2
Type "help", "copyright", "credits" or "license" for more
    information.
Using Spark's default log4j profile: org/apache/spark/log4j-
    defaults.properties
```

```
Setting default log level to "WARN".
To adjust logging level use sc.setLogLevel(newLevel).
16/08/06 22:16:15 WARN NativeCodeLoader: Unable to load native-
    hadoop library for your platform... using builtin-java classes
    where applicable
16/08/06 22:16:15 WARN Utils: Your hostname, ubuntu resolves to a
    loopback address: 127.0.1.1; using 192.168.22.180 instead (on
    interface eth1)
16/08/06 22:16:15 WARN Utils: Set SPARK_LOCAL_IP if you need to
    bind to another address
16/08/06 22:16:16 WARN Utils: Service 'SparkUI' could not bind on
    port 4040. Attempting port 4041.
Welcome to


      ____              __
     / __/__  ___ _____/ /__
    _\ \/ _ \/ _ `/ __/  '_/
   /__ / .__/\_,_/_/ /_/\_\   version 2.0.0
      /_/


Using Python version 2.7.6 (default, Jun 22 2015 17:58:13)
SparkSession available as 'spark'.
>>>
```

R is a language and has a runtime environment for statistical computing and graphics. It is a GNU project. R is a different implementation of **S** (a language developed by Bell Labs).

R provides statistical (linear and nonlinear modeling, classical statistical tests, time-series analysis, classification, and clustering) and graphical techniques. It is considered to be highly extensible.

To use Spark using R, run the following command to open Spark-R shell:

```
$ ~/work/spark-2.0.0-bin-hadoop2.7/bin/sparkR
R version 3.0.2 (2013-09-25) -- "Frisbee Sailing"
Copyright (C) 2013 The R Foundation for Statistical Computing
Platform: x86_64-pc-linux-gnu (64-bit)

R is free software and comes with ABSOLUTELY NO WARRANTY.
You are welcome to redistribute it under certain conditions.
Type 'license()' or 'licence()' for distribution details.

  Natural language support but running in an English locale

R is a collaborative project with many contributors.
Type 'contributors()' for more information and
'citation()' on how to cite R or R packages in publications.

Type 'demo()' for some demos, 'help()' for on-line help, or
```

```
'help.start()' for an HTML browser interface to help.
Type 'q()' to quit R.

Launching java with spark-submit command /home/ubuntu/work/spark-
    2.0.0-bin-hadoop2.7/bin/spark-submit    "sparkr-shell"
    /tmp/RtmppzWD8S/backend_porta6366144af4f
Using Spark's default log4j profile: org/apache/spark/log4j-
    defaults.properties
Setting default log level to "WARN".
To adjust logging level use sc.setLogLevel(newLevel).
16/08/06 22:26:22 WARN NativeCodeLoader: Unable to load native-
    hadoop library for your platform... using builtin-java classes
    where applicable
16/08/06 22:26:22 WARN Utils: Your hostname, ubuntu resolves to a
    loopback address: 127.0.1.1; using 192.168.22.186 instead (on
    interface eth1)
16/08/06 22:26:22 WARN Utils: Set SPARK_LOCAL_IP if you need to
    bind to another address
16/08/06 22:26:22 WARN Utils: Service 'SparkUI' could not bind on
    port 4040. Attempting port 4041.

 Welcome to
      ____              __
     / __/__  ___ _____/ /__
    _ / _ / _ `/ __/  '_/
   /___/ .__/\_,_/_/ /_/\_\   version  2.0.0
      /_/

 SparkSession available as 'spark'.
During startup - Warning message:
package 'SparkR' was built under R version 3.1.1
>
```

Resilient Distributed Datasets

The core of Spark is a concept called the **Resilient Distributed Dataset (RDD)**. An RDD is a collection of *records* (strictly speaking, objects of some type) that are distributed or partitioned across many nodes in a cluster (for the purposes of the Spark local mode, the single multithreaded process can be thought of in the same way). An RDD in Spark is fault-tolerant; this means that if a given node or task fails (for some reason other than erroneous user code, such as hardware failure, loss of communication, and so on), the RDD can be reconstructed automatically on the remaining nodes and the job will still be completed.

Creating RDDs

RDDs can be Scala Spark shells that you launched earlier:

```
val collection = List("a", "b", "c", "d", "e")
val rddFromCollection = sc.parallelize(collection)
```

RDDs can also be created from Hadoop-based input sources, including the local filesystem, HDFS, and Amazon S3. A Hadoop-based RDD can utilize any input format that implements the Hadoop `InputFormat` interface, including text files, other standard Hadoop formats, HBase, Cassandra, tachyon, and many more.

The following code is an example of creating an RDD from a text file located on the local filesystem:

```
val rddFromTextFile = sc.textFile("LICENSE")
```

The preceding `textFile` method returns an RDD where each record is a `String` object that represents one line of the text file. The output of the preceding command is as follows:

```
rddFromTextFile: org.apache.spark.rdd.RDD[String] = LICENSE
MapPartitionsRDD[1] at textFile at <console>:24
```

The following code is an example of how to create an RDD from a text file located on the HDFS using `hdfs://` protocol:

```
val rddFromTextFileHDFS = sc.textFile("hdfs://input/LICENSE ")
```

The following code is an example of how to create an RDD from a text file located on the Amazon S3 using `s3n://` protocol:

```
val rddFromTextFileS3 = sc.textFile("s3n://input/LICENSE ")
```

Spark operations

Once we have created an RDD, we have a distributed collection of records that we can manipulate. In Spark's programming model, operations are split into transformations and actions. Generally speaking, a transformation operation applies some function to all the records in the dataset, changing the records in some way. An action typically runs some computation or aggregation operation and returns the result to the driver program where `SparkContext` is running.

Spark operations are functional in style. For programmers familiar with functional programming in Scala, Python, or Lambda expressions in Java 8, these operations should seem natural. For those without experience in functional programming, don't worry; the Spark API is relatively easy to learn.

One of the most common transformations that you will use in Spark programs is the map operator. This applies a function to each record of an RDD, thus *mapping* the input to some new output. For example, the following code fragment takes the RDD we created from a local text file and applies the `size` function to each record in the RDD. Remember that we created an RDD of Strings. Using `map`, we can transform each string to an integer, thus returning an RDD of `Int`s:

```
val intsFromStringsRDD = rddFromTextFile.map(line => line.size)
```

You should see output similar to the following line in your shell; this indicates the type of the RDD:

```
intsFromStringsRDD: org.apache.spark.rdd.RDD[Int] =
MapPartitionsRDD[2] at map at <console>:26
```

In the preceding code, we saw the use of the => syntax. This is the Scala syntax for an anonymous function, which is a function that is not a named method (that is, one defined using the `def` keyword in Scala or Python, for example).

While a detailed treatment of anonymous functions is beyond the scope of this book, they are used extensively in Spark code in Scala and Python, as well as in Java 8 (both in examples and real-world applications), so it is useful to cover a few practicalities.

The line => `line.size` syntax means that we are applying a function where => is the operator, and the output is the result of the code to the right of the => operator. In this case, the input is line, and the output is the result of calling `line.size`. In Scala, this function that maps a string to an integer is expressed as `String => Int`.

This syntax saves us from having to separately define functions every time we use methods such as map; this is useful when the function is simple and will only be used once, as in this example.

Now, we can apply a common action operation, count, to return the number of records in our RDD:

```
intsFromStringsRDD.count
```

The result should look something like the following console output:

```
res0: Long = 299
```

Perhaps we want to find the average length of each line in this text file. We can first use the sum function to add up all the lengths of all the records and then divide the sum by the number of records:

```
val sumOfRecords = intsFromStringsRDD.sum
val numRecords = intsFromStringsRDD.count
val aveLengthOfRecord = sumOfRecords / numRecords
```

The result will be as follows:

```
scala> intsFromStringsRDD.count
res0: Long = 299

scala> val sumOfRecords = intsFromStringsRDD.sum
sumOfRecords: Double = 17512.0

scala> val numRecords = intsFromStringsRDD.count
numRecords: Long = 299

scala> val aveLengthOfRecord = sumOfRecords / numRecords
aveLengthOfRecord: Double = 58.5685618729097
```

Spark operations, in most cases, return a new RDD, with the exception of most actions, which return the result of a computation (such as Long for count and Double for sum in the preceding example). This means that we can naturally chain together operations to make our program flow more concise and expressive. For example, the same result as the one in the preceding line of code can be achieved using the following code:

```
val aveLengthOfRecordChained = rddFromTextFile.map(line => line.size).sum /
rddFromTextFile.count
```

An important point to note is that Spark transformations are lazy. That is, invoking a transformation on an RDD does not immediately trigger a computation. Instead, transformations are chained together and are effectively only computed when an action is called. This allows Spark to be more efficient by only returning results to the driver when necessary so that the majority of operations are performed in parallel on the cluster.

This means that if your Spark program never uses an action operation, it will never trigger an actual computation, and you will not get any results. For example, the following code will simply return a new RDD that represents the chain of transformations:

```
val transformedRDD = rddFromTextFile.map(line => line.size).filter(size =>
size > 10).map(size => size * 2)
```

This returns the following result in the console:

```
transformedRDD: org.apache.spark.rdd.RDD[Int] =
MapPartitionsRDD[6] at map at <console>:26
```

Notice that no actual computation happens and no result is returned. If we now call an action, such as sum, on the resulting RDD, the computation will be triggered:

```
val computation = transformedRDD.sum
```

You will now see that a Spark job is run, and it results in the following console output:

```
computation: Double = 35006.0
```

> The complete list of transformations and actions possible on RDDs, as well as a set of more detailed examples, are available in the Spark programming guide (located at http://spark.apache.org/docs/latest /programming-guide.html#rdd-operations), and the API documentation (the Scala API documentation) is located at (http://spark.apache.org/docs/latest/api/scala/index.html#org.ap ache.spark.rdd.RDD).

Caching RDDs

One of the most powerful features of Spark is the ability to cache data in memory across a cluster. This is achieved through the use of the cache method on an RDD:

```
rddFromTextFile.cache
res0: rddFromTextFile.type = MapPartitionsRDD[1] at textFile at
<console>:27
```

Calling `cache` on an RDD tells Spark that the RDD should be kept in memory. The first time an action is called on the RDD that initiates a computation, the data is read from its source and put into memory. Hence, the first time such an operation is called, the time it takes to run the task is partly dependent on the time it takes to read the data from the input source. However, when the data is accessed the next time (for example, in subsequent queries in analytics or iterations in a machine learning model), the data can be read directly from memory, thus avoiding expensive I/O operations and speeding up the computation, in many cases, by a significant factor.

If we now call the `count` or `sum` function on our cached RDD, the RDD is loaded into memory:

```
val aveLengthOfRecordChained = rddFromTextFile.map(line =>
line.size).sum / rddFromTextFile.count
```

 Spark also allows more fine-grained control over caching behavior. You can use the persist method to specify what approach Spark uses to cache data. More information on RDD caching can be found here: http://spark.apache.org/docs/latest/programmingguide.html#rdd-persistence

Broadcast variables and accumulators

Another core feature of Spark is the ability to create two special types of variables-- broadcast variables and accumulators.

A **broadcast variable** is a *read-only* variable that is created from the driver program object and made available to the nodes that will execute the computation. This is very useful in applications that need to make the same data available to the worker nodes in an efficient manner, such as distributed systems. Spark makes creating broadcast variables as simple as calling a method on `SparkContext`, as follows:

```
val broadcastAList = sc.broadcast(List("a", "b", "c", "d", "e"))
```

A broadcast variable can be accessed from nodes other than the driver program that created it (that is, the worker nodes) by calling `value` on the variable:

```
sc.parallelize(List("1", "2", "3")).map(x => broadcastAList.value ++
  x).collect
```

This code creates a new RDD with three records from a collection (in this case, a Scala `List`) of (`"1"`, `"2"`, `"3"`). In the map function, it returns a new collection with the relevant rom our new RDD appended to the `broadcastAList` that is our broadcast variable:

```
. . .
res1: Array[List[Any]] = Array(List(a, b, c, d, e, 1), List(a, b,
c, d, e, 2), List(a, b, c, d, e, 3))
```

Notice the `collect` method in the preceding code. This is a Spark *action* that returns the entire RDD to the driver as a Scala (or Python or Java) collection.

We will often use when we wish to apply further processing to our results locally within the driver program.

Note that `collect` should generally only be used in cases where we really want to return the full result set to the driver and perform further processing. If we try to call `collect` on a very large dataset, we might run out of memory on the driver and crash our program.
It is preferable to perform as much heavy-duty processing on our Spark cluster as possible, preventing the driver from becoming a bottleneck. In many cases, however, such as during iterations in many machine learning models, collecting results to the driver is necessary.

On inspecting the result, we will see that for each of the three records in our new RDD, we now have a record that is our original broadcasted `List`, with the new element appended to it (that is, there is now `"1"`, `"2"`, or `"3"` at the end):

An **accumulator** is also a variable that is broadcasted to the worker nodes. The key difference between a broadcast variable and an accumulator is that while the `broadcast` variable is read-only, the accumulator can be added to. There are limitations to this, that is, in particular, the addition must be an associative operation so that the global accumulated value can be correctly computed in parallel and returned to the driver program. Each worker node can only access and add to its own local accumulator value, and only the driver program can access the global value. Accumulators are also accessed within the Spark code using the value method.

For more details on broadcast variables and accumulators, refer to the *Shared Variables* section of the *Spark Programming Guide* at
`http://spark.apache.org/docs/latest/programming-guide.html#share d-variables`.

SchemaRDD

SchemaRDD is a combination of RDD and schema information. It also offers many rich and easy-to-use APIs (that is, the `DataSet` API). SchemaRDD is not used with 2.0 and is internally used by `DataFrame` and `Dataset` APIs.

A schema is used to describe how structured data is logically organized. After obtaining the schema information, the SQL engine is able to provide the structured query capability for the corresponding data. The `DataSet` API is a replacement for Spark SQL parser's functions. It is an API to achieve the original program logic tree. Subsequent processing steps reuse Spark SQL's core logic. We can safely consider `DataSet` API's processing functions as completely equivalent to that of SQL queries.

SchemaRDD is an RDD subclass. When a program calls the `DataSet` API, a new SchemaRDD object is created, and a logic plan attribute of the new object is created by adding a new logic operation node on the original logic plan tree. Operations of the `DataSet` API (like RDD) are of two types--**Transformation** and **Action**.

APIs related to the relational operations are attributed to the Transformation type.

Operations associated with data output sources are of Action type. Like RDD, a Spark job is triggered and delivered for cluster execution, only when an Action type operation is called.

Spark data frame

In Apache Spark, a `Dataset` is a distributed collection of data. The `Dataset` is a new interface added since Spark 1.6. It provides the benefits of RDDs with the benefits of Spark SQL's execution engine. A `Dataset` can be constructed from JVM objects and then manipulated using functional transformations (`map`, `flatMap`, `filter`, and so on). The `Dataset` API is available only for in Scala and Java. It is not available for Python or R.

A `DataFrame` is a dataset with named columns. It is equivalent to a table in a relational database or a data frame in R/Python, with richer optimizations. `DataFrame` is constructed from structured data files, tables in Hive, external databases, or existing RDDs. The `DataFrame` API is available in Scala, Python, Java, and R.

A Spark `DataFrame` needs the Spark session instantiated first:

```
import org.apache.spark.sql.SparkSession
val spark = SparkSession.builder().appName("Spark
SQL").config("spark.some.config.option", "").getOrCreate()
import spark.implicits._
```

Next, we create a `DataFrame` from a Json file using the `spark.read.json` function:

```
scala> val df = spark.read.json("/home/ubuntu/work/ml-resources
   /spark-ml/Chapter_01/data/example_one.json")
```

Note that Spark `Implicits` are being used to implicitly convert RDD to Data Frame types:

```
org.apache.spark.sql
Class SparkSession.implicits$
Object org.apache.spark.sql.SQLImplicits
Enclosing class: SparkSession
```

Implicit methods available in Scala for converting common Scala objects into `DataFrames`.

Output will be similar to the following listing:

```
df: org.apache.spark.sql.DataFrame = [address: struct<city:
string, state: string>, name: string]
```

Now we want to see how this is actually loaded in the `DataFrame`:

```
scala> df.show
+-----------------+-------+
|          address|   name|
+-----------------+-------+
|   [Columbus,Ohio]|    Yin|
|[null,California]|Michael|
+-----------------+-------+
```

The first step to a Spark program in Scala

We will now use the ideas we introduced in the previous section to write a basic Spark program to manipulate a dataset. We will start with Scala and then write the same program in Java and Python. Our program will be based on exploring some data from an online store, about which users have purchased which products. The data is contained in a **Comma-Separated-Value (CSV)** file called `UserPurchaseHistory.csv`. This file is expected to be in the `data` directory.

The contents are shown in the following snippet. The first column of the CSV is the username, the second column is the product name, and the final column is the price:

```
John,iPhone Cover,9.99
John,Headphones,5.49
Jack,iPhone Cover,9.99
Jill,Samsung Galaxy Cover,8.95
Bob,iPad Cover,5.49
```

For our Scala program, we need to create two files-our Scala code and our project build configuration file-using the build tool **Scala Build Tool** (**SBT**). For ease of use, we recommend that you use -spark-app for this chapter. This code also contains the CSV file under the data directory. You will need SBT installed on your system in order to run this example program (we use version 0.13.8 at the time of writing this book).

> Setting up SBT is beyond the scope of this book; however, you can find more information at http://www.scala-sbt.org/release/docs/Getting -Started/Setup.html.

Our SBT configuration file, build.sbt, looks like this (note that the empty lines between each line of code are required):

```
name := "scala-spark-app"

version := "1.0"

scalaVersion := "2.11.7"

libraryDependencies += "org.apache.spark" %% "spark-core" % "2.0.0"
```

The last line adds the dependency on Spark to our project.

Our Scala program is contained in the ScalaApp.scala file. We will walk through the program piece by piece. First, we need to import the required Spark classes:

```
import org.apache.spark.SparkContext
import org.apache.spark.SparkContext._

/**
 * A simple Spark app in Scala
 */
object ScalaApp {
```

In our main method, we need to initialize our SparkContext object and use this to access our CSV data file with the textFile method. We will then map the raw text by splitting the string on the delimiter character (a comma in this case) and extracting the relevant records for username, product, and price:

```
def main(args: Array[String]) {
  val sc = new SparkContext("local[2]", "First Spark App")
  // we take the raw data in CSV format and convert it into a
  set of records of the form (user, product, price)
  val data = sc.textFile("data/UserPurchaseHistory.csv")
    .map(line => line.split(","))
    .map(purchaseRecord => (purchaseRecord(0),
      purchaseRecord(1), purchaseRecord(2)))
```

Now that we have an RDD, where each record is made up of (`user`, `product`, `price`), we can compute various interesting metrics for our store, such as the following ones:

- The total number of purchases
- The number of unique users who purchased
- Our total revenue
- Our most popular product

Let's compute the preceding metrics:

```
// let's count the number of purchases
val numPurchases = data.count()
// let's count how many unique users made purchases
val uniqueUsers = data.map{ case (user, product, price) => user
}.distinct().count()
// let's sum up our total revenue
val totalRevenue = data.map{ case (user, product, price) =>
price.toDouble }.sum()
// let's find our most popular product
val productsByPopularity = data
  .map{ case (user, product, price) => (product, 1) }
  .reduceByKey(_ + _)
  .collect()
  .sortBy(-_._2)
val mostPopular = productsByPopularity(0)
```

This last piece of code to compute the most popular product is an example of the *Map/Reduce* pattern made popular by Hadoop. First, we mapped our records of (user, product, price) to the records of (product, 1). Then, we performed a reduceByKey operation, where we summed up the 1s for each unique product.

Once we have this transformed RDD, which contains the number of purchases for each product, we will call collect, which returns the results of the computation to the driver program as a local Scala collection. We will then sort these counts locally (note that in practice, if the amount of data is large, we will perform the sorting in parallel, usually with a Spark operation such as sortByKey).

Finally, we will print out the results of our computations to the console:

```
println("Total purchases: " + numPurchases)
println("Unique users: " + uniqueUsers)
println("Total revenue: " + totalRevenue)
println("Most popular product: %s with %d
purchases".format(mostPopular._1, mostPopular._2))
}
}
```

We can run this program by running sbt run in the project's base directory or by running the program in your Scala IDE if you are using one. The output should look similar to the following:

```
...
[info] Compiling 1 Scala source to ...
[info] Running ScalaApp
...
Total purchases: 5
Unique users: 4
Total revenue: 39.91
Most popular product: iPhone Cover with 2 purchases
```

We can see that we have 5 purchases from four different users with total revenue of 39.91. Our most popular product is an iPhone cover with 2 purchases.

The first step to a Spark program in Java

The Java API is very similar in principle to the Scala API. However, while Scala can call the Java code quite easily, in some cases, it is not possible to call the Scala code from Java. This is particularly the case when Scala code makes use of Scala features such as implicit conversions, default parameters, and the Scala reflection API.

Spark makes heavy use of these features in general, so it is necessary to have a separate API specifically for Java that includes Java versions of the common classes. Hence, `SparkContext` becomes `JavaSparkContext` and RDD becomes JavaRDD.

Java versions prior to version 8 do not support anonymous functions and do not have succinct syntax for functional-style programming, so functions in the Spark Java API must implement a `WrappedFunction` interface with the `call` method signature. While it is significantly more verbose, we will often create one-off anonymous classes to pass to our Spark operations, which implement this interface and the `call` method to achieve much the same effect as anonymous functions in Scala.

Spark provides support for Java 8's anonymous function (or *lambda*) syntax. Using this syntax makes a Spark program written in Java 8 look very close to the equivalent Scala program.

In Scala, an RDD of key/value pairs provides special operators (such as `reduceByKey` and `saveAsSequenceFile`, for example) that are accessed automatically via implicit conversions. In Java, special types of `JavaRDD` classes are required in order to access similar functions. These include `JavaPairRDD` to work with key/value pairs and `JavaDoubleRDD` to work with numerical records.

In this section, we covered the standard Java API syntax. For more details and examples related to working RDDs in Java, as well as the Java 8 lambda syntax, refer to the Java sections of the *Spark Programming Guide* found at `http://spark.apache.org/docs/latest/programming-guide.html#rdd-operations`.

We will see examples of most of these differences in the following Java program, which is included in the example code of this chapter in the directory named `java-spark-app`. The `code` directory also contains the CSV data file under the `data` subdirectory.

We will build and run this project with the **Maven** build tool, which we assume you have installed on your system.

Installing and setting up Maven is beyond the scope of this book. Usually, Maven can easily be installed using the package manager on your Linux system or HomeBrew or MacPorts on Mac OS X.
Detailed installation instructions can be found at `http://maven.apache.org/download.cgi`.

The project contains a Java file called `JavaApp.java`, which contains our program code:

```java
import org.apache.spark.api.java.JavaRDD;
import org.apache.spark.api.java.JavaSparkContext;
import scala.Tuple2;
import java.util.*;
import java.util.stream.Collectors;


/**
 * A simple Spark app in Java
 */
public class JavaApp {
  public static void main(String[] args) {
```

As in our Scala example, we first need to initialize our context. Note that we will use the `JavaSparkContext` class here instead of the `SparkContext` class that we used earlier. We will use the `JavaSparkContext` class in the same way to access our data using `textFile` and then split each row into the required fields. Note how we used an anonymous class to define a split function that performs the string processing in the highlighted code:

```java
JavaSparkContext sc = new JavaSparkContext("local[2]",
    "First Spark App");
// we take the raw data in CSV format and convert it into a
// set of records of the form (user, product, price)
JavaRDD<String[]> data =
sc.textFile("data/UserPurchaseHistory.csv").map(s ->        s.split(","));
```

Now, we can compute the same metrics as we did in our Scala example. Note how some methods are the same (for example, `distinct` and `count`) for the Java and Scala APIs. Also note the use of anonymous classes that we pass to the map function. This code is highlighted here:

```java
// let's count the number of purchases
long numPurchases = data.count();
// let's count how many unique users made purchases
long uniqueUsers = data.map(strings ->
    strings[0]).distinct().count();
// let's sum up our total revenue
Double totalRevenue = data.map(strings ->
    Double.parseDouble(strings[2])).reduce((Double v1,
Double v2) -> new Double(v1.doubleValue() + v2.doubleValue()));
```

In the following lines of code, we can see that the approach to compute the most popular product is the same as that in the Scala example. The extra code might seem complex, but it is mostly related to the Java code required to create the anonymous functions (which we have highlighted here). The actual functionality is the same:

```
// let's find our most popular product
List<Tuple2<String, Integer>> pairs = data.mapToPair(strings -> new
Tuple2<String, Integer>(strings[1], 1)).reduceByKey((Integer i1, Integer
i2) -> i1 + i2).collect();

Map<String, Integer> sortedData = new HashMap<>();
Iterator it = pairs.iterator();
while (it.hasNext()) {
    Tuple2<String, Integer> o = (Tuple2<String, Integer>) it.next();
    sortedData.put(o._1, o._2);
}
List<String> sorted = sortedData.entrySet()
        .stream()
        .sorted(Comparator.comparing((Map.Entry<String, Integer>
          entry) -> entry.getValue()).reversed())
        .map(Map.Entry::getKey)
        .collect(Collectors.toList());
String mostPopular = sorted.get(0);
            int purchases = sortedData.get(mostPopular);
    System.out.println("Total purchases: " + numPurchases);
    System.out.println("Unique users: " + uniqueUsers);
    System.out.println("Total revenue: " + totalRevenue);
    System.out.println(String.format("Most popular product:
      %s with %d purchases", mostPopular, purchases));
    }
}
```

As can be seen, the general structure is similar to the Scala version, apart from the extra boilerplate code used to declare variables and functions via anonymous inner classes. It is a good exercise to work through both examples and compare lines of Scala code to those in Java to understand how the same result is achieved in each language.

This program can be run with the following command executed from the project's base directory:

```
$ mvn exec:java -Dexec.mainClass="JavaApp"
```

You will see output that looks very similar to the Scala version with identical results of the computation:

```
...
14/01/30 17:02:43 INFO spark.SparkContext: Job finished: collect
```

```
at JavaApp.java:46, took 0.039167 s
Total purchases: 5
Unique users: 4
Total revenue: 39.91
Most popular product: iPhone Cover with 2 purchases
```

The first step to a Spark program in Python

Spark's Python API exposes virtually all the functionalities of Spark's Scala API in the Python language. There are some features that are not yet supported (for example, graph processing with GraphX and a few API methods here and there). Refer to the Python section of *Spark Programming Guide* (http://spark.apache.org/docs/latest/programming-guide.html) for more details.

PySpark is built using Spark's Java API. Data is processed in native Python, cached, and shuffled in JVM. Python driver program's SparkContext uses Py4J to launch a JVM and create a JavaSparkContext. The driver uses Py4J for local communication between the Python and Java SparkContext objects. RDD transformations in Python map to transformations on PythonRDD objects in Java. PythonRDD object launches Python sub-processes on remote worker machines, communicate with them using pipes. These sub-processes are used to send the user's code and to process data.

Following on from the preceding examples, we will now write a Python version. We assume that you have Python version 2.6 and higher installed on your system (for example, most Linux and Mac OS X systems come with Python preinstalled).

The example program is included in the sample code for this chapter, in the directory named python-spark-app, which also contains the CSV data file under the data subdirectory. The project contains a script, pythonapp.py, provided here.

A simple Spark app in Python:

```
from pyspark import SparkContext

sc = SparkContext("local[2]", "First Spark App")
# we take the raw data in CSV format and convert it into a set of
    records of the form (user, product, price)
data = sc.textFile("data/UserPurchaseHistory.csv").map(lambda
    line: line.split(",")).map(lambda record: (record[0], record[1],
    record[2]))
# let's count the number of purchases
numPurchases = data.count()
# let's count how many unique users made purchases
```

```
uniqueUsers = data.map(lambda record: record[0]).distinct().count()
# let's sum up our total revenue
totalRevenue = data.map(lambda record: float(record[2])).sum()
# let's find our most popular product
products = data.map(lambda record: (record[1],
    1.0)).reduceByKey(lambda a, b: a + b).collect()
mostPopular = sorted(products, key=lambda x: x[1], reverse=True)[0]

print "Total purchases: %d" % numPurchases
print "Unique users: %d" % uniqueUsers
print "Total revenue: %2.2f" % totalRevenue
print "Most popular product: %s with %d purchases" %
    (mostPopular[0], mostPopular[1])
```

If you compare the Scala and Python versions of our program, you will see that generally, the syntax looks very similar. One key difference is how we express anonymous functions (also called `lambda` functions; hence, the use of this keyword for the Python syntax). In Scala, we've seen that an anonymous function mapping an input x to an output y is expressed as x => y, while in Python, it is `lambda x: y`. In the highlighted line in the preceding code, we are applying an anonymous function that maps two inputs, a and b, generally of the same type, to an output. In this case, the function that we apply is the plus function; hence, `lambda a, b: a + b`.

The best way to run the script is to run the following command from the base directory of the sample project:

$SPARK_HOME/bin/spark-submit pythonapp.py

Here, the SPARK_HOME variable should be replaced with the path of the directory in which you originally unpacked the Spark prebuilt binary package at the start of this chapter.

Upon running the script, you should see output similar to that of the Scala and Java examples, with the results of our computation being the same:

```
. . .
14/01/30 11:43:47 INFO SparkContext: Job finished: collect at
pythonapp.py:14, took 0.050251 s
Total purchases: 5
Unique users: 4
Total revenue: 39.91
Most popular product: iPhone Cover with 2 purchases
```

The first step to a Spark program in R

SparkR is an R package which provides a frontend to use Apache Spark from R. In Spark 1.6.0; SparkR provides a distributed data frame on large datasets. SparkR also supports distributed machine learning using MLlib. This is something you should try out while reading machine learning chapters.

SparkR DataFrames

`DataFrame` is a collection of data organized into names columns that are distributed. This concept is very similar to a relational database or a data frame of R but with much better optimizations. Source of these data frames could be a CSV, a TSV, Hive tables, local R data frames, and so on.

Spark distribution can be run using the `./bin/sparkR` shell.

Following on from the preceding examples, we will now write an R version. We assume that you have R (R version 3.0.2 (2013-09-25)-*Frisbee Sailing*), R Studio and higher installed on your system (for example, most Linux and Mac OS X systems come with Python preinstalled).

The example program is included in the sample code for this chapter, in the directory named `r-spark-app`, which also contains the CSV data file under the `data` subdirectory. The project contains a script, `r-script-01.R`, which is provided in the following. Make sure you change `PATH` to appropriate value for your environment.

```
Sys.setenv(SPARK_HOME = "/PATH/spark-2.0.0-bin-hadoop2.7")
.libPaths(c(file.path(Sys.getenv("SPARK_HOME"), "R", "lib"),
 .libPaths()))
#load the Sparkr library
library(SparkR)
sc <- sparkR.init(master = "local", sparkPackages="com.databricks:spark-
csv_2.10:1.3.0")
sqlContext <- sparkRSQL.init(sc)

user.purchase.history <- "/PATH/ml-resources/spark-ml/Chapter_01/r-spark-
app/data/UserPurchaseHistory.csv"
data <- read.df(sqlContext, user.purchase.history,
"com.databricks.spark.csv", header="false")
head(data)
count(data)

parseFields <- function(record) {
  Sys.setlocale("LC_ALL", "C") # necessary for strsplit() to work correctly
```

```
  parts <- strsplit(as.character(record), ",")
  list(name=parts[1], product=parts[2], price=parts[3])
}

parsedRDD <- SparkR:::lapply(data, parseFields)
cache(parsedRDD)
numPurchases <- count(parsedRDD)

sprintf("Number of Purchases : %d", numPurchases)
getName <- function(record){
  record[1]
}

getPrice <- function(record){
  record[3]
}

nameRDD <- SparkR:::lapply(parsedRDD, getName)
nameRDD = collect(nameRDD)
head(nameRDD)

uniqueUsers <- unique(nameRDD)
head(uniqueUsers)

priceRDD <- SparkR:::lapply(parsedRDD, function(x) {
as.numeric(x$price[1])})
take(priceRDD,3)

totalRevenue <- SparkR:::reduce(priceRDD, "+")

sprintf("Total Revenue : %.2f", s)

products <- SparkR:::lapply(parsedRDD, function(x) { list(
toString(x$product[1]), 1) })
take(products, 5)
productCount <- SparkR:::reduceByKey(products, "+", 2L)
productsCountAsKey <- SparkR:::lapply(productCount, function(x) { list(
as.integer(x[2][1]), x[1][1])})

productCount <- count(productsCountAsKey)
mostPopular <- toString(collect(productsCountAsKey)[[productCount]][[2]])
sprintf("Most Popular Product : %s", mostPopular)
```

Run the script with the following command on the bash terminal:

```
$ Rscript r-script-01.R
```

Your output will be similar to the following listing:

```
> sprintf("Number of Purchases : %d", numPurchases)
[1] "Number of Purchases : 5"

> uniqueUsers <- unique(nameRDD)
> head(uniqueUsers)
[[1]]
[[1]]$name
[[1]]$name[[1]]
[1] "John"
[[2]]
[[2]]$name
[[2]]$name[[1]]
[1] "Jack"
[[3]]
[[3]]$name
[[3]]$name[[1]]
[1] "Jill"
[[4]]
[[4]]$name
[[4]]$name[[1]]
[1] "Bob"

> sprintf("Total Revenue : %.2f", totalRevenueNum)
[1] "Total Revenue : 39.91"

> sprintf("Most Popular Product : %s", mostPopular)
[1] "Most Popular Product : iPad Cover"
```

Getting Spark running on Amazon EC2

The Spark project provides scripts to run a Spark cluster in the cloud on Amazon's EC2 service. These scripts are located in the ec2 directory. You can run the spark-ec2 script contained in this directory with the following command:

```
>./ec2/spark-ec2
```

Running it in this way without an argument will show the help output:

```
Usage: spark-ec2 [options] <action> <cluster_name>
<action> can be: launch, destroy, login, stop, start, get-master

Options:
...
```

Before creating a Spark EC2 cluster, you will need to ensure that you have an
Amazon account.

 If you don't have an Amazon Web Services account, you can sign up at
`http://aws.amazon.com/`.
The AWS console is available at `http://aws.amazon.com/console/`.

You will also need to create an Amazon EC2 key pair and retrieve the relevant security
credentials. The Spark documentation for EC2 (available at
`http://spark.apache.org/docs/latest/ec2-scripts.html`) explains the requirements:

> *Create an Amazon EC2 key pair for yourself. This can be done by logging into your
> Amazon Web Services account through the AWS console, clicking on* **Key Pairs** *on the
> left sidebar, and creating and downloading a key. Make sure that you set the permissions
> for the private key file to 600 (that is, only you can read and write it) so that ssh will work.*

> *Whenever you want to use the spark-ec2 script, set the environment variables*
> AWS_ACCESS_KEY_ID *and* AWS_SECRET_ACCESS_KEY *to your Amazon EC2 access
> key* ID *and secret access key, respectively. These can be obtained from the AWS homepage
> by clicking* **Account** | **Security Credentials** | **Access Credentials**.

When creating a key pair, choose a name that is easy to remember. We will simply use the
name *spark* for the key pair. The key pair file itself will be called `spark.pem`. As mentioned
earlier, ensure that the key pair file permissions are set appropriately and that the
environment variables for the AWS credentials are exported using the following
commands:

```
$ chmod 600 spark.pem
$ export AWS_ACCESS_KEY_ID="..."
$ export AWS_SECRET_ACCESS_KEY="..."
```

You should also be careful to keep your downloaded key pair file safe and not lose it, as it
can only be downloaded once when it is created!

Note that launching an Amazon EC2 cluster in the following section will *incur costs* to your
AWS account.

Launching an EC2 Spark cluster

We're now ready to launch a small Spark cluster by changing into the `ec2` directory and
then running the cluster launch command:

```
$  cd ec2
$  ./spark-ec2 --key-pair=rd_spark-user1 --identity-file=spark.pem
   --region=us-east-1 --zone=us-east-1a launch my-spark-cluster
```

This will launch a new Spark cluster called test-cluster with one master and one slave node of instance type m3.medium. This cluster will be launched with a Spark version built for Hadoop 2. The key pair name we used is spark, and the key pair file is spark.pem (if you gave the files different names or have an existing AWS key pair, use that name instead).

It might take quite a while for the cluster to fully launch and initialize. You should see something like the following immediately after running the launch command:

```
Setting up security groups...
Creating security group my-spark-cluster-master
Creating security group my-spark-cluster-slaves
Searching for existing cluster my-spark-cluster in region
    us-east-1...
Spark AMI: ami-5bb18832
Launching instances...
Launched 1 slave in us-east-1a, regid = r-5a893af2
Launched master in us-east-1a, regid = r-39883b91
Waiting for AWS to propagate instance metadata...
Waiting for cluster to enter 'ssh-ready' state..........
Warning: SSH connection error. (This could be temporary.)
Host: ec2-52-90-110-128.compute-1.amazonaws.com
SSH return code: 255
SSH output: ssh: connect to host ec2-52-90-110-128.compute-
    1.amazonaws.com port 22: Connection refused
Warning: SSH connection error. (This could be temporary.)
Host: ec2-52-90-110-128.compute-1.amazonaws.com
SSH return code: 255
SSH output: ssh: connect to host ec2-52-90-110-128.compute-
    1.amazonaws.com port 22: Connection refused
Warnig: SSH connection error. (This could be temporary.)
Host: ec2-52-90-110-128.compute-1.amazonaws.com
SSH return code: 255
SSH output: ssh: connect to host ec2-52-90-110-128.compute-
    1.amazonaws.com port 22: Connection refused
Cluster is now in 'ssh-ready' state. Waited 510 seconds.
```

If the cluster has launched successfully, you should eventually see a console output similar to the following listing:

```
./tachyon/setup.sh: line 5: /root/tachyon/bin/tachyon:
    No such file or directory
./tachyon/setup.sh: line 9: /root/tachyon/bin/tachyon-start.sh:
    No such file or directory
```

```
[timing] tachyon setup:  00h 00m 01s
Setting up rstudio
spark-ec2/setup.sh: line 110: ./rstudio/setup.sh:
    No such file or directory
[timing] rstudio setup:  00h 00m 00s
Setting up ganglia
RSYNC'ing /etc/ganglia to slaves...
ec2-52-91-214-206.compute-1.amazonaws.com
Shutting down GANGLIA gmond:                    [FAILED]
Starting GANGLIA gmond:                         [ OK  ]
Shutting down GANGLIA gmond:                    [FAILED]
Starting GANGLIA gmond:                         [ OK  ]
Connection to ec2-52-91-214-206.compute-1.amazonaws.com closed.
Shutting down GANGLIA gmetad:                   [FAILED]
Starting GANGLIA gmetad:                        [ OK  ]
Stopping httpd:                                 [FAILED]
Starting httpd: httpd: Syntax error on line 154 of /etc/httpd
    /conf/httpd.conf: Cannot load /etc/httpd/modules/mod_authz_core.so
    into server: /etc/httpd/modules/mod_authz_core.so: cannot open
    shared object file: No such file or directory     [FAILED]
[timing] ganglia setup:  00h 00m 03s
Connection to ec2-52-90-110-128.compute-1.amazonaws.com closed.
Spark standalone cluster started at
    http://ec2-52-90-110-128.compute-1.amazonaws.com:8080
Ganglia started at http://ec2-52-90-110-128.compute-
    1.amazonaws.com:5080/ganglia
Done!
ubuntu@ubuntu:~/work/spark-1.6.0-bin-hadoop2.6/ec2$
```

This will create two VMs - Spark Master and Spark Slave of type **m1.large** as shown in the following screenshot :

	Name	Instance ID	Instance Type	Availability Zone	Instance State	Status Checks
	my-spark-clu...	i-35e1b5b4	m1.large	us-east-1a	running	Initializing
	rd-app	i-f13c33de	t2.micro	us-east-1e	running	2/2 checks ...
	my-spark-clu...	i-f4e3b775	m1.large	us-east-1a	running	Initializing

To test whether we can connect to our new cluster, we can run the following command:

```
$ ssh -i spark.pem root@ ec2-52-90-110-128.compute-1.amazonaws.com
```

Remember to replace the public domain name of the master node (the address after `root@` in the preceding command) with the correct Amazon EC2 public domain name that will be shown in your console output after launching the cluster.

You can also retrieve your cluster's master public domain name by running this line of code:

```
$ ./spark-ec2 -i spark.pem get-master test-cluster
```

After successfully running the `ssh` command, you will be connected to your Spark master node in EC2, and your terminal output should match the following screenshot:

```
ec2-52-91-214-206.compute-1.amazonaws.com
./tachyon/setup.sh: line 5: /root/tachyon/bin/tachyon: No such file or directory
./tachyon/setup.sh: line 9: /root/tachyon/bin/tachyon-start.sh: No such file or directory
[timing] tachyon setup:  00h 00m 01s
Setting up rstudio
spark-ec2/setup.sh: line 110: ./rstudio/setup.sh: No such file or directory
[timing] rstudio setup:  00h 00m 00s
Setting up ganglia
RSYNC'ing /etc/ganglia to slaves...
ec2-52-91-214-206.compute-1.amazonaws.com
Shutting down GANGLIA gmond:                            [FAILED]
Starting GANGLIA gmond:                                 [  OK  ]
Shutting down GANGLIA gmond:                            [FAILED]
Starting GANGLIA gmond:                                 [  OK  ]
Connection to ec2-52-91-214-206.compute-1.amazonaws.com closed.
Shutting down GANGLIA gmetad:                           [FAILED]
Starting GANGLIA gmetad:                                [  OK  ]
Stopping httpd:                                         [FAILED]
Starting httpd: httpd: Syntax error on line 154 of /etc/httpd/conf/httpd.conf: Cannot load
/etc/httpd/modules/mod_authz_core.so into server: /etc/httpd/modules/mod_authz_core.so: cannot open shared object file:
No such file or directory
                                                       [FAILED]
[timing] ganglia setup:  00h 00m 03s
Connection to ec2-52-90-110-128.compute-1.amazonaws.com closed.
Spark standalone cluster started at http://ec2-52-90-110-128.compute-1.amazonaws.com:8080
Ganglia started at http://ec2-52-90-110-128.compute-1.amazonaws.com:5080/ganglia
Done!
ubuntu@ubuntu:~/work/spark-1.6.0-bin-hadoop2.6/ec2$
```

We can test whether our cluster is correctly set up with Spark by changing into the `Spark` directory and running an example in the local mode:

```
$ cd spark
$ MASTER=local[2] ./bin/run-example SparkPi
```

You should see output similar to what you would get on running the same command on your local computer:

```
...
14/01/30 20:20:21 INFO SparkContext: Job finished: reduce at
SparkPi.scala:35, took 0.864044012 s
Pi is roughly 3.14032
...
```

Now that we have an actual cluster with multiple nodes, we can test Spark in the cluster mode. We can run the same example on the cluster, using our one slave node by passing in the master URL instead of the local version:

```
$ MASTER=spark:// ec2-52-90-110-128.compute-
1.amazonaws.com:7077 ./bin/run-example SparkPi
```

Note that you will need to substitute the preceding master domain name with the correct domain name for your specific cluster.

Again, the output should be similar to running the example locally; however, the log messages will show that your driver program has connected to the Spark master:

```
. . .
14/01/30 20:26:17 INFO client.Client$ClientActor: Connecting to
    master spark://ec2-54-220-189-136.eu-
    west-1.compute.amazonaws.com:7077
14/01/30 20:26:17 INFO cluster.SparkDeploySchedulerBackend:
    Connected to Spark cluster with app ID app-20140130202617-0001
14/01/30 20:26:17 INFO client.Client$ClientActor: Executor added:
    app-20140130202617-0001/0 on worker-20140130201049-
    ip-10-34-137-45.eu-west-1.compute.internal-57119
    (ip-10-34-137-45.eu-west-1.compute.internal:57119) with 1 cores
14/01/30 20:26:17 INFO cluster.SparkDeploySchedulerBackend:
    Granted executor ID app-20140130202617-0001/0 on hostPort
    ip-10-34-137-45.eu-west-1.compute.internal:57119 with 1 cores,
    2.4 GB RAM
14/01/30 20:26:17 INFO client.Client$ClientActor:
    Executor updated: app-20140130202617-0001/0 is now RUNNING
14/01/30 20:26:18 INFO spark.SparkContext: Starting job: reduce at
    SparkPi.scala:39
. . .
```

Feel free to experiment with your cluster. Try out the interactive console in Scala, for example:

```
$ ./bin/spark-shell --master spark:// ec2-52-90-110-128.compute-
1.amazonaws.com:7077
```

Once you've finished, type exit to leave the console. You can also try the PySpark console by running the following command:

```
$ ./bin/pyspark --master spark:// ec2-52-90-110-128.compute-
1.amazonaws.com:7077
```

You can use the Spark Master web interface to see the applications registered with the master. To load the Master Web UI, navigate to `ec2-52-90-110-128.compute-1.amazonaws.com:8080` (again, remember to replace this domain name with your own master domain name).

Remember that *you will be charged by Amazon* for usage of the cluster. Don't forget to stop or terminate this test cluster once you're done with it. To do this, you can first exit the `ssh` session by typing `exit` to return to your own local system and then run the following command:

```
$ ./ec2/spark-ec2 -k spark -i spark.pem destroy test-cluster
```

You should see the following output:

```
Are you sure you want to destroy the cluster test-cluster?
The following instances will be terminated:
Searching for existing cluster test-cluster...
Found 1 master(s), 1 slaves
> ec2-54-227-127-14.compute-1.amazonaws.com
> ec2-54-91-61-225.compute-1.amazonaws.com
ALL DATA ON ALL NODES WILL BE LOST!!
Destroy cluster test-cluster (y/N): y
Terminating master...
Terminating slaves...
```

Hit *Y* and then *Enter* to destroy the cluster.

Congratulations! You've just set up a Spark cluster in the cloud, run a fully parallel example program on this cluster, and terminated it. If you would like to try out any of the example code in the subsequent chapters (or your own Spark programs) on a cluster, feel free to experiment with the Spark EC2 scripts and launch a cluster of your chosen size and instance profile. (Just be mindful of the costs and remember to shut it down when you're done!)

Configuring and running Spark on Amazon Elastic Map Reduce

Launch a Hadoop cluster with Spark installed using the Amazon Elastic Map Reduce. Perform the following steps to create an EMR cluster with Spark installed:

1. Launch an Amazon EMR Cluster.
2. Open the Amazon EMR UI console at `https://console.aws.amazon.com/elasticmapreduce/`.

3. Choose **Create cluster**:

4. Choose appropriate Amazon AMI Version 3.9.0 or later as shown in the following screenshot:

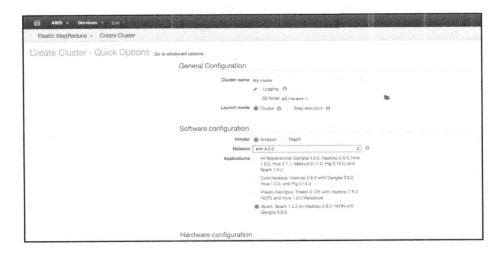

5. For the applications to be installed field, choose **Spark 1.5.2** or later from the list shown on the **User Interface** and click on **Add**.

6. Select other hardware options as necessary:
    - The **Instance Type**
    - The keypair to be used with SSH
    - **Permissions**
    - IAM roles (**Default** or**Custom**)

    Refer to the following screenshot:

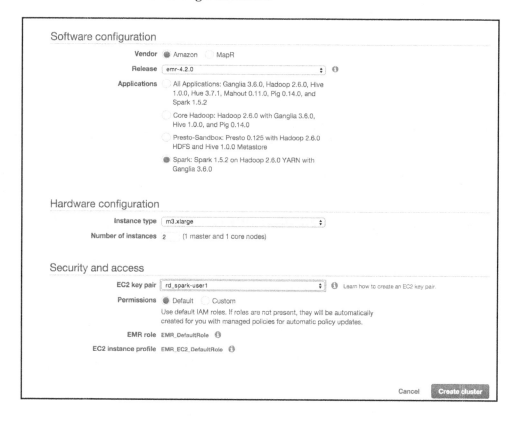

7. Click on **Create cluster**. The cluster will start instantiating as shown in the following screenshot:

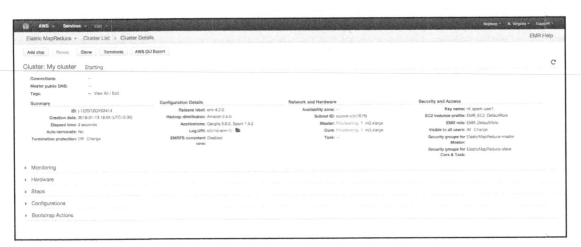

8. Log in into the master. Once the EMR cluster is ready, you can SSH into the master:

```
$ ssh -i rd_spark-user1.pem
hadoop@ec2-52-3-242-138.compute-1.amazonaws.com
```

The output will be similar to following listing:
```
Last login: Wed Jan 13 10:46:26 2016
```
```
     __|  __|_  )
     _|  (     /   Amazon Linux AMI
    ___|___|___|
```
```
https://aws.amazon.com/amazon-linux-ami/2015.09-release-notes/
23 package(s) needed for security, out of 49 available
Run "sudo yum update" to apply all updates.
[hadoop@ip-172-31-2-31 ~]$
```

9. Start the Spark Shell:

```
[hadoop@ip-172-31-2-31 ~]$ spark-shell
16/01/13 10:49:36 INFO SecurityManager: Changing view acls to:
    hadoop
16/01/13 10:49:36 INFO SecurityManager: Changing modify acls to:
    hadoop
16/01/13 10:49:36 INFO SecurityManager: SecurityManager:
    authentication disabled; ui acls disabled; users with view
```

```
    permissions: Set(hadoop); users with modify permissions:
    Set(hadoop)
16/01/13 10:49:36 INFO HttpServer: Starting HTTP Server
16/01/13 10:49:36 INFO Utils: Successfully started service 'HTTP
    class server' on port 60523.
Welcome to
      ____              __
     / __/__  ___ _____/ /__
    _\ \/ _ \/ _ `/ __/  '_/
   /___/ .__/\_,_/_/ /_/\_\   version 1.5.2
      /_/
scala> sc
```

10. Run Basic Spark sample from the EMR:

```
scala> val textFile = sc.textFile("s3://elasticmapreduce/samples
    /hive-ads/tables/impressions/dt=2009-04-13-08-05
    /ec2-0-51-75-39.amazon.com-2009-04-13-08-05.log")
scala> val linesWithCartoonNetwork = textFile.filter(line =>
    line.contains("cartoonnetwork.com")).count()
```

Your output will be as follows:

```
linesWithCartoonNetwork: Long = 9
```

UI in Spark

Spark provides a web interface which can be used to monitor jobs, see the environment, and run SQL commands.

`SparkContext` launches a web UI on port `4040` that displays useful information about the application. This includes the following:

- A list of scheduler stages and tasks
- A summary of RDD sizes and memory usage
- Environmental information
- Information about the running executors

This interface can be accessed by going to `http://<driver-node>:4040` in a web browser. If multiple `SparkContext`s are running on the same host, they will bind to ports beginning with port `4040` (`4041`, `4042`, and so on).

The following screenshots display some of the information provided by the Web UI:

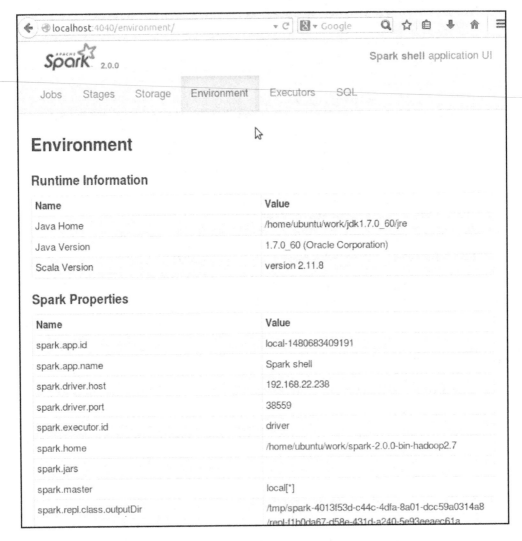

UI showing the Environment of the Spark Content

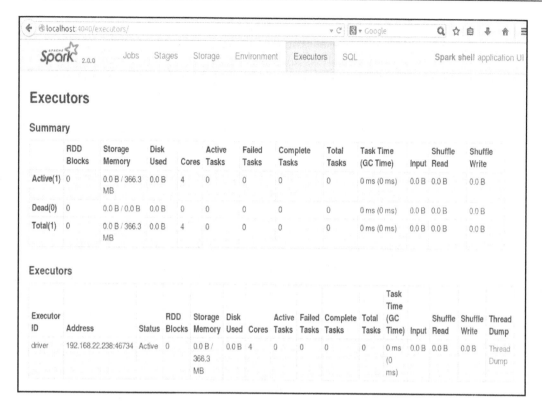

UI table showing Executors available

Supported machine learning algorithms by Spark

The following algorithms are supported by Spark ML:

- **Collaborative filtering**
  - **Alternating Least Squares (ALS):** Collaborative filtering is often used for recommender systems. These techniques aim to fill the missing entries of a user-item association matrix. The spark.mllib currently supports model-based collaborative filtering. In this implementation, users and products are described by a small set of latent factors that can be used to predict missing entries. The spark.mllib uses the ALS algorithm to learn these latent factors.

- **Clustering**: This is an unsupervised learning problem where the aim is to group subsets of entities with one another based on the notion of similarity. Clustering is used for exploratory analysis and as a component of a hierarchical supervised learning pipeline. When used in a learning pipeline, distinct classifiers or regression models are trained for each cluster. The following clustering techniques are implemented in Spark:

  - **k-means**: This is one of the commonly used clustering algorithms that cluster the data points into a predefined number of clusters. It is up to the user to choose the number of clusters. The `spark.mllib` implementation includes a parallelized variant of the k-means++ method (http://theory.stanford.edu/~sergei/papers/vldb12-kmpar.pdf).

  - **Gaussian mixture**: A **Gaussian Mixture Model (GMM)** represents a composite distribution where points are taken from one of the k Gaussian sub-distributions. Each of these distributions has its own probability. The `spark.mllib` implementation uses the expectation-maximization algorithm to induce the maximum-likelihood model given a set of samples.

  - **Power Iteration Clustering (PIC)**: This is a scalable algorithm for clustering vertices of a graph given pairwise similarities as edge properties. It computes a pseudo-eigenvector of the (affinity matrix which is normalized) of the graph using power iteration.

  Power iteration is an eigenvalue algorithm. Given a matrix X, the algorithm will produce a number λ (eigenvalue) and a non-zero vector v (the eigenvector), such that $Xv = \lambda v$.

  Pseudo eigenvectors of a matrix can be thought of as the eigenvectors of a nearby matrix. More specifically, pseudo eigenvectors are defined as:

  Let A be an n by n matrix. Let E be any matrix such that $||E|| = \epsilon$. Then the eigenvectors of $A + E$ are defined to be pseudo-eigenvectors of A. This eigenvector uses it to cluster graph vertices.

The `spark.mllib` includes an implementation of PIC using *GraphX*. It takes an RDD of tuples and outputs a model with the clustering assignments. The similarities must be non-negative. PIC makes the assumption that the similarity measure is symmetric.

(In statistics, a similarity measure or similarity function is a real-valued function that quantifies the similarity between two objects. Such measures are inverse of distance metrics; an example of this is the Cosine similarity)

A pair (`srcId`, `dstId`) regardless of the ordering should appear at the most once in the input data.

- **Latent Dirichlet Allocation (LDA)**: This is a form of a topic model that infers topics from a collection of text documents. LDA is a form clustering algorithm. The following points explain the topics:

  Topics are cluster centers and documents correspond to examples in a dataset Topics and documents both exist in a feature space, where feature vectors are vectors of word counts (also known as bag of words)
  Instead of estimating a clustering using a traditional distance approach, LDA uses a function based on a model of how text documents are generated

- **Bisecting k-means**: This is a type of hierarchical clustering. **Hierarchical Cluster Analysis (HCA)** is a method of cluster analysis that builds a hierarchy of clusters*top down*. In this approach, all observations start in one cluster and splits are performed recursively as one moves down the hierarchy.

  Hierarchical clustering is one of the commonly used methods of cluster analysis that seek to build a hierarchy of clusters.

- **Streaming k-means**: When data arrives in a stream, we want to estimate clusters dynamically and update them as new data arrives. The `spark.mllib` supports streaming k-means clustering, with parameters to control the decay of the estimates. The algorithm uses a generalization of the mini-batch k-means update rule.

- **Classification**
    - **Decision Trees:** Decision trees and their ensembles are one of the methods for classification and regression. Decision trees are popular as they are easy to interpret, handle categorical features, and extend to the multiclass classification setting. They do not require feature scaling and are also able to capture non-linearities and feature interactions. Tree ensemble algorithms, random forests and boosting are among the top performers for classification and regression scenarios.

        The `spark.mllib` implements decision trees for binary and multiclass classification and regression. It supports both continuous and categorical features. The implementation partitions data by rows, which allows distributed training with millions of instances.

    - **Naive Bayes**: Naive Bayes classifiers are a family of simple probabilistic classifiers based on applying Bayes' theorem (`https://en.wikipedia.org/wiki/Bayes%27_theorem`) with strong (naive) independence assumptions between the features.

        Naive Bayes is a multiclass classification algorithm with the assumption of independence between every pair of features. In a single pass of training data, the algorithm computes the conditional probability distribution of each feature given the label, and then it applies Bayes' theorem to compute the conditional probability distribution of a label given an observation, which is then used for prediction. The `spark.mllib` supports multinomial naive Bayes and Bernoulli Naive Bayes. These models are generally used for document classification.

    - **Probability Classifier**: In machine learning, a probabilistic classifier is a classifier that can predict, given an input, a probability distribution over a set of classes, rather than outputting the most likely class that the sample should belong to. Probabilistic classifiers provide classification with some certainty, which can be useful on its own or when combining classifiers into ensembles.

    - **Logistical Regression**: This is a method used to predict a binary response. Logistic regression measures the relationship between the categorical dependent variable and independent variables by estimating probabilities using a logistical function. This function is a cumulative logistic distribution.

It is a special case of **Generalized Linear Models (GLM)** that predicts the probability of the outcome. For more background and more details about the implementation, refer to the documentation on the logistic regression in `spark.mllib`.

GLM is considered a generalization of linear regression that allows for response variables that have an error distribution other than a normal distribution.

- **Random Forest**: This algorithms use ensembles of decision trees to decide decision boundaries. Random forests combine many decision trees. This reduces the risk of overfitting the result.

  Spark ML supports random forest for binary and multi-class classification as well as regression. It can use used for continuous or categorical values.

- **Dimensionality reduction**: This is the process of reducing the number of variables on which machine learning will be done. It can be used to extract latent features from raw features or to compress data while maintaining the overall structure. MLlib provides support dimensionality reduction on top of the `RowMatrix` class.

  - **Singular value decomposition (SVD)**: Singular value decomposition of a matrix $M: m \times n$ (real or complex) is a factorization of the form $U\Sigma V^*$, where U is an $m \times R$ matrix. Σ is an $R \times R$ rectangular diagonal matrix with non-negative real numbers on the diagonal, and V is an $n \times r$ unitary matrix. r is equal to the rank of the matrix M.

  - **Principal component analysis (PCA)**: This is a statistical method used to find a rotation to find largest variance in the first coordinate. Each succeeding coordinate, in turn, has the largest variance possible. The columns of the rotation matrix are called principal components. PCA is used widely in dimensionality reduction.

    MLlib supports PCA for tall-and-skinny matrices stored in row-oriented format using `RowMatrix`.
    Spark supports features extraction and transforation using TF-IDF, ChiSquare, Selector, Normalizer, and Word2Vector.

- **Frequent pattern mining**:
    - **FP-growth**: FP stands for frequent pattern. Algorithm first counts item occurrences (attribute and value pairs) in the dataset and stores them in the header table.

        In the second pass, the algorithm builds the FP-tree structure by inserting instances (made of items). Items in each instance are sorted by descending order of their frequency in the dataset; this ensures that the tree can be processed quickly. Items in each instance that do not meet minimum coverage threshold are discarded. For a use case where many instances share most frequent items, the FP-tree provides high compression close to the tree root.

    - **Association rules**: Association rule learning is a mechanism for discovering interesting relations between variables in large databases.

        It implements a parallel rule generation algorithm for constructing rules that have a single item as the consequent.

- **PrefixSpan**: This is a sequential pattern mining algorithm.
- **Evaluation metrics**: The `spark.mllib` comes with a suite of metrics for evaluating the algorithms.
- **PMML model export**: The **Predictive Model Markup Language** (**PMML**) is an XML-based predictive model interchange format. PMML provides a mechanism for analytic applications to describe and exchange predictive models produced by machine learning algorithms.

    The `spark.mllib` allows the export of its machine learning models to PMML and their equivalent PMML models.

- **Optimization (Developer)**
    - **Stochastic Gradient Descent**: This is used to optimize gradient descent to minimize an objective function; this function is a sum of differentiable functions.

Gradient descent methods and the **Stochastic Subgradient Descent (SGD)** are included as a low-level primitive in MLlib, on top of which various ML algorithms are developed.

- **Limited-Memory BFGS (L-BFGS)**: This is an optimization algorithm and belongs to the family of quasi-Newton methods that approximates the **Broyden-Fletcher-Goldfarb-Shanno (BFGS)** algorithm. It uses a limited amount of computer memory. It is used for parameter estimation in machine learning.

  The BFGS method approximates Newton's method, which is a class of hill-climbing optimization techniques that seeks a stationary point of a function. For such problems, a necessary optimal condition is that the gradient should be zero.

Benefits of using Spark ML as compared to existing libraries

AMQ Lab at Berkley Evaluated Spark, and RDDs were evaluated through a series of experiments on Amazon EC2 as well as benchmarks of user applications.

- **Algorithms used**: Logistical Regression and k-means
- **Use case**: First iteration, multiple iterations.

All the tests used `m1.xlarge` EC2 nodes with 4 cores and 15 GB of RAM. HDFS was for storage with 256 MB blocks. Refer to the following graph:

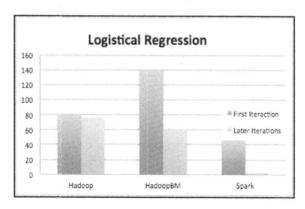

The preceding graph shows the comparison between the performance of Hadoop and Spark for the first and subsequent iteration for **Logistical Regression**:

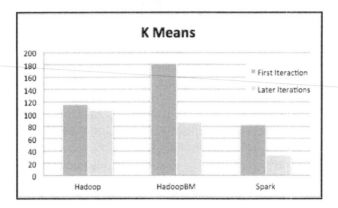

The preceding graph shows the comparison between the performance of Hadoop and Spark for the first and subsequent iteration for K Means clustering algorithm.

The overall results show the following:

- Spark outperforms Hadoop by up to 20 times in iterative machine learning and graph applications. The speedup comes from avoiding I/O and deserialization costs by storing data in memory as Java objects.
- The applications written perform and scale well. Spark can speed up an analytics report that was running on Hadoop by 40 times.
- When nodes fail, Spark can recover quickly by rebuilding only the lost RDD partitions.
- Spark was be used to query a 1-TB dataset interactively with latencies of 5-7 seconds.

For more information, go to `http://people.csail.mit.edu/matei/pape rs/2012/nsdi_spark.pdf`.

Spark versus Hadoop for a SORT Benchmark--In 2014, the Databricks team participated in a SORT benchmark test (`http://sortbenchmark.org/`). This was done on a 100-TB dataset. Hadoop was running in a dedicated data center and a Spark cluster of over 200 nodes was run on EC2. Spark was run on HDFS distributed storage.

Spark was 3 times faster than Hadoop and used 10 times fewer machines. Refer to the following graph:

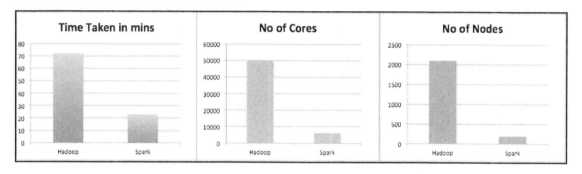

Spark Cluster on Google Compute Engine - DataProc

Cloud Dataproc is a Spark and Hadoop service running on Google Compute Engine. It is a managed service. Cloud Dataproc automation helps create clusters quickly, manage them easily, and save money by turning clusters off when you don't need them.

In this section, we will learn how to create a Spark cluster using DataProc and running a Sample app on it.

Make sure that you have created a Google Compute Engine account and installed Google Cloud SDK (https://cloud.google.com/sdk/gcloud/).

Hadoop and Spark Versions

DataProc supports the following Hadoop and Spark versions. Note that this will change with time as new versions come out:

- Spark 1.5.2
- Hadoop 2.7.1
- Pig 0.15.0
- Hive 1.2.1
- GCS connector 1.4.3-hadoop2
- BigQuery connector 0.7.3-hadoop2 (https://github.com/GoogleCloudPlatform/bigdata-interop)

For more information, go to
`http://cloud.google.com/dataproc-versions.`

In the following steps, we will use Google Cloud Console (the user interface used to create a Spark Cluster and submit a job).

Creating a Cluster

You can create a Spark cluster by going to the Cloud Platform Console. Select the project, and then click **Continue** to open the **Clusters** page. You would see the Cloud Dataproc clusters that belong to your project, if you have created any.

Click on the **Create a cluster** button to open the Create a Cloud Data pros cluster page. Refer to the following screenshot:

Once you click on **Create a cluster**, a detailed form, which is as shown in the following screenshot, shows up:

The previous screenshot shows the Create a Cloud Dataproc cluster page with the default fields automatically filled in for a new **cluster-1** cluster. Take a look at the following screenshot:

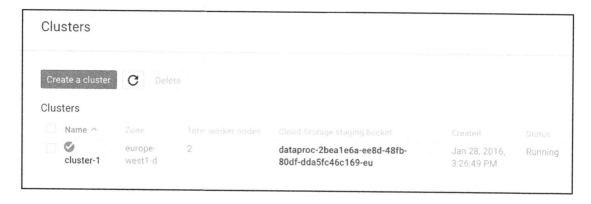

You can expand the workers, bucket, network, version, initialization, and access options panel to specify one or more worker nodes, a staging bucket, network, initialization, the Cloud Dataproc image version, actions, and project-level access for your cluster. Providing these values is optional.

The default cluster is created with no worker nodes, an auto-created staging bucket, and a default network It also has the latest released Cloud Dataproc image version. You can change these default settings:

Once you have configured all fields on the page, click on the **Create** button to create the cluster. The cluster name created appears on the **Clusters** page. The status is updated to **Running** once the spark cluster is created.

Click on the cluster name created earlier to open the cluster details page. It also has a **Overview** tab and the **CPU utilization** graph selected.

You can examine jobs, instances, and so on for the cluster from the other tabs.

Submitting a Job

To submit a job from the Cloud Platform Console to the cluster, go to the Cloud Platform UI. Select the appropriate project and then click on **Continue**. The first time you submit a job, the following dialog appears:

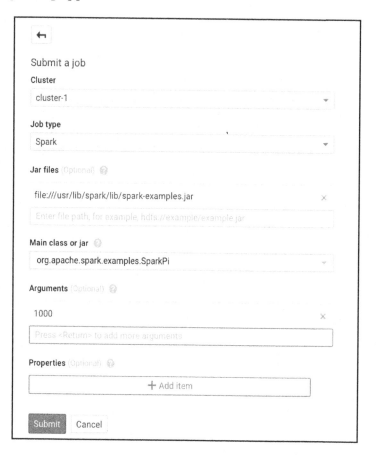

Click on **Submit** a job:

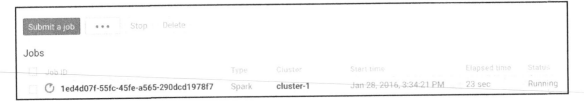

To submit a Spark sample job, fill the fields on the **Submit** a job page, as follows:

1. Select a cluster name from the cluster list on the screen.
2. Set **Job type** to**Spark**.
3. Add `file:///usr/lib/spark/lib/spark-examples.jar` to Jar files. Here, `file:///` denotes a Hadoop `LocalFileSystem` scheme; Cloud Dataproc installs `/usr/lib/spark/lib/spark-examples.jar` on the cluster's master node when it creates the cluster. Alternatively, you can specify a Cloud Storage path (`gs://my-bucket/my-jarfile.jar`) or an HDFS path (`hdfs://examples/myexample.jar`) to one of the custom jars.
4. Set `Main` class or jar to `org.apache.spark.examples.SparkPi`.
5. Set **Arguments** to the single argument `1000`.

Click on **Submit** to start the job.

Once the job starts, it is added to the **Jobs** list. Refer to the following screenshot:

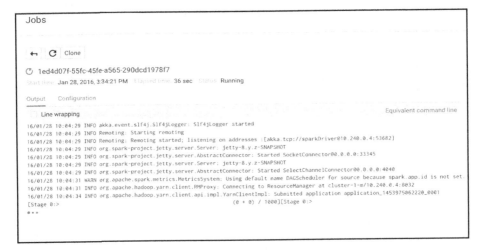

Once the job is complete, its status changes:

Take a look at the `job` output as listed here.

Execute the command from the terminal with the appropriate Job ID.

In our case, the Job ID was `1ed4d07f-55fc-45fe-a565-290dcd1978f7` and project-ID was `rd-spark-1`; hence, the command looks like this:

```
$ gcloud beta dataproc --project=rd-spark-1 jobs wait 1ed4d07f-
  55fc-45fe-a565-290dcd1978f7
```

The (abridged) output is shown here:

```
Waiting for job output...
16/01/28 10:04:29 INFO akka.event.slf4j.Slf4jLogger: Slf4jLogger
    started
16/01/28 10:04:29 INFO Remoting: Starting remoting
...
Submitted application application_1453975062220_0001
Pi is roughly 3.14157732
```

You can also SSH into the Spark Instance and run spark-shell in the interactive mode.

Summary

In this chapter, we covered how to set up Spark locally on our own computer as well as in the cloud as a cluster running on Amazon EC2. You learned how to run Spark on top of Amazon's **Elastic Map Reduce** (**EMR**). You also learned how to use Google Compute Engine's Spark Service to create a cluster and run a simple job. We discussed the basics of Spark's programming model and API using the interactive Scala console, and we wrote the same basic Spark program in Scala, Java, R, and Python. We also compared the performance metrics of Hadoop versus Spark for different machine learning algorithms as well as SORT benchmark tests.

In the next chapter, we will consider how to go about using Spark to create a machine learning system.

2

Math for Machine Learning

A machine learning user needs to have a fair understanding of machine learning concepts and algorithms. Familiarity with mathematics is an important aspect of machine learning. We learn to program by understanding the fundamental concepts and constructs of a language. Similarly, we learn machine learning by understanding concepts and algorithms using Mathematics, which is used to solve complex computational problems, and is a discipline for understanding and appreciating many computer science concepts. Mathematics plays a fundamental role in grasping theoretical concepts and in choosing the right algorithm. This chapter covers the basics of **linear algebra** and **calculus** for **machine learning**.

In this chapter, we will cover the following topics:

- Linear algebra
- Environment setup
    - Setting up the Scala environment in Intellij
    - Setting up the Scala environment on the command line
- Fields
- Vectors
    - Vector spaces
    - Vector types:
        - Dense vector
        - Sparse vector
        - Vectors in Spark
    - Vector operations
    - Hyperplanes
    - Vectors in machine learning

- Matrices
  - Introduction
  - Matrices types:
    - Dense matrix
    - CSC matrix
    - Matrix in Spark
  - Matrix operations
  - Determinant
  - Eigenvalues and eigenvectors
  - Singular value decomposition
  - Matrices in machine learning
- Functions
  - Definition
  - Function types:
    - Linear functions
    - Polynomial functions
    - Identity functions
    - Constant functions
    - Probability distribution functions
    - Gaussian functions
  - Functional composition
  - Hypothesis
  - Gradient descent
  - Prior, likelihood, and posterior
- Calculus
  - Differential calculus
  - Integral calculus
  - Lagrange multipliers
- Plotting

Linear algebra

Linear algebra is the study of solving a system of linear equations and transformations. Vectors, matrices, and determinants are the fundamental tools of linear algebra. We will learn each of these in detail using **Breeze**. Breeze is the underlying linear algebra library used for numerical processing. Respective Spark objects are wrappers around Breeze, and act as a public interface to ensure the consistency of the Spark ML library even if Breeze changes internally.

Setting up the Scala environment in Intellij

It is best to use an IDE like IntelliJ to edit Scala code, which provides faster development tools and coding assistance. Code completion and inspection makes coding and debugging faster and simpler, ensuring you focus on the end goal of learning math for machine learning.

IntelliJ 2016.3 brings Akka, Scala.meta, Memory view, Scala.js, and Migrators to the IntelliJ IDE as part of the Scala plugin. Now, let's set up the Scala environment in Intellij as follows:

1. Go to Under **Preferences** | **Plugins**, and verify if the Scala plugin is installed. SBT, which is a build tool for Scala, is configured by default as shown in the following screenshot:

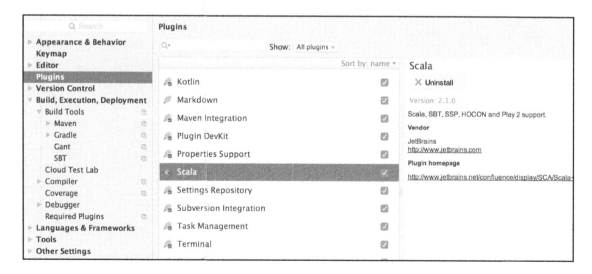

2. Select **File | New | Project from Existing resources | $GIT_REPO/Chapter_02/breeze or $GIT_REPO/Chapter_02/spark**. Here, **$GIT_REPO** is the repository path where you have cloned the source code of the book.

3. Import project by selecting the **SBT** option:

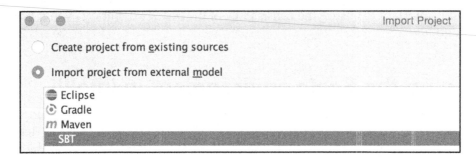

4. Keep the default options of SBT, and click on **Finish**.

5. SBT will take a while to import references from `build.sbt`.

```
name := "maths-for-ml"

version := "1.0"

val sparkVersion = "2.0.0"

libraryDependencies ++= Seq(
  // other dependencies here
  "org.scalanlp" %% "breeze" % "0.12",
  // native libraries are not included by default. add this if you want them (as of 0.7)
  // native libraries greatly improve performance, but increase jar sizes.
  // It also packages various blas implementations, which have licenses that may or may not
  // be compatible with the Apache License. No GPL code, as best I know.
  "org.scalanlp" %% "breeze-natives" % "0.12",
  // the visualization library is distributed separately as well.
  // It depends on LGPL code.
  "org.scalanlp" %% "breeze-viz" % "0.12",
  "org.apache.spark" %% "spark-core" % sparkVersion,
  "org.apache.spark" %% "spark-mllib" % sparkVersion
)


resolvers ++= Seq(
  // other resolvers here
  // if you want to use snapshot builds (currently 0.12-SNAPSHOT), use this.
  "Sonatype Snapshots" at "https://oss.sonatype.org/content/repositories/snapshots/",
  "Sonatype Releases" at "https://oss.sonatype.org/content/repositories/releases/"
)

scalaVersion := "2.11.7"
```

6. Finally, right click on the source file and select **Run 'Vector'**.

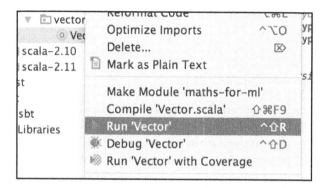

Setting up the Scala environment on the Command Line

To set up the environment locally, follow the steps listed next:

1. Go to the root directory of Chapter 2, and choose the appropriate folder.

   ```
   $ cd /PATH/spark-ml/Chapter_02/breeze
   ```

   Alternatively, choose the following:
   ```
   $ cd /PATH/spark-ml/Chapter_02/spark
   ```

2. Compile the code.

   ```
   $ sbt compile
   ```

3. Run the compiled code, and choose the program to run (classes shown depend on whether sbt run is executed in the Spark or Breeze folder).

   ```
   $ sbt run

   Multiple main classes detected, select one to run:
   . . . .
   Enter number:
   ```

Fields

Fields are fundamental structures of mathematics defined in many different ways. We will now look at the most basic types.

Real numbers

A real number is any number we can think of; real numbers include whole numbers (0, 1, 2, 3), rational numbers (2/6, 0.768, 0.222..., 3.4), and irrational numbers (π, √3). Real numbers can be positive, negative, or zero. Imaginary numbers, on the other hand, are like √−1 (the square root of minus 1); note that infinity is not a real number.

Complex numbers

Our understanding is that the square of a number can never be negative. In that case, how do we solve $x2 = -9$? Sensibly, in math we have the concept of i, as a solution, that is, $x = 3i$. Numbers such as i, -i, 3i, and 2.27i are called imaginary numbers. "A real number" + "an imaginary number" forms a "complex number".

Complex number = (real part) + (imaginary part) I

The following examples show complex number representation using the Breeze library for Mathematics:

```
import breeze.linalg.DenseVector
import breeze.math.Complex
val i = Complex.i

// add
println((1 + 2 * i) + (2 + 3 * i))

// sub
println((1 + 2 * i) - (2 + 3 * i))

// divide
println((5 + 10 * i) / (3 - 4 * i))

// mul
println((1 + 2 * i) * (-3 + 6 * i))
println((1 + 5 * i) * (-3 + 2 * i))

// neg
println(-(1 + 2 * i))
```

```
// sum of complex numbers
val x = List((5 + 7 * i), (1 + 3 * i), (13 + 17 * i))
println(x.sum)
// product of complex numbers
val x1 = List((5 + 7 * i), (1 + 3 * i), (13 + 17 * i))
println(x1.product)
// sort list of complex numbers
val x2 = List((5 + 7 * i), (1 + 3 * i), (13 + 17 * i))
println(x2.sorted)
```

This preceding code gives us the following result:

```
3.0 + 5.0i
-1.0 + -1.0i
-1.0 + 2.0i
-15.0 + 0.0i
-13.0 + -13.0i
-1.0 + -2.0i
19.0 + 27.0i
-582.0 + 14.0i
List(1.0 + 3.0i, 5.0 + 7.0i, 13.0 + 17.0i)
```

Vectors

A vector is a mathematical object described as an ordered set of numbers. It is similar to a Set, except that order is maintained in vectors. All members are part of real numbers. A vector having dimension n is geometrically represented as a point in *n*-dimensional space. The origin of a vector starts from zero.

Example:

```
[2, 4, 5, 9, 10]
[3.14159, 2.718281828, -1.0, 2.0]
[1.0, 1.1, 2.0]
```

Vector spaces

Linear algebra is well known as an algebra of vector spaces. Vector objects of field type real or complex can be added and scaled by multiplying the vector with the scalar number α.

Vector space is a collection of vector objects, which can be added and multiplied together. Two vectors can be combined to produce a third vector or another object in a vector space. The axioms of vector space have useful properties. Space in vector space helps in studying the properties of physical space, for example, to find how near or far away an object is. One of the examples of vector space is a collection of vectors in a three-dimensional Euclidean space. Vector space V over field F has the following properties:

- Vector addition: denoted by $v + w$, where v and w are element of space V
- Scalar multiplication: denoted by $\alpha * v$, where α is an element of F
- Associativity: represented by $u + (v + w) = (u + v) + w$, where u, v, and w are elements of space V
- Commutative: indicated by $v + w = w + v$
- Distributive: denoted by $\alpha * (v + w) = \alpha * v + \alpha * w$

In machine learning, features are the dimensions of vector space.

Vector types

In Scala, we will use the Breeze library to represent a vector. The vector can be represented as a dense or a sparse vector.

Vectors in Breeze

Breeze uses two basic vector types-`breeze.linalg.DenseVector` and `breeze.linalg.SparseVector`-to represent the two vector types shown earlier.

`DenseVector` is a wrapper around an array which supports numeric operations. Let's first look at the dense vector computation; we will create a dense vector object using Breeze, and then update index three to a new value.

```
import breeze.linalg.DenseVector
val v = DenseVector(2f, 0f, 3f, 2f, -1f)
v.update(3, 6f)
println(v)
```

This gives us the following result: `DenseVector (2.0, 0.0, 3.0, 6.0, -1.0)`

`SparseVector` is a vector with most of its values at zero, and supports numeric operations. Let's look at the sparse vector computation; we will a create sparse vector object using Breeze, and then update the values by one.

```
import breeze.linalg.SparseVectorval sv:SparseVector[Double] =
SparseVector(5)()
sv(0) = 1
sv(2) = 3
sv(4) = 5
val m:SparseVector[Double] = sv.mapActivePairs((i,x) => x+1)
println(m)
```

This gives us the following result: `SparseVector((0,2.0), (2,4.0), (4,6.0))`

Vectors in Spark

Spark MLlib uses Breeze and JBlas for internal linear algebraic operations. It uses its own class to represent a vector defined using the `org.apache.spark.mllib.linalg.Vector` factory. A local vector has integer-typed and 0-based indices. Its values are stored as double-typed. A local vector is stored on a single machine, and cannot be distributed. Spark MLlib supports two types of local vectors, dense and sparse, created using factory methods.

The following code snippet shows how to create basic sparse and dense vectors in Spark:

```
val dVectorOne: Vector = Vectors.dense(1.0, 0.0, 2.0)
println("dVectorOne:" + dVectorOne)
//  Sparse vector (1.0, 0.0, 2.0, 3.0)
// corresponding to nonzero entries.
val sVectorOne: Vector = Vectors.sparse(4,  Array(0, 2,3),
    Array(1.0, 2.0, 3.0))
// Create a sparse vector (1.0, 0.0, 2.0, 2.0) by specifying its
// nonzero entries.
val sVectorTwo: Vector = Vectors.sparse(4, Seq((0, 1.0), (2, 2.0),
    (3, 3.0)))
```

The preceding code produces the following output:

```
dVectorOne:[1.0,0.0,2.0]
sVectorOne:(4,[0,2,3],[1.0,2.0,3.0])
sVectorTwo:(4,[0,2,3],[1.0,2.0,3.0])
```

There are various methods exposed by Spark for accessing and discovering vector values as shown next:

```
val sVectorOneMax = sVectorOne.argmax
val sVectorOneNumNonZeros = sVectorOne.numNonzeros
val sVectorOneSize = sVectorOne.size
val sVectorOneArray = sVectorOne.toArray
val sVectorOneJson = sVectorOne.toJson

println("sVectorOneMax:" + sVectorOneMax)
println("sVectorOneNumNonZeros:" + sVectorOneNumNonZeros)
println("sVectorOneSize:" + sVectorOneSize)
println("sVectorOneArray:" + sVectorOneArray)
println("sVectorOneJson:" + sVectorOneJson)
val dVectorOneToSparse = dVectorOne.toSparse
```

The preceding code produces the following output:

```
sVectorOneMax:3
sVectorOneNumNonZeros:3
sVectorOneSize:4
sVectorOneArray:[D@38684d54
sVectorOneJson:{"type":0,"size":4,"indices":[0,2,3],"values":
   [1.0,2.0,3.0]}
dVectorOneToSparse:(3,[0,2],[1.0,2.0])
```

Vector operations

Vectors can be added together, subtracted, and multiplied by scalars. Other operations on vectors include finding the mean, normalization, comparison, and geometrical representation.

- **The Add operation**: This code shows an element-wise add operation on vector objects:

```
// vector's
val v1 = DenseVector(3, 7, 8.1, 4, 5)
val v2 = DenseVector(1, 9, 3, 2.3, 8)
// elementwise add operation
def add(): Unit = {
  println(v1 + v2)
}
```

This last code gives us the result as follows: `DenseVector(4.0, 16.0, 11.1, 6.3, 13.0)`

- **Multiply and Dot operation**: It is an algebraic operation, which takes two sequences of an equal length of numbers, and returns a single number; algebraically, it is the sum of the products of the corresponding entries of the two sequences of numbers. It is mathematically represented as follows:

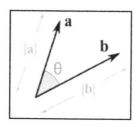

```
a   b = |a| × |b| × cos(θ) OR a   b = ax × bx + ay × by
```

```
import breeze.linalg.{DenseVector, SparseVector}
val a = DenseVector(0.56390, 0.36231, 0.14601, 0.60294,
    0.14535)
val b = DenseVector(0.15951, 0.83671, 0.56002, 0.57797,
    0.54450)
println(a.t * b)
println(a dot b)
```

This preceding code gives us the following result:

```
0.9024889161, 0.9024889161
```

```
import breeze.linalg.{DenseVector, SparseVector}
val sva =
    SparseVector(0.56390,0.36231,0.14601,0.60294,0.14535)
val svb =
    SparseVector(0.15951,0.83671,0.56002,0.57797,0.54450)
println(sva.t * svb)
println(sva dot svb)
```

The last code gives us the result as follows: `0.9024889161, 0.9024889161`

- **Finding the Mean:** This operation returns the mean of the elements of the vector along the first array dimension, whose size does not equal 1. It is mathematically represented as follows:

```
import breeze.linalg.{DenseVector, SparseVector}
import breeze.stats.mean
val mean = mean(DenseVector(0.0,1.0,2.0))
println(mean)
```

This gives us the result as follows:

```
1.0
import breeze.linalg.{DenseVector, SparseVector}
import breeze.stats.mean
val svm = mean(SparseVector(0.0,1.0,2.0))
val svm1 = mean(SparseVector(0.0,3.0))
println(svm, svm1)
```

This gives us the result as follows:

```
(1.0,1.5)
```

- **Normalized vector:** Every vector has a magnitude, which is calculated using the Pythagoras theorem as $|v| = sqrt(x^2 + y^2 + z^2)$; this magnitude is a length of a line from the origin point $(0, 0, 0)$ to the point indicated by the vector. A vector is normal if its magnitude is 1. Normalizing a vector means changing it so that it points in the same direction (beginning from the origin), but its magnitude is one. Hence, a normalized vector is a vector in the same direction, but with norm (length) 1. It is denoted by ^X and is given by the following formula:

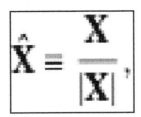

Where $|X|$ is the norm of X. It is also called a unit vector.

```
import breeze.linalg.{norm, DenseVector, SparseVector}
import breeze.stats.mean
val v = DenseVector(-0.4326, -1.6656, 0.1253, 0.2877, -
  1.1465)
val nm = norm(v, 1)
```

```
//Normalizes the argument such that its norm is 1.0
val nmlize = normalize(v)
// finally check if the norm of normalized vector is 1 or not
println(norm(nmlize))
```

This gives us the following result:

```
Norm(of dense vector) = 3.6577


Normalized vector is = DenseVector(-0.2068389122442966,
-0.7963728438143791, 0.05990965257561341, 0.1375579173663526,
-0.5481757117154094)


Norm(of normalized vector) = 0.999999999999999
```

- **Displaying the minimum and maximum element in a vector:**

```
import breeze.linalg._
val v1 = DenseVector(2, 0, 3, 2, -1)
println(argmin(v1))
println(argmax(v1))
println(min(v1))
println(max(v1))
```

This gives us the result as follows:

```
4, 2, -1, 3
```

- **Compare operation**: This compares two vectors for equality and for less than, or greater than, operations:

```
import breeze.linalg._
val a1 = DenseVector(1, 2, 3)
val b1 = DenseVector(1, 4, 1)
println((a1 :== b1))
println((a1 :<= b1))
println((a1 :>= b1))
println((a1 :< b1))
println((a1 :> b1))
```

This gives us the following result:

```
BitVector(0), BitVector(0, 1), BitVector(0, 2),
BitVector(1),
BitVector(2)
```

- **Geometrical representation of a vector:**

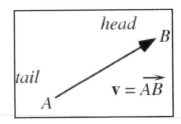

Hyperplanes

Vectors of field type real numbers are difficult to visualize if n is not 1,2, or 3. Familiar objects like lines and planes make sense for any value of n. Line L along the direction defined by a vector v, through a point P labeled by a vector u, can be written as follows:

$$L = \{u + tv \mid t \ \∈ \ R\}$$

Given two non-zero vectors, u and v, they determine a plane if both the vectors are not in the same line, and one of the vectors is a scalar multiple of the other. The addition of two vectors is accomplished by laying the vectors head to tail in a sequence to create a triangle. If u and v lie in a plane, then their sum lies in the plane of u and v. The plane represented by two vectors u and v can be mathematically shown as follows:

$$\{P + su + tv \mid s, t \ \∈ \ R\}$$

We can generalize the notion of a plane as a set of $x + 1$ vectors and $P, v1, \ldots, vx$ in R, n with $x \leq n$ determines a x-dimensional hyperplane:

$$(P + X x i=1 \ \lambda ivi \mid \lambda i \ \∈ \ R)$$

Vectors in machine learning

Features in machine learning are represented using the n-dimensional vector. In machine learning, data objects are required to be represented in the numeric format to allow processing and statistic analysis. For example, images are represented using the pixel vector.

Matrix

A matrix over a field F is a two-dimensional array whose entries are elements of F. An example of a matrix over the field of real numbers is given as follows:

1 2 3

10 20 30

The previous matrix has two rows and three columns; we call it a 2 × 3 matrix. It is traditional to refer to the rows and columns by numbers. Row 1 is (*1 2 3*), and row 2 is (*10 20 30*); column 1 is (*1 10*) , column 2 is (*2 20*), and column 3 is (*3 30*). In general, a matrix with m rows and n columns is called an $m \times n$ matrix. For matrix A, the element (i, j) is defined to be the element in the ith row and the jth column, and is indexed using the Ai, j or Aij notation. We will often use the pythonese notation, *A[i, j]*. Row i is the vector (*A[i, 0]*, *A[i, 1]*, *A[i, 2]*, , *A[i, m − 1]*) and column j is the vector (*A[0, j]*, *A[1, j]*, *A[2, j]*, , *A[n − 1, j]*).

Types of matrices

In Scala, we will use the Breeze library to represent a matrix. A matrix can be represented as a dense or a CSC matrix.

- **Dense matrix**: A dense matrix is created with a constructor method call. Its elements can be accessed and updated. It is a column major, and can be transposed to convert to row major.

  ```
  val a = DenseMatrix((1,2),(3,4))
    println("a : n" + a)
   val m = DenseMatrix.zeros[Int](5,5)
  ```

  The columns of a matrix can be accessed as Dense Vectors, and the rows as Dense Matrices.

  ```
    println( "m.rows :" + m.rows + " m.cols : "  + m.cols)
    m(::,1)
   println("m : n" + m)
  ```

- **Transposing a matrix**: Transposing a matrix means swapping its rows and columns. The transpose of a P × Q matrix, written MT, is a Q × P matrix such that (MT) j, I = Mi, j for every I ∈ P, j ∈ Q. Vector transpose to create a matrix row.

  ```
   m(4,::)  := DenseVector(5,5,5,5,5).t
   println(m)
  ```

The output of the preceding program is as follows:

```
a :
1   2
3   4
Created a 5x5 matrix
0  0  0  0  0
0  0  0  0  0
0  0  0  0  0
0  0  0  0  0
0  0  0  0  0
m.rows :5 m.cols : 5
First Column of m :
        DenseVector(0, 0, 0, 0, 0)
        Assigned 5,5,5,5,5 to last row of m.
0  0  0  0  0
0  0  0  0  0
0  0  0  0  0
0  0  0  0  0
5  5  5  5  5
```

- **CSC matrix:** The **CSC** matrix is known as the **Compressed Sparse Columns** matrix. Each column within the CSC matrix represents a sparse vector. The CSC matrix supports all matrix operations, and is constructed using `Builder`.

```
val builder = new CSCMatrix.Builder[Double](rows=10,
    cols=10)
builder.add(3,4, 1.0)
// etc.
val myMatrix = builder.result()
```

Matrix in Spark

A local matrix in Spark has integer-typed row and column indices. Values are double-typed. All the values are stored on a single machine. MLlib supports the following matrix types:

- **Dense matrices:** Matrices where entry values stored are in a single, double array in a column-major order.

- **Sparse matrices**: Matrices where non-zero entry values are stored in the CSC format in a column-major order. For example, the following dense matrix is stored in a one-dimensional array [2.0, 3.0, 4.0, 1.0, 4.0, 5.0] for the matrix size (3, 2):

```
2.0 3.0
4.0 1.0
4.0 5.0
```

This is an example of a dense and sparse matrix:

```
val dMatrix: Matrix = Matrices.dense(2, 2, Array(1.0, 2.0, 3.0,
    4.0))
println("dMatrix: n" + dMatrix)

val sMatrixOne: Matrix = Matrices.sparse(3, 2, Array(0, 1, 3),
    Array(0, 2, 1), Array(5, 6, 7))
println("sMatrixOne: n" + sMatrixOne)

val sMatrixTwo: Matrix = Matrices.sparse(3, 2, Array(0, 1, 3),
    Array(0, 1, 2), Array(5, 6, 7))
println("sMatrixTwo: n" + sMatrixTwo)
```

The output of the preceding code is as follows:

```
[info] Running linalg.matrix.SparkMatrix
dMatrix:
1.0   3.0
2.0   4.0
sMatrixOne:
3 x 2 CSCMatrix
(0,0) 5.0
(2,1) 6.0
(1,1) 7.0
sMatrixTwo:
3 x 2 CSCMatrix
(0,0) 5.0
(1,1) 6.0
(2,1) 7.0
```

Distributed matrix in Spark

A distributed matrix has long-type row and column indices. It has double-typed values, stored distributively in one or more RDDs. Four different types of distributed matrices have been implemented in Spark. All of them are subclasses of `DistributedMatrix`.

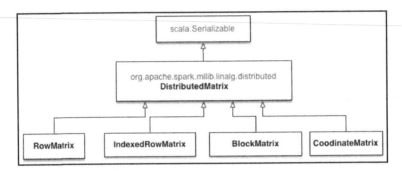

`RowMatrix`: A `RowMatrix` is a row-oriented distributed matrix without meaningful row indices. (In a row-oriented matrix, consecutive elements of the rows of an array are contiguous in memory). `RowMatrix` is implemented as an RDD of its rows. Each row is a local vector. The number of columns must be less than or equal to 2^31 for a `RowMatrix` so that a single local vector is communicated to the driver, and can also be stored or operated on using a single node.

The following example shows how a row matrix (dense and sparse) is created from the `Vectors` class:

```
val spConfig = (new
    SparkConf).setMaster("local").setAppName("SparkApp")
    val sc = new SparkContext(spConfig)
    val denseData = Seq(
      Vectors.dense(0.0, 1.0, 2.1),
      Vectors.dense(3.0, 2.0, 4.0),
      Vectors.dense(5.0, 7.0, 8.0),
      Vectors.dense(9.0, 0.0, 1.1)
    )
    val sparseData = Seq(
      Vectors.sparse(3, Seq((1, 1.0), (2, 2.1))),
      Vectors.sparse(3, Seq((0, 3.0), (1, 2.0), (2, 4.0))),
      Vectors.sparse(3, Seq((0, 5.0), (1, 7.0), (2, 8.0))),
      Vectors.sparse(3, Seq((0, 9.0), (2, 1.0)))
    )

val denseMat = new RowMatrix(sc.parallelize(denseData, 2))
val sparseMat = new RowMatrix(sc.parallelize(sparseData, 2))
```

```
println("Dense Matrix - Num of Rows :" + denseMat.numRows())
println("Dense Matrix - Num of Cols:" + denseMat.numCols())
println("Sparse Matrix - Num of Rows :" + sparseMat.numRows())
println("Sparse Matrix - Num of Cols:" + sparseMat.numCols())

sc.stop()
```

Output of the preceding code is as follows:

```
Using Spark's default log4j profile:
org/apache/spark/log4j-
defaults.properties
16/01/27 04:51:59 INFO SparkContext: Running Spark version
1.6.0
Dense Matrix - Num of Rows :4
Dense Matrix - Num of Cols:3
...
Sparse Matrix - Num of Rows :4
Sparse Matrix - Num of Cols :3
```

IndexedRowMatrix: IndexedRowMatrix is similar to a RowMatrix, but with row indices, which can be used for identifying rows and executing joins. In the following code listing, we create a 4x3 IndexedMatrix with appropriate row indices:

```
val data = Seq(
(0L, Vectors.dense(0.0, 1.0, 2.0)),
(1L, Vectors.dense(3.0, 4.0, 5.0)),
(3L, Vectors.dense(9.0, 0.0, 1.0))
).map(x => IndexedRow(x._1, x._2))
val indexedRows: RDD[IndexedRow] = sc.parallelize(data, 2)
val indexedRowsMat = new IndexedRowMatrix(indexedRows)
 println("Indexed Row Matrix - No of Rows: " +
indexedRowsMat.numRows())
 println("Indexed Row Matrix - No of Cols: " +
indexedRowsMat.numCols())
```

Output of the code listing above is as follows:

```
Indexed Row Matrix - No of Rows: 4
Indexed Row Matrix - No of Cols: 3
```

CoordinateMatrix: This is a distributed matrix stored in a coordinate list (COO) format, backed by an RDD of its entries.

The COO format stores a list of (row, column, value) tuples. Entries are sorted (row index, then column index) to improve random access times. This format is good for incremental matrix construction.

```
val entries = sc.parallelize(Seq(
        (0, 0, 1.0),
        (0, 1, 2.0),
        (1, 1, 3.0),
        (1, 2, 4.0),
        (2, 2, 5.0),
        (2, 3, 6.0),
        (3, 0, 7.0),
        (3, 3, 8.0),
        (4, 1, 9.0)), 3).map { case (i, j, value) =>
        MatrixEntry(i, j, value)
    }
val coordinateMat = new CoordinateMatrix(entries)
println("Coordinate Matrix - No of Rows: " +
    coordinateMat.numRows())
println("Coordinate Matrix - No of Cols: " +
    coordinateMat.numCols())
```

The output of the preceding code is as follows:

```
Coordinate Matrix - No of Rows: 5
Coordinate - No of Cols: 4
```

Matrix operations

There are different kinds of operations which can be performed on matrices.

- **Elementwise addition**: Given two matrices, a and b, addition of the two (a + b) means adding each element of two matrices.

Breeze

```
val a = DenseMatrix((1,2),(3,4))
val b = DenseMatrix((2,2),(2,2))
val c = a + b
println("a: n" + a)
println("b: n" + b)
println("a + b : n" + c)
```

The output of the last code is given as follows:

```
a:
1   2
3   4
b:
2   2
2   2
```

```
a + b :
3   4
5   6
```

- **Elementwise multiplication**: In this operation, each element of the matrix *a* is multiplied by matrix

Breeze

```
a :* b
val d = a*b
println("Dot product a*b : n" + d)
```

The output of the preceding code is given as follows:

```
Dot product a*b :
6    6
14   14
```

- **Elementwise comparison**: In this operation, each element of a is compared with b. The code in Breeze is given as follows:

Breeze
```
a :< b
```

The output for the preceding code is give as follows:

```
a :< b
false   false
false   false
```

- **Inplace addition**: This implies adding each element of a by 1.

Breeze
The following is the output of the preceding code:
```
Inplace Addition : a :+= 1
2   3
4   5
value = a :+= 1
println("Inplace Addition : a :+= 1n" + e)
```

- **Element-wise sum**: This is used to add all the elements of a matrix. The code in Breeze is given as follows:

Breeze

```
val sumA = sum(a)
```

```
println("sum(a):n" + sumA)
```

The following is the output for the preceding code:

sum(a):
14

- **Element-wise max**: To find the maximum value out of all the elements in a matrix, we use

  ```
  a.max
  ```

  Breeze
  The code in Breeze can be written as follows:
  ```
  println("a.max:n" + a.max)
  ```

- **Element-wise argmax**: This is used to get the position of the element with the maximum value.

Breeze

  Code:
  ```
  println("argmax(a):n" + argmax(a))
  ```

The output of the preceding command is as follows:

argmax(a):
(1,1)

- **Ceiling**: This rounds off each element of the matrix to the next integer.

  Breeze
  Code:
  ```
  val g = DenseMatrix((1.1, 1.2), (3.9, 3.5))
  println("g: n" + g)
  val gCeil =ceil(g)
  println("ceil(g)n " + gCeil)
  ```

The output of the preceding code is as follows:

```
g:
    1.1   1.2
    3.9   3.5

ceil(g)
    2.0   2.0
    4.0   4.0
```

- **Floor**: Floor rounds off the value of each element to the nearest integer of a lower value.

    Breeze
    Code:
    ```
    val gFloor =floor(g)
    println("floor(g)n" + gFloor)
    ```

The output will be as follows:

```
floor(g)
1.0   1.0
3.0   3.0
```

Determinant

The `tr` M denotes the trace of a matrix M; it is the sum of the elements along the diagonal. The trace of a matrix is normally used as a measure of the "size" of a matrix. The determinant is known as the product of the elements along its diagonal.

$$\det \begin{bmatrix} a & b \\ c & d \end{bmatrix} = ad - bc$$

The determinant is majorly used in the system of linear equations; it indicates if the columns are linearly related, and it also helps to find the inverse of a matrix. For large matrices, the determinant is calculated using laplace expansion.

```
val detm: Matrix = Matrices.dense(3, 3, Array(1.0, 3.0, 5.0, 2.0,
    4.0, 6.0, 2.0, 4.0, 5.0))
print(det(detm))
```

Eigenvalues and eigenvectors

$Ax = b$ is a linear equation which emerges from static problems. Eigenvalues, on the other hand, are used for dynamic problems. Let's consider A as a matrix with x as a vector; we will now solve the new equation in linear algebra, $Ax = \lambda x$.

As A multiplies x, the vector x changes its direction. But there are certain vectors in the same direction as Ax-these are known as **eigenvectors,** for which the following equation holds good:

$Ax = \lambda x$

In the last equation, vector Ax is lambda times the vector x, and λ is known as eigenvalue. Eigenvalue λ gives the direction of a vector-if it is reversed, or is in the same direction.

$Ax = \lambda x$ also conveys that $det(A - \lambda I) = 0$, where I is the identity matrix. This determines n eigenvalues.

The eigenvalue problem is defined as follows:

$A\,x = \lambda\,x$

$A\,x - \lambda\,x = 0$

$A\,x - \lambda\,I\,x = 0$

$(A - \lambda\,I)\,x = 0$

If x is non-zero, the preceding equation will have a solution only if $|A - \lambda I| = 0$. Using this equation, we can find eigenvalues.

```
val A = DenseMatrix((9.0,0.0,0.0),(0.0,82.0,0.0),(0.0,0.0,25.0))
val es = eigSym(A)
val lambda = es.eigenvalues
val evs = es.eigenvectors
println("lambda is : " + lambda)
println("evs is : " + evs)
```

This last code gives us the following result:

```
lambda is : DenseVector(9.0, 25.0, 82.0)
evs is : 1.0  0.0  0.0
0.0  0.0  1.0
0.0  1.0  -0.0
```

Singular value decomposition

Singular value decomposition of a matrix M: $m \times n$ (real or complex) is a factorization with the form $U\Sigma V^*$, where U is an $m \times R$ matrix. Σ is an $R \times R$ rectangular diagonal matrix with non-negative real numbers on the diagonal, and V is an $n \times r$ unitary matrix. r is equal to the rank of the matrix M.

The diagonal entries Σii of Sigma are known as the singular values of M. The columns of U and the columns of V are called the left-singular vectors and right-singular vectors of M respectively.

The following is an example of an SVD in Apache Spark:

```
package linalg.svd

import org.apache.spark.{SparkConf, SparkContext}
import org.apache.spark.mllib.linalg.distributed.RowMatrix
import org.apache.spark.mllib.linalg.{Matrix,
SingularValueDecomposition, Vector, Vectors}
object SparkSVDExampleOne {

  def main(args: Array[String]) {
    val denseData = Seq(
      Vectors.dense(0.0, 1.0, 2.0, 1.0, 5.0, 3.3, 2.1),
      Vectors.dense(3.0, 4.0, 5.0, 3.1, 4.5, 5.1, 3.3),
      Vectors.dense(6.0, 7.0, 8.0, 2.1, 6.0, 6.7, 6.8),
      Vectors.dense(9.0, 0.0, 1.0, 3.4, 4.3, 1.0, 1.0)
    )
    val spConfig = (new
      SparkConf).setMaster("local").setAppName("SparkSVDDemo")
    val sc = new SparkContext(spConfig)
    val mat: RowMatrix = new RowMatrix(sc.parallelize(denseData, 2))


    // Compute the top 20 singular values and corresponding
      singular vectors.
    val svd: SingularValueDecomposition[RowMatrix, Matrix] =
    mat.computeSVD(7, computeU = true)
    val U: RowMatrix = svd.U // The U factor is a RowMatrix.
    val s: Vector = svd.s // The singular values are stored in a
      local dense  vector.
    val V: Matrix = svd.V // The V factor is a local dense matrix.
    println("U:" + U)
    println("s:" + s)
    println("V:" + V)
    sc.stop()
```

```
        }
    }
```

Matrices in machine learning

Matrices are used as mathematical objects to represent images, datasets for real world machine learning applications like a face or text recognition, medical imaging, principal component analysis, numerical accuracy, and so on.

As an example, eigen decomposition is explained here. Many mathematical objects can be understood better by breaking them into constituent parts, or by finding properties which are universal.

Like when integers are decomposed into prime factors, matrix decomposition is called eigen decomposition, where we decompose a matrix into eigenvectors and eigenvalues.

Eigenvector v of a matrix A is such that multiplication by A alters only the scale of v, as shown next:

$Av = \lambda v$

The scalar λ is known as the eigenvalue corresponding to this eigenvector. The eigen decomposition of A is then given by the following:

$A = V\,diag(\lambda)V^{-1}$

The eigen decomposition of a matrix shares many facts about the matrix. The matrix is singular if and only if any of the eigenvalues is 0. The eigen decomposition of a real symmetric matrix can also be used to optimize quadratic expressions and much more. Eigenvectors and eigenvalues are used for **Principal Component Analysis**.

The following example shows how a DenseMatrix is used to get eigenvalues and eigen vectors:

```
// The data
val msData = DenseMatrix(
    (2.5,2.4), (0.5,0.7), (2.2,2.9), (1.9,2.2), (3.1,3.0),
    (2.3,2.7), (2.0,1.6), (1.0,1.1), (1.5,1.6), (1.1,0.9))


def main(args: Array[String]): Unit = {
        val pca = breeze.linalg.princomp(msData)

        print("Center" , msData(*,::) - pca.center)
```

```
//the covariance matrix of the data

print("covariance matrix", pca.covmat)

// the eigenvalues of the covariance matrix, IN SORTED ORDER
print("eigen values",pca.eigenvalues)

// eigenvectors
print("eigen vectors",pca.loadings)
print(pca.scores)
}
```

This gives us the following result:

```
eigen values = DenseVector(1.2840277121727839, 0.04908339893832732)
eigen vectors = -0.6778733985280118  -0.735178655544408
```

Functions

To define a mathematical object like a function, we must first understand what a set is.

A set is an unordered collection of objects like S = {-4, 4, -3, 3, -2, 2, -1, 1, 0}. If a set S is not infinite, we use |S| to denote the number of elements, which is known as the Cardinality of the set. If *A* and *B* are finite sets, then $|A$ ⇥ $B|=|A|$ ⇥ $|B|$, which is known as the Cartesian product.

For each input element in a set A, a function assigns a single output element from another set B. A is called the domain of the function, and B, the codomain. A function is a set of pairs *(x, y)*, with none of these pairs having the same first element.

Example: The function with domain {1, 2, 3, . . .}, which doubles its input is the set {(1,2),(2,4),(3,6),(4,8),...}

Example: The function with domain {1, 2, 3, . . .} ⇥ {1, 2, 3, . . .}, which multiplies the numbers forming its input is {((1,1),1),((1,2),2)),....,((2,1),2),((2,2),4),((2,3),6),... ((3,1),3),((3,2),6),((3,3),9),...

The output of a given input is known as the image of that input. The image of q under a function f is denoted by $f(q)$. If $f(q)=s$, we say q maps to s under f. We write this as $q{\to}s$. The set from which all the outputs are chosen is a codomain.

We write this as $f: D \to F$ when we want to say that f is a function with domain D and codomain F.

Function types

Procedures versus Functions:

A procedure is a description of a computation that, given an input, produces an output.

Functions or computational problems don't indicate how to compute the output from the given input.

Many methods might exist for the same specification.

A computational problem may allow several possible outputs for each input.

We will write procedures in Breeze; often, these are called functions, but we will reserve that term for the mathematical objects.

- **One to One function:**

    $f: D \to F$ is one-to-one if $f(x) = f(y)$ implies $x = y$; that is, both x and y are in D.

- **Onto function:**

    $F: D \to F$ is onto if for every z element of F, there exists an element a in D such that $f(a) = z$.

A function is invertible if it is one-to-one and onto.

- **Linear functions:** Linear functions are the functions whose graph is a straight line. A linear function has the form $z = f(x) = a + bx$. A linear function has one dependent variable, and one independent variable. The dependent variable is z, and the independent variable is x.

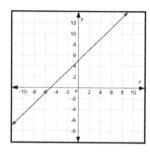

- **Polynomial function**: A polynomial function involves only non-negative integer powers of x such as a quadratic, a cubic, a quartic, and so on. We can give a general definition of a polynomial, and define its degree. A polynomial of degree n is a function of the form $f(x) = a_n x^n + a_{n-1} x^{n-1} + \ldots + a_2 x^2 + a_1 x + a_0$, where a's are real numbers, also known as coefficients of polynomials.

For example: $f(x) = 4x^3 - 3x^2 + 2$

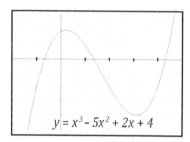

$$y = x^3 - 5x^2 + 2x + 4$$

- **Identity function**: For any domain D, $id_D: D \rightarrow D$ maps each domain element d to itself.

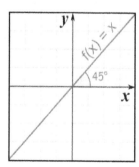

- **Constant function**: this is a special function represented as a horizontal line.

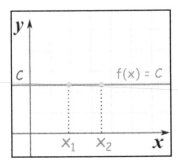

- **Probability distribution function** : This used to define the relative likelihood of different outcomes of a particular experiment. It assigns a probability to each potential outcome. Probabilities of all outcomes must sum equal to 1. Often, probability distribution is a uniform distribution. That means, it assigns the same probability to each outcome. When we roll a die, the possible outcomes are 1, 2, 3, 4, 5, and probabilities are defined as $Pr(1) = Pr(2) = Pr(3) = Pr(4) = Pr(5) = 1/5$.

- **Gaussian Function**: When the number of events is large, then the Gaussian function can be used to describe events. Gaussian distribution is described as a continuous function, also known as normal distribution. Normal distribution has the mean equal to median, and has symmetry about the center.

Functional composition

For functions $f: A \rightarrow B$ and $g: B \rightarrow C$, the functional composition of function f and function g is the function $(g \circ f): A \rightarrow C$, defined by $(g \circ f)(x) = g(f(x))$. For example, if $f : \{1,2,3\} \rightarrow \{A,B,C,D\}$ and $g : \{A,B,C,D\} \rightarrow \{4,5\}$, the composition of $g(y)=y2$ and $f(x)=x+1$ is $(g \circ f)(x)=(x+1)2$.

Function composition is applying a function to the results of another function. So, in $(g \circ f)(x) = g(f(x))$, first apply $f()$, and then $g()$. Some functions can be decomposed into two (or more) simpler functions.

Hypothesis

X denotes the input variables, also called input features, and y denotes the output or target variable that we are trying to predict. The pair (x, y) is called a training example, and the dataset used to learn is a list of m training examples, where $\{(x, y)\}$ is a training set. We will also use X to denote the space of input values, and Y to denote the space of output values. For a training set, to learn a function, $h: X \rightarrow Y$ so that $h(x)$ is a predictor for the value of y. Function h is called a **hypothesis**.

When the target variable to be predicted is continuous, we call the learning problem a regression problem. When y can take a small number of discrete values, we call it a classification problem.

Let's say we choose to approximate y as a linear function of x.

The hypothesis function is as follows:

$$h_\theta(x) = \theta_0 + \theta_1 x_1 + \theta_2 x_2$$

In this last hypothesis function, the θi 's are parameters, also known as weights, which parameterize the space of linear functions mapping from X to Y. To simplify the notation, we also introduce the convention of letting $x0 = 1$ (this is the intercept term), such that:

$$h(x) = \sum_{i=0}^{n} \theta_i x_i = \theta^T x,$$

On the RHS, we view θ and x both as vectors, and n is the number of input variables.

Now before we proceed any further, it's important to note that we will now be transitioning from mathematical fundamentals to learning algorithms. Optimizing the cost function and learning θ will lay the foundation to understand machine learning algorithms.

Given a training set, how do we learn the parameters θ? One method that looks possible is to get $h(x)$ close to y for the given training examples. We shall define a function that measures, for each value of the θs, how close the $h(x(i))$s are to the corresponding y *(i)* s. We define this as a cost function.

$$J(\theta) = \frac{1}{2} \sum_{i=1}^{m} (h_\theta(x^{(i)}) - y^{(i)})^2.$$

Gradient descent

An SGD implementation of gradient descent uses a simple distributed sampling of the data examples. Loss is a part of the optimization problem, and therefore, is a true sub-gradient.

$$\frac{1}{n} \sum_{i=1}^{n} L(\mathbf{w}; \mathbf{x}_i, y_i)$$

This requires access to the full dataset, which is not optimal.

$$\frac{1}{n} \sum_{i=1}^{n} L'_{\mathbf{w},i}$$

The parameter *miniBatchFraction* specifies the fraction of the full data to use. The average of the gradients over this subset

$$\frac{1}{|S|} \sum_{i \in S} L'_{\mathbf{w},i}$$

is a stochastic gradient. S is a sampled subset of size $|S| = $ *miniBatchFraction*.

In the following code, we show how to use stochastic gardient descent on a mini batch to calculate the weights and the loss. The output of this program is a vector of weights and loss.

```
object SparkSGD {
 def main(args: Array[String]): Unit = {
    val m = 4
    val n = 200000
    val sc = new SparkContext("local[2]", "")
    val points = sc.parallelize(0 until m,
      2).mapPartitionsWithIndex { (idx, iter) =>
      val random = new Random(idx)
      iter.map(i => (1.0,
        Vectors.dense(Array.fill(n)(random.nextDouble())))))
    }.cache()
    val (weights, loss) = GradientDescent.runMiniBatchSGD(
      points,
      new LogisticGradient,
      new SquaredL2Updater,
      0.1,
      2,
      1.0,
      1.0,
      Vectors.dense(new Array[Double](n)))
    println("w:" + weights(0))
    println("loss:" + loss(0))
    sc.stop()
  }
```

Prior, likelihood, and posterior

Bayes theorem states the following:

*Posterior = Prior * Likelihood*

This can also be stated as $P(A \mid B) = (P(B \mid A) * P(A)) / P(B)$, where $P(A|B)$ is the probability of A given B, also called posterior.

Prior: Probability distribution representing knowledge or uncertainty of a data object prior or before observing it

Posterior: Conditional probability distribution representing what parameters are likely after observing the data object

Likelihood: The probability of falling under a specific category or class.

This is represented as follows:

$$p(\theta|y) = \frac{p(y|\theta)p(\theta)}{p(y)} = \frac{p(y|\theta)p(\theta)}{\int p(y|\theta')p(\theta')d\theta'},$$

Calculus

Calculus is a mathematical tool which helps the study of how things change. It provides a framework for modeling systems in which there is change, and a way to deduce the predictions of such models.

Differential calculus

At the core of calculus lie derivatives, where the derivative is defined as the instantaneous rate of change of a given function with respect to one of its variables. The study of finding a derivative is known as differentiation. Geometrically, the derivative at a known point is given by the slope of a tangent line to the graph of the function, provided that the derivative exists, and is defined at that point.

Differentiation is the reverse of Integration. Differentiation has several applications; like in physics, the derivative of displacement is velocity, and the derivative of velocity is acceleration. Derivatives are mainly used to find maxima or minima of a function.

Within machine learning, we deal with the functions that operate on variables or features having hundreds or more dimensions. We calculate derivatives of the function in each dimension of the variable, and combine these partial derivatives into a vector, which gives us what is called a gradient. Similarly, taking the second-order derivative of a gradient gives us a matrix termed as **Hessian**.

The knowledge of gradients and hessians helps us define things like directions of descent and rate of descent, which tell us how we should travel in our function space in order to get to the bottom-most point, in order to minimize the function.

The following is an example of a simple objective function (linear regression with weights x, N data points, and D dimensions in a vectorized notation:

$$J(w) = \frac{1}{2} \|\mathbf{A}x - b\|^2$$

The method of Lagrange multipliers is a standard way in calculus to maximize or minimize functions when there are constraints involved.

Integral calculus

Integral calculus joins (integrates) the granular pieces together to find the total. It is also known as anti-differential, where differential is to divide into small chunks and study how it changes as described in the previous section.

Integral is often used to find the area underneath the graph of a function.

Lagranges multipliers

In the math optimization problem, the method of Lagrange multipliers is used as a tool for finding the local minima and maxima of a function subject to equality constraints. An example involves finding the maximum entropy distribution subject to given constraints.

This is best explained with an example. Let's say we have to maximize K (x, y) = -x2 -y2 *subject to y = x + 1.*

The constraint function is *g (x, y) = x-y+1=0*. The *L* multiplier then becomes this:

$$L(x, y, \lambda) = -x^2 - y^2 + \lambda(x - y + 1)$$

Differentiating with respect to *x, y,* and lambda, and setting to *0* we get the following:

$$\frac{\partial L}{\partial x}(x, y, \lambda) = -2x + \lambda x = 0$$

$$\frac{\partial L}{\partial y}(x, y, \lambda) = -2y + \lambda x = 0$$

$$\frac{\partial L}{\partial \lambda}(x, y, \lambda) = x - y + 1 = 0$$

Solving the preceding equations, we get *x=-0.5, y=0.5, lambda=-1.*

Plotting

In this segment, we will see how to use Breeze to create a simple line plot from the Breeze `DenseVector`.

Breeze uses most of the functionality of Scala's plotting facilities, although the API is different. In the following example, we create two vectors x1 and y with some values, and plot a line and save it to a PNG file:

```
package linalg.plot
import breeze.linalg._
import breeze.plot._

object BreezePlotSampleOne {
  def main(args: Array[String]): Unit = {

    val f = Figure()
    val p = f.subplot(0)
    val x = DenseVector(0.0,0.1,0.2,0.3,0.4,0.5,0.6,0.7,0.8)
    val y = DenseVector(1.1, 2.1, 0.5, 1.0,3.0, 1.1, 0.0, 0.5,2.5)
    p += plot(x,  y)
    p.xlabel = "x axis"
    p.ylabel = "y axis"
    f.saveas("lines-graph.png")
  }
}
```

The preceding code generates the following Line Plot:

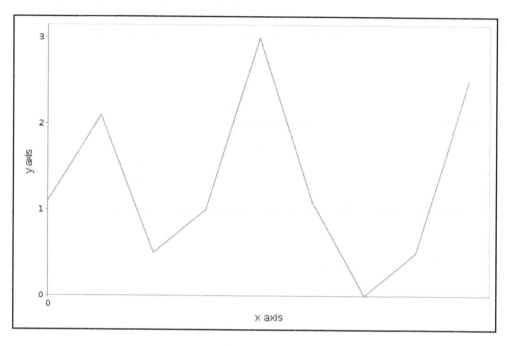

Breeze also supports histogram. This is drawn for various sample sizes $100,000,$ and $100,0000$ normally distributed random numbers into 100 buckets.

```
package linalg.plot
import breeze.linalg._
import breeze.plot._

object BreezePlotGaussian {
  def main(args: Array[String]): Unit = {
    val f = Figure()
    val p = f.subplot(2, 1, 1)
    val g = breeze.stats.distributions.Gaussian(0, 1)
    p += hist(g.sample(100000), 100)
    p.title = "A normal distribution"
    f.saveas("plot-gaussian-100000.png")
  }
}
```

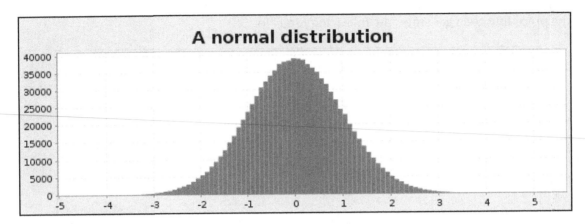

A Gaussian distribution with 1000000 elements is shown in this next image:

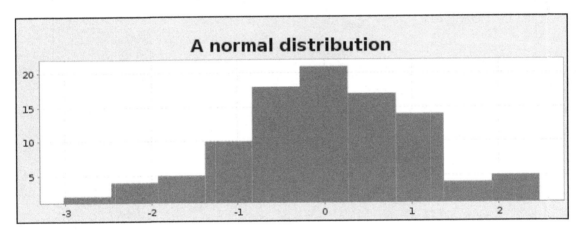

A Gaussian distribution with 100 elements

Summary

In this chapter, you learnt the basics of linear algebra, which is useful for machine learning, and the basic constructs like vectors and matrix. You also learnt how to use Spark and Breeze to do basic operations on these constructs. We looked at techniques like SVD to transform data. We also looked at the importance of the function types in linear algebra. In the end, you learnt how to plot basic charts using Breeze. In the next chapter, we will cover an overview of Machine Learning systems, components and architecture.

3
Designing a Machine Learning System

In this chapter, we will design a high-level architecture for an intelligent, distributed machine learning system that uses Spark as its core computation engine. The problem we will focus on will be taking the existing architecture for a web-based business and redesigning it to use automated machine learning systems to power key areas of the business.

Before we dig deeper into our scenario, we will spend some time understanding what machine learning is.

Then we will:

- Introduce a hypothetical business scenario
- Provide an overview of the current architecture
- Explore various ways in which machine learning systems can enhance or replace certain business functions
- Provide a new architecture based on these ideas

A modern large-scale data environment includes the following requirements:

- It must integrate with the other components of the system, especially with data collection and storage systems, analytics and reporting, and frontend applications
- It should be easily scalable and independent of the rest of the architecture. Ideally, this should be in the form of horizontal as well as vertical scalability
- It should allow efficient computation with respect to the type of workload in mind, that is, machine learning and iterative analytics applications
- If possible, it should support both batch and real-time workload

As a framework, Spark meets these criteria. However, we must ensure that the machine learning systems designed on Spark also meet this criteria. There is no good in implementing an algorithm that ends up having bottlenecks that cause our system to fail in terms of one or more of these requirements.

What is Machine Learning?

Machine learning is a subfield of data mining. While data mining has been around for more than 50+ years, machine learning is a subset where a large cluster of machines is used to analyze and extract knowledge from large datasets.

Machine learning is closely related to computational statistics. It has strong ties to mathematical optimization; it provides methods, theory, and application domains to the field. Machine learning is employed in various types of computing tasks where designing and programming explicit algorithms are infeasible. Example applications are spam filtering, **optical character recognition** (**OCR**), search engine, and computer vision. Machine learning is sometimes combined with data mining, which focuses more on exploratory data analysis and is known as unsupervised learning.

Machine learning systems can be classified into three categories, depending on the nature of the learning signal available to a learning system. Learning algorithm discovers structure from the input provided. It can have a goal (hidden patterns), or it could be a means try to find features.

- **Unsupervised learning**: No labels of outputs are given to the learning system. It finds structure on its own from the inputs given to
- **Supervised learning**: The system is presented with inputs and desired outputs by a human and the goal is to learn a model to map inputs to outputs
- **Reinforcement learning**: The system interacts with an environment in which it performs a stated goal without a human explicitly telling it whether it has come close to its goal

In the later sections, we will map supervised and unsupervised learning to various chapters.

Introducing MovieStream

To better illustrate the design of our architecture, we will introduce a practical scenario. Let's assume that we have just been appointed to head the data science team of MovieStream, a fictitious Internet business that streams movies and television shows to its users.

MovieStream system is outlined in the following diagram:

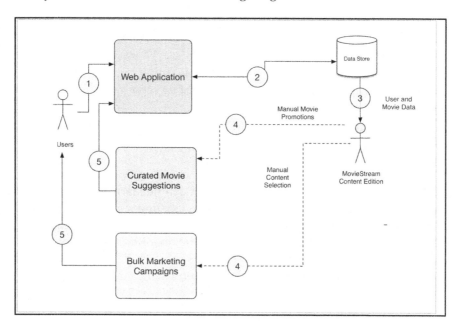

MovieStream's current architecture

As we can see in the preceding diagram, currently, MovieStream's content editorial team is responsible for deciding which movies and shows are promoted and shown in various parts of the site. They are also responsible for creating the content for MovieStream's bulk marketing campaigns, which include e-mail and other direct marketing channels. Currently, MovieStream collects basic data on what titles are viewed by users on an aggregate basis and has access to some demographic data collected from users when they sign up to the service. In addition, they have access to some basic metadata about the titles in their catalog.

MovieStream can handle many of the functions currently handled by the content team in an automated manner.

Business use cases for a machine learning system

Perhaps the first question we should answer is, *Why to use machine learning at all?*

Why doesn't MovieStream simply continue with human-driven decisions? There are many reasons to use machine learning (and certainly some reasons not to), but the most important ones are mentioned here:

- The scale of data involved means that full human involvement quickly becomes infeasible as MovieStream grows
- Model-driven approaches such as machine learning and statistics can often benefit from uncovering patterns that cannot be seen by humans (due to the size and complexity of the datasets)
- Model-driven approaches can avoid human and emotional biases (as long as the correct processes are carefully applied)

However, there is no reason why both model-driven and human-driven processes and decision making cannot coexist. For example, many machine learning systems rely on receiving labeled data in order to train models. Often, labeling such data is costly, time consuming, and requires human input. A good example of this is classifying textual data into categories or assigning a sentiment indicator to the text. Many real-world systems use some form of human-driven system to generate labels for such data (or at least part of it) to provide training data to models. These models are then used to make predictions in the live system at a larger scale.

In the context of MovieStream, we need not fear that our machine learning system will make the content team redundant. Indeed, we will see that our aim is to lift the burden of time-consuming tasks where machine learning might be able to perform better while providing tools to allow the team to better understand the users and content. This might, for example, help them in selecting which new content to acquire for the catalog (which involves a significant amount of cost and is, therefore, a critical aspect of the business).

Personalization

Perhaps one of the most important potential applications of machine learning in MovieStream's business is personalization. Generally speaking, personalization refers to adapting the experience of a user and the content presented to them based on various factors, which might include user behavior data as well as external factors.

Recommendations are essentially a subset of personalization. Recommendation generally refers to presenting a user with a list of items that we hope the user will be interested in. Recommendations might be used in web pages (for example, recommendation-related products), via e-mails or other direct marketing channels, via mobile apps, and so on.

Personalization is very similar to recommendations, but while recommendations are usually focused on an *explicit* presentation of products or content to the user, personalization is more generic and, often, more *implicit*. For example, applying personalization to search on the MovieStream site might allow us to adapt the search results for a given user, based on the data available about that user. This might include recommendation-based data (in the case of a search for products or content) but might also include various other factors such as geolocation and past search history. It might not be apparent to the user that the search results are adapted to their specific profile; this is why personalization tends to be more implicit.

Targeted marketing and customer segmentation

In a manner similar to recommendations, targeted marketing uses a model to select what to target at users. While generally recommendations and personalization are focused on a one-to-one situation, segmentation approaches might try to assign users into groups based on characteristics and, possibly, behavioral data. The approach might be fairly simple or might involve approaches that try to assign users into groups based on characteristics and, possibly, behavioral data. The approach might be fairly simple or might involve a machine-learning model such as clustering. Either way, the result is a set of segment assignments that might allow us to understand the broad characteristics of each group of users, what makes them similar to each other within a group, and what makes them different from others in different groups.

This could help MovieStream to better understand the drivers of user behavior and might also allow a broader targeting approach where groups are targeted as opposed to (or more likely, in addition to) direct one-to-one targeting with personalization.

These methods can also help when we don't necessarily have labeled data available (as is the case with certain user and content profile data), but we still wish to perform more focused targeting than a complete one-size-fits-all approach.

Predictive modeling and analytics

A third area where machine learning can be applied is in predictive analytics. This is a very broad term, and in some ways, it encompasses recommendations, personalization, and targeting too. In this context, since recommendations and segmentation are somewhat distinct, we use the term **predictive modeling** to refer to other models that seek to make predictions. An example of this can be a model that predicts the potential viewing activity and revenue of new titles before any data is available on how popular the title might be. MovieStream can use past activity and revenue data, together with content attributes, to create a regression model that can be used to make predictions for brand new titles.

As another example, we can use a **classification model** to automatically assign tags, keywords, or categories to new titles for which we only have partial data.

Types of machine learning models

While we have one example, there are many other examples, some of which we will touch on in the relevant chapters when we introduce each machine learning task.

However, we can broadly divide the preceding use cases and methods into two categories of machine learning:

- **Supervised learning**: These types of models use labeled data to learn. Recommendation engines, regression, and classification are examples of supervised learning methods. The labels in these models can be user--movie ratings (for the recommendation), movie tags (in the case of the preceding classification example), or revenue figures (for regression). We will cover supervised learning models in Chapter 4, *Building a Recommendation Engine with Spark*, Chapter 6, *Building a Classification Model with Spark*, and Chapter 7, *Building a Regression Model with Spark*.
- **Unsupervised learning**: When a model does not require labeled data, we refer to unsupervised learning. These types of models try to learn or extract some underlying structure in the data or reduce the data down to its most important features. Clustering, dimensionality reduction, and some forms of feature extraction, such as text processing, are all unsupervised techniques and will be dealt with in Chapter 8, *Building a Clustering Model with Spark*, Chapter 9, *Dimensionality Reduction with Spark*, and Chapter 10, *Advanced Text Processing with Spark*.

The components of a data-driven machine learning system

The high-level components of our machine learning system are outlined in the following diagram. This diagram illustrates the machine learning pipeline from which we obtain data and in which we store data. We then transform it into a form that is usable as input to a machine learning model; train, test, and refine our model; and then, deploy the final model to our production system. The process is then repeated as new data is generated.

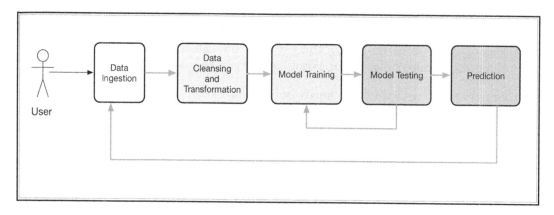

A general machine-learning pipeline

Data ingestion and storage

The first step in our machine learning pipeline will be taking in the data that we require for training our models. Like many other businesses, MovieStream's data is typically generated by user activity, other systems (this is commonly referred to as machine-generated data), and external sources (for example, the time of day and weather during a particular user's visit to the site).

This data can be ingested in various ways, for example, gathering user activity data from the browser and mobile application event logs or accessing external web APIs to collect data on geolocation or weather.

Once the collection mechanisms are in place, the data usually needs to be stored. This includes the raw data, data resulting from intermediate processing, and final model results to be used in production.

Data storage can be complex and involve a wide variety of systems, including HDFS, Amazon S3, and other filesystems; SQL databases such as MySQL or PostgreSQL; distributed NoSQL data stores such as HBase, Cassandra, and DynamoDB; and search engines such as Solr or Elasticsearch to stream data systems such as Kafka, Flume, or Amazon Kinesis.

For the purposes of this book, we will assume that the relevant data is available to us, so we will focus on the processing and modeling steps in the following pipeline.

Data cleansing and transformation

The majority of machine learning algorithms operate on features, which are typically numerical representations of the input variables that will be used for the model.

While we might want to spend the majority of our time exploring machine learning models, data collected via various systems and sources in the preceding ingestion step is, in most cases, in a raw form. For example, we might log user events such as details of when a user views the information page for a movie, when they watch a movie, or when they provide some other feedback. We might also collect external information such as the location of the user (as provided through their IP address, for example). These event logs will typically contain some combination of textual and numeric information about the event (and also, perhaps, other forms of data such as images or audio).

In order to use this raw data in our models, in almost all cases, we need to perform preprocessing, which might include:

- **Filtering data**: Let's assume that we want to create a model from a subset of raw data, such as only the most recent few months of activity data or only events that match certain criteria.
- **Dealing with missing, incomplete, or corrupted data**: Many real-world datasets are incomplete in some way. This might include data that is missing (for example, due to a missing user input) or data that is incorrect or flawed (for example, due to an error in data ingestion or storage, technical issues or bugs, or software or hardware failure). We might need to filter out bad data or alternatively decide a method to fill in missing data points (such as using the average value from the dataset for missing points, for example).
- **Dealing with potential anomalies, errors, and outliers**: Erroneous or outlier data might skew the results of model training, so we might wish to filter these cases out or use techniques that are able to deal with outliers.

- **Joining together disparate data sources**: For example, we might need to match up the event data for each user with different internal data sources, such as user profiles, as well as external data, such as geolocation, weather, and economic data.
- **Aggregating data**: Certain models might require input data that is aggregated in some way, such as computing the sum of a number of different event types per user.

Once we have performed initial preprocessing on our data, we often need to transform the data into a representation that is suitable for machine learning models. For many model types, this representation will take the form of a vector or matrix structure that contains numerical data. Common challenges during data transformation and feature extraction include:

- Taking categorical data (such as country for geolocation or category for a movie) and encoding it in a numerical representation.
- Extracting useful features from text data.
- Dealing with image or audio data.
- Converting numerical data into categorical data to reduce the number of values a variable can take on. An example of this is converting a variable for age into buckets (such as 25-35, 45-55, and so on).
- Transforming numerical features; for example, applying a log transformation to a numerical variable can help deal with variables that take on a very large range of values.
- Normalizing and standardizing numerical features ensures that all the different input variables for a model have a consistent scale. Many machine learning models require standardized input to work properly.
- Feature engineering, which is the process of combining or transforming the existing variables to create new features. For example, we can create a new variable that is the average of some other data, such as the average number of times a user watches a movie.

We will cover all of these techniques through the examples in this book.

This data-cleansing, exploration, aggregation, and transformation steps can be carried out using both Spark's core API functions as well as the SparkSQL engine, not to mention other external Scala, Java, or Python libraries. We can take advantage of Spark's Hadoop compatibility to read data from and write data to the various storage systems mentioned earlier.

We can also leverage Spark streaming in case the streaming input is involved.

Model training and testing loop

Once we have our training data in a form that is suitable for our model, we can proceed with the model's training and testing phase. During this phase, we are primarily concerned with model selection. This can refer to choosing the best modeling approach for our task, or the best parameter settings for a given model. In fact, the term model selection often refers to both of these processes, as, in many cases, we might wish to try out various models and select the best performing model (with the best performing parameter settings for each model). It is also common to explore the application of combinations of different models (known as ensemble methods) in this phase.

This is typically a fairly straightforward process of running our chosen model on our training dataset and testing its performance on a test dataset (that is, a set of data that is held out for the evaluation of the model that the model has not seen in the training phase). This process is referred to as cross-validation.

Sometimes, the model tends to overfit or doesn't converge fully depending on the type of the dataset and the number of Iterations used.

Using Ensemble methods such as Gradient Boosted Trees and Random forest are techniques used in ML and Spark to avoid overfitting.

However, due to the large scale of data we are typically working with, it is often useful to carry out this initial train-test loop on a smaller representative sample of our full dataset or perform model selection using parallel methods where possible.

For this part of the pipeline, Spark's built-in machine learning library, MLlib, is a perfect fit. We will focus most of our attention in this book on the model training, evaluation, and cross-validation steps for various machine learning techniques, using MLlib and Spark's core features.

Model deployment and integration

Once we have found the optimal train-test loop, we might still face the task of deploying the model to a production system so that it can be used to make actionable predictions.

Usually, this process involves exporting the trained model to a central data store from where the production-serving system can obtain the latest version. Thus, the live system *refreshes* the model periodically as a new model is trained.

Model monitoring and feedback

It is critically important to monitor the performance of our machine learning system in production. Once we deploy our optimal-trained model, we wish to understand how it is doing in the "wild". Is it performing as we expect on new, unseen data? Is its accuracy good enough? The reality is, regardless of how much model selection and tuning we try to do in the earlier phases, the only way to measure true performance is to observe what happens in our production system.

In addition to the batch mode model creation, there are also models built with Spark streaming which are real-time in nature.

Also, bear in mind that model accuracy and predictive performance is only one aspect of a real-world system. Usually, we are concerned with other metrics related to business performance (for example, revenue and profitability) or user experience (such as the time spent on our site and how active our users are overall). In most cases, we cannot easily map model-predictive performance to these business metrics. The accuracy of a recommendation or targeting system might be important, but it relates only indirectly to the true metrics we are concerned about, namely, whether we are improving user experience, activity, and ultimately, revenue.

So, in real-world systems, we should monitor both model-accuracy metrics as well as business metrics. If possible, we should be able to experiment with different models running in production to allow us to optimize against these business metrics by making changes to the models. This is often done using live split tests. However, doing this correctly is not an easy task, and live testing and experimentation is expensive, in the sense that mistakes, poor performance, and using baseline models (they provide a control against which we test our production models) can negatively impact user experience and revenue.

Another important aspect of this phase is **model feedback**. This is the process where the predictions of our model feed through into user behavior; this, in turn, feeds through into our model. In a real-world system, our models are essentially influencing their own future training data by impacting decision-making and potential user behavior.

For example, if we have deployed a recommendation system, then, by making recommendations, we might be influencing user behavior because we are only allowing users a limited selection of choices. We hope that this selection is relevant for our model; however, this feedback loop, in turn, can influence our model's training data. This, in turn, feeds back into real-world performance. It is possible to get into an ever-narrowing feedback loop; ultimately, this can negatively affect both model accuracy and our important business metrics.

Fortunately, there are mechanisms by which we can try to limit the potential negative impact of this feedback loop. These include providing some unbiased training data by having a small portion of data coming from users who are not exposed to our models or by being principled in the way we balance exploration, to learn more about our data, and exploitation, to use what we have learned to improve our system's performance.

We will briefly cover in Chapter 11, *Real-time Machine Learning with Spark Streaming.*

Batch versus real time

In the previous sections, we outlined the common batch processing approach, where the model is retrained using all data or a subset of all data, periodically. As the preceding pipeline takes some time to complete, it might not be possible to use this approach to update models immediately as new data arrives.

While we will be mostly covering batch machine learning approaches in this book, there is a class of machine learning algorithms known as **online learning**; they update immediately as new data is fed into the model, thus enabling a real-time system. A common example is an online-optimization algorithm for a linear model, such as stochastic gradient descent. We can learn this algorithm using examples. The advantages of these methods are that the system can react very quickly to new information and also that the system can adapt to changes in the underlying behavior (that is, if the characteristics and distribution of the input data are changing over time, which is almost always the case in real-world situations).

However, online-learning models come with their own unique challenges in a production context. For example, it might be difficult to ingest and transform data in real-time. It can also be complex to properly perform model selection in a purely online setting. The latency of the online training and the model selection and deployment phases might be too high for true real-time requirements (for example, in online advertising, latency requirements are measured in single-digit milliseconds). Finally, batch-oriented frameworks might make it awkward to handle real-time processes of a streaming nature.

Fortunately, Spark's real-time stream processing is a good potential fit for real-time machine learning workflows. We will explore Spark Streaming and online learning in Chapter 11, *Real-time Machine Learning with Spark Streaming*

Due to the complexities inherent in a true real-time machine learning system, in practice, many systems target near real-time operations. This is essentially a hybrid approach where models are not necessarily updated immediately as new data arrives; instead, the new data is collected into mini batches of a small set of training data. These mini batches can be fed to an online-learning algorithm. In many cases, this approach is combined with a periodic batch process that might recompute the model on the entire dataset and perform more complex processing and model selection. This can help ensure that the real-time model does not degrade over time.

Another similar approach involves making approximate updates to a more complex model as new data arrives while recomputing the entire model in a batch process periodically. In this way, the model can learn from new data, with a short delay (usually measured in seconds or, perhaps, a few minutes), but will become more and more inaccurate over time due to the approximation applied. The periodic recomputation takes care of this by retraining the model on all available data.

Data Pipeline in Apache Spark

As we have seen the movie lens use case, it is quite common to run a sequence of machine learning algorithms to process and learn from data. Another example is a simple text document processing workflow, which can include several stages:

- Split the document's text into words
- Convert the document's words into a numerical feature vector
- Learn a prediction model from feature vectors and labels

Spark MLlib represents such a workflow as a Pipeline; it consists of Pipeline Stages in sequence (Transformers and Estimators), which are run in a specific order.

A Pipeline is specified as a sequence of stages. Each stage is a Transformer or an Estimator. Transform converts one data frame into another. Estimator, on the other hand, is a learning algorithm. Pipeline stages are run in order, and the input DataFrame is transformed as it passes through each stage.

In Transformer stages, the `transform()` method is called on the DataFrame. For Estimator stages, the `fit()` method is called to produce a Transformer (which becomes part of the PipelineModel or fitted Pipeline). The transformer's `transform()` method is executed on the DataFrame.

An architecture for a machine learning system

Now that we have explored how our machine learning system might work in the context of MovieStream, we can outline a possible architecture for our system:

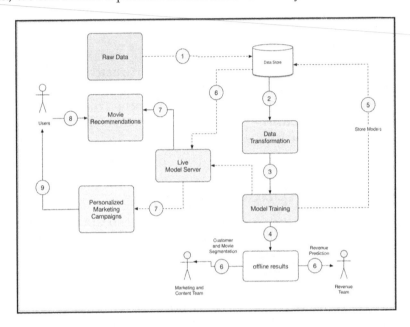

MovieStream's future architecture

As we can see, our system incorporates the machine learning pipeline outlined in the preceding diagram; this system also includes:

- Collecting data about users, their behavior, and our content titles
- Transforming this data into features
- Training our models, including our training-testing and model-selection phases
- Deploying the trained models to both our live model-serving system as well as using these models for offline processes
- Feeding back the model results into the MovieStream website through recommendation and targeting pages

- Feeding back the model results into MovieStream's personalized marketing channels
- Using the offline models to provide tools to MovieStream's various teams to better understand user behavior, characteristics of the content catalogue, and drivers of revenue for the business

In the next section, we digress a little from Movie Stream and give an overview of MLlib-Spark's machine learning module.

Spark MLlib

Apache Spark is an open-source platform for large dataset processing. It is well suited for iterative machine learning tasks as it leverages in-memory data structures such as RDDs. MLlib is Spark's machine learning library. MLlib provides functionality for various learning algorithms-supervised and unsupervised. It includes various statistical and linear algebra optimizations. It is shipped along with Apache Spark and hence saves on installation headaches like some other libraries. MLlib supports several higher languages such as Scala, Java, Python and R. It also provides a high-level API to build machine-learning pipelines.

MLlib's integration with Spark has quite a few benefits. Spark is designed for iterative computation cycles; it enables efficient implementation platform for large machine learning algorithms, as these algorithms are themselves iterative.

Any improvement in Spark's data structures results in direct gains for MLlib. Spark's large community contributions have helped bring new algorithms to MLlib faster.

Spark also has other APIs such as Pipeline APIs GraphX, which can be used in conjunction with MLlib; it makes building interesting use cases on top of MLlib easier.

Performance improvements in Spark ML over Spark MLlib

Spark 2.0 uses Tungsten Engine, which is built using ideas of modern compilers and MPP databases. It emits optimized bytecode at runtime, which collapses the query into a single function. Hence, there is no need for virtual function calls. It also uses CPU registers to store intermediate data.

This technique has been called whole stage code generation.

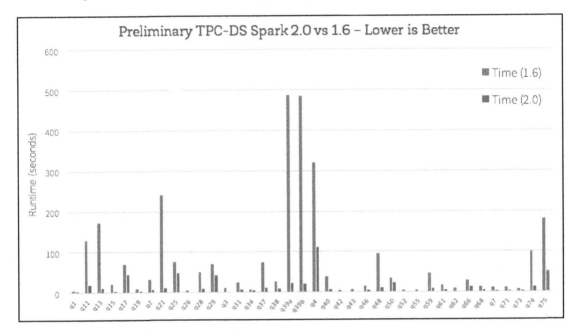

Reference : https://databricks.com/blog/2016/05/11/apache-spark-2-0-technical-preview-easier-faster-and-smarter.htmlSource: https://databricks.com/blog/2016/05/11/apache-spark-2-0-technical-preview-easier-faster-and-smarter.html

The upcoming table and graph show single function improvements between Spark 1.6 and Spark 2.0:

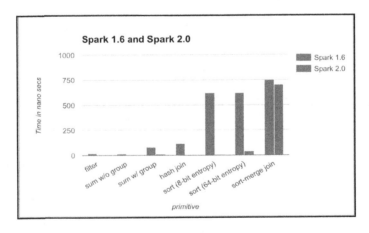

Chart comparing Performance improvements in Single line functions between Spark 1.6 and Spark 2.0

primitive	Spark 1.6	Spark 2.0
filter	15	1.1
sum w/o group	14	0.9
sum w/ group	79	10.7
hash join	115	4
sort (8-bit entropy)	620	5.3
sort (64-bit entropy)	620	40
sort-merge join	750	700

Table comparing Performance improvements in Single line functions between Spark 1.6 and Spark 2.0.

Comparing algorithms supported by MLlib

In this section, we look at various algorithms supported by MLlib versions.

Classification

In 1.6, there are over 10 algorithms supported for classification, whereas when Spark MLversion 1.0 was announced, only 3 algorithms were supported.

Algorithm Type	SNo	Name	Spark Version							
			1.0.0	1.1.0	1.2.0	1.3.0	1.4.0	1.5.0	1.6.0	2.0.0
Classification	1	Binary Classification	y	y	y	y	y	y	y	y
	2	Naive Bayes	y	y	y	y	y	y	y	y
	3	Linear Regression	n	y	y	y	y	y	y	y
	4	Logistical Regression	y	y	y	y	y	y	y	y
	5	RandomForrest Classifier	n	n	n		y	y	y	y
	6	Probabilistic Classifier	n	n	n	n	n	y	y	y
	7	GBT Classifier	n	n	n	n	y	y	y	y
	8	SVMwithSGD	y	y	y	y	y			y
	9	Decision Tree Classifier	n	n	n	n	y	y	y	y
	10	Multi Layer Perceptron Classifier	n	n	n	n	n	y	y	y

Clustering

There has been quite a bit of investment in Clustering algorithms, moving from 1 algo support in 1.0.0 to supporting 6 implementations in 1.6.0.

Algorithm Type	SNo	Name	Spark Version							
			1.0.0	1.1.0	1.2.0	1.3.0	1.4.0	1.5.0	1.6.0	2.0.0
Clustering	1	K Means	y	y	y	y	y	y	y	y
	2	Bisecting K Means	n	n	n	n	n	n	y	y
	3	LDA	n	n	n	y	y	y	y	y
	4	PowerIteration Clusting	n	n	n	y	y	y	y	y
	5	Streaming K Means	n	y	y	y	y	y	y	y
	6	Gaussian Mixture	n	n	n	y	y	y	y	y

Regression

Traditionally, regression was not the main area of focus but has become of late with 3-4 new algorithms from 1.2.0 version to 1.3.0 version.

Algorithm Type	SNo	Name	Spark Version							
			1.0.0	1.1.0	1.2.0	1.3.0	1.4.0	1.5.0	1.6.0	2.0.0
Regression	1	GeneralizedLinearAlgorithm	y	y	y	y	y	y	y	y
	2	Isotonic Regression	n	n	n	y	y	y	y	y
	3	LassowithSGD	y	y	y	y	y	y	y	y
	4	Linear Regression	y	y	y	y	y	y	y	y
	5	Ridge Regression	y	y	y	y	y	y	y	y
	6	Ridge Regression with SGD	y	y	y	y	y	y	y	y
	7	Streaming Linear Algorithm	n	y	y	y	y	y	y	y

MLlib supported methods and developer APIs

MLlib provides fast and distributed implementations of learning algorithms, including various linear models, Naive Bayes, SVM, and Ensembles of Decision Trees (also known as Random Forests) for classification and regression problems, alternating.

Least Squares (explicit and implicit feedback) are used for collaborative filtering. It also supports k-means clustering and **principal component analysis** (**PCA**) for clustering and dimensionality reduction.

The library provides some low-level primitives and basic utilities for convex optimization (`http://spark.apache.org/docs/latest/mllib-optimization.html`), distributed linear algebra (with support for Vectors and Matrix), statistical analysis (using Breeze and also native functions), and feature extraction, and supports various I/O formats, including native support for LIBSVM format.

It also supports data integration via Spark SQL as well as PMML (`https://en.wikipedia.org/wiki/Predictive_Model_Markup_Language`) (Guazzelli et al., 2009). You can find more information about PMML support at this link: `https://spark.apache.org/docs/1.6.0/mllib-pmml-model-export.html`.

Algorithmic Optimizations involves MLlib that includes many optimizations to support efficient distributed learning and prediction.

The ALS algorithm for recommendation makes use of blocking to reduce JVM garbage collection overhead and to utilize higher-level linear algebra operations. Decision trees use ideas from the PLANET project (reference: `http://dl.acm.org/citation.cfm?id=1687569`), such as data-dependent feature discretization to reduce communication costs, and tree ensembles parallelize learning both within trees and across trees.

Generalized linear models are learned using optimization algorithms, which parallelize gradient computation, using fast C++-based linear algebra libraries for worker.

Computations. Algorithms benefit from efficient communication primitives. In particular, tree-structured aggregation prevents the driver from being a bottleneck.

Model updates are combined partially on a small set of executors. These are then sent to the driver. This implementation reduces the load the driver has to handle. Tests showed that these functions reduce the aggregation time by an order of magnitude, especially on datasets with a large number of partitions.

(Reference: `https://databricks.com/blog/2014/09/22/spark-1-1-mllib-performance-improvements.html`)

Pipeline API includes practical machine learning pipelines that often involve a sequence of data preprocessing, feature extraction, model fitting, and validation stages.

Most of the machine learning libraries do not provide native support for the diverse set of functionalities for pipeline construction. When handling large-scale datasets, the process of wiring together an end-to-end pipeline is both labor-intensive and expensive from the perspective of network overheads.

Leveraging Spark's ecosystem: MLlib includes a package aimed to address these concerns.

The `spark.ml` package eases the development and tuning of multistage learning pipelines by providing a uniform set of high-level APIs (`http://arxiv.org/pdf/1505.06807.pdf`). It includes APIs that enable users to swap out a standard learning approach in place of their specialized algorithms.

Spark Integration

MLlib benefits from the components within the Spark ecosystem. Spark core provides an execution engine with over 80 operators for transforming data (data cleaning and featurization).

MLlib uses other high-level libraries packaged with Spark-like Spark SQL. It provides integration data functionality, SQL, and structured data processing, which simplifies data cleaning and preprocessing. It supports the DataFrame abstraction, which is fundamental to the `spark.ml` package.

GraphX (`https://www.usenix.org/system/files/conference/osdi14/osdi14-paper-gonzalez.pdf`) supports large-scale graph processing and has a powerful API for implementing learning algorithms that can be viewed as large sparse graph problems, for example, LDA.

Spark Streaming
(`https://www.cs.berkeley.edu/~matei/papers/2013/sosp_spark_streaming.pdf`) allows processing of real-time data streams and enabling the development of learning algorithms which are online, as in Freeman (2015). We will cover streaming in some of the later chapters of this book.

MLlib vision

MLlib's vision is to provide a scalable machine learning platform, which can handle large datasets at scale and fastest processing time as compared to the existing systems such as Hadoop.

It also strives to provide support for as many algorithms as possible in the domain of supervised and unsupervised learning classification, regression such as Classification, Regression, and clustering.

MLlib versions compared

In this section, we will compare various versions of MLlib and new functionality, which has been added.

Spark 1.6 to 2.0

The DataFrame-based API will be the primary API.

The RDD-based API is entering maintenance mode. The MLlib guide (`http://spark.apache.org/docs/2.0.0/ml-guide.html`) provides more details.

The following are the new features introduced in Spark 2.0:

- **ML persistence**: The DataFrames-based API provides support for saving and loading ML models and Pipelines in Scala, Java, Python, and R
- **MLlib in R**: SparkR offers MLlib APIs for generalized linear models, naive Bayes, k-means clustering, and survival regression in this release
- **Python**: PySpark in 2.0 supports new MLlib algorithms, LDA, Generalized Linear Regression, Gaussian Mixture Model, among others

Algorithms added to DataFrames-based API are GMM, Bisecting K-Means clustering, MaxAbsScaler feature transformer.

Summary

In this chapter, we learnt about the components that are inherent in a data-driven, automated machine learning system. We also outlined how a possible high-level architecture for such a system might look in a real-world situation. We also got an overview of MLlib-Spark's machine learning library-compared to other machine learning implementations from a performance perspective. In the end, we looked at new features in various versions of Spark starting from Spark 1.6 to Spark 2.0.

In next chapter, we shall discuss how to obtain publicly-available datasets for common machine learning tasks. We will also explore general concepts to process, clean, and transform data so that it can be used to train a machine learning model.

4

Obtaining, Processing, and Preparing Data with Spark

Machine learning is an extremely broad field, and these days, applications can be found across areas that include web and mobile applications, the Internet of Things and sensor networks, financial services, healthcare, and various scientific fields, to name just a few.

Therefore, the range of data available for potential use in machine learning is enormous. In this book, we will focus mostly on business applications. In this context, the data available often consists of data internal to an organization (such as transactional data for a financial services company) as well as external data sources (such as financial asset price data for the same financial services company).

For example, you'll recall from `Chapter 3`, *Designing a Machine Learning System*, that the main internal source of data for our hypothetical internet business, Movie Stream, consists of data on the movies available on the site, the users of the service, and their behavior. This includes data about movies and other content (for example, title, categories, description, images, actors, and directors), user information (for example, demographics, location, and so on), and user activity data (for example, web page views, title previews and views, ratings, reviews, and social data such as *likes*, *shares*, and social network profiles on services, including Facebook and Twitter).

External data sources in this example may include weather and geolocation services, third-party movie ratings, and review sites such as *IMDB* and *Rotten Tomatoes*, and so on.

Generally speaking, it is quite difficult to obtain data of an internal nature for real-world services and businesses, as it is commercially sensitive (in particular, data on purchasing activity, user or customer behavior, and revenue) and of great potential value to the organization concerned. This is why it is also often the most useful and interesting data on which to apply machine learning--a good machine learning model that can make accurate predictions can be highly valuable (witness the success of machine learning competitions, such as *Netflix Prize* and *Kaggle*).

In this book, we will make use of datasets that are publicly available to illustrate concepts around data processing and training of machine learning models.

In this chapter, we will:

- Briefly cover the types of data typically used in machine learning.
- Provide examples of where to obtain interesting datasets, often publicly available on the internet. We will use some of these datasets throughout the book to illustrate the use of the models we introduce.
- Discover how to process, clean, explore, and visualize our data.
- Introduce various techniques to transform our raw data into features that can be used as input to machine learning algorithms.
- Learn how to normalize input features using external libraries as well as Spark's built-in functionality.

Accessing publicly available datasets

Fortunately, while commercially sensitive data can be hard to come by, there are still a number of useful datasets available publicly. Many of these are often used as benchmark datasets for specific types of machine learning problems. Examples of common data sources include:

- **UCI Machine Learning Repository**: This is a collection of almost 300 datasets of various types and sizes for tasks, including classification, regression, clustering, and recommender systems. The list is available at
  `http://archive.ics.uci.edu/ml/`.
- **Amazon AWS public datasets**: This is a set of often very large datasets that can be accessed via Amazon S3. These datasets include the Human Genome Project, the Common Crawl web corpus, Wikipedia data, and Google Books Ngrams. Information on these datasets can be found at
  `http://aws.amazon.com/publicdatasets/`.

- **Kaggle**: This is a collection of datasets used in machine learning competitions run by Kaggle. Areas include classification, regression, ranking, recommender systems, and image analysis. These datasets can be found under the Competitions section at `http://www.kaggle.com/competitions`.
- **KDnuggets**: This has a detailed list of public datasets, including some of those mentioned earlier. The list is available at `http://www.kdnuggets.com/datasets/index.html`.

 There are many other resources to find public datasets depending on the specific domain and machine-learning task. Hopefully, you might also have exposure to some interesting academic or commercial data of your own!

To illustrate a few key concepts related to data processing, transformation, and feature extraction in Spark, we will download a commonly used dataset for movie recommendations; this dataset is known as the **MovieLens** dataset. As it is applicable to recommender systems as well as potentially other machine learning tasks, it serves as a useful example dataset.

The MovieLens 100k dataset

The MovieLens 100k dataset is a set of 100,000 data points related to ratings given by a set of users to a set of movies. It also contains movie metadata and user profiles. While it is a small dataset, you can quickly download it and run Spark code on it. This makes it ideal for illustrative purposes.

You can download the dataset from `http://files.grouplens.org/datasets/movielens/ml-100k.zip`.

Once you have downloaded the data, unzip it using your terminal:

```
>unzip ml-100k.zip
   inflating: ml-100k/allbut.pl
   inflating: ml-100k/mku.sh
   inflating: ml-100k/README
      ...
   inflating: ml-100k/ub.base
   inflating: ml-100k/ub.test
```

This will create a directory called `ml-100k`. Change into this directory and examine the contents. The important files are `u.user` (user profiles), `u.item` (movie metadata), and `u.data` (the ratings given by users to movies):

```
>cd ml-100k
```

The README file contains more information on the dataset, including the variables present in each data file. We can use the head command to examine the contents of the various files.

For example, we can see that the `u.user` file contains the user ID, age, gender, occupation, and ZIP code fields, separated by a pipe (`|` character):

```
$ head -5 u.user
1|24|M|technician|85711
2|53|F|other|94043
3|23|M|writer|32067
4|24|M|technician|43537
5|33|F|other|15213
```

The `u.item` file contains the movie ID, title, release data, and IMDB link fields and a set of fields related to movie category data. It is also separated by a `|` character:

```
$head -5 u.item
1|Toy Story (1995)|01-Jan-1995||http://us.imdb.com/M/title-
exact?Toy%20Story%20(1995)|0|0|0|1|1|1|1|0|0|0|0|0|0|0|0|0|0|0|0
2|GoldenEye (1995)|01-Jan-1995||http://us.imdb.com/M/title-
exact?GoldenEye%20(1995)|0|1|1|0|0|0|0|0|0|0|0|0|0|0|0|0|0|1|0|0
3|Four Rooms (1995)|01-Jan-1995||http://us.imdb.com/M/title-
exact?Four%20Rooms%20(1995)|0|0|0|0|0|0|0|0|0|0|0|0|0|0|0|0|0|1|0|0
4|Get Shorty (1995)|01-Jan-1995||http://us.imdb.com/M/title-
exact?Get%20Shorty%20(1995)|0|1|0|0|0|1|0|0|1|0|0|0|0|0|0|0|0|0|0
5|Copycat (1995)|01-Jan-1995||http://us.imdb.com/M/title-
exact?Copycat%20(1995)|0|0|0|0|0|0|1|0|1|0|0|0|0|0|0|0|1|0|0
```

The previous data listed has the following format:

```
movie id | movie title | release date | video release date | IMDb
URL | unknown | Action | Adventure | Animation | Children's |
Comedy | Crime | Documentary | Drama | Fantasy | Film-Noir |
Horror | Musical | Mystery | Romance | Sci-Fi | Thriller | War |
Western |
```

The last 19 fields are the genres, a 1 indicates the movie is of that genre, a 0 indicates it is not; movies can be in several genres at once.

The movie IDs are the ones used in the `u.data` dataset. It contains100000 ratings by 943 users on 1682 items. Each user has rated at least 20 movies. Users and items are numbered consecutively from 1. The data is randomly ordered. This is a tab separated list of following fields:

```
user id | item id | rating | timestamp
```

The time stamps are Unix seconds since 1/1/1970 UTC.

Let's look at some data from the u.data file:

```
>head -5 u.data
1962423881250949
1863023891717742
223771878887116
244512880606923
1663461886397596
```

Exploring and visualizing your data

Source code for the chapter can be found at `PATH/spark-ml/Chapter04`:

- Python code is available at `/MYPATH/spark-ml/Chapter_04/python`
- Scala code is available at`/MYPATH/spark-ml/Chapter_04/scala`

Pythons Samples are available for both version 1.6.2 and 2.0.0; we will focus on 2.0.0 in this book:

```
├── 1.6.2
│   ├── com
│   │   ├── __init__.py
│   │   └── sparksamples
│   │       ├── __init__.py
│   │       ├── movie_data.py
│   │       ├── plot_user_ages.py
│   │       ├── plot_user_occupations.py
│   │       ├── rating_data.py
│   │       ├── user_data.py
│   │       └── util.py
│   │
│   └── __init__.py
├── 2.0.0
│   └── com
│       ├── __init__.py
│       └── sparksamples
```

```
|                      ├── __init__.py
|                      ├── movie_data.py
|                      ├── plot_user_ages.py
|                      ├── plot_user_occupations.py
|                      ├── rating_data.py
|                      ├── spark-warehouse
|                      ├── user_data.py
|                      └── util.py
|
```

Scala samples are structured as shown in the following:

```
├── 1.6.2
|   ├── build.sbt
|   ├── spark-warehouse
|   ├── src
|   |   └── main
|   |       └── scala
|   |           └── org
|   |               └── sparksamples
|   |                   ├── CountByRatingChart.scala
|   |                   ├── exploredataset
|   |                   |   ├── explore_movies.scala
|   |                   |   ├── explore_ratings.scala
|   |                   |   └── explore_users.scala
|   |                   ├── featureext
|   |                   |   ├── ConvertWordsToVectors.scala
|   |                   |   ├── StandardScalarSample.scala
|   |                   |   └── TfIdfSample.scala
|   |                   ├── MovieAgesChart.scala
|   |                   ├── MovieDataFillingBadValues.scala
|   |                   ├── MovieData.scala
|   |                   ├── RatingData.scala
|   |                   ├── UserAgesChart.scala
|   |                   ├── UserData.scala
|   |                   ├── UserOccupationChart.scala
|   |                   ├── UserRatingsChart.scala
|   |                   └── Util.scala
```

Scala 2.0.0 Samples:

```
├── 2.0.0
|   ├── build.sbt
|   ├── src
|   |   └── main
|   |       └── scala
|   |           └── org
|   |               └── sparksamples
```

```
│  │                        ├── CountByRatingChart.scala
│  │                        ├── df
│  │                        ├── exploredataset
│  │                        │    ├── explore_movies.scala
│  │                        │    ├── explore_ratings.scala
│  │                        │    └── explore_users.scala
│  │                        ├── featureext
│  │                        │    ├── ConvertWordsToVectors.scala
│  │                        │    ├── StandardScalarSample.scala
│  │                        │    └── TfIdfSample.scala
│  │                        ├── MovieAgesChart.scala
│  │                        ├── MovieDataFillingBadValues.scala
│  │                        ├── MovieData.scala
│  │                        ├── RatingData.scala
│  │                        ├── UserAgesChart.scala
│  │                        ├── UserData.scala
│  │                        ├── UserOccupationChart.scala
│  │                        ├── UserRatingsChart.scala
│  │                        └── Util.scala
```

Go to the following directory and run the following commands to run the samples:

```
$ cd /MYPATH/spark-ml/Chapter_04/scala/2.0.0
$ sbt compile
$ sbt run
```

Exploring the user dataset

First, we will analyze the characteristics of MovieLens users.

We use a custom_schema to load the | delimited data into a DataFrame. This Python code is in com/sparksamples/Util.py:

```
def get_user_data():
  custom_schema = StructType([
  StructField("no", StringType(), True),
  StructField("age", IntegerType(), True),
  StructField("gender", StringType(), True),
  StructField("occupation", StringType(), True),
  StructField("zipCode", StringType(), True)
])
frompyspark.sql import SQLContext
frompyspark.sql.types import *

sql_context = SQLContext(sc)
```

```
user_df = sql_context.read
  .format('com.databricks.spark.csv')
  .options(header='false', delimiter='|')
  .load("%s/ml-100k/u.user"% PATH, schema =
custom_schema)
returnuser_df
```

This function is called from `user_data.py` as show following:

```
user_data = get_user_data()
print(user_data.first)
```

You should see output similar to this:

u'1|24|M|technician|85711'

Code-listing:

- https://github.com/ml-resources/spark-ml/blob/branch-ed2/Chapter_04/py thon/2.0.0/com/sparksamples/user_data.py
- https://github.com/ml-resources/spark-ml/blob/branch-ed2/Chapter_04/py thon/2.0.0/com/sparksamples/util.py

Similar code in Scala for loading data into a DataFrame is listed as follows. This code is in `Util.scala`:

```
val customSchema = StructType(Array(
StructField("no", IntegerType, true),
StructField("age", StringType, true),
StructField("gender", StringType, true),
StructField("occupation", StringType, true),
StructField("zipCode", StringType, true)));
val spConfig = (new
 SparkConf).setMaster("local").setAppName("SparkApp")
val spark = SparkSession
  .builder()
  .appName("SparkUserData").config(spConfig)
  .getOrCreate()

val user_df = spark.read.format("com.databricks.spark.csv")
  .option("delimiter", "|").schema(customSchema)
  .load("/home/ubuntu/work/ml-resources/spark-ml/data/ml-
 100k/u.user")
val first = user_df.first()
println("First Record : " + first)
```

You should see output similar to this:

```
u'1|24|M|technician|85711'
```

The code listing is at :
https://github.com/ml-resources/spark-ml/blob/branch-ed2/Chapter
_04/scala/2.0.0/src/main/scala/org/sparksamples/UserData.scala

As we can see, this is the first line of our user data file, separated by the " | " character.

The `first` function is similar to `collect`, but it only returns the first element of the RDD to the driver. We can also use `take(k)` to collect only the first *k* elements of the RDD to the driver.

We will use the DataFrame created earlier and use the `groupBy` function followed by `count()` and `collect()` to calculate number of users, genders, ZIPcodes, and occupations. We will then count the number of users, genders, occupations, and ZIP codes. We can achieve this by running the following code. Note that we do not cache the data, as it is unnecessary for this small size:

```
num_users = user_data.count()
num_genders =
 len(user_data.groupBy("gender").count().collect())
num_occupation =
 len(user_data.groupBy("occupation").count().collect())
num_zipcodes =
 len(user_data.groupby("zipCode").count().collect())
print("Users: "+ str(num_users))
print("Genders: "+ str(num_genders))
print("Occupation: "+ str(num_occupation))
print("ZipCodes: "+ str(num_zipcodes))
```

You will see the following output:

```
Users: 943
Genders: 2
Occupations: 21
ZIPCodes: 795
```

Similarly, we can implement the logic of getting number of users, genders, occupations, and zip codes using Scala.

```
val num_genders = user_df.groupBy("gender").count().count()
val num_occupations =
 user_df.groupBy("occupation").count().count()
```

```
val num_zipcodes = user_df.groupBy("zipCode").count().count()

println("num_users : "+ user_df.count())
println("num_genders : "+ num_genders)
println("num_occupations : "+ num_occupations)
println("num_zipcodes: "+ num_zipcodes)
println("Distribution by Occupation")
println(user_df.groupBy("occupation").count().show())
```

You will see the following output:

num_users: 943
num_genders: 2
num_occupations: 21
num_zipcodes: 795

Find the code listing at:
https://github.com/ml-resources/spark-ml/blob/branch-ed2/Chapter
_04/scala/2.0.0/src/main/scala/org/sparksamples/UserData.scala

Next, we will create a histogram to analyze the distribution of user ages.

In Python, first we get the DatFrame into variable user_data. Next, we'll call select('age') and collect the result into List of Row object. Then, we iterate and extract age parameter and populate user_ages_list.

We will be using Python matplotlib library's hist function.

```
user_data = get_user_data()
user_ages = user_data.select('age').collect()
user_ages_list = []
user_ages_len = len(user_ages)
for i in range(0, (user_ages_len - 1)):
    user_ages_list.append(user_ages[i].age)
plt.hist(user_ages_list, bins=20, color='lightblue', normed=True)
fig = matplotlib.pyplot.gcf()
fig.set_size_inches(16, 10)
plt.show()
```

Find the code listing at:
https://github.com/ml-resources/spark-ml/blob/branch-ed2/Chapter
_04/python/2.0.0/com/sparksamples/plot_user_ages.py

We passed in the `user_ages_list`, together with the number of bins for our histogram (20 in this case), to the `hist` function. Using the `normed=True` argument, we also specified that we want the histogram to be normalized so that each bucket represents the percentage of the overall data that falls into that bucket.

You will see an image containing the histogram chart, which looks something like the one shown here. As we can see, the ages of MovieLens users are somewhat skewed toward younger viewers. A large number of users are between the ages of about 15 and 35.

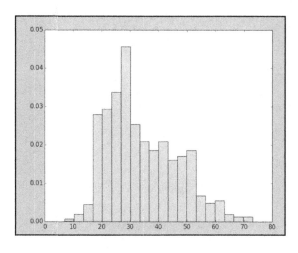

Distribution of user ages

For Scala Histogram Chart, we are using a JFreeChart-based library. We divided the data into 16 bins to the show the distribution.

We are using the `https://github.com/wookietreiber/scala-chart` library to create a barchart from the Scala map `m_sorted`.

First we extract the `ages_array` from `userDataFrame` using the `select("age")` function.

Then, we populate the mx Map, which is the bins for displaying. We sort the mx Map to create a ListMap, which is then used to populate DefaultCategorySet ds:

```scala
val userDataFrame = Util.getUserFieldDataFrame()
val ages_array = userDataFrame.select("age").collect()

val min = 0
val max = 80
val bins = 16
val step = (80/bins).toInt
var mx = Map(0 ->0)
for (i <- step until (max + step) by step) {
  mx += (i -> 0)
}
for( x <- 0 until ages_array.length) {
  val age = Integer.parseInt(
    ages_array(x)(0).toString)
  for(j <- 0 until (max + step) by step) {
    if(age >= j && age < (j + step)){
      mx = mx + (j -> (mx(j) + 1))
    }
  }
}

val mx_sorted =  ListMap(mx.toSeq.sortBy(_._1):_*)
val ds = new org.jfree.data.category.DefaultCategoryDataset
mx_sorted.foreach{ case (k,v) => ds.addValue(v,"UserAges", k)}
val chart = ChartFactories.BarChart(ds)
chart.show()
Util.sc.stop()
```

The complete code can be found in UserAgesChart.scalafile and is listed here:

Find the code listing at:
https://github.com/ml-resources/spark-ml/blob/branch-ed2/Chapter_04/scala/2.0.0/src/main/scala/org/sparksamples/UserAgesChart.scala

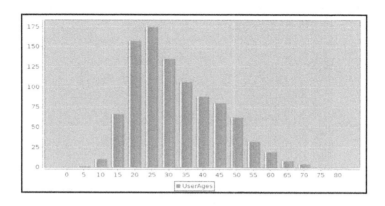

Count by occupation

We count a number of the various occupations of our users.

The following steps were implemented to get the occupation DataFrame and populate the list, which was displayed using Matplotlib.

1. Get `user_data`.
2. Extract occupation count using `groupby("occupation")` and calling `count()` on it.
3. Extract list of `tuple("occupation","count")` from the list of rows.
4. Create a `numpy` array of values in `x_axis` and `y_axis`.
5. Create a plot of type bar.
6. Display the chart.

The complete code listing can be found following:

```
user_data = get_user_data()
user_occ = user_data.groupby("occupation").count().collect()

user_occ_len = len(user_occ)
user_occ_list = []
for i in range(0, (user_occ_len - 1)):
element = user_occ[i]
count = element. __getattr__('count')
tup = (element.occupation, count)
    user_occ_list.append(tup)

x_axis1 = np.array([c[0] for c in user_occ_list])
y_axis1 = np.array([c[1] for c in user_occ_list])
```

```
x_axis = x_axis1[np.argsort(y_axis1)]
y_axis = y_axis1[np.argsort(y_axis1)]

pos = np.arange(len(x_axis))
width = 1.0

ax = plt.axes()
ax.set_xticks(pos + (width / 2))
ax.set_xticklabels(x_axis)

plt.bar(pos, y_axis, width, color='lightblue')
plt.xticks(rotation=30)
fig = matplotlib.pyplot.gcf()
fig.set_size_inches(20, 10)
plt.show()
```

The image you have generated should look like the one here. It appears that the most prevalent occupations are **student**, **other**, **educator**, **administrator**, **engineer**, and **programmer**.

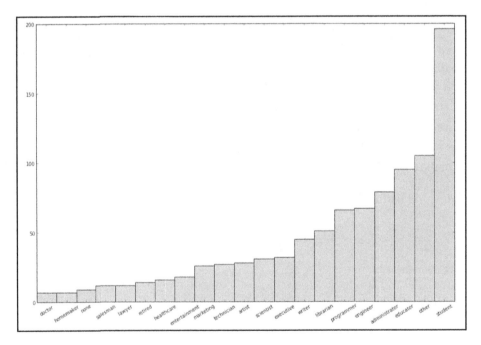

Distribution of user occupations

Find the code listing at:
`https://github.com/ml-resources/spark-ml/blob/branch-ed2/Chapter`
`_04/python/2.0.0/com/sparksamples/plot_user_occupations.py`

In Scala, we follow the following steps:

1. First get the `userDataFrame`
2. We extract occupation column:

```
userDataFrame.select("occupation")
```

3. Group the rows by occupation:

```
val occupation_groups =
   userDataFrame.groupBy("occupation").count()
```

4. Sort the rows by count:

```
val occupation_groups_sorted =
   occupation_groups.sort("count")
```

5. Populate Default category set ds from: `occupation_groups_collection`
6. Display the Jfree Bar Chart

The complete code listing is given following:

```
val userDataFrame = Util.getUserFieldDataFrame()
val occupation = userDataFrame.select("occupation")
val occupation_groups =
 userDataFrame.groupBy("occupation").count()
val occupation_groups_sorted = occupation_groups.sort("count")
occupation_groups_sorted.show()
val occupation_groups_collection =
 occupation_groups_sorted.collect()

val ds = new org.jfree.data.category.DefaultCategoryDataset
val mx = scala.collection.immutable.ListMap()

for( x <- 0 until occupation_groups_collection.length) {
  val occ = occupation_groups_collection(x)(0)
  val count = Integer.parseInt(
    occupation_groups_collection(x)(1).toString)
  ds.addValue(count,"UserAges", occ.toString)
}
```

```
val chart = ChartFactories.BarChart(ds)
val font = new Font("Dialog", Font.PLAIN,5);

chart.peer.getCategoryPlot.getDomainAxis().
setCategoryLabelPositions(CategoryLabelPositions.UP_90);
chart.peer.getCategoryPlot.getDomainAxis.setLabelFont(font)
chart.show()
Util.sc.stop()
```

The output of this code is shown here:

```
+-------------+-----+
|   occupation|count|
+-------------+-----+
|    homemaker|    7|
|       doctor|    7|
|         none|    9|
|     salesman|   12|
|       lawyer|   12|
|      retired|   14|
|   healthcare|   16|
|entertainment|   18|
|    marketing|   26|
|    technician|  27|
|       artist|   28|
|     scientist|  31|
|     executive|  32|
|       writer|   45|
|     librarian|  51|
|    programmer|  66|
|      engineer|  67|
|administrator|   79|
|      educator|  95|
|        other|  105|
+-------------+-----+
only showing top 20 rows
```

The following figure shows the JFreeChart generated from the previous source code:

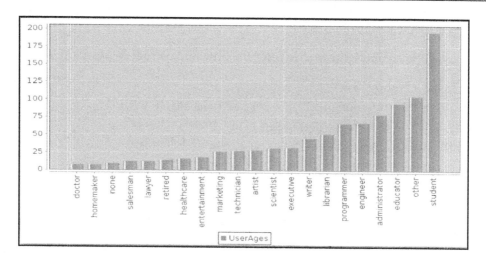

 Find the code listing at:
`https://github.com/ml-resources/spark-ml/blob/branched2/Chapter_04/scala/2.0.0/src/main/scala/org/sparksamples/UserOccupationChart.scala`

Movie dataset

Next, we will investigate a few properties of the movie catalog. We can inspect a row of the movie data file, as we did for the user data earlier, and then count the number of movies:

We will create a DataFrame of movie data by parsing using the format `com.databrick.spark.csv` and giving a | delimiter. Then, we use a `CustomSchema` to populate the DataFrame and return it:

```
def getMovieDataDF() : DataFrame = {
  val customSchema = StructType(Array(
  StructField("id", StringType, true),
  StructField("name", StringType, true),
  StructField("date", StringType, true),
  StructField("url", StringType, true)));
  val movieDf = spark.read.format(
    "com.databricks.spark.csv")
    .option("delimiter", "|").schema(customSchema)
    .load(PATH_MOVIES)
  return movieDf
}
```

This method is then called from the `MovieData` Scala Object.

The following steps are implemented to filter the date and format it into a `Year`:

1. Create a Temp View.
2. Register the function `Util.convertYear` as a UDF with `SparkSession.Util.spark` (this is our custom class).
3. Execute SQLon this `SparkSession` as shown following.
4. Group the resulting DataFrame by `Year` and call `count()` function.

The complete code listing for the logic is given here:

```scala
def getMovieYearsCountSorted(): scala.Array[(Int,String)] = {
  val movie_data_df = Util.getMovieDataDF()
  movie_data_df.createOrReplaceTempView("movie_data")
  movie_data_df.printSchema()

  Util.spark.udf.register("convertYear", Util.convertYear _)
  movie_data_df.show(false)

  val movie_years = Util.spark.sql(
    "select convertYear(date) as year from movie_data")
  val movie_years_count = movie_years.groupBy("year").count()
  movie_years_count.show(false)
  val movie_years_count_rdd = movie_years_count.rdd.map(
   row => (Integer.parseInt(row(0).toString), row(1).toString))
  val movie_years_count_collect = movie_years_count_rdd.collect()
  val movie_years_count_collect_sort =
  movie_years_count_collect.sortBy(_._1)
}

def main(args: Array[String]) {
  val movie_years = MovieData.getMovieYearsCountSorted()
  for( a <- 0 to (movie_years.length -1)){
    print(movie_years(a))
  }
}
```

The output will be similar as shown here:

```
(1900,1)
(1922,1)
(1926,1)
(1930,1)
(1931,1)
(1932,1)
```

```
(1933,2)
(1934,4)
(1935,4)
(1936,2)
(1937,4)
(1938,3)
(1939,7)
(1940,8)
(1941,5)
(1942,2)
(1943,4)
(1944,5)
(1945,4)
(1946,5)
(1947,5)
(1948,3)
(1949,4)
(1950,7)
(1951,5)
(1952,3)
(1953,2)
(1954,7)
(1955,5)
(1956,4)
(1957,8)
(1958,9)
(1959,4)
(1960,5)
(1961,3)
(1962,5)
(1963,6)
(1964,2)
(1965,5)
(1966,2)
(1967,5)
(1968,6)
(1969,4)
(1970,3)
(1971,7)
(1972,3)
(1973,4)
(1974,8)
(1975,6)
(1976,5)
(1977,4)
(1978,4)
(1979,9)
(1980,8)
```

```
(1981,12)
(1982,13)
(1983,5)
(1984,8)
(1985,7)
(1986,15)
(1987,13)
(1988,11)
(1989,15)
(1990,24)
(1991,22)
(1992,37)
(1993,126)
(1994,214)
(1995,219)
(1996,355)
(1997,286)
(1998,65)
```

Find the code listing at:
https://github.com/ml-resources/spark-ml/blob/branch-ed2/Chapter
_04/scala/2.0.0/src/main/scala/org/sparksamples/MovieData.scala

Next, we draw the graph of ages of movies collection created earlier. We use JFreeChart in Scala and populate `org.jfree.data.category.DefaultCategoryDataset` from the collection created by `MovieData.getMovieYearsCountSorted()`.

```scala
object MovieAgesChart {
  def main(args: Array[String]) {
    val movie_years_count_collect_sort =
    MovieData.getMovieYearsCountSorted()

    val ds = new
      org.jfree.data.category.DefaultCategoryDataset
    for(i <- movie_years_count_collect_sort){
      ds.addValue(i._2.toDouble,"year", i._1)
    }
    val  chart = ChartFactories.BarChart(ds)
    chart.show()
    Util.sc.stop()
  }
}
```

Note that most of the movies are from 1996. The graph created is shown here:

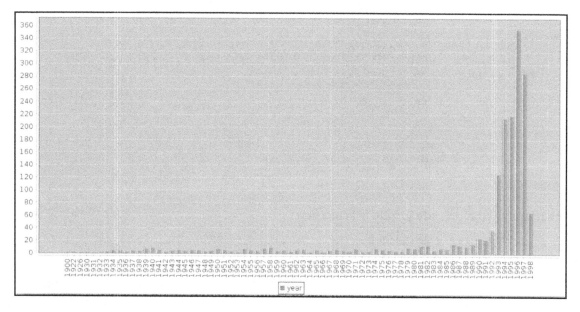

Distribution of movie ages

 Find the code listing at:
https://github.com/ml-resources/spark-ml/blob/branch-ed2/Chapter
_04/scala/2.0.0/src/main/scala/org/sparksamples/MovieAgesChart.s
cala

Exploring the rating dataset

Let's now take a look at the rating data:

The code is located under `RatingData`:

```scala
object RatingData {
  def main(args: Array[String]) {
    val customSchema = StructType(Array(
      StructField("user_id", IntegerType, true),
      StructField("movie_id", IntegerType, true),
      StructField("rating", IntegerType, true),
      StructField("timestamp", IntegerType, true)))

    val spConfig = (new SparkConf).setMaster("local").
      setAppName("SparkApp")
```

```
val spark = SparkSession.builder()
  .appName("SparkRatingData").config(spConfig)
  .getOrCreate()

val rating_df = spark.read.format("com.databricks.spark.csv")
  .option("delimiter", "t").schema(customSchema)
  .load("../../data/ml-100k/u.data")
rating_df.createOrReplaceTempView("df")
val num_ratings = rating_df.count()
val num_movies = Util.getMovieDataDF().count()
val first = rating_df.first()
println("first:" + first)
println("num_ratings:" + num_ratings)
  }
}
```

The output of the preceding code is listed here:

```
First: 196 242 3 881250949
num_ratings:100000
```

There are 100,000 ratings, and unlike the user and movie datasets, these records are split with a tab character ("t"). As you might have guessed, we'd probably want to compute some basic summary statistics and frequency histograms for the rating values. Let's do this now.

Data is separated. As you might have guessed, we'd probably want to compute some basic summary statistics and frequency histograms for the rating values. Let's do this now:). As you might have guessed, we probably want to compute some basic summary statistics and frequency histograms for the rating values. Let's do this now:

We will calculate the max, min, and average ratings. We will also calculate ratings per user and ratings per movie. We are using Spark SQL to extract the max, min, and average value of movie ratings.

```
val max = Util.spark.sql("select max(rating)  from df")
max.show()

val min = Util.spark.sql("select min(rating)  from df")
min.show()

val avg = Util.spark.sql("select avg(rating)  from df")
avg.show()
```

The output of the preceding code is listed here:

```
+----------------+
| . max(rating) |
+----------------+
|              5 |
+----------------+

+----------------+
| . min(rating) |
+----------------+
|              1 |
+----------------+

+----------------+
| . avg(rating) |
+----------------+
|        3.52986 |
+----------------+
```

> Find the code listing at:
> https://github.com/ml-resources/spark-ml/blob/branch-ed2/Chapter
> _04/scala/2.0.0/src/main/scala/org/sparksamples/RatingData.scala

Rating count bar chart

Looking at the results, the average rating given by a user to a movie is around 3.5, so we might expect that the distribution of ratings will be skewed towards slightly higher ratings. Let's see whether this is true, by creating a bar chart of rating values using a similar procedure as we did for occupations.

The code for plotting ratings versus count is shown here. This is available in the file `CountByRatingChart.scala`:

```scala
object CountByRatingChart {
  def main(args: Array[String]) {
    val customSchema = StructType(Array(
      StructField("user_id", IntegerType, true),
      StructField("movie_id", IntegerType, true),
      StructField("rating", IntegerType, true),
      StructField("timestamp", IntegerType, true)))

    val  spConfig = (new SparkConf).setMaster("local").
      setAppName("SparkApp")
    val  spark = SparkSession
```

```
        .builder()
        .appName("SparkRatingData").config(spConfig)
        .getOrCreate()
    val rating_df = spark.read.format("com.databricks.spark.csv")
        .option("delimiter", "t").schema(customSchema)

    val rating_df_count = rating_df.groupBy("rating").
        count().sort("rating")

    rating_df_count.show()
    val rating_df_count_collection = rating_df_count.collect()

    val ds = new org.jfree.data.category.DefaultCategoryDataset
    val mx = scala.collection.immutable.ListMap()

    for( x <- 0 until rating_df_count_collection.length) {
        val occ = rating_df_count_collection(x)(0)
        val count = Integer.parseInt(
          rating_df_count_collection(x)(1).toString)
        ds.addValue(count,"UserAges", occ.toString)
     }

    val chart = ChartFactories.BarChart(ds)
    val font = new Font("Dialog", Font.PLAIN,5);
    chart.peer.getCategoryPlot.getDomainAxis().
    setCategoryLabelPositions(CategoryLabelPositions.UP_90);
    chart.peer.getCategoryPlot.getDomainAxis.setLabelFont(font)
    chart.show()
    Util.sc.stop()
  }
}
```

On executing the previous code, you will get the bar chart as follows:

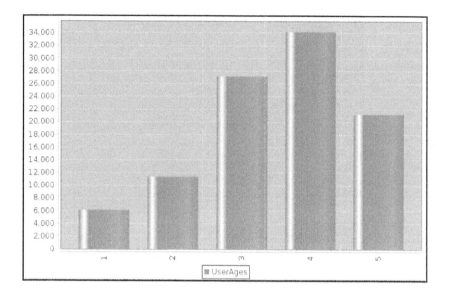

Distribution of number ratings

We can also look at the distribution of the number of ratings made by each user. Recall that we previously computed the `rating_data` RDD used in the preceding code by splitting the ratings with the tab character. We will now use the `rating_data` variable again in the following code.

Code resides in the class `UserRatingChart`. We will create a DataFrame from `u.data` file which is tab separated and then `groupbyuser_id` and sort by the count of ratings given by each user in ascending order.

```
object UserRatingsChart {
  def main(args: Array[String]) {

  }
}
```

Let us first try to show the ratings.

```
val customSchema = StructType(Array(
  StructField("user_id", IntegerType, true),
  StructField("movie_id", IntegerType, true),
  StructField("rating", IntegerType, true),
  StructField("timestamp", IntegerType, true)))

val spConfig = (new
```

```
        SparkConf).setMaster("local").setAppName("SparkApp")
val spark = SparkSession
    .builder()
    .appName("SparkRatingData").config(spConfig)
    .getOrCreate()

val rating_df = spark.read.format("com.databricks.spark.csv")
    .option("delimiter", "t").schema(customSchema)
    .load("../../data/ml-100k/u.data")

val rating_nos_by_user =
    rating_df.groupBy("user_id").count().sort("count")
val ds = new org.jfree.data.category.DefaultCategoryDataset
  rating_nos_by_user.show(rating_nos_by_user.collect().length)
```

The output of the preceding code is listed here:

```
+-------+-----+
|user_id|count|
+-------+-----+
|    636|   20|
|    572|   20|
|    926|   20|
|    824|   20|
|    166|   20|
|    685|   20|
|    812|   20|
|    418|   20|
|    732|   20|
|    364|   20|
....
     222|  387|
|    293|  388|
|     92|  388|
|    308|  397|
|    682|  399|
|     94|  400|
|      7|  403|
|    846|  405|
|    429|  414|
|    279|  434|
|    181|  435|
|    393|  448|
|    234|  480|
|    303|  484|
|    537|  490|
|    416|  493|
|    276|  518|
```

```
|    450|   540|
|     13|   636|
|    655|   685|
|    405|   737|
+-------+-----+
```

After showing the data textually, let's show it using JFreeChart by loading
`DefaultCategorySet` **with data from the** `rating_nos_by_user DataFrame`.

```
val step = (max/bins).toInt
for(i <- step until (max + step) by step) {
  mx += (i -> 0);
}
for( x <- 0 until rating_nos_by_user_collect.length) {
  val user_id =
    Integer.parseInt(rating_nos_by_user_collect(x)(0).toString)
  val count =
    Integer.parseInt(rating_nos_by_user_collect(x)(1).toString)
  ds.addValue(count,"Ratings", user_id)
}

val chart = ChartFactories.BarChart(ds)
chart.peer.getCategoryPlot.getDomainAxis().setVisible(false)

chart.show()
Util.sc.stop()
```

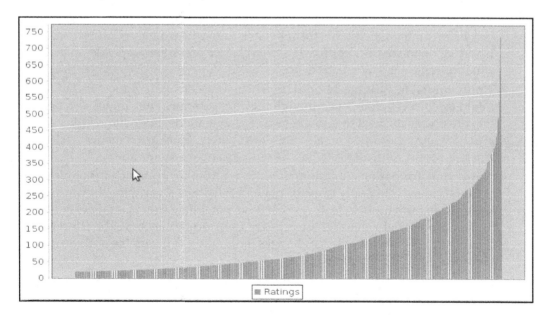

In the previous graph, x-axis is the user ID and y-axis is the number of ratings, which varies from minimum rating of 20 to a maximum of 737.

Processing and transforming your data

In order to make the raw data usable in a machine learning algorithm, we first need to clean it up and possibly transform it in various ways before extracting useful features from the transformed data. The transformation and feature extraction steps are closely linked, and in some cases, certain transformations are themselves a case of feature extraction.

We have already seen an example of the need to clean data in the movie dataset. Generally, real-world datasets contain bad data, missing data points, and outliers. Ideally, we would correct bad data; however, this is often not possible, as many datasets derive from some form of collection process that cannot be repeated (this is the case, for example, in web activity data and sensor data). Missing values and outliers are also common and can be dealt with in a manner similar to bad data. Overall, the broad options are as follows:

- **Filter out or remove records with bad or missing values**: This is sometimes unavoidable; however, this means losing the good part of a bad or missing record.
- **Fill in bad or missing data**: We can try to assign a value to bad or missing data based on the rest of the data we have available. Approaches can include assigning a zero value, assigning the global mean or median, interpolating nearby or similar data points (usually, in a time-series dataset), and so on. Deciding on the correct approach is often a tricky task and depends on the data, situation, and one's own experience.
- **Apply robust techniques to outliers**: The main issue with outliers is that they might be correct values, even though they are extreme. They might also be errors. It is often very difficult to know which case you are dealing with. Outliers can also be removed or filled in, although fortunately, there are statistical techniques (such as robust regression) to handle outliers and extreme values.
- **Apply transformations to potential outliers**: Another approach for outliers or extreme values is to apply transformations, such as a logarithmic or Gaussian kernel transformation, to features that have potential outliers, or display large ranges of potential values. These types of transformations have the effect of dampening the impact of large changes in the scale of a variable and turning a nonlinear relationship into one that is linear.

Filling in bad or missing data

Let's take a looks at the year of movie review and clean it up.

We have already seen an example of filtering out bad data. Following on from the preceding code, the following code snippet applies the fill-in approach to the bad release date record by assigning a value which is Empty String as 1900 (this will be later replaced by the Median):

```
Util.spark.udf.register("convertYear", Util.convertYear _)
movie_data_df.show(false)

val movie_years = Util.spark.sql("select convertYear(date) as year from
movie_data")

movie_years.createOrReplaceTempView("movie_years")
Util.spark.udf.register("replaceEmptyStr", replaceEmptyStr _)

val years_replaced =  Util.spark.sql("select replaceEmptyStr(year)
  as r_year from movie_years")
```

In the previous code, we used the `replaceEmtryStr` function described here:

```
def replaceEmptyStr(v : Int): Int = {
  try {
    if(v.equals("") ) {
      return 1900
    } else {
      returnv
    }
  }catch{
    case e: Exception => println(e)
     return 1900
  }
}
```

Next, we extract filtered years which are not 1900, replace `Array[Row]` with `Array[int]` and calculate various metrics:

- Total sum of Entries
- Total No. of Entries
- Mean value of Year
- Median value of Year
- Total Years after conversion
- Count of 1900

```
val movie_years_filtered = movie_years.filter(x =>(x == 1900) )
val years_filtered_valid = years_replaced.filter(x => (x !=
  1900)).collect()
val years_filtered_valid_int = new
  Array[Int](years_filtered_valid.length)
for( i <- 0 until years_filtered_valid.length -1){
  val x = Integer.parseInt(years_filtered_valid(i)(0).toString)
  years_filtered_valid_int(i) = x
}
val years_filtered_valid_int_sorted =
  years_filtered_valid_int.sorted

val years_replaced_int = new Array[Int]
  (years_replaced.collect().length)

val years_replaced_collect = years_replaced.collect()

for( i <- 0 until years_replaced.collect().length -1){
  val x = Integer.parseInt(years_replaced_collect(i)(0).toString)
  years_replaced_int(i) = x
}

val years_replaced_rdd = Util.sc.parallelize(years_replaced_int)

val num = years_filtered_valid.length
var sum_y = 0
years_replaced_int.foreach(sum_y += _)
println("Total sum of Entries:"+ sum_y)
println("Total No of Entries:"+ num)
val mean = sum_y/num
val median_v = median(years_filtered_valid_int_sorted)
Util.sc.broadcast(mean)
println("Mean value of Year:"+ mean)
println("Median value of Year:"+ median_v)
val years_x = years_replaced_rdd.map(v => replace(v , median_v))
println("Total Years after conversion:"+ years_x.count())
var count = 0
Util.sc.broadcast(count)
val years_with1900 = years_x.map(x => (if(x == 1900) {count +=1}))
println("Count of 1900: "+ count)
```

The output of the previous code is listed in the following; values with 1900 after replacement with median shows that our processing has been successful

```
Total sum of Entries:3344062
Total No of Entries:1682
Mean value of Year:1988
Median value of Year:1995
```

```
Total Years after conversion:1682
Count of 1900: 0
Count of 1900: 0
```

Find the code listing at:
https://github.com/ml-resources/spark-ml/blob/branch-ed2/Chapter
_04/scala/2.0.0/src/main/scala/org/sparksamples/MovieDataFilling
BadValues.scala

We computed both the mean and the median year of release here. As can be seen from the output, the median release year is considerably higher, because of the skewed distribution of the years. While it is not always straightforward to decide on precisely which fill-in value to use for a given situation, in this case, it is certainly feasible to use the median due to this skew.

Note that the preceding code example is, strictly speaking, not very scalable, as it requires collecting all the data to the driver. We can use Spark's `mean` function for numeric RDDs to compute the mean, but there is no median function available currently. We can solve this by creating our own or by computing the median on a sample of the dataset created using the `sample` function (we will see more of this in the upcoming chapters).

Extracting useful features from your data

Once we are done with the cleaning of our data, we are ready to get down to the business of extracting actual features from the data, with which our machine learning model can be trained.

Features refer to the variables that we use to train our model. Each row of data contains information that we would like to extract into a training example.

Almost all machine learning models ultimately work on numerical representations in the form of a vector; hence, we need to convert raw data into numbers.

Features broadly fall into a few categories, which are as follows:

- **Numerical features**: These features are typically real or integer numbers, for example, the user age that we used in an example earlier.
- **Categorical features**: These features refer to variables that can take one of a set of possible states at any given time. Examples from our dataset might include a user's gender or occupation or movie categories.

- **Text features**: These are features derived from the text content in the data, for example, movie titles, descriptions, or reviews.
- **Other features**: Most other types of features are ultimately represented numerically. For example, images, video, and audio can be represented as sets of numerical data. Geographical locations can be represented as latitude and longitude or geohash data.

Here we will cover numerical, categorical, and text features.

Numerical features

What is the difference between any old number and a numerical feature? Well, in reality, any numerical data can be used as an input variable. However, in a machine learning model, you learn about a vector of weights for each feature. The weights play a role in mapping feature values to an outcome or target variable (in the case of supervised learning models).

Thus, we want to use features that make sense, that is, where the model can learn the relationship between feature values and the target variable. For example, age might be a reasonable feature. Perhaps there is a direct relationship between increasing age and a certain outcome. Similarly, height is a good example of a numerical feature that can be used directly.

We will often see that numerical features are less useful in their raw form but can be turned into representations that are more useful. The location is an example of such a case.

Using raw locations (say, latitude and longitude) might not be that useful unless our data is very dense indeed since our model might not be able to learn about a useful relationship between the raw location and an outcome. However, a relationship might exist between some aggregated or binned representation of the location (for example, a city or country) and the outcome.

Categorical features

Categorical features cannot be used as input in their raw form, as they are not numbers; instead, they are members of a set of possible values that the variable can take. In the example mentioned earlier, user occupation is a categorical variable that can take the value of student, programmer, and so on.

To transform categorical variables into a numerical representation, we can use a common approach known as **1-of-k** encoding. An approach such as 1-of-k encoding is required to represent.

An approach such as 1-of-k encoding is required to represent nominal variables in a way that makes sense for machine learning tasks. Ordinal variables might be used in their raw form but are often encoded in the same way as nominal variables.

Assume that there are k possible values that the variable can take. If we assign each possible value an index from the set of 1 to k, then we can represent a given state of the variable using a binary vector of length k; here, all entries are zero, except the entry at the index that corresponds to the given state of the variable. This entry is set to one.

e.g. student is [0], programmer is [1]

so values of:

student become [1, 0]

programmer become [0,1]

Extract the binary encoding for two occupations, followed by binary feature vector creation with a length of 21:

```
val ratings_grouped = rating_df.groupBy("rating")
ratings_grouped.count().show()
val ratings_byuser_local = rating_df.groupBy("user_id").count()
val count_ratings_byuser_local = ratings_byuser_local.count()
ratings_byuser_local.show(ratings_byuser_local.collect().length)
val movie_fields_df = Util.getMovieDataDF()
val user_data_df = Util.getUserFieldDataFrame()
val occupation_df = user_data_df.select("occupation").distinct()
occupation_df.sort("occupation").show()
val occupation_df_collect = occupation_df.collect()

var all_occupations_dict_1:Map[String, Int] = Map()
var idx = 0;
// for loop execution with a range
for( idx <- 0 to (occupation_df_collect.length -1)){
  all_occupations_dict_1 +=
    occupation_df_collect(idx)(0).toString() -> idx
}

println("Encoding of 'doctor : " +
 all_occupations_dict_1("doctor"))
println("Encoding of 'programmer' : " +
 all_occupations_dict_1("programmer"))
```

The output of the previous `println` statements is listed here:

```
Encoding of 'doctor : 20
Encoding of 'programmer' : 5

var k = all_occupations_dict_1.size
var binary_x = DenseVector.zeros[Double](k)
var k_programmer = all_occupations_dict_1("programmer")
binary_x(k_programmer) = 1
println("Binary feature vector: %s" + binary_x)
println("Length of binary vector: " + k)
```

The output of the previous commands, which show the binary feature vector and length of binary vector is listed here:

```
Binary feature vector: %sDenseVector(0.0, 0.0, 0.0, 0.0, 0.0, 1.0, 0.0,
0.0, 0.0, 0.0, 0.0, 0.0, 0.0, 0.0, 0.0, 0.0, 0.0, 0.0, 0.0, 0.0, 0.0)
Length of binary vector: 21
```

Find the code listing at:
https://github.com/ml-resources/spark-ml/blob/branch-ed2/Chapter
_04/scala/2.0.0/src/main/scala/org/sparksamples/RatingData.scala

Derived features

As we mentioned earlier, it is often useful to compute a derived feature from one or more available variables. We hope that the derived feature can add more information than only using the variable in its raw form available variables. We hope that the derived feature can add more information than only using the variable in its raw form.

For instance, we can compute the average rating given by each user to all the movies they rated. This would be a feature that could provide a *user-specific* intercept in our model (in fact, this is a commonly used approach in recommendation models). We have taken the raw rating data and created a new feature that can allow us to learn a better model.

Examples of features derived from raw data include computing average values, median values, variances, sums, differences, maximums or minimums, and counts. We have already seen a case of this when we created a new `movie age` feature from the year of release of the movie and the current year. Often, the idea behind using these transformations is to summarize the numerical data in some way that might make it easier for a model to learn features, for example, by binning features. Common examples of these include variables such as age, geolocation, and time.

Transforming timestamps into categorical features

Extract time of Day

To illustrate how to derive categorical features from numerical data, we will use the times of the ratings given by users to movies. Extract the date and time from the timestamp and, in turn, extract the hour of the day.

We will need a function to extract a datetime representation of the rating timestamp (in seconds); we will create this function now: extract the date and time from the timestamp and, in turn, extract the hour of the day. This will result in an RDD of the hour of the day for each rating.

Scala

First, we define a function which extracts currentHour from a date string:

```
def getCurrentHour(dateStr: String) : Integer = {
  var currentHour = 0
  try {
    val date = new Date(dateStr.toLong)
    return int2Integer(date.getHours)
  } catch {
    case _ => return currentHour
  }
  return 1
}
```

The output of the preceding code is listed here:

Timestamps DataFrame is extracted from rating_df by creating a TempView df and running a select statement.

Relevant code listing:

```
val customSchema = StructType(Array(
StructField("user_id", IntegerType, true),
StructField("movie_id", IntegerType, true),
StructField("rating", IntegerType, true),
StructField("timestamp", IntegerType, true)))

val spConfig = (new
  SparkConf).setMaster("local").setAppName("SparkApp")
val spark = SparkSession
  .builder()
  .appName("SparkRatingData").config(spConfig)
  .getOrCreate()
```

```
val rating_df = spark.read.format("com.databricks.spark.csv")
  .option("delimiter", "t").schema(customSchema)
  .load("../../data/ml-100k/u.data")
rating_df.createOrReplaceTempView("df")
Util.spark.udf.register("getCurrentHour", getCurrentHour _)

val timestamps_df =
  Util.spark.sql("select getCurrentHour(timestamp) as hour from
  df")
timestamps_df.show()
```

Find the code listing at:
https://github.com/ml-resources/spark-ml/blob/branch-ed2/Chapter
_04/scala/2.0.0/src/main/scala/org/sparksamples/RatingData.scala

Extract time of day

We have transformed the raw time data into a categorical feature that represents the hour of the day in which the rating was given.

Now, say that we decide this is too coarse a representation. Perhaps we want to further refine the transformation. We can assign each hour-of-the-day value into a defined bucket that represents a time of day.

For example, we can say that morning is from 7 a.m. to 11 a.m., while lunch is from 11 a.m. to 1 a.m., and so on. Using these buckets, we can create a function to assign a time of day, given the hour of the day as input.

Scala

In Scala, we define a function which takes inputer as absolute HR in 24 HR format and returns time of day: morning, lunch, afternoon, evening, or night:

```
def assignTod(hr : Integer) : String = {
if(hr >= 7 && hr < 12){
return"morning"
}else if ( hr >= 12 && hr < 14) {
return"lunch"
  } else if ( hr>= 14 && hr < 18) {
return"afternoon"
  } else if ( hr>= 18 && hr.<(23)) {
return"evening"
  } else if ( hr>= 23 && hr <= 24) {
return"night"
  } else if (  hr< 7) {
```

```
return"night"
   } else {
return"error"
   }
}
```

We register this function as a UDF and call it on temp view timestamps within a select call.

```
Util.spark.udf.register("assignTod", assignTod _)
timestamps_df.createOrReplaceTempView("timestamps")
val tod = Util.spark.sql("select assignTod(hour) as tod from
 timestamps")
tod.show()
```

Find the code listing at:
https://github.com/ml-resources/spark-ml/blob/branch-ed2/Chapter _04/scala/2.0.0/src/main/scala/org/sparksamples/RatingData.scala

We have now transformed the timestamp variable (which can take on thousands of values and is probably not useful to a model in its raw form) into hours (taking on 24 values) and then into a time of day (taking on five possible values). Now that we have a categorical feature, we can use the same 1-of-k encoding method outlined earlier to generate a binary feature vector.

Text features

In some ways, text features are a form of categorical and derived features. Let's take the example of the description for a movie (which we do not have in our dataset). Here, the raw text could not be used directly, even as a categorical feature, since there are virtually unlimited possible combinations of words that could occur if each piece of text was a possible value `true`, since there are virtually unlimited possible combinations of words that could occur if each piece of text was a possible value. Our model would almost never see two occurrences of the same feature and would not be able to learn effectively. Therefore, we would like to turn raw text into a form that is more amenable to machine learning, since there are virtually unlimited possible combinations of words that could occur if each piece of text was a possible value.

There are numerous ways of dealing with text, and the field of natural language processing is dedicated to processing, representing, and modeling textual content. A full treatment is beyond the scope of this book, but we will introduce a simple and standard approach for text-feature extraction; this approach is known as the bag-of-words representation.

The bag-of-words approach treats a piece of text content as a set of the words, and possibly numbers, in the text (these are often referred to as terms). The process of the bag-of-words approach is as follows:

- **Tokenization**: First, some form of tokenization is applied to the text to split it into a set of tokens (generally words, numbers, and so on). An example of this is simple whitespace tokenization, which splits the text on each space and might remove punctuation and other characters that are not alphabetical or numerical.
- **Stop word removal**: Next, it is usual to remove very common words such as "the", "and", and "but" (these are known as stop words).
- **Stemming**: The next step can include stemming, which refers to taking a term and reducing it to its base form or stem. A common example is plural terms becoming singular (for example, dogs becomes dog, and so on). There are many approaches to stemming, and text-processing libraries often contain various stemming algorithms, for example, OpenNLP, NLTK and so on. Covering stemming in detail is outside the scope of this book, but feel free to explore these libraries on your own.
- **Vectorization**: The final step is turning the processed terms into a vector representation. The simplest form is, perhaps, a binary vector representation, where we assign a value of one if a term exists in the text and zero if it does not. This is essentially identical to the categorical 1-of-k encoding we encountered earlier. Like 1-of-k encoding, this requires a dictionary of terms mapping a given term to an index number. As you might gather, there are potentially millions of individual possible terms (even after stop word removal and stemming). Hence, it becomes critical to use a sparse vector representation compute `time.computetime.computetime.compute` time.

In `Chapter 10`, *Advanced Text Processing with Spark*, we will cover more complex text processing and feature extraction, including methods to weight terms; these methods go beyond the basic binary encoding we saw earlier.

Simple text feature extraction

To show an example of extracting textual features in the binary vector representation, we can use the movie titles that we have available.

First, we will create a function to strip away the year of release for each movie, if the year is present, leaving only the title of the movie.

We will use a regular expression, to search for the year between parentheses in the movie titles. If we find a match with this regular expression, we will extract only the title up to the index of the first match (that is, the index in the title string of the opening parenthesis).

Scala

First, we create a function which takes the input string and filters the output with a regular expression.

```
def processRegex(input:String):String= {
   val pattern = "^[^(]*".r
   val output = pattern.findFirstIn(input)
   return output.get
}
```

Extract DataFrame with only the raw title and create a temp view `titles`. Register the function created above with Spark and then run it on the DataFrame within the `select` statement.

```
val raw_title =
  org.sparksamples.Util.getMovieDataDF().select("name"
  raw_title.show()
raw_title.createOrReplaceTempView("titles")
Util.spark.udf.register("processRegex", processRegex _)
val processed_titles = Util.spark.sql(
"select processRegex(name) from titles")
processed_titles.show()
val titles_rdd = processed_titles.rdd.map(r => r(0).toString)
titles_rdd.take(5).foreach(println)
```

The output of the preceding code is listed here:

```
//Output of raw_title.show()
+--------------------+
|          UDF(name) |
+--------------------+
|          Toy Story |
|          GoldenEye |
|         Four Rooms |
|         Get Shorty |
|            Copycat |
|     Shanghai Triad |
|      Twelve Monkeys |
|               Babe |
|    Dead Man Walking |
|         Richard III |
|              Seven |
```

```
|Usual Suspects, The |
|    Mighty Aphrodite |
|          Postino, Il |
| Mr. Holland's Opus |
|         French Twist |
|From Dusk Till Dawn |
| White Balloon, The |
|       Antonia's Line |
| Angels and Insects |
+--------------------+

//titles_rdd.take(5).foreach(println)
Toy Story
GoldenEye
Four Rooms
Get Shorty
Copycat
```

Then, to apply our function to the raw titles and apply a tokenization scheme to the extracted titles to convert them to terms, we will use the simple whitespace tokenization we covered earlier:

Next, we split the `titles` into single words

```
val title_terms = titles_rdd.map(x => x.split(""))
title_terms.take(5).foreach(_.foreach(println))
println(title_terms.count())
```

Applying this simple tokenization gives the following result:

```
Toy
Story
GoldenEye
Four
Rooms
Get
Shorty
Copycat
```

Then, we convert the rdd of words and find the total number of words--we get the collection of total words and index of "Dead" and "Rooms".

```
val all_terms_dic = new ListBuffer[String]()
val all_terms = title_terms.flatMap(title_terms =>
title_terms).distinct().collect()
for (term <- all_terms){
  all_terms_dic += term
}
```

```
println(all_terms_dic.length)
println(all_terms_dic.indexOf("Dead"))
println(all_terms_dic.indexOf("Rooms"))
```

This will result in the following output:

```
Total number of terms: 2645
Index of term 'Dead': 147
Index of term 'Rooms': 1963
```

We can also achieve the same result more efficiently using Spark's `zipWithIndex` function. This function takes an RDD of values and merges them together with an index to create a new RDD of key-value pairs, where the key will be the term and the value will be the index in the term dictionary. We will use `collectAsMap` to collect the key-value RDD to the driver as a Python `dict` method:

Scala

```
val all_terms_withZip = title_terms.flatMap(title_terms =>
  title_terms).distinct().zipWithIndex().collectAsMap()
println(all_terms_withZip.get("Dead"))
println(all_terms_withZip.get("Rooms"))
```

The output is as follows:

```
Index of term 'Dead': 147
Index of term 'Rooms': 1963
```

Sparse Vectors from Titles

The final step is to create a function that converts a set of terms into a sparse vector representation. To do this, we will create an empty sparse matrix with one row and a number of columns equal to the total number of terms in our dictionary. We will then step through each term in the input list of terms and check whether this term is in our term dictionary. If it is, we assign a value of 1 to the vector at the index that corresponds to the term in our dictionary mapping:

extracted terms:

Scala

```
def create_vector(title_terms:Array[String],
  all_terms_dic:ListBuffer[String]): CSCMatrix[Int] = {
  var idx = 0
  val x = CSCMatrix.zeros[Int](1, all_terms_dic.length)
  title_terms.foreach(i => {
```

```
      if (all_terms_dic.contains(i)) {
        idx = all_terms_dic.indexOf(i)
        x.update(0, idx, 1)
      }
   })
   return x
}

val term_vectors = title_terms.map(title_terms =>
 create_vector(title_terms, all_terms_dic))
term_vectors.take(5).foreach(println)
```

We can then inspect the first few records of our new RDD of sparse vectors:

```
1 x 2453 CSCMatrix
(0,622) 1
(0,1326) 1
1 x 2453 CSCMatrix
(0,418) 1
1 x 2453 CSCMatrix
(0,729) 1
(0,996) 1
1 x 2453 CSCMatrix
(0,433) 1
(0,1414) 1
1 x 2453 CSCMatrix
(0,1559) 1
```

Find the code listing at:
https://github.com/ml-resources/spark-ml/blob/branch-ed2/Chapter_04/scala/2.0.0/src/main/scala/org/sparksamples/exploredataset/explore_movies.scala

We can see that each movie title has now been transformed into a sparse vector. We can see that the titles where we extracted two terms have two non-zero entries in the vector, titles where we extracted only one term have one non-zero entry, and so on.

Note the use of Spark's `broadcast` method in the preceding example code to create a broadcast variable that contains the term dictionary. In real-world applications, such term dictionaries can be extremely large, so using a broadcast variable is not advisable.

Normalizing features

Once the features have been extracted into the form of a vector, a common preprocessing step is to normalize the numerical data. The idea behind this is to transform each numerical feature in a way that scales it to a standard size. We can perform different kinds of normalization, which are as follows:

- Normalize a feature: This is usually a transformation applied to an individual feature across the dataset, for example, subtracting the mean (centering the feature) or applying the standard normal transformation (such that the feature has a mean of zero and a standard deviation of 1).
- Normalize a feature vector: This is usually a transformation applied to all features in a given row of the dataset such that the resulting feature vector has a normalized length. That is, we will ensure that each feature in the vector is scaled such that the vector has a norm of 1 (typically, on an L1 or L2 norm).

We will use the second case as an example. We can use the `norm` function of `numpy` to achieve the vector normalization by first computing the L2 norm of a random vector and then dividing each element in the vector by this norm to create our normalized vector:

```
//val vector = DenseVector.rand(10)
val vector = DenseVector(0.49671415, -0.1382643,
  0.64768854,1.52302986, -0.23415337, -0.23413696, 1.57921282,
  0.76743473, -0.46947439, 0.54256004)
val norm_fact = norm(vector)
val vec = vector/norm_fact
println(norm_fact)
println(vec)
```

The output of the preceding code is listed here:

```
2.5908023998401077
DenseVector(0.19172212826059407, -0.053367366036303286,
  0.24999534508690138, 0.5878602938201672, -0.09037870661786127, -
  0.09037237267282516, 0.6095458380374597, 0.2962150760889223, -
  0.18120810372453483, 0.20941776186153152)
```

Using ML for feature normalization

Spark provides some built-in functions for feature scaling and standardization in its machine learning library. These include `StandardScaler`, which applies the standard normal transformation, and `Normalizer`, which applies the same feature vector normalization we showed you in our preceding example code.lization we showed you in our preceding example code.lization, we showed you in our preceding example code.

We will explore the use of these methods in the upcoming chapters, but for now, let's simply compare the results of using MLlib's `Normalizer` to our own results:

```
from pyspark.mllib.feature import Normalizer
normalizer = Normalizer()
vector = sc.parallelize([x])
```

After importing the required class, we will instantiate `Normalizer` (by default, it will use the L2 norm as we did earlier). Note that, as in most situations in Spark, we need to provide `Normalizer` with an RDD as input (it contains `numpy` arrays or MLlib vectors); hence, we will create a single-element RDD from our vector x for illustrative purposes.

We will then use the `transform` function of `Normalizer` on our RDD. Since the RDD only has one vector in it, we will return our vector to the driver by calling `first` and finally by calling the `toArray` function to convert the vector back into a `numpy` array:

```
normalized_x_mllib =
  normalizer.transform(vector).first().toArray()
```

Finally, we can print out the same details as we did previously, comparing the results:

```
print"x:n%s" % x
print"2-Norm of x: %2.4f" % norm_x_2
print"Normalized x MLlib:n%s" % normalized_x_mllib
print"2-Norm of normalized_x_mllib: %2.4f" %
  np.linalg.norm(normalized_x_mllib)
```

You will end up with exactly the same normalized vector as we did with our own code. However, using MLlib's built-in methods is certainly more convenient and efficient than writing our own functions! Equivalent Scala implementation is as follows:

```
object FeatureNormalizer {
  def main(args: Array[String]): Unit = {
    val v = Vectors.dense(0.49671415, -0.1382643, 0.64768854,
      1.52302986, -0.23415337, -0.23413696, 1.57921282,
      0.76743473, -0.46947439, 0.54256004)
    val normalizer = new Normalizer(2)
    val norm_op = normalizer.transform(v)
```

```
        println(norm_op)
    }
}
```

The output of the preceding code is listed following:

```
[0.19172212826059407,-
 0.053367366036303286,0.24999534508690138,0.5878602938201672,-
 0.09037870661786127,-
 0.09037237267282516,0.6095458380374597,0.2962150760889223,-
 0.18120810372453483,0.20941776186153152]
```

Using packages for feature extraction

While from these common tasks each and every time. Certainly, we can create our own reusable code libraries for this purpose; however, fortunately, we can rely on the existing tools and packages. Since Spark supports Scala, Java, and Python bindings, we can use packages available in these languages that provide sophisticated tools to process and extract features and represent them as vectors. A few examples of packages for feature extraction include scikit-learn, gensim, scikit-image, matplotlib, and NLTK in Python, OpenNLP in Java, and Breeze and Chalk in Scala. In fact, Breeze has been part of Spark MLlib since version 1.0, and we will see how to use some Breeze functionality for linear algebra in the later chapters.

TFID

tf-idf is short term for **term frequency-inverse document frequency**. It is a numerical statistic that is intended to reflect how important a word is to a document in a collection or corpus. It is used as a weighting factor in information retrieval and text mining. The tf-idf value increases in proportion to the number of times a word appears in a document. It is offset by the frequency of the word in the corpus, that helps to adjust for some words which appear more frequently in general.

tf-idf is used by search engines or text processing engines as a tool in scoring and ranking a document's relevance for a user query.

The simplest ranking functions are computed by summing the tf-idf for each query term; more sophisticated ranking functions are variants of this simple model.

In the term frequency $tf(t,d)$ calculation, one choice is to use the raw frequency of a term in a document: the number of times term t occurs in document d. If raw frequency of t is $f(t,d)$, then the simple tf scheme is $tf(t,d) = f_{t,d}$.

Spark's implementation of tf(t.d) uses the hashing. A raw word is mapped into an index (term) by applying a hash function.The term frequencies are calculated using the mapped indices.

References:

- https://spark.apache.org/docs/1.6.0/api/scala/index.html#org.apache.spark.mllib.feature.HashingTF
- https://en.wikipedia.org/wiki/Tf%E2%80%93idf
- https://spark.apache.org/docs/1.6.0/mllib-feature-extraction.html

IDF

The **inverse document frequency(IDF)**represents how much information the word provides: is the term common or rare across the corpus. It is the log scaled inverse fraction of the documents containing the word, calculated by division of the total number of documents by the number of documents containing the term**TF-IDF**

TF-IDF is calculated by multiplying TF and IDF.

$$TFIDF(t,d,D) = TF(t,d) * IDF(t,D)$$

The following example calculates TFIDF for each term in the Apache Spark README.md file:

```
object TfIdfSample{
  def main(args: Array[String]) {
    // TODO replace with path specific to your machine
    val file = Util.SPARK_HOME + "/README.md"
    val spConfig = (new
      SparkConf).setMaster("local").setAppName("SparkApp")
    val sc = new SparkContext(spConfig)
    val documents: RDD[Seq[String]] =
      sc.textFile(file).map(_.split("").toSeq)
    print("Documents Size:" + documents.count)
    val hashingTF = new HashingTF()
    val tf = hashingTF.transform(documents)
    for(tf_ <- tf) {
      println(s"$tf_")
    }
    tf.cache()
    val idf = new IDF().fit(tf)
    val tfidf = idf.transform(tf)
```

```
    println("tfidf size : " + tfidf.count)
    for(tfidf_ <- tfidf) {
      println(s"$tfidf_")
    }
  }
}
```

Find the code listing at:
https://github.com/ml-resources/spark-ml/blob/branch-ed2/Chapter
_04/scala2.0.0/src/main/scala/org/sparksamples/featureext/TfIdfS
ample.scala

Word2Vector

The Word2Vec tools take text data as input and produce the word vectors as output. This tool constructs a vocabulary from the training text data and learns vector representation of words. The resulting word vector file can be used as features for many natural language processing and machine learning applications.

The easiest way to investigate the learned representations is to find the closest words for a user-specified word.

Word2Vec implementation in Apache Spark computes distributed vector representation of words. Apache Spark's implementation is a more scalable approach as compared to single machine Word2Vec implementations provided by Google).

(https://code.google.com/archive/p/word2vec/)

Word2Vec can be implemented using two learning algorithms: continuous bag-of-words and continuous skip-gram.

Skip-gram model

The training objective of the skip-gram model is to find word representations useful for predicting the surrounding words in a document or a sentence. Given a sequence of words *w1, w2, w3, .., wT*, skip-gram model maximizes the average log probability shown as following:

$$\frac{1}{T} \sum_{t=0}^{t=T} \sum_{-c \leq j \leq c, j! = 0} \log_p \left(w_{t+j} / w_t \right)$$

c is the size of the training context (which can be a function of the center word *wt*). Larger *c* results in more training examples leading to a higher accuracy, at the expense of the training time. The basic skip-gram formulation defines *p(wt+j |wt)* using the `softmax` function:

$$p(^wo/w_l) = \frac{exp(v'_{w_o}{}^T v_{w_l})}{\sum_{w=1}^{w=W} exp(v'_w{}^T v_{w_l})}$$

v_w, v' and, *w* are the *input* and *output* vector representations of *w*, and *W* is the number of words in the vocabulary

In Spark Hierarchical soft-max approach is used to predicting word *wi* given word *wj*.

The following example shows how to create word vectors using Apache Spark.

```scala
object ConvertWordsToVectors{
  def main(args: Array[String]) {
    val file =
      "/home/ubuntu/work/ml-resources/" +
      "spark-ml/Chapter_04/data/text8_10000"
    val conf = new SparkConf().setMaster("local").
      setAppName("Word2Vector")
    val sc = new SparkContext(conf)
    val input = sc.textFile(file).map(line => line.split("").toSeq)
    val word2vec = new Word2Vec()
    val model = word2vec.fit(input)
    val vectors = model.getVectors
    vectors foreach (
      (t2) =>println (t2._1 + "-->" + t2._2.mkString(""))
    )
  }
}
```

Find the code listing at:
`https://github.com/ml-resources/spark-ml/blob/branch-ed2/Chapter_04/scala/2.0.0/src/main/scala/org/sparksamples/featureext/ConvertWordsToVectors.scala`

The output of the preceding code:

```
ideas-->0.0036772825 -9.474439E-4 0.0018383651 -6.24215E-4 -
0.0042944895 -5.839545E-4 -0.004661157 -0.0024960344 0.0046632644 -
0.00237432 -5.5691406E-5 -0.0033026629 0.0032463844 -0.0019799764 -
0.0016042799 0.0016129494 -4.099998E-4 0.0031266063 -0.0051537985
```

```
0.004354736 -8.4361364E-4 0.0016157745 -0.006367187 0.0037806155 -
4.4071436E-4 8.62155E-4 0.0051918332 0.004437387 -0.0012511226 -
8.7162864E-4 -0.0035564564 -4.2263913E-4 -0.0020519749 -
0.0034343079 0.0035128237 -0.0014698022 -7.263344E-4 -0.0030510207
-1.05513E-4 0.003316195 0.001853326 -0.003090298 -7.3562167E-4 -
0.004879414 -0.007057088 1.1937474E-4 -0.0017973455 0.0034448127
0.005289607 9.6152216E-4 0.002103868 0.0016721261 -9.6310966E-4
0.0041839285 0.0035658625 -0.0038187192 0.005523701 -1.8146896E-4 -
0.006257453 6.5041234E-4 -0.006894542 -0.0013860351 -4.7463065E-4
0.0044280654 -7.142674E-4 -0.005085546 -2.7047616E-4 0.0026938762 -
0.0020157609 0.0051508015 -0.0027767695 0.003554946 -0.0052921847
0.0020432177 -0.002188367 -0.0010223344 -0.0031813548 -0.0032866944
0.0020323955 -0.0015844131 -0.0041034482 0.0044767153 -2.5071128E-4
0.0022343954 0.004051373 -0.0021706335 8.161181E-4 0.0042591896
0.0036099665 -0.0024891358 -0.0043153367 -0.0037649528 -
0.0033249175 -9.5358933E-4 -0.0041675125 0.0029751007 -0.0017840122
-5.3287676E-4 1.983675E-4 -1.9737136E-5
```

Standard scalar

Standard scalar standardizes features of the data set by scaling to unit variance and removing the mean (optionally) using column summary statistics on the samples in the training set.

This process is a very common pre-processing step.

Standardization improves the convergence rate during the optimization process. It also prevents features with large variances from exerting an overly large influence during model training.

StandardScaler class has the following parameters in the constructor:

new StandardScaler(withMean: Boolean, withStd: Boolean)

- withMean: False by default. Centers the data with mean before scaling. It will build a dense output, does not work on sparse input and will raise an exception.
- withStd: True by default. It Scales the data to unit standard deviation.

Annotations

Available @Since("1.1.0")

```
object StandardScalarSample {
  def main(args: Array[String]) {
    val conf = new SparkConf().setMaster("local").
```

```
    setAppName("Word2Vector")
  val sc = new SparkContext(conf)
  val data = MLUtils.loadLibSVMFile( sc,
    org.sparksamples.Util.SPARK_HOME +
    "/data/mllib/sample_libsvm_data.txt")

  val scaler1 = new StandardScaler().fit(data.map(x => x.features)
  val scaler2 = new StandardScaler(withMean = true,
    withStd = true).fit(data.map(x => x.features))
  // scaler3 is an identical model to scaler2, and will produce
  //identical transformations
  val scaler3 = new StandardScalerModel(scaler2.std, scaler2.mean)

  // data1 will be unit variance.
  val data1 = data.map(x =>
    (x.label, scaler1.transform(x.features)))
  println(data1.first())
  // Without converting the features into dense vectors,
  //transformation with zero mean will raise
  // exception on sparse vector.
  // data2 will be unit variance and zero mean.
  val data2 = data.map(x => (x.label,
    scaler2.transform(Vectors.dense(x.features.toArray))))
  println(data2.first())
  }
}
```

 Find the code listing at:
https://github.com/ml-resources/spark-ml/blob/branch-ed2/Chapter
_04/scala/2.0.0/src/main/scala/org/sparksamples/featureext/Stand
ardScalarSample.scala

Summary

In this chapter, we saw how to find common, publicly available datasets that can be used to test various machine learning models. You learned how to load, process, and clean data, as well as how to apply common techniques to transform raw data into feature vectors that can be used as training examples for our models.

In the next chapter, you will learn the basics of recommender systems and explore how to create a recommendation model, use the model to make predictions, and evaluate the model.

5
Building a Recommendation Engine with Spark

Now that you have learned the basics of data processing and feature extraction, we will move on to explore individual machine learning models in detail, starting with recommendation engines.

Recommendation engines are probably among the best types of machine learning models known to the general public. Even if people do not know exactly what a recommendation engine is, they have most likely experienced one through the use of popular websites, such as Amazon, Netflix, YouTube, Twitter, LinkedIn, and Facebook. Recommendations are a core part of all these businesses, and in some cases, they drive significant percentages of their revenue.

The idea behind recommendation engines is to predict what people might like and to uncover relationships between items to aid in the discovery process; in this way, they are similar and, in fact, often complementary to search engines, which also play a role in discovery. However, unlike search engines, recommendation engines try to present people with relevant content that they did not necessarily search for or that they might have not even heard of.

Typically, a recommendation engine tries to model the connections between users and some type of item. In our movie stream scenario from Chapter 3, *Designing a Machine Learning System*, for example, we can use a recommendation engine to show our users movies that they might enjoy. If we can do this well, we could keep our users engaged using our service, which is good for both our users and us. Similarly, if we can do a good job of showing our users movies related to a given movie, we could aid in discovery and navigation on our site, again improving our users' experience, engagement, and the relevance of our content to them.

However, recommendation engines are not limited to movies, books, or products. The techniques we will explore in this chapter can be applied to just about any user-to-item relationship as well as user-to-user connections, such as those found on social networks, allowing us to make recommendations, such as people you may know or who to follow.

Recommendation engines are most effective in two general scenarios, which are not mutually exclusive. They are explained here:

- **Large number of available options for users**: When there are a very large number of available items, it becomes increasingly difficult for the user to find something they want. Searching can help when the user knows what they are looking for, but often, the right item might be something previously unknown to them. In this case, being recommended relevant items that the user may not already know about can help them discover new items.
- **A significant degree of personal taste involved**: When personal taste plays a large role in selection, recommendation models, which often utilize a wisdom-of-the-crowd approach, can be helpful in discovering items based on the behavior of others that have similar taste profiles.

In this chapter, we will cover the following topics:

- Introduce the various types of recommendation engines
- Build a recommendation model using data about user preferences
- Use the trained model to compute recommendations for a given user as well compute similar items for a given item, that is, related items
- Apply standard evaluation metrics to the model that we created to measure how well it performs in terms of predictive capability

Types of recommendation models

Recommender systems are widely studied, and there are many approaches used, but there are two that are probably most prevalent: content-based filtering and collaborative filtering. Recently, other approaches, such as ranking models, have also gained in popularity. In practice, many approaches are hybrids, incorporating elements of many different methods into a model or combination of models.

Content-based filtering

Content-based methods try to use the content or attributes of an item, together with some notion of similarity between two pieces of content, to generate items similar to a given item. These attributes are often textual content, such as titles, names, tags, and other metadata attached to an item, or in the case of media, they could include other features of the item, such as attributes extracted from audio and video content.

In a similar manner, user recommendations can be generated based on attributes of users or user profiles, which are then matched to item attributes using the same measure of similarity. For example, a user can be represented by the combined attributes of the items they have interacted with. This becomes their user profile, which is then compared to item attributes to find items that match the user profile.

These are a few examples of creating a profile for each user or item to characterize its nature:

- Movie profile includes attributes regarding actors, genre, popularity, and so on.
- User profile includes demographic information or answers given to specific questions.
- Content filtering uses profiles to associate users or items.
- Compute similarity of a new item with the user profile based on keyword overlap example using Dice coefficient. There are other approaches as well.

Collaborative filtering

Collaborative filtering relies only on past behavior, such as previous ratings or transactions. The idea behind this is the notion of similarity.

The basic idea is that the user gives ratings to items, implicitly or explicitly. Users who had a similar taste in the past will have a similar taste in the future.

In a user-based approach, if two users have exhibited similar preferences, that is, patterns of interacting with the same items in broadly the same way, then we would assume that they are similar to each other in terms of taste. To generate recommendations for unknown items for a given user, we can use the known preferences of other users that exhibit similar behavior. We can do this by selecting a set of similar users and computing some form of combined score based on the items they have shown a preference for. The overall logic is that if others have tastes similar to a set of items, these items would tend to be good candidates for recommendation.

We can also take an item-based approach that computes some measure of similarity between items. This is usually based on the existing user-item preferences or ratings. Items that tend to be rated the same by similar users will be classed as similar under this approach. Once we have these similarities, we can represent a user in terms of the items they have interacted with and find items that are similar to these known items, which we can then recommend to the user. Again, a set of items similar to the known items is used to generate a combined score to estimate for an unknown item.

The user- and item-based approaches are usually referred to as nearest-neighbor models, since the estimated scores are computed based on the set of most similar users or items, that is, their neighbors.

A traditional collaborative filtering algorithm represents a user as an N-dimensional vector of items, where N is the number of distinct items. The components of the vector are positive or negative items. To calculate for best items, the algorithm typically multiplies the vector components by the inverse frequency, that is, the inverse of the number of users who have rated the item, making less well-known items much more relevant. For most users, this vector is extremely sparse. The algorithm generates recommendations based on a few users who are most similar to the user. It can measure the similarity of two users, X and Y, using a common method called cosine of the angle between the two vectors:

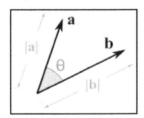

Finally, there are many model-based methods that attempt to model the user-item preferences themselves, so that new preferences can be estimated directly by applying the model to unknown user-item combinations.

Two primary modeling methods for collaborative filtering are as follows:

- **Neighborhood methods**:
    - The user-oriented approach is centered on computing the relationships between users
    - The item-oriented approach evaluates a user's preference for an item based on ratings of a neighboring item by the same user

- Use centered cosine distance for similarity calculation, which is also known as **Pearson correlation coefficients**
- **Latent factor models**:
    - The **Latent factor model** (**LFM**) approach explains ratings by characterizing both users and items to find the hidden latent features
    - In movies, features such as action or drama, type of actors, and so on, are the latent factors
    - In users, features such as liking the score for movie is an example of a latent factor
    - Types are neural networks, latent dirichlet allocation, matrix factorization

In the next section, we will discuss Matrix Factorization models.

Matrix factorization

Since Spark's recommendation models currently only include an implementation of Matrix factorization, we will focus our attention on this class of models. This focus is with good reason; however, these types of models have consistently been shown to perform extremely well in collaborative filtering and were among the best models in well-known competitions, such as the Netflix prize.

Matrix Factorization assumes that:

- Each user can be described by n attributes or features. For example, feature one might be a number that says how much each user likes action movies.
- Each item can be described by a set of n attributes or features. To connect with the preceding example, feature one for the movie might be a number that says how close the movie is to pure action.
- If we multiply each feature of the user by the corresponding feature of the item and add everything together, this will be a good approximation for the rating the user would give that item.

For more information on and a brief overview of the performance of the best algorithms for the Netflix prize, see
http://techblog.netflix.com/2012/04/netflix-recommendations-beyond-5-stars.html.

Explicit matrix factorization

When we deal with data that consists of preferences of users, which are provided by the users themselves, we refer to explicit preference data. This includes, for example, ratings, thumbs up, likes, and so on that are given by users to items.

We can take these ratings and form a two-dimensional matrix with users as rows and items as columns. Each entry represents a rating given by a user to a certain item. Since, in most cases, each user has only interacted with a relatively small set of items, this matrix has only a few non-zero entries, that is, it is very sparse.

As a simple example, let's assume that we have the following user ratings for a set of movies:

Tom: Star Wars, 5

Jane: Titanic, 4

Bill: Batman, 3

Jane: Star Wars, 2

Bill: Titanic, 3

We will form the following ratings matrix:

User / Item	Batman	Star Wars	Titanic
Bill	3	3	
Jane		2	4
Tom		5	

A simple movie-rating matrix

Matrix Factorization (or matrix completion) attempts to directly model this user-item matrix by representing it as a product of two smaller matrices of lower dimension. Thus, it is a dimensionality-reduction technique. If we have **U** users and **I** items, then our user-item matrix is of dimension U x I and might look something like the one shown in the following diagram:

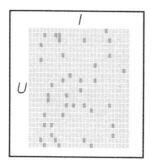

A sparse ratings matrix

If we want to find a lower dimension (low-rank) approximation to our user-item matrix with the dimension **k**, we would end up with two matrices: one for users of size U x k and one for items of size I x k; these are known as factor matrices. If we multiply these two factor matrices, we will reconstruct an approximate version of the original ratings matrix. Note that while the original ratings matrix is typically very sparse, each factor matrix is dense, as shown in the following diagram:

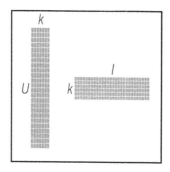

The user- and item-factor matrices

These models are often also called latent feature models, as we are trying to discover some form of hidden features (which are represented by the factor matrices) that account for the structure of behavior inherent in the user-item rating matrix. While the latent features or factors are not directly interpretable, they might, perhaps, represent things such as the tendency of a user to like movies from a certain director, genre, style, or group of actors.

As we are directly modeling the user-item matrix, the prediction in these models is relatively straightforward: to compute a predicted rating for a user and item, we will compute the vector dot product between the relevant row of the user-factor matrix, that is, the user's factor vector, and the relevant row of the item-factor matrix, that is, the item's factor vector.

This is illustrated with the highlighted vectors in the following diagram:

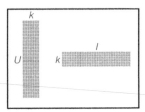

Computing recommendations from user- and item-factor vectors

To find out the similarity between two items, we can use the same measures of similarity as we would use in the nearest-neighbor models, except that we can use the factor vectors directly by computing the similarity between two item-factor vectors, as illustrated in the following diagram:

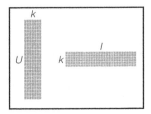

Computing similarity with item-factor vectors

The benefit of factorization models is the relative ease of computing recommendations once the model is created. However, for very large user and item sets, this can become a challenge, as it requires storage and computation across potentially many millions of user- and item-factor vectors. Another advantage, as mentioned earlier, is that they tend to offer very good performance.

 Projects such as Oryx (`https://github.com/OryxProject/oryx`) and Prediction.io (`https://github.com/PredictionIO/PredictionIO`) focus on model serving for large-scale models, including recommenders based on matrix factorization.

On the down side, factorization models are relatively more complex to understand and interpret compared to nearest-neighbor models and are often more computationally intensive during the model's training phase.

Implicit Matrix Factorization

So far, we have dealt with explicit preferences such as ratings. However, much of the preference data that we might be able to collect is implicit feedback, where the preferences between a user and item are not given to us, but are, instead, implied from the interactions they might have with an item. Examples include binary data, such as whether a user viewed a movie, whether they purchased a product, and so on, as well as count data, such as the number of times a user watched a movie.

There are many different approaches to deal with implicit data. MLlib implements a particular approach that treats the input rating matrix as two matrices: a binary preference matrix, **P**, and a matrix of confidence weights, **C**.

For example, let's assume that the user-movie ratings we saw previously were, in fact, the number of times each user had viewed that movie. The two matrices would look something like the ones shown in the following screenshot. Here, the matrix **P** informs us that a movie was viewed by a user, and the matrix **C** represents the confidence weighting, in the form of the view counts--generally, the more a user has watched a movie, the higher the confidence that they actually like it.

P					C			
User / Item	Batman	Star Wars	Titanic		User / Item	Batman	Star Wars	Titanic
Bill	1	1			Bill	3	3	
Jane		1	1		Jane		2	4
Tom		1			Tom		5	

Representation of an implicit preference and confidence matrix

The implicit model still creates a user- and item-factor matrix. In this case, however, the matrix that the model is attempting to approximate is not the overall ratings matrix, but the preference matrix **P**. If we compute a recommendation by calculating the dot product of a user- and item-factor vector, the score will not be an estimate of a rating directly. It will rather be an estimate of the preference of a user for an item; although, not strictly between 0 and 1, these scores will generally be fairly close to a scale of 0 to 1.

In a nutshell, Matrix Factorization methods characterize both users and items by vectors of factors inferred from a rating pattern. High confidence or correspondence between user and item factors leads to a recommendation. Two main data types are Explicit feedback, such as ratings (represented by sparse matrix), and Implicit feedback, such as purchase history, search patterns, browse history, and clickstream data (represented by dense matrix).

Basic model for Matrix Factorization

Both users and items are mapped to a joint latent factor space of dimensionality f, where user-item interaction is modeled as inner product in this space. Item i is associated with vector q where q measures the extent to which the item possesses the latent factors and User u is associated with vector p, where p measures the extent of interest the user has in the item.

The dot product $q_i^T p_u$ between q and p captures the interaction between user u and item I, that is, a user's interest in an item. Key to model is finding vectors q and p.

To design the model, get latent relationship between users and items. Produce a low dimensional representation of rating matrix. Perform SVD on thye rating matrix to get Q, S, P. Reduce matrix S to dimension k to get q and p.

$$Q_k S_k (q^T), S_k P_k (p)$$

Now, calculate the recommendations:

$$\hat{r}_{ui} = q_i^T p_u$$

Optimization function (on observed ratings) is shown in the following diagram; learn the latent factor vectors q and p, the system minimizes the regularized squared error on set of ratings.

$$\min_{q,p} \sum_{(u,i)\in k} (r_{ui} - q_i^T p_u)^2 + \lambda$$

Learning algorithms used are **stochastic gradient descent (SGD)** or **alternating least squares (ALS)**.

Alternating least squares

ALS is an optimization technique to solve Matrix Factorization problems; this technique is powerful, achieves good performance, and has proven to be relatively easy to implement in a parallel fashion. Hence, it is well suited for platforms such as Spark. At the time of writing this book, it is the only recommendation model implemented in Spark ML.

ALS works by iteratively solving a series of least squares regression problems. In each iteration, one of the user- or item-factor matrices is treated as fixed, while the other one is updated using the fixed factor and the rating data. Then, the factor matrix that was solved for is, in turn, treated as fixed, while the other one is updated. This process continues until the model has converged (or for a fixed number of iterations):

$$\min_{q,p} \sum_{(u,i)\in k} (r_{ui} - q_i^T p_u)^2 + \lambda$$

Objective function is not convex since both q and p are not known, but if we fix one of the unknown optimization can be solved. ALS rotates between fixing q's and p's as explained earlier.

Spark's documentation for collaborative filtering contains references to the papers that underlie the ALS algorithms implemented each component of explicit and implicit data. You can view the documentation at http://spark.apache.org/docs/latest/ml-collaborative-filtering.html.

The following code explains how to implement ALS algorithm from scratch.

Let's take an example and show how it is implemented and look at a real matrix of 3 movies and 3 users:

```
Array2DRowRealMatrix
```

```
{{0.5306513708,0.5144338501,0.5183049},
{0.0612665269,0.0595122885,0.0611548878},
{0.3215637836,0.2964382622,0.1439834964}}
```

The first iteration of movie matrix is chosen randomly:

```
ms = {RealVector[3]@3600}
 0 = {ArrayRealVector@3605} "{0.489603683; 0.5979051631}"
 1 = {ArrayRealVector@3606} "{0.2069873135; 0.4887559609}"
 2 = {ArrayRealVector@3607} "{0.5286582698; 0.6787608323}"
```

The first iteration of user matrix is chosen randomly:

```
us = {RealVector[3]@3602}
 0 = {ArrayRealVector@3611} "{0.7964247309; 0.091570682}"
 1 = {ArrayRealVector@3612} "{0.4509758768; 0.0684475614}"
 2 = {ArrayRealVector@3613} "{0.7812240904; 0.4180722562}"
```

Pickup the first row of user matrix us, Calculate XtX (matrix) and Xty (a vector) as shown in the following code:

```
m: {0.489603683; 0.5979051631}
us: [Lorg.apache.commons.math3.linear.RealVector;@75961f16
 XtX: Array2DRowRealMatrix{{0.0,0.0},{0.0,0.0}}
 Xty: {0; 0}
```

j:0

```
u: {0.7964247309; 0.091570682}
u.outerProduct(u):
   Array2DRowRealMatrix{{0.634292352,0.0729291558},
   {0.0729291558,0.0083851898}}
XtX = XtX.add(u.outerProduct(u)):
   Array2DRowRealMatrix{{0.634292352,0.0729291558},
   {0.0729291558,0.0083851898}}
R.getEntry(i, j)):0.5306513708051035
u.mapMultiply(R.getEntry(i, j): {0.4226238752; 0.0485921079}
Xty = Xty.add(u.mapMultiply(R.getEntry(i, j))): {0.4226238752;
   0.0485921079}
```

Pickup the second row of user matrix us, and add values to XtX (matrix) and Xty (a vector) as shown in the folowing code:

j:1

```
u: {0.4509758768; 0.0684475614}
u.outerProduct(u):
Array2DRowRealMatrix{{0.2033792414,0.030868199},{0.030868199,0.0046850687}}
```

```
XtX = XtX.add(u.outerProduct(u)):
Array2DRowRealMatrix{{0.8376715935,0.1037973548},{0.1037973548,0.0130702585
}}
R.getEntry(i, j)):0.5144338501354986
u.mapMultiply(R.getEntry(i, j): {0.2319972566; 0.0352117425}
Xty = Xty.add(u.mapMultiply(R.getEntry(i, j))): {0.6546211318;
0.0838038505}
```

j:2

```
u: {0.7812240904; 0.4180722562}
u.outerProduct(u):
    Array2DRowRealMatrix{{0.6103110794,0.326608118},
    {0.326608118,0.1747844114}}
XtX = XtX.add(u.outerProduct(u)):
    Array2DRowRealMatrix{{1.4479826729,0.4304054728},
    {0.4304054728,0.1878546698}}
R.getEntry(i, j)):0.5183049000396933
u.mapMultiply(R.getEntry(i, j): {0.4049122741; 0.2166888989}
Xty = Xty.add(u.mapMultiply(R.getEntry(i, j))): {1.0595334059;
    0.3004927494}
After Regularization XtX:
    Array2DRowRealMatrix{{1.4779826729,0.4304054728},
    {0.4304054728,0.1878546698}}
After Regularization XtX:
Array2DRowRealMatrix{{1.4779826729,0.4304054728},{0.4304054728,0.2178546698
}}
```

Calculate value of first row of ms (movie matrix using Cholesky decomposition of XtX and XtY:

```
CholeskyDecomposition{0.7422344051; -0.0870718111}
```

After going through each row of us and following the steps above we arrive at:

```
ms = {RealVector[3]@5078}
 0 = {ArrayRealVector@5125} "{0.7422344051; -0.0870718111}"
 1 = {ArrayRealVector@5126} "{0.0856607011; -0.007426896}"
 2 = {ArrayRealVector@5127} "{0.4542083563; -0.392747909}"
```

Listing the following source code for the mathematical implementation explained previously:

```
object AlternatingLeastSquares {

  var movies = 0
  var users = 0
  var features = 0
```

```scala
var ITERATIONS = 0
val LAMBDA = 0.01 // Regularization coefficient

private def vector(n: Int): RealVector =
  new ArrayRealVector(Array.fill(n)(math.random))

private def matrix(rows: Int, cols: Int): RealMatrix =
  new Array2DRowRealMatrix(Array.fill(rows, cols)(math.random))

def rSpace(): RealMatrix = {
  val mh = matrix(movies, features)
  val uh = matrix(users, features)
  mh.multiply(uh.transpose())
}

def rmse(targetR: RealMatrix, ms: Array[RealVector], us:
 Array[RealVector]): Double = {
  val r = new Array2DRowRealMatrix(movies, users)
  for (i <- 0 until movies; j <- 0 until users) {
    r.setEntry(i, j, ms(i).dotProduct(us(j)))
  }
  val diffs = r.subtract(targetR)
  var sumSqs = 0.0
  for (i <- 0 until movies; j <- 0 until users) {
    val diff = diffs.getEntry(i, j)
    sumSqs += diff * diff
  }
  math.sqrt(sumSqs / (movies.toDouble * users.toDouble))
}

def update(i: Int, m: RealVector, us: Array[RealVector], R:
 RealMatrix) : RealVector = {
  val U = us.length
  val F = us(0).getDimension
  var XtX: RealMatrix = new Array2DRowRealMatrix(F, F)
  var Xty: RealVector = new ArrayRealVector(F)
  // For each user that rated the movie
  for (j <- 0 until U) {
    val u = us(j)
    // Add u * u^t to XtX
    XtX = XtX.add(u.outerProduct(u))
    // Add u * rating to Xty
    Xty = Xty.add(u.mapMultiply(R.getEntry(i, j)))
  }
  // Add regularization coefs to diagonal terms
  for (d <- 0 until F) {
    XtX.addToEntry(d, d, LAMBDA * U)
  }
```

```scala
    // Solve it with Cholesky
    new CholeskyDecomposition(XtX).getSolver.solve(Xty)
  }

  def main(args: Array[String]) {

    movies = 100
    users = 500
    features = 10
    ITERATIONS = 5
    var slices = 2

    val spark =
      SparkSession.builder.master("local[2]").
      appName("AlternatingLeastS
    quares").getOrCreate()
    val sc = spark.sparkContext

    val r_space = rSpace()

    // Initialize m and u randomly
    var ms = Array.fill(movies)(vector(features))
    var us = Array.fill(users)(vector(features))

    // Iteratively update movies then users
    val Rc = sc.broadcast(r_space)
    var msb = sc.broadcast(ms)
    var usb = sc.broadcast(us)
    for (iter <- 1 to ITERATIONS) {
      println(s"Iteration $iter:")
      ms = sc.parallelize(0 until movies, slices)
        .map(i => update(i, msb.value(i), usb.value, Rc.value))
        .collect()
      msb = sc.broadcast(ms) // Re-broadcast ms because it was
    updated
      us = sc.parallelize(0 until users, slices)
        .map(i => update(i, usb.value(i), msb.value,
    Rc.value.transpose()))
        .collect()
      usb = sc.broadcast(us) // Re-broadcast us because it was
    updated
      println("RMSE = " + rmse(r_space, ms, us))
      println()
    }

    spark.stop()
  }
}
```

You can find the code listing at:
`https://github.com/ml-resources/spark-ml/blob/branch-ed2/Chapter_05/2.0.0/scala-spark-app/src/main/scala/com/spark/recommendation/AlternatingLeastSquares.scala`

Extracting the right features from your data

In this section, we will use explicit rating data, without additional user, item metadata, or other information related to the user-item interactions. Hence, the features that we need as inputs are simply the user IDs, movie IDs, and the ratings assigned to each user and movie pair.

Extracting features from the MovieLens 100k dataset

In this example, we will use the same MovieLens dataset that we used in the previous chapter. Use the directory in which you placed the MovieLens 100k dataset as the input path in the following code.

First, let's inspect the raw ratings dataset:

```
object FeatureExtraction {

def getFeatures(): Dataset[FeatureExtraction.Rating] = {
  val spark =
SparkSession.builder.master("local[2]").appName("FeatureExtraction").getOrC
reate()

  import spark.implicits._
  val ratings = spark.read.textFile("/data/ml-100k
2/u.data").map(parseRating)
  println(ratings.first())

  return ratings
}

case class Rating(userId: Int, movieId: Int, rating: Float)
def parseRating(str: String): Rating = {
  val fields = str.split("t")
  Rating(fields(0).toInt, fields(1).toInt, fields(2).toFloat)
}
```

You can find the code listing at:
https://github.com/ml-resources/spark-ml/blob/branch-ed2/Chapter
_05/2.0.0/scala-spark-app/src/main/scala/com/spark/recommendatio
n/FeatureExtraction.scala

You will see an output similar to these lines of code:

```
16/09/07 11:23:38 INFO CodeGenerator: Code generated in 7.029838 ms
16/09/07 11:23:38 INFO Executor: Finished task 0.0 in stage 0.0 (TID
   0). 1276 bytes result sent to driver
16/09/07 11:23:38 INFO TaskSetManager: Finished task 0.0 in stage 0.0
   (TID 0) in 82 ms on localhost (1/1)
16/09/07 11:23:38 INFO TaskSchedulerImpl: Removed TaskSet 0.0, whose
   tasks have all completed, from pool
16/09/07 11:23:38 INFO DAGScheduler: ResultStage 0 (first at
   FeatureExtraction.scala:25) finished in 0.106 s
16/09/07 11:23:38 INFO DAGScheduler: Job 0 finished: first at
   FeatureExtraction.scala:25, took 0.175165 s
16/09/07 11:23:38 INFO CodeGenerator: Code generated in 6.834794 ms
Rating(196,242,3.0)
```

Recall that this dataset (mapped to the `Rating` class using case) consisted of the `userID`, `movieID`, `rating`, and `timestamp` fields separated by a tab ("t") character. We don't need the time when the rating was made to train our model, so in the following code snippet we simply extracted the first three fields:

```
case class Rating(userId: Int, movieId: Int, rating: Float)
def parseRating(str: String): Rating = {
  val fields = str.split("t")
  Rating(fields(0).toInt, fields(1).toInt, fields(2).toFloat)
}
```

 You can find the code listing at:
https://github.com/ml-resources/spark-ml/blob/branch-ed2/Chapter
_05/2.0.0/scala-spark-
app/src/main/scala/com/spark/recommendation/FeatureExtraction.sc
ala

We will first split each record on the "t" character, which gives us a `String[]` array. We will then use case class to map and keep only the first 3 elements of the array, which correspond to `userID`, `movieID`, and `rating`, respectively.

Training the recommendation model

Once we have extracted these simple features from our raw data, we are ready to proceed with model training; ML takes care of this for us. All we have to do is provide the correctly-parsed input dataset we just created as well as our chosen model parameters.

Split the dataset in to training and testing sets with ratio 80:20, as shown in the following lines of code:

```
def createALSModel() {
  val ratings = FeatureExtraction.getFeatures();

  val Array(training, test) = ratings.randomSplit(Array(0.8, 0.2))
  println(training.first())
}
```

 You can find the code listing at:
https://github.com/ml-resources/spark-ml/blob/branch-ed2/Chapter
_05/2.0.0/scala-spark-
app/src/main/scala/com/spark/recommendation/ALSModeling.scala

You will see the following output:

```
16/09/07 13:23:28 INFO Executor: Finished task 0.0 in stage 1.0 (TID
  1). 1768 bytes result sent to driver
16/09/07 13:23:28 INFO TaskSetManager: Finished task 0.0 in stage 1.0
  (TID 1) in 459 ms on localhost (1/1)
16/09/07 13:23:28 INFO TaskSchedulerImpl: Removed TaskSet 1.0, whose
  tasks have all completed, from pool
16/09/07 13:23:28 INFO DAGScheduler: ResultStage 1 (first at
  FeatureExtraction.scala:34) finished in 0.459 s
16/09/07 13:23:28 INFO DAGScheduler: Job 1 finished: first at
  FeatureExtraction.scala:34, took 0.465730 s
Rating(1,1,5.0)
```

Training a model on the MovieLens 100k dataset

We're now ready to train our model! The other inputs required for our model are as follows:

- `rank`: This refers to the number of factors in our ALS model, that is, the number of hidden features in our low-rank approximation matrices. Generally, the greater the number of factors, the better, but this has a direct impact on memory usage, both for computation and to store models for serving, particularly for large numbers of users or items. Hence, this is often a trade-off in real-world use cases. It also impacts the amount of training data required.
- A rank in the range of 10 to 200 is usually reasonable.
- `iterations`: This refers to the number of iterations to run. While each iteration in ALS is guaranteed to decrease the reconstruction error of the ratings matrix, ALS models will converge to a reasonably good solution after relatively little iterations. So, we don't need to run too many iterations in most cases--around 10 is often a good default.
- `numBlocks`: This is the number of blocks the users and items will be partitioned into, to parallelize computation (defaults to 10). The number depends on the number of cluster nodes as well as how data is partitioned.
- `regParam`: This specifies the regularization parameter in ALS (defaults to 1.0). The constant λ is called the regularization parameter and essentially penalizes the components of the user and item matrices if they get too large (in magnitude). This is important for numerical stability, and some kind of regularization is almost always used.
- `implicitPrefs`: This specifies whether to use the Explicit feedback ALS variant or one adapted for Implicit feedback data; it defaults to false, which means using Explicit feedback.
- `alpha`: This is a parameter applicable to the Implicit feedback variant of ALS that governs the *baseline* confidence in preference observations (defaults to 1.0).
- `nonnegative`: This specifies whether or not to use nonnegative constraints for least squares (defaults to `false`).

We'll use default `rank`, `5maxIter`, and a `regParam` parameter of `0.01` to illustrate how to train our model which is shown in the following code:

```
// Build the recommendation model using ALS on the training data
val als = new ALS()
  .setMaxIter(5)
  .setRegParam(0.01)
  .setUserCol("userId")
  .setItemCol("movieId")
  .setRatingCol("rating")

val model = als.fit(training)
```

You can find the code listing at
`https://github.com/ml-resources/spark-ml/blob/branch-ed2/Chapter`
`_05/2.0.0/scala-spark-app/src/main/scala/com/spark/recommendatio`
`n/ALSModeling.scala`.

This returns a `ALSModel` object, which contains the user and item factors. These are called `userFactors` and `itemFactors`, respectively.

For example, `model.userFactors`.

You will see the output as follows:

```
16/09/07 13:08:16 INFO MapPartitionsRDD: Removing RDD 16 from
    persistence list
16/09/07 13:08:16 INFO BlockManager: Removing RDD 16
16/09/07 13:08:16 INFO Instrumentation: ALS-als_1ca69e2ffef7-
    10603412-1: training finished
16/09/07 13:08:16 INFO SparkContext: Invoking stop() from shutdown
    hook
[id: int, features: array<float>]
```

We can see that the factors are in the form of `Array[float]`.

Note that the operations used in MLlib's ALS implementation are lazy transformations, so the actual computation will only be performed once we call some sort of action on the resulting DataFrame of the user and item factors. In the following code we can force the computation using a Spark action such as `count`:

```
model.userFactors.count()
```

This will trigger the computation, and we will see quite a bit of output texts similar to the following lines of code:

```
16/09/07 13:21:54 INFO Executor: Running task 0.0 in stage 53.0 (TID
    166)
16/09/07 13:21:54 INFO ShuffleBlockFetcherIterator: Getting 10 non-
    empty blocks out of 10 blocks
16/09/07 13:21:54 INFO ShuffleBlockFetcherIterator: Started 0 remote
    fetches in 0 ms
16/09/07 13:21:54 INFO Executor: Finished task 0.0 in stage 53.0 (TID
    166). 1873 bytes result sent to driver
16/09/07 13:21:54 INFO TaskSetManager: Finished task 0.0 in stage
    53.0 (TID 166) in 12 ms on localhost (1/1)
16/09/07 13:21:54 INFO TaskSchedulerImpl: Removed TaskSet 53.0, whose
    tasks have all completed, from pool
16/09/07 13:21:54 INFO DAGScheduler: ResultStage 53 (count at
    ALSModeling.scala:25) finished in 0.012 s
```

```
16/09/07 13:21:54 INFO DAGScheduler: Job 7 finished: count at
    ALSModeling.scala:25, took 0.123073 s
16/09/07 13:21:54 INFO CodeGenerator: Code generated in 11.162514 ms
943
```

If we call `count` for the movie factors, it will be done with the help of following code:

```
model.itemFactors.count()
```

This will trigger the computation, and we will get the following output:

```
16/09/07 13:23:32 INFO TaskSetManager: Starting task 0.0 in stage
    68.0 (TID 177, localhost, partition 0, ANY, 5276 bytes)
16/09/07 13:23:32 INFO Executor: Running task 0.0 in stage 68.0 (TID
    177)
16/09/07 13:23:32 INFO ShuffleBlockFetcherIterator: Getting 10 non-
    empty blocks out of 10 blocks
16/09/07 13:23:32 INFO ShuffleBlockFetcherIterator: Started 0 remote
    fetches in 0 ms
16/09/07 13:23:32 INFO Executor: Finished task 0.0 in stage 68.0 (TID
    177). 1873 bytes result sent to driver
16/09/07 13:23:32 INFO TaskSetManager: Finished task 0.0 in stage
    68.0 (TID 177) in 3 ms on localhost (1/1)
16/09/07 13:23:32 INFO TaskSchedulerImpl: Removed TaskSet 68.0, whose
    tasks have all completed, from pool
16/09/07 13:23:32 INFO DAGScheduler: ResultStage 68 (count at
    ALSModeling.scala:26) finished in 0.003 s
16/09/07 13:23:32 INFO DAGScheduler: Job 8 finished: count at
    ALSModeling.scala:26, took 0.072450 s
```

```
1651
```

As expected, we have a factor array for each user (`943` factors) and each movie (`1651` factors).

Training a model using Implicit feedback data

The standard Matrix Factorization approach in MLlib deals with explicit ratings. To work with implicit data, you can use the `trainImplicit` method. It is called in a manner similar to the standard `train` method. There is an additional parameter, `alpha`, that can be set (and in the same way, the regularization parameter, `lambda`, should be selected via testing and cross-validation methods).

The `alpha` parameter controls the baseline level of confidence, weighting applied. A higher level of `alpha` tends to make the model more confident about the fact that missing data equates to no preference for the relevant user-item pair.

From Spark version 2.0, if the rating matrix is derived from another source of information that is, it is inferred from other signals, you can `setImplicitPrefs` to `true` to get better results, as shown in the following example:

```
val als = new ALS()
  .setMaxIter(5)
  .setRegParam(0.01)
  .setImplicitPrefs(true)
  .setUserCol("userId")
  .setItemCol("movieId")
  .setRatingCol("rating")
```

 As an exercise, try to take the existing MovieLens dataset and convert it into an implicit dataset. One possible approach is to convert it to binary feedback (0s and 1s) by applying a threshold on the ratings at some level.

 Another approach could be to convert the ratings' values into confidence weights (for example, perhaps, low ratings could imply zero weights, or even negative weights, which are supported by MLlib's implementation).

 Train a model on this dataset and compare the results of the following section with those generated by your implicit model.

Using the recommendation model

Now that we have our trained model, we're ready to use it to make predictions.

ALS Model recommendations

Starting Spark v2.0, `org.apache.spark.ml.recommendation.ALS` modeling is a blocked implementation of the factorization algorithm that groups "users" and "products" factors into blocks and decreases communication by sending only one copy of each user vector to each product block at each iteration, and only for the product blocks that need that user's feature vector.

Here, we will load the rating data from the movies dataset where each row consists of a user, movie, rating, and a timestamp. We will then train an ALS model by default works on explicit preferences (`implicitPrefs` is `false`). We will evaluate the recommendation model by measuring the root-mean-square error of rating prediction as follows:

```scala
object ALSModeling {

  def createALSModel() {
    val ratings = FeatureExtraction.getFeatures();

    val Array(training, test) = ratings.randomSplit(Array(0.8,
0.2))
    println(training.first())

    // Build the recommendation model using ALS on the training
    data
    val als = new ALS()
      .setMaxIter(5)
      .setRegParam(0.01)
      .setUserCol("userId")
      .setItemCol("movieId")
      .setRatingCol("rating")

    val model = als.fit(training)
    println(model.userFactors.count())
    println(model.itemFactors.count())

    val predictions = model.transform(test)
    println(predictions.printSchema())

  }
```

You can find the code listing at:
https://github.com/ml-resources/spark-ml/blob/branch-ed2/Chapter_05/2.0.0/scala-spark-app/src/main/scala/com/spark/recommendation/ALSModeling.scala

The following is the output for the preceding code:

```
16/09/07 17:58:42 INFO SparkContext: Created broadcast 26 from
   broadcast at DAGScheduler.scala:1012
16/09/07 17:58:42 INFO DAGScheduler: Submitting 1 missing tasks from
   ResultStage 67 (MapPartitionsRDD[138] at count at
   ALSModeling.scala:31)
16/09/07 17:58:42 INFO TaskSchedulerImpl: Adding task set 67.0 with 1
   tasks
16/09/07 17:58:42 INFO TaskSetManager: Starting task 0.0 in stage
   67.0 (TID 176, localhost, partition 0, ANY, 5276 bytes)
16/09/07 17:58:42 INFO Executor: Running task 0.0 in stage 67.0 (TID
   176)
16/09/07 17:58:42 INFO ShuffleBlockFetcherIterator: Getting 10 non-
   empty blocks out of 10 blocks
16/09/07 17:58:42 INFO ShuffleBlockFetcherIterator: Started 0 remote
   fetches in 0 ms
16/09/07 17:58:42 INFO Executor: Finished task 0.0 in stage 67.0 (TID
   176). 1960 bytes result sent to driver
16/09/07 17:58:42 INFO TaskSetManager: Finished task 0.0 in stage
   67.0 (TID 176) in 3 ms on localhost (1/1)
16/09/07 17:58:42 INFO TaskSchedulerImpl: Removed TaskSet 67.0, whose
   tasks have all completed, from pool
16/09/07 17:58:42 INFO DAGScheduler: ResultStage 67 (count at
   ALSModeling.scala:31) finished in 0.003 s
16/09/07 17:58:42 INFO DAGScheduler: Job 7 finished: count at
   ALSModeling.scala:31, took 0.060748 s
100
root
 |-- userId: integer (nullable = true)
 |-- movieId: integer (nullable = true)
 |-- rating: float (nullable = true)
 |-- timestamp: long (nullable = true)
 |-- prediction: float (nullable = true)
```

 Before we proceed further, please note that the following examples for User and Item recommendations use MLlib from Spark v1.6. Kindly follow the code listing to get the details of creating recommendation models using `org.apache.spark.mllib.recommendation.ALS`.

User recommendations

In this case, we would like to generate recommended items for a given user. This usually takes the form of a *top-K* list, that is, the *K* items that our model predicts will have the highest probability of the user liking them. This is done by computing the predicted score for each item and ranking the list based on this score.

The exact method to perform this computation depends on the model involved. For example, in user-based approaches, the ratings of similar users on items are used to compute the recommendations for a user; while in an item-based approach, the computation is based on the similarity of items the user has rated to the candidate items.

In matrix factorization, because we are modeling the ratings matrix directly, the predicted score can be computed as the vector dot product between a user-factor vector and an item-factor vector.

Generating movie recommendations from the MovieLens 100k dataset

As MLlib's recommendation model is based on matrix factorization, we can use the factor matrices computed by our model to compute predicted scores (or ratings) for a user. We will focus on the explicit rating case using MovieLens data; however, the approach is the same when using the implicit model.

The MatrixFactorizationModel class has a convenient predict method that will compute a predicted score for a given user and item combination as shown in the following code:

```
val predictedRating = model.predict(789, 123)
```

The output is as follows:

```
14/03/30 16:10:10 INFO SparkContext: Starting job: lookup at
    MatrixFactorizationModel.scala:45
14/03/30 16:10:10 INFO DAGScheduler: Got job 30 (lookup at
    MatrixFactorizationModel.scala:45) with 1 output partitions
    (allowLocal=false)
. . .
14/03/30 16:10:10 INFO SparkContext: Job finished: lookup at
    MatrixFactorizationModel.scala:46, took 0.023077 s
predictedRating: Double = 3.128545693368485
```

As we can see, this model predicts a rating of 3.12 for user 789 and movie 123.

Note that you might see different results than those shown in this section because the ALS model is initialized randomly. So, different runs of the model will lead to different solutions.

The `predict` method can also take an RDD of (`user`, `item`) IDs as the input and will generate predictions for each of these. We can use this method to make predictions for many users and items at the same time.

To generate the *top-K* recommended items for a user, `MatrixFactorizationModel` provides a convenience method called `recommendProducts`. This takes two arguments: `user` and `num`, where `user` is the user ID and `num` is the number of items to recommend.

It returns the top `num` items ranked in the order of the predicted score. Here, the scores are computed as the dot product between the user-factor vector and each item-factor vector.

Let's generate the top 10 recommended items for user 789 as follows:

```
val userId = 789
val K = 10
val topKRecs = model.recommendProducts(userId, K)
```

We now have a set of predicted ratings for each movie for user 789. If we print this out, by writing the following line of code, we could inspect the top 10 recommendations for this user:

```
println(topKRecs.mkString("n"))
```

You should see the following output on your console:

```
Rating(789,715,5.931851273771102)
Rating(789,12,5.582301095666215)
Rating(789,959,5.516272981542168)
Rating(789,42,5.458065302395629)
Rating(789,584,5.449949837103569)
Rating(789,750,5.348768847643657)
Rating(789,663,5.30832117499004)
Rating(789,134,5.278933936827717)
Rating(789,156,5.250959077906759)
Rating(789,432,5.169863417126231)
```

Inspecting the recommendations

We can give these recommendations a sense check by taking a quick look at the titles of the movies a user has rated and the recommended movies. First, we will need to load the movie data, which is one of the datasets we explored in the previous chapter. In the following code we'll collect this data as a `Map[Int, String]` method, mapping the movie ID to the title:

```
val movies = sc.textFile("/PATH/ml-100k/u.item")
val titles = movies.map(line =>
  line.split("|").take(2)).map(array => (array(0).toInt,
```

```
      array(1))).collectAsMap()
titles(123)
```

The preceding code will produce the following output:

res68: String = Frighteners, The (1996)

For our user `789`, we can find out what movies they have rated, take the `10` movies with the highest rating, and then check the titles. We will do this now by first using the `keyBy` Spark function to create an RDD of key-value pairs from our `ratings` RDD, where the key will be the user ID. We will then use the `lookup` function to return just the ratings for this key (that is, that particular user ID) to the driver which is described as follows:

```
val moviesForUser = ratings.keyBy(_.user).lookup(789)
```

Let's see how many movies this user has rated. This will be the `size` of the `moviesForUser` collection:

```
println(moviesForUser.size)
```

We will see that this user has rated `33` movies.

Next, we will take the 10 movies with the highest ratings by sorting the `moviesForUser` collection using the `rating` field of the `Rating` object. We will then extract the movie title for the relevant product ID attached to the `Rating` class from our mapping of movie titles and print out the top `10` titles with their ratings as shown next:

```
moviesForUser.sortBy(-_.rating).take(10).map(rating =>
    (titles(rating.product), rating.rating)).foreach(println)
```

You will see the following output displayed:

```
(Godfather, The (1972),5.0)
(Trainspotting (1996),5.0)
(Dead Man Walking (1995),5.0)
(Star Wars (1977),5.0)
(Swingers (1996),5.0)
(Leaving Las Vegas (1995),5.0)
(Bound (1996),5.0)
(Fargo (1996),5.0)
(Last Supper, The (1995),5.0)
(Private Parts (1997),4.0)
```

Now, let's take a look at the top 10 recommendations for this user and see what the titles are, using the same approach as the one we used earlier (note that the recommendations are already sorted):

```
topKRecs.map(rating => (titles(rating.product),
    rating.rating)).foreach(println)
```

The output is as follows:

```
(To Die For (1995),5.931851273771102)
(Usual Suspects, The (1995),5.582301095666215)
(Dazed and Confused (1993),5.516272981542168)
(Clerks (1994),5.458065302395629)
(Secret Garden, The (1993),5.449949837103569)
(Amistad (1997),5.348768847643657)
(Being There (1979),5.30832117499004)
(Citizen Kane (1941),5.278933936827717)
(Reservoir Dogs (1992),5.250959077906759)
(Fantasia (1940),5.169863417126231)
```

We leave it for you to decide whether these recommendations make sense.

Item recommendations

Item recommendations are about answering the following question: for a certain item, what are the items most similar to it? Here, the precise definition of similarity is dependent on the model involved. In most cases, similarity is computed by comparing the vector representation of two items using some similarity measure. Common similarity measures include Pearson correlation and cosine similarity for real-valued vectors, and Jaccard similarity for binary vectors.

Generating similar movies for the MovieLens 100k dataset

The current `MatrixFactorizationModel` API does not directly support item-to-item similarity computations. Therefore, we will need to create our own code to do this.

We will use the cosine similarity metric, and we will use the jblas linear algebra library (a dependency of MLlib) to compute the required vector dot products. This is similar to how the existing `predict` and `recommendProducts` methods work, except that we will use cosine similarity as opposed to just the dot product.

We would like to compare the factor vector of our chosen item with each of the other items using our similarity metric. In order to perform linear algebra computations, we will first need to create a vector object out of the factor vectors, which are in the form of `Array[Double]`. The JBLAS class, `DoubleMatrix`, takes `Array[Double]` as the constructor argument, as follows:

```
import org.jblas.DoubleMatrix
```

Use the following constructor to instantiate `DoubleMatrix` from an array.

The `jblas` class is a linear algebra library written in Java. It is based on BLAS and LAPACK, the de-facto industry standard for matrix computations, and uses implementations like ATLAS for its computational routines, making jBLAS very fast.

It is a light-weight wrapper around the BLAS and LAPACK routines. BLAS and LAPACK packages have originated in the Fortran community.

Let's see an example of it:

```
public DoubleMatrix(double[] newData)
```

Create a column vector using `newData` as the data array. Any change in the created `DoubleMatrix` will change in input array `newData`.

Let's create a simple `DoubleMatrix`:

```
val aMatrix = new DoubleMatrix(Array(1.0, 2.0, 3.0))
```

Here is the output of the preceding code:

```
aMatrix: org.jblas.DoubleMatrix = [1.000000; 2.000000; 3.000000]
```

Note that using jblas, vectors are represented as a one-dimensional `DoubleMatrix` class, while matrices are a two-dimensional `DoubleMatrix` class.

We will need a method to compute the cosine similarity between two vectors. Cosine similarity is a measure of the angle between two vectors in an *n*-dimensional space. It is computed by first calculating the dot product between the vectors and then dividing the result by a denominator, which is the norm (or length) of each vector multiplied together (specifically, the L2-norm is used in cosine similarity).

In linear algebra, the size of a vector $\vec{v}$ is called the norm of $\vec{v}$. We will discuss a few different kinds of norms. For this discussion, we will define a vector v as an ordered tuple of numbers.

$$\vec{v} = (v_1, v_2, ... v_n) \ (v_i \in \mathbb{C} \ for \ i = 1, 2, ..., n)$$

One Norm: The one-norm (also known as the L1-norm, or mean norm) of vector $\vec{v}$ is denoted as shown in the following diagram and is defined as the sum of the absolute values of its components:

$$\left\| \vec{v} \right\|_1 = \sum_{i=1}^{n} |v_i|$$

Two-norm (also known as the L2-norm, mean-square norm, least-squares norm)

of a $\vec{v}$ vector is denoted as shown in this diagram::

Moreover, it is defined as the square root of the sum of the squares of the absolute values of its components:

$$\left\|\vec{v}\right\|_2 = \sqrt{\sum_{i=1}^{n}\left|v_i\right|^2}$$

In this way, cosine similarity is a normalized dot product. The cosine similarity measure takes on values between –1 and 1. A value of 1 implies completely similarity, while a value of 0 implies independence (that is, no similarity). This measure is useful because it also captures negative similarity, that is, a value of –1 implies that not only are the vectors not similar, but they are also completely dissimilar:

$$\text{similarity} = \cos(\theta) = \frac{\mathbf{A}\cdot\mathbf{B}}{\|\mathbf{A}\|\|\mathbf{B}\|} = \frac{\sum_{i=1}^{n} A_i B_i}{\sqrt{\sum_{i=1}^{n} A_i^2}\sqrt{\sum_{i=1}^{n} B_i^2}}$$

Let's create our `cosineSimilarity` function here:

```
def cosineSimilarity(vec1: DoubleMatrix, vec2: DoubleMatrix): Double = {
  vec1.dot(vec2) / (vec1.norm2() * vec2.norm2())
}
```

Note that we defined a return type for this function of `Double`. We are not required to do this since Scala features type inference. However, it can often be useful to document return types for Scala functions.

Let's try it out on one of our item factors for item 567. We will need to collect an item factor from our model; we will do this using the `lookup` method in a similar way that we did earlier to collect the ratings for a specific user. In the following lines of code, we will also use the `head` function, since `lookup` returns an array of values, and we will only need the first value (in fact, there will only be one value, which is the factor vector for this item).

Since this will be an constructor `Array[Double]`, we will then need to create a `DoubleMatrix` object from it and compute the cosine similarity with itself which is shown as follows:

```
val itemId = 567
val itemFactor = model.productFeatures.lookup(itemId).head
val itemVector = new DoubleMatrix(itemFactor)
cosineSimilarity(itemVector, itemVector)
```

A similarity metric should measure how close, in some sense, two vectors are to each other. In the following example, we can see that our cosine similarity metric tells us that this item vector is identical to itself, which is what we would expect:

```
res113: Double = 1.0
```

Now, we are ready to apply our similarity metric to each item which is shown as follows:

```
val sims = model.productFeatures.map{ case (id, factor) =>
  val factorVector = new DoubleMatrix(factor)
  val sim = cosineSimilarity(factorVector, itemVector)
  (id, sim)
}
```

Next, we can compute the top 10 most similar items by sorting out the similarity score for each item:

```
// recall we defined K = 10 earlier
val sortedSims = sims.top(K)(Ordering.by[(Int, Double), Double] {
    case (id, similarity) => similarity })
```

In the preceding code snippet, we used Spark's `top` function, which is an efficient way to compute *top-K* results in a distributed fashion, instead of using `collect` to return all the data to the driver and sorting it locally (remember that we could be dealing with millions of users and items in the case of recommendation models).

We will need to tell Spark how to sort the `(item id, similarity score)` pairs in the `sims` RDD. To do this, we will pass an extra argument to `top`, which is a Scala `Ordering` object that tells Spark that it should sort by the value in the key-value pair (that is, sort by `similarity`).

Finally, we can print the 10 items with the highest computed similarity metric to our given item:

```
println(sortedSims.take(10).mkString("n"))
```

You will see an output like the following one:

```
(567,1.0000000000000002)
(1471,0.6932331537649621)
(670,0.6898690594544726)
(201,0.6897964975027041)
```

```
(343,0.6891221044611473)
(563,0.6864214133620066)
(294,0.6812075443259535)
(413,0.6754663844488256)
(184,0.6702643811753909)
(109,0.6594872765176396)
```

Not surprisingly, we can see that the top-ranked similar item is our item. The rest are the other items in our set of items, ranked in order of our similarity metric.

Inspecting the similar items

Let's see what the title of our chosen movie is:

```
println(titles(itemId))
```

The preceding code will print the following output:

Wes Craven's New Nightmare (1994)

As we did for user recommendations, we can sense check our item-to-item similarity computations and take a look at the titles of the most similar movies. This time, we will take the top 11, so that we can exclude our given movie. So, we will take the numbers 1 to 11 in the list:

```
val sortedSims2 = sims.top(K + 1)(Ordering.by[(Int, Double),
    Double] { case (id, similarity) => similarity })
sortedSims2.slice(1, 11).map{ case (id, sim) => (titles(id), sim)
    }.mkString("n")
```

You will see the movie titles and scores displayed similar to this output:

```
(Hideaway (1995),0.6932331537649621)
(Body Snatchers (1993),0.6898690594544726)
(Evil Dead II (1987),0.6897964975027041)
(Alien: Resurrection (1997),0.6891221044611473)
(Stephen King's The Langoliers (1995),0.6864214133620066)
(Liar Liar (1997),0.6812075443259535)
(Tales from the Crypt Presents: Bordello of Blood
(1996),0.6754663844488256)
(Army of Darkness (1993),0.6702643811753909)
(Mystery Science Theater 3000: The Movie (1996),0.6594872765176396)
(Scream (1996),0.6538249646863378)
```

Once again, note that you might see quite different results due to random model initialization.

Now that you have computed similar items using cosine similarity, see if you can do the same with the user-factor vectors to compute similar users for a given user.

Evaluating the performance of recommendation models

How do we know whether the model we have trained is a good model? We will need to be able to evaluate its predictive performance in some way. Evaluation metrics are measures of a model's predictive capability or accuracy. Some are direct measures of how well a model predicts the model's target variable, such as Mean Squared Error, while others are concerned with how well the model performs at predicting things that might not be directly optimized in the model, but are often closer to what we care about in the real world, such as Mean Average Precision.

Evaluation metrics provide a standardized way of comparing the performance of the same model with different parameter settings and of comparing performance across different models. Using these metrics, we can perform model selection to choose the best-performing model from the set of models we wish to evaluate.

Here, we will show you how to calculate two common evaluation metrics used in recommender systems and collaborative filtering models: **Mean Squared Error (MSE)** and **Mean Average Precision at K (MAPK)**.

ALS Model Evaluation

From Spark v2.0, we will use `org.apache.spark.ml.evaluation.RegressionEvaluator` for regression problems. Regression evaluation is a metric to measure how well a fitted model does on held-out test data. Here, we will use **Root Mean Squared Error (RMSE)**, which is just the square root of the MSE metric:

```
object ALSModeling {

  def createALSModel() {
    val ratings = FeatureExtraction.getFeatures();
```

```
    val Array(training, test) = ratings.randomSplit(Array(0.8, 0.2))
    println(training.first())

    // Build the recommendation model using ALS on the training data
    val als = new ALS()
      .setMaxIter(5)
      .setRegParam(0.01)
      .setUserCol("userId")
      .setItemCol("movieId")
      .setRatingCol("rating")

    val model = als.fit(training)
    println(model.userFactors.count())
    println(model.itemFactors.count())

    val predictions = model.transform(test)
    println(predictions.printSchema())

    val evaluator = new RegressionEvaluator()
      .setMetricName("rmse")
      .setLabelCol("rating")
      .setPredictionCol("prediction")
    val rmse = evaluator.evaluate(predictions)

    println(s"Root-mean-square error = $rmse")
  }

  def main(args: Array[String]) {
    createALSModel()
  }

}
```

 You can find the code-listing at
https://github.com/ml-resources/spark-ml/blob/branch-ed2/Chapter
_05/2.0.0/scala-spark-
app/src/main/scala/com/spark/recommendation/ALSModeling.scala.

You will see an output like the following one:

```
16/09/07 17:58:45 INFO ShuffleBlockFetcherIterator: Getting 4 non-
    empty blocks out of 200 blocks
16/09/07 17:58:45 INFO ShuffleBlockFetcherIterator: Getting 2 non-
    empty blocks out of 200 blocks
16/09/07 17:58:45 INFO ShuffleBlockFetcherIterator: Started 0 remote
    fetches in 0 ms
16/09/07 17:58:45 INFO ShuffleBlockFetcherIterator: Started 0 remote
    fetches in 0 ms
```

```
16/09/07 17:58:45 INFO ShuffleBlockFetcherIterator: Getting 1 non-
    empty blocks out of 10 blocks
16/09/07 17:58:45 INFO ShuffleBlockFetcherIterator: Getting 1 non-
    empty blocks out of 10 blocks
16/09/07 17:58:45 INFO ShuffleBlockFetcherIterator: Started 0 remote
    fetches in 0 ms
16/09/07 17:58:45 INFO ShuffleBlockFetcherIterator: Started 0 remote
    fetches in 0 ms
Root-mean-square error = 2.1487554400294777
```

Before we proceed further, please note that the following evaluation examples use MLLib from Spark v1.6. Kindly follow the code listing to get the details of creating recommendation model using `org.apache.spark.mllib.recommendation.ALS`.

Mean Squared Error

The MSE is a direct measure of the reconstruction error of the user-item rating matrix. It is also the objective function being minimized in certain models, specifically many matrix-factorization techniques, including ALS. As such, it is commonly used in explicit ratings settings.

It is defined as the sum of the squared errors divided by the number of observations. The squared error, in turn, is the square of the difference between the predicted rating for a given user-item pair and the actual rating.

We will use our user 789 as an example. Let's take the first rating for this user from the `moviesForUser` set of `Ratings` that we previously computed:

```
val actualRating = moviesForUser.take(1)(0)
```

Here is the output:

```
actualRating: org.apache.spark.mllib.recommendation.Rating =
    Rating(789,1012,4.0)
```

We will see that the rating for this user-item combination is 4. Next, we will compute the model's predicted rating:

```
val predictedRating = model.predict(789, actualRating.product)
```

The output of the model's predicted rating is as follows:

```
...
14/04/13 13:01:15 INFO SparkContext: Job finished: lookup at
```

```
MatrixFactorizationModel.scala:46, took 0.025404 s
predictedRating: Double = 4.001005374200248
```

We will see that the predicted rating is about 4, very close to the actual rating. Finally, we will compute the squared error between the actual rating and the predicted rating:

```
val squaredError = math.pow(predictedRating - actualRating.rating,
    2.0)
```

The preceding code will output the squared error:

```
squaredError: Double = 1.010777282523947E-6
```

So, in order to compute the overall MSE for the dataset, we will need to compute this squared error for each (user, movie, actual rating, predicted rating) entry, sum them up, and divide them by the number of ratings. We will do this in the following code snippet.

> Note: the following code is adapted from the Apache Spark programming guide for ALS at
> http://spark.apache.org/docs/latest/mllib-collaborative-filterin g.html.

First, we will extract the user and product IDs from the ratings RDD and make predictions for each user-item pair using model.predict. We will use the user-item pair as the key and the predicted rating as the value:

```
val usersProducts = ratings.map{ case Rating(user, product,
    rating)  => (user, product)}
val predictions = model.predict(usersProducts).map{
    case Rating(user, product, rating) => ((user, product),
    rating)
}
```

Next, we will extract the actual ratings and also map the ratings RDD so that the user-item pair is the key and the actual rating is the value. Now that we have two RDDs with the same form of key, we can join them together to create a new RDD with the actual and predicted ratings for each user-item combination:

```
val ratingsAndPredictions = ratings.map{
    case Rating(user, product, rating) => ((user, product), rating)
}.join(predictions)
```

Finally, we will compute the MSE by summing up the squared errors using reduce and dividing by the count method of the number of records:

```
val MSE = ratingsAndPredictions.map{
    case ((user, product), (actual, predicted)) =>  math.pow((actual -
predicted), 2)
}.reduce(_ + _) / ratingsAndPredictions.count
println("Mean Squared Error = " + MSE)
```

The output is as follows:

Mean Squared Error = 0.08231947642632852

It is common to use the RMSE, which is just the square root of the MSE metric. This is somewhat more interpretable, as it is in the same units as the underlying data (that is, the ratings in this case). It is equivalent to the standard deviation of the differences between the predicted and actual ratings. We can compute it simply as follows:

```
val RMSE = math.sqrt(MSE)
println("Root Mean Squared Error = " + RMSE)
```

The preceding code will print the RMSE:

Root Mean Squared Error = 0.2869137090247319

To interpret the preceding result, keep following the definition in mind. Lowering the value of RMSE closer is the fit of predicted value to the actual value. While interpreting RMSE, keep the minimum and maximum of the actual data in mind.

Mean Average Precision at K

Mean Average Precision at *K* is the mean of the **average precision at K (APK)** metric across all instances in the dataset. APK is a metric commonly used for information retrieval. APK is a measure of the average relevance scores of a set of the *top-K* documents presented in response to a query. For each query instance, we will compare the set of *top-K* results with the set of actual relevant documents, that is, a ground truth set of relevant documents for the query.

In the APK metric, the order of the result set matters, in that the APK score would be higher if the result documents are both relevant and the relevant documents are presented higher in the results. It is, thus, a good metric for recommender systems; in that, typically, we would compute the *top-K* recommended items for each user and present these to the user. Of course, we prefer models where the items with the highest predicted scores, which are presented at the top of the list of recommendations, are, in fact, the most relevant items for the user. APK and other ranking-based metrics are also more appropriate evaluation measures for implicit datasets; here, MSE makes less sense.

In order to evaluate our model, we can use APK, where each user is the equivalent of a query, and the set of *top-K* recommended items is the document result set. The relevant documents, that is, the ground truth, in this case, is the set of items that a user interacted with. Hence, APK attempts to measure how good our model is at predicting items that a user will find relevant and choose to interact with.

The code for the following average precision computation is based on https://github.com/benhamner/Metrics.

More information on MAPK can be found at https://www.kaggle.com/wiki/MeanAveragePrecision.

Our function to compute the APK is shown here:

```
def avgPrecisionK(actual: Seq[Int], predicted: Seq[Int], k: Int):
    Double = {
     val predK = predicted.take(k)
     var score = 0.0
     var numHits = 0.0
     for ((p, i) <- predK.zipWithIndex) {
       if (actual.contains(p)) {
         numHits += 1.0
         score += numHits / (i.toDouble + 1.0)
       }
     }
     if (actual.isEmpty) {
       1.0
     } else {
       score / scala.math.min(actual.size, k).toDouble
     }
    }
```

As you can see, this takes as input a list of `actual` item IDs that are associated with the user and another list of `predicted` IDs so that our estimate will be relevant for the user.

We can compute the APK metric for our example user `789` as follows. First, we will extract the actual movie IDs for the user, as follows:

```
val actualMovies = moviesForUser.map(_.product)
```

The output is as follows:

```
actualMovies: Seq[Int] = ArrayBuffer(1012, 127, 475, 93, 1161, 286,
    293, 9, 50, 294, 181, 1, 1008, 508, 284, 1017, 137, 111, 742, 248,
    249, 1007, 591, 150, 276, 151, 129, 100, 741, 288, 762, 628, 124)
```

We will then use the movie recommendations we made previously to compute the APK score using K = 10:

```
val predictedMovies = topKRecs.map(_.product)
```

Here is the output:

```
predictedMovies: Array[Int] = Array(27, 497, 633, 827, 602, 849, 401,
    584, 1035, 1014)
```

The following code will produce the average precision:

```
val apk10 = avgPrecisionK(actualMovies, predictedMovies, 10)
```

The preceding code will print the following command line:

```
apk10: Double = 0.0
```

In this case, we can see that our model is not doing a very good job of predicting relevant movies for this user, as the APK score is 0.

In order to compute the APK for each user and average them to compute the overall MAPK, we will need to generate the list of recommendations for each user in our dataset. While this can be fairly intensive on a large scale, we can distribute the computation using our Spark functionality. However, one limitation is that each worker must have the full item-factor matrix available so that it can compute the dot product between the relevant user vector and all item vectors. This can be a problem when the number of items is extremely high, as the item matrix must fit in the memory of one machine.

There is actually no easy way around this limitation. One possible approach is to only compute recommendations for a subset of items from the total item set, using approximate techniques such as Locality Sensitive Hashing (`http://en.wikipedia.org/wiki/Locality-sensitive_hashing`).

We will now see how to go about this. First, we will collect the item factors and form a `DoubleMatrix` object from them:

```
val itemFactors = model.productFeatures.map { case (id, factor) =>
    factor }.collect()
```

```
val itemMatrix = new DoubleMatrix(itemFactors)
println(itemMatrix.rows, itemMatrix.columns)
```

The output of the preceding code is as follows:

(1682,50)

This gives us a matrix with 1682 rows and 50 columns, as we would expect from 1682 movies with a factor dimension of 50. Next, we will distribute the item matrix as a broadcast variable so that it is available on each worker node:

```
val imBroadcast = sc.broadcast(itemMatrix)
```

You will see the output as follows:

```
14/04/13 21:02:01 INFO MemoryStore: ensureFreeSpace(672960) called
   with curMem=4006896, maxMem=311387750
14/04/13 21:02:01 INFO MemoryStore: Block broadcast_21 stored as
   values to memory (estimated size 657.2 KB, free 292.5 MB)
imBroadcast:
   org.apache.spark.broadcast.Broadcast[org.jblas.DoubleMatrix] =
   Broadcast(21)
```

Now we are ready to compute the recommendations for each user. We will do this by applying a map function to each user factor within which we will perform a matrix multiplication between the user-factor vector and the movie-factor matrix. The result is a vector (of length 1682, that is, the number of movies we have) with the predicted rating for each movie. We will then sort these predictions by the predicted rating:

```
val allRecs = model.userFeatures.map{ case (userId, array) =>
  val userVector = new DoubleMatrix(array)
  val scores = imBroadcast.value.mmul(userVector)
  val sortedWithId = scores.data.zipWithIndex.sortBy(-_._1)
  val recommendedIds = sortedWithId.map(_._2 + 1).toSeq
  (userId, recommendedIds)
}
```

You will see the following on the screen:

```
allRecs: org.apache.spark.rdd.RDD[(Int, Seq[Int])] = MappedRDD[269]
   at map at <console>:29
```

As we can see, we now have an RDD that contains a list of movie IDs for each user ID. These movie IDs are sorted in order of the estimated rating.

Note that we needed to add 1 to the returned movie IDs (as highlighted in the preceding code snippet), as the item-factor matrix is 0-indexed, while our movie IDs start at 1.

We will also need the list of movie IDs for each user to pass into our APK function as the `actual` argument. We already have the `ratings` RDD ready, so we can extract just the user and movie IDs from it.

If we use Spark's `groupBy` operator, we will get an RDD that contains a list of (`userid`, `movieid`) pairs for each user ID (as the user ID is the key on which we perform the `groupBy` operation) shown as follows:

```
val userMovies = ratings.map{ case Rating(user, product, rating)
    => (user, product) }.groupBy(_._1)
```

The output of the preceding code is as follows:

```
userMovies: org.apache.spark.rdd.RDD[(Int, Seq[(Int, Int)])] =
    MapPartitionsRDD[277] at groupBy at <console>:21
```

Finally, we can use Spark's `join` operator to join these two RDDs together on the user ID key. Then, for each user, we have the list of actual and predicted movie IDs that we can pass to our APK function. In a manner similar to how we computed MSE, we will sum each of these APK scores using a `reduce` action and divide by the number of users, that is, the count of the `allRecs` RDD as shown in the following code:

```
val K = 10
val MAPK = allRecs.join(userMovies).map{ case (userId, (predicted,
actualWithIds)) =>
  val actual = actualWithIds.map(_._2).toSeq
  avgPrecisionK(actual, predicted, K)
}.reduce(_ + _) / allRecs.count
println("Mean Average Precision at K = " + MAPK)
```

The preceding code will print the Mean Average Precision at K as follows:

```
Mean Average Precision at K = 0.030486963254725705
```

Our model achieves a fairly low MAPK. However, note that typical values for recommendation tasks are usually relatively low, especially if the item set is extremely large.

Try out a few parameter settings for `lambda` and `rank` (and `alpha`, if you are using the implicit version of ALS) and see whether you can find a model that performs better based on the RMSE and MAPK evaluation metrics.

Using MLlib's built-in evaluation functions

While we have computed MSE, RMSE, and MAPK from scratch, and it's a useful learning exercise to do so, MLlib provides convenience functions to do this for us in the `RegressionMetrics` and `RankingMetrics` classes.

RMSE and MSE

First, we will compute the MSE and RMSE metrics using `RegressionMetrics`. We will instantiate a `RegressionMetrics` instance by passing in an RDD of key-value pairs that represent the predicted and true values for each data point, as shown in the following code snippet. Here, we will again use the `ratingsAndPredictions` RDD we computed in our earlier example:

```
import org.apache.spark.mllib.evaluation.RegressionMetrics
val predictedAndTrue = ratingsAndPredictions.map { case ((user,
    product), (predicted, actual)) => (predicted, actual) }
val regressionMetrics = new RegressionMetrics(predictedAndTrue)
```

We can then access various metrics, including MSE and RMSE. We will print out these metrics here:

```
println("Mean Squared Error = " +
    regressionMetrics.meanSquaredError)
println("Root Mean Squared Error = " +
    regressionMetrics.rootMeanSquaredError)
```

In the following command lines, you will see that the output for MSE and RMSE, is exactly the same as the metrics we computed earlier:

```
Mean Squared Error = 0.08231947642632852
Root Mean Squared Error = 0.2869137090247319
```

MAP

As we did for MSE and RMSE, we can compute ranking-based evaluation metrics using MLlib's `RankingMetrics` class. Similarly, to our own average precision function, we will need to pass in an RDD of key-value pairs, where the key is `Array` of predicted item IDs for a user, while the value is an array of actual item IDs.

The implementation of the average precision at the K function in `RankingMetrics` is slightly different from ours, so we will get different results. However, the computation of the overall Mean Average Precision (MAP, which does not use a threshold at K) is the same as our function if we select K to be very high (say, at least as high as the number of items in our item set).

First, we will calculate MAP using `RankingMetrics` as follows:

```
import org.apache.spark.mllib.evaluation.RankingMetrics
val predictedAndTrueForRanking = allRecs.join(userMovies).map{
    case (userId, (predicted, actualWithIds)) =>
     val actual = actualWithIds.map(_._2)
     (predicted.toArray, actual.toArray)
}
val rankingMetrics = new
    RankingMetrics(predictedAndTrueForRanking)
println("Mean Average Precision = " +
    rankingMetrics.meanAveragePrecision)
```

You will see the following output:

```
Mean Average Precision = 0.07171412913757183
```

Next, we will use our function to compute the MAP in exactly the same way as we did previously, except that we set K to a very high value, say 2000:

```
val MAPK2000 = allRecs.join(userMovies).map{ case (userId,
    (predicted, actualWithIds)) =>
  val actual = actualWithIds.map(_._2).toSeq
  avgPrecisionK(actual, predicted, 2000)
}.reduce(_ + _) / allRecs.count
println("Mean Average Precision = " + MAPK2000)
```

You will see that the MAP from our own function is the same as the one computed using `RankingMetrics`:

Mean Average Precision = 0.07171412913757186.

 We will not cover cross-validation in this chapter, as we will provide a detailed treatment in the next few chapters. However, note that the same techniques for cross-validation that are explored in the upcoming chapters can be used to evaluate recommendation models using the performance metrics such as MSE, RMSE, and MAP, which we covered in this section.

FP-Growth algorithm

We will apply the FP-Growth algorithm to find frequently recommended movies.

The FP-Growth algorithm has been described in the paper by Han et al., *Mining frequent patterns without candidate generation* available at: `http://dx.doi.org/10.1145/335191.335372`, where **FP** stands for the **frequent pattern**. For given a dataset of transactions, the first step of FP-Growth is to calculate item frequencies and identify frequent items. The second step of FP-Growth algorithm implementation uses a suffix tree (FP-tree) structure to encode transactions; this is done without generating candidate sets explicitly, which are usually expensive to generate for large datasets.

FP-Growth Basic Sample

Let's start with a very simple dataset of random numbers:

```
val transactions = Seq(
    "r z h k p",
    "z y x w v u t s",
    "s x o n r",
    "x z y m t s q e",
    "z",
    "x z y r q t p")
    .map(_.split(" "))
```

We will find out the most frequent items (character in this case). First, we will get the spark context as follows:

```
val sc = new SparkContext("local[2]", "Chapter 5 App")
```

Convert our data in an RDD:

```
val rdd = sc.parallelize(transactions, 2).cache()
```

Initialize the `FPGrowth` instance:

```
val fpg = new FPGrowth()
```

 FP-Growth can be configured with the following parameters:

- `minSupport`: the minimum support number for an itemset to be identified as frequent. For example, if an item appears in 3 out of 10 transactions, it has a support of 3/10=0.3.
- `numPartitions`: the number of partitions to distribute the work.

Set `minsupport` and number of partitions for the FP-Growth instance and call run on the RDD object. Number of partitions should be set to the number of partitions in the dataset-- number of worker nodes from where data will be loaded, as follows:

```
val model = fpg.setMinSupport(0.2).setNumPartitions(1).run(rdd)
```

Get the item sets of the output and print:

```
model.freqItemsets.collect().foreach {
itemset =>
        println(itemset.items.mkString(
"[", ",", "]") + ", " + itemset.freq
  )
```

The output for the preceding code is listed as follows, as you can see `[Z]` occurs the most:

```
[s], 3
[s,x], 3
[s,x,z], 2
[s,z], 2
[r], 3
[r,x], 2
[r,z], 2
[y], 3
[y,s], 2
[y,s,x], 2
[y,s,x,z], 2
[y,s,z], 2
[y,x], 3
[y,x,z], 3
[y,t], 3
[y,t,s], 2
```

```
[y,t,s,x], 2
[y,t,s,x,z], 2
[y,t,s,z], 2
[y,t,x], 3
[y,t,x,z], 3
[y,t,z], 3
[y,z], 3
[q], 2
[q,y], 2
[q,y,x], 2
[q,y,x,z], 2
[q,y,t], 2
[q,y,t,x], 2
[q,y,t,x,z], 2
[q,y,t,z], 2
[q,y,z], 2
[q,x], 2
[q,x,z], 2
[q,t], 2
[q,t,x], 2
[q,t,x,z], 2
[q,t,z], 2
[q,z], 2
[x], 4
[x,z], 3
[t], 3
[t,s], 2
[t,s,x], 2
[t,s,x,z], 2
[t,s,z], 2
[t,x], 3
[t,x,z], 3
[t,z], 3
[p], 2
[p,r], 2
[p,r,z], 2
[p,z], 2
[z], 5
```

FP-Growth Applied to Movie Lens Data

Let's apply the algorithm to Movie Lens data to find our frequent movie titles:

1. Instantiate the `SparkContext` by writing the following lines of code:

```
val sc = Util.sc
val rawData = Util.getUserData()
rawData.first()
```

2. Get raw ratings and print first by writing the following lines of code:

```
val rawRatings = rawData.map(_.split("t").take(3))
rawRatings.first()
val ratings = rawRatings.map { case Array(user, movie,
    rating) =>
Rating(user.toInt, movie.toInt, rating.toDouble) }
    val ratingsFirst = ratings.first()
println(ratingsFirst)
```

3. Load the movie data and get the titles as follows:

```
val movies = Util.getMovieData()
val titles = movies.map(line =>
line.split("|").take(2)).map(array
=> (array(0).toInt, array(1))).collectAsMap()
titles(123)
```

4. Next, we will find out the most frequent movies for 400 users from 501 to 900 using the FP-Growth algorithm.

5. The FP-Growth model is created first by writing the following lines of code:

```
val model = fpg
        .setMinSupport(0.1)
        .setNumPartitions(1)
        .run(rddx)
```

6. Where `0.1` is the minimum cutoff to be considered, `rddx` is the RDD with raw movie ratings loaded into RDD for 400 users. Once we have the model we can iterate `overitemsetr`, the `itemset` and print the results.

6.

6. The complete code listing is given here and can also be found at `https://github.com/ml-resources/spark-ml/blob/branch-ed2/Chapter_05/scala-spark-app/src/main/scala/MovieLensFPGrowthApp.scala`.

This can be done by writing the following lines of code:

```scala
var eRDD = sc.emptyRDD
var z = Seq[String]()
val l = ListBuffer()
val aj = new Array[String](400)
var i = 0
for( a <- 501 to 900) {
  val moviesForUserX = ratings.keyBy(_.user).
    lookup(a)
 val moviesForUserX_10 =
   moviesForUserX.sortBy(-_.rating).take(10)
 val moviesForUserX_10_1 = moviesForUserX_10.map
   (r => r.product)
 var temp = ""
 for( x <- moviesForUserX_10_1){
    if(temp.equals(""))
      temp = x.toString
    else {
      temp =  temp + " " + x
    }
 }
 aj(i) = temp
 i += 1
}
z = aj
val transaction = z.map(_.split(" "))
val rddx = sc.parallelize(transaction, 2).cache()
val fpg = new FPGrowth()
val model = fpg
  .setMinSupport(0.1)
  .setNumPartitions(1)
  .run(rddx)
model.freqItemsets.collect().foreach { itemset =>
  println(itemset.items.mkString("[", ",", "]")
    + ", " + itemset.freq)
}
sc.stop()
```

The output of the preceding sample is as follows:

```
[302], 40
[258], 59
[100], 49
[286], 50
[181], 45
[127], 60
[313], 59
[300], 49
[50], 94
```

This provides movies with the maximum frequency for user IDs 501 to 900.

Summary

In this chapter, we used Spark's ML and MLlib library to train a collaborative filtering recommendation model, and you learned how to use this model to make predictions for the items that a given user may have a preference for. We also used our model to find items that are similar or related to a given item. Finally, we explored common metrics to evaluate the predictive capability of our recommendation model.

In the next chapter, you will learn how to use Spark to train a model to classify your data and to use standard evaluation mechanisms to gauge the performance of your model.

6
Building a Classification Model with Spark

In this chapter, you will learn the basics of classification models, and how they can be used in a variety of contexts. Classification generically refers to classifying things into distinct categories or classes. In the case of a classification model, we typically wish to assign classes based on a set of features. The features might represent variables related to an item or object, an event or context, or some combination of these.

The simplest form of classification is when we have two classes; this is referred to as **binary classification**. One of the classes is usually labeled as the **positive class** (assigned a label of 1), while the other is labeled as the **negative class** (assigned a label of -1, or, sometimes, 0). A simple example with two classes is shown in the following figure. The input features, in this case, have two dimensions, and the feature values are represented on the x and y-axes in the figure. Our task is to train a model that can classify new data points in this two-dimensional space as either one class (red) or the other (blue).

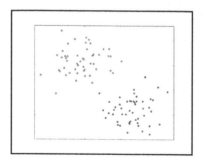

A simple binary classification problem

If we have more than two classes, we would refer to multiclass classification, and classes are typically labeled using integer numbers starting at 0 (for example, five different classes would range from label 0 to 4). An example is shown in the following figure. Again, the input features are assumed to be two-dimensional for ease of illustration:

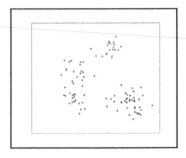

A simple multiclass classification problem

Classification is a form of supervised learning, where we train a model with training examples that include known targets or outcomes of interest (that is, the model is supervised with these example outcomes). Classification models can be used in many situations, but a few common examples include the ones listed next:

- Predicting the probability of Internet users clicking on an online advert; here, the classes are binary in nature (that is, click or no click)
- Detecting fraud; again, in this case, the classes are commonly binary (fraud or no fraud)
- Predicting defaults on loans (binary)
- Classifying images, video, or sounds (most often multiclass, with potentially very many different classes)
- Assigning categories or tags to news articles, web pages, or other content (multiclass)
- Discovering e-mail and web spam, network intrusions, and other malicious behavior (binary or multiclass)
- Detecting failure situations, for example, in computer systems or networks
- Ranking customers or users in order of probability that they might purchase a product or use a service
- Predicting customers or users who might stop using a product, service, or provider (called churn)

These are just a few possible use cases. In fact, it is probably safe to say that classification is one of the most widely used machine learning and statistical techniques in modern businesses, especially, online businesses.

In this chapter, we will do the following:

- Discuss the types of classification models available in ML library
- Use Spark to extract appropriate features from raw input data
- Train a number of classification models using ML library
- Make predictions with our classification models
- Apply a number of standard evaluation techniques to assess the predictive performance of our models
- Illustrate how to improve model performance using some of the feature extraction approaches from `Chapter 4`, *Obtaining, Processing, and Preparing Data with Spark*
- Explore the impact of parameter tuning on model performance, and learn how to use cross-validation to select the most optimal model parameters

Types of classification models

We will explore three common classification models available in Spark: linear models, decision trees, and naive Bayes models. Linear models, while less complex, are relatively easier to scale to very large datasets. Decision tree is a powerful non-linear technique, which can be a little more difficult to scale up (fortunately, ML library takes care of this for us!) and more computationally intensive to train, but delivers leading performance in many situations. The naive Bayes models are more simple, but are easy to train efficiently and parallelize (in fact, they require only one pass over the dataset). They can also give reasonable performance in many cases where appropriate feature engineering is used. A naive Bayes model also provides a good baseline model against which we can measure the performance of other models.

Currently, Spark's ML library supports binary classification for linear models, decision trees, and naive Bayes models, and multiclass classification for decision trees and naive Bayes models. In this book, for simplicity in illustrating the examples, we will focus on the binary case.

Linear models

The core idea of linear models (or generalized linear models) is that we model the predicted outcome of interest (often called the **target** or **dependent variable**) as a function of a simple linear predictor applied to the input variables (also referred to as features or independent variables).

$$y = f(W^T x)$$

Here, y is the target variable, w is the vector of parameters (known as the **weight vector**), and x is the vector of input features.

wTx is the linear predictor (or vector dot product) of the weight vector w and feature vector x. To this linear predictor, we applied a function f (called the **link function**).

Linear models can, in fact, be used for both classification and regression, simply by changing the link function. Standard linear regression (covered in the next chapter) uses an identity link (that is, $y = W^T x$ directly), while binary classification uses alternative link functions as discussed here.

Let's take a look at the example of online advertising. In this case, the target variable would be 0 (often assigned the class label of -1 in mathematical treatments) if no click was observed for a given advert displayed on a web page (called an **impression**). The target variable would be 1 if a click occurred. The feature vector for each impression would consist of variables related to the impression event (such as features relating to the user, web page, advert and advertiser, and various other factors relating to the context of the event, such as the type of device used, time of the day, and geolocation).

Thus, we would like to find a model that maps a given input feature vector (advert impression) to a predicted outcome (click or not). To make a prediction for a new data point, we will take the new feature vector (which is unseen, and hence, we do not know what the target variable is), and compute the dot product with our weight vector. We will then apply the relevant link function, and the result is our predicted outcome (after applying a threshold to the prediction, in the case of some models).

Given a set of input data in the form of feature vectors and target variables, we would like to find the weight vector that is the best fit for the data, in the sense that we minimize some error between what our model predicts and the actual outcomes observed. This process is called model fitting, training, or optimization.

More formally, we seek to find the weight vector that minimizes the sum, over all the training examples, of the loss (or error) computed from some loss function. The loss function takes the weight vector, feature vector, and the actual outcome for a given training example as input, and outputs the loss. In fact, the loss function itself is effectively specified by the link function; hence, for a given type of classification or regression (that is, a given link function), there is a corresponding loss function.

> For further details on linear models and loss functions, see the linear methods section related to binary classification in the *Spark Programming Guide* at `http://spark.apache.org/docs/latest/mllib-linear-methods.html#binary-classification`and `http://spark.apache.org/docs/latest/ml-classification-regression.html#linear-methods`. Also, see the Wikipedia entry for generalized linear models at `http://en.wikipedia.org/wiki/Generalized_linear_model`.

While a detailed treatment of linear models and loss functions is beyond the scope of this book, Spark ML provides two loss functions suitable to binary classification (you can learn more about them from the Spark documentation). The first one is a logistic loss, which equates to a model known as **logistic regression**, while the second one is the hinge loss, which is equivalent to a linear **Support Vector Machine (SVM)**. Note that the SVM does not strictly fall into the statistical framework of generalized linear models, but can be used in the same way as it essentially specifies a loss and link function.

In the following figure, we show the logistic loss and hinge loss relative to the actual zero-one loss. The zero-one loss is the true loss for binary classification--it is either zero if the model predicts correctly, or one if the model predicts incorrectly. The reason it is not actually used is that it is not a differentiable loss function, so it is not possible to easily compute a gradient and, thus, very difficult to optimize.

The other loss functions are approximations to the zero-one loss, which make optimization possible:

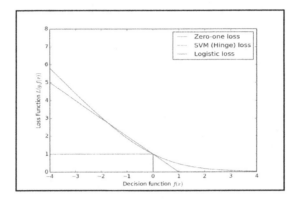

The logistic, hinge, and zero-one loss functions

The preceding loss diagram is adapted from the scikit-learn example at `ht tp://scikit-learn.org/stable/auto_examples/linear_model/plot_s gd_loss_functions.html`.

Logistic regression

Logistic regression is a probabilistic model that is, its predictions are bounded between 0 and 1, and for binary classification, equate to the model's estimate of the probability of the data point belonging to the positive class. Logistic regression is one of the most widely used linear classification models.

As mentioned earlier, the link function used in logistic regression is this logit link:

$$1 / (1 + exp(- W^T x)) \ a$$

The related loss function for logistic regression is the logistic loss:

$$log(1 + exp(-y \ W^T x))$$

Here, y is the actual target variable (either 1 for the positive class or -1 for the negative class).

Multinomial logistic regression

Multinomial logistic regression generalizes to multiclass problems; it allows for more than two categories of the outcome variable. Just like binary logistic regression, multinomial logistic regression also uses maximum likelihood estimation to evaluate the probability.

Multinomial logistic regression is mainly used when the dependent variable in question is nominal. Multinomial logistic regression is a classification problem in which a linear combination of the observed features and parameters can be utilized to calculate the probability of each particular outcome of the dependent variable.

In this chapter, we will use a different dataset from the one we used for our recommendation model, as the MovieLens data doesn't have much for us to work with in terms of a classification problem. We will use a dataset from a competition on Kaggle. The dataset was provided by StumbleUpon, and the problem relates to classifying whether a given web page is ephemeral (that is, short-lived, and will cease being popular soon), or evergreen (that is, persistently popular) on their web content recommendation pages.

The dataset used here can be downloaded from `http://www.kaggle.com/c/stumbleupon/data`.

Download the training data (`train.tsv`)-you will need to accept the terms and conditions before downloading the dataset.

You can find more information about the competition at `http://www.kaggle.com/c/stumbleupon`.

The code listing to get started is available at `https://github.com/ml-resources/spark-ml/tree/branch-ed2/Chapter_06/2.0.0/src/scala/org/sparksamples/classification/stumbleupon`.

A glimpse of the StumbleUpon dataset stored as a temporary table using Spark SQLContext is given in the following screenshot:

url	urlid		boilerplate	alchemy_category	alchemy_category_score	avglinksize	commonlinkratio_1	commonlinkratio_2	commonlinkratio_3	commonlinkratio_4	
http://www.cpnven...	7018	{"url":"conven...	?		?	119.0	0.745454545	0.581818182	0.290909091	0.018181818	
http://www.inside...	3402	{"url":"insidersh...	?		?	1.883333333	0.71969697	0.265151515	0.113636364	0.015151515	
http://www.valetm...	477	{"title":"Valet T...	?		?	0.471502591	0.190721649	0.036082474	0.0	0.0	
http://www.howswe...	6731	{"url":"howsweete...	?		?	2.41011236	0.469325153	0.101226994	0.018404908	0.003067485	
http://www.thedai...	1063	{"title":" ","bod...	?		?	0.0	0.0	0.0	0.0	0.0	
http://www.monice...	8945	{"title":"Origina...	?		?	4.327655311	0.978757515	0.895791583	0.669138277	0.422044088	
http://blogs.babb...	2839	{"title":" ","bod...	?		?	1.786407767	0.552631579	0.149122807	0.052631579	0.01754386	
http://humor.cool...	2949	{"title":"Supermo...	?		?	3.417910448	0.541176471	0.270588235	0.176470588	0.117647059	
http://sportsillu...	4156	{"title":"Genevie...	?		?	1.154761905	0.584424779	0.427728614	0.02359882	0.0	
http://www.chican...	8004	{"title":"Ten way...	?		?	1.292682927	0.421965318	0.306358382	0.011560694	0.0	
http://nerdsmagaz...	3201	{"url":"nerdsmaga...	?		?	1.888888889	0.59375	0.171875	0.0625	0.046875	
http://bitten.blo...	6704	{"title":"Microwa...	?		?	2.618902439	0.707317073	0.33604336	0.119241192	0.051490515	
http://www.peta.o...	3561	{"title":"Creamy ...	?		?	2.881944444	0.54822335	0.23857868	0.106598985	0.040609137	
http://www.refine...	8136	{"title":"Photo 1...	?		?	1.76969697	0.381818182	0.181818182	0.048484848	0.006060606	
http://sportsillu...	1754	{"title":"Alyssa ...	?		?	1.158208955	0.50591716	0.428994083	0.023668639	0.0	
http://twentylf.com/	4881	{"title":"Twentyl...	?		?	2.133333333	0.655737705	0.213114754	0.196721311	0.196721311	
http://allrecipes...	5483	{"title":"Apple D...	?		?	2.328502415	0.427777778	0.205555556	0.061111111	0.019444444	
http://hypersapie...	4781	{"url":"hypersapi...	?		?	2.85483871	0.428571429	0.103896104	0.038961039	0.0	
http://www.phoeni...	7053	{"title":" ","bod...	?		?	2.278481013	0.552419355	0.266129032	0.052419355	0.02016129	
http://www.comple...	1033	{"title":"The 25 ...	?		?	1.127156779	0.636363636	0.048484848	0.0	0.0	

only showing top 20 rows

Visualizing the StumbleUpon dataset

We ran custom logic to reduce the number of features to two, so that we can visualize the dataset in a two-dimensional plane, keeping the lines in the dataset constant.

```
{
  val sc = new SparkContext("local[1]", "Classification")

  // get StumbleUpon dataset 'https://www.kaggle.com/c/stumbleupon'
  val records = sc.textFile(
    SparkConstants.PATH + "data/train_noheader.tsv").map(
    line => line.split("\t"))

  val data_persistent = records.map { r =>
    val trimmed = r.map(_.replaceAll("\"", ""))
    val label = trimmed(r.size - 1).toInt
    val features = trimmed.slice(4, r.size - 1).map(
      d => if (d == "?") 0.0 else d.toDouble)
    val len = features.size.toInt
    val len_2 = math.floor(len/2).toInt
    val x = features.slice(0,len_2)

    val y = features.slice(len_2 -1 ,len )
    var i=0
    var sum_x = 0.0
    var sum_y = 0.0
    while (i < x.length) {
    sum_x += x(i)
    i += 1
}

i = 0
while (i < y.length) {
  sum_y += y(i)
  i += 1
}

if (sum_y != 0.0) {
  if(sum_x != 0.0) {
    math.log(sum_x) + "," + math.log(sum_y)
  }else {
    sum_x + "," + math.log(sum_y)
  }
}else {
  if(sum_x != 0.0) {
    math.log(sum_x) + "," + 0.0
  }else {
    sum_x + "," + 0.0
```

```
      }
    }

  }
  val dataone = data_persistent.first()
    data_persistent.saveAsTextFile(SparkConstants.PATH +
      "/results/raw-input-log")
    sc.stop()

  }
```

Once we have the data in a two-dimensional format, log scale is applied to both x and y for plotting convenience. In our case, we used D3.js for plotting as shown next. This data will be classified into two classes, and we will use the same base image to show the classification:

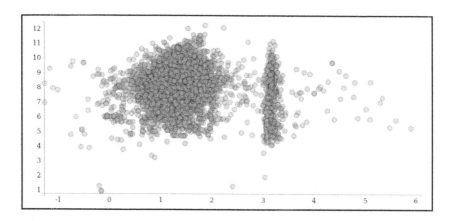

Extracting features from the Kaggle/StumbleUpon evergreen classification dataset

Before we begin, we will remove the column name header from the first line of the file to make it easier for us to work with the data in Spark. Change to the directory in which you downloaded the data (referred to as PATH here), run the following command to remove the first line, and pipe the result to a new file called `train_noheader.tsv`:

```
> sed 1d train.tsv > train_noheader.tsv
```

Now, we are ready to start up our Spark shell (remember to run this command from your Spark installation directory):

```
>./bin/spark-shell --driver-memory 4g
```

You can type in the code that follows for the remainder of this chapter directly into your Spark shell.

In a manner similar to what we did in the earlier chapters, we will load the raw training data into an RDD, and inspect it as follows:

```
val rawData = sc.textFile("/PATH/train_noheader.tsv")
val records = rawData.map(line => line.split("\t"))
records.first()
```

You will see the following on the screen:

```
Array[String] =
Array("http://www.bloomberg.com/news/2010-12-23/ibm-predicts-holographic-ca
lls-air-breathing-batteries-by-2015.html", "4042", ...
```

You can check the fields that are available by reading through the overview on the dataset page as mentioned earlier. The first two columns contain the URL and ID of the page. The next column contains some raw textual content. The next column contains the category assigned to the page. The next 22 columns contain numeric or categorical features of various kinds. The final column contains the target--1 is evergreen, while 0 is non-evergreen.

We'll start off with a simple approach of using only the available numeric features directly. As each categorical variable is binary, we already have a *1-of-k* encoding for these variables, so we don't need to do any further feature extraction.

Due to the way the data is formatted, we will have to do a bit of data cleaning during our initial processing by trimming out the extra quotation characters ("). There are also missing values in the dataset; they are denoted by the "?" character. In this case, we will simply assign a zero value to these missing values.

```
import org.apache.spark.mllib.regression.LabeledPoint
import org.apache.spark.mllib.linalg.Vectors
val data = records.map { r =>
  val trimmed = r.map(_.replaceAll("\"", ""))
  val label = trimmed(r.size - 1).toInt
  val features = trimmed.slice(4, r.size - 1).map(d => if (d ==   "?") 0.0
else d.toDouble)
  LabeledPoint(label, Vectors.dense(features))
}
```

In the preceding code, we extracted the `label` variable from the last column, and an array of `features` for columns 5 to 25 after cleaning and dealing with missing values. We converted the `label` variable to an integer value, and the `features` variable to an `Array[Double]`. Finally, we wrapped `label` and `features` in a `LabeledPoint` instance, converting the features into an MLlib vector.

We will also cache the data and count the number of data points as follows:

```
data.cache
val numData = data.count
```

You will see that the value of `numData` is `7395`.

We will explore the dataset in more detail a little later, but we will tell you now that there are some negative feature values in the numeric data. As we saw earlier, the naive Bayes model requires non-negative features, and will throw an error if it encounters negative values. So, for now, we will create a version of our input feature vectors for the naive Bayes model by setting any negative feature values to zero.

```
val nbData = records.map { r =>
  val trimmed = r.map(_.replaceAll("\"", ""))
  val label = trimmed(r.size - 1).toInt
  val features = trimmed.slice(4, r.size - 1).map(d => if (d ==
  "?") 0.0 else d.toDouble).map(d => if (d < 0) 0.0 else d)
  LabeledPoint(label, Vectors.dense(features))
}
```

StumbleUponExecutor

The StumbleUponExecutor (https://github.com/ml-resources/spark-ml/blob/branch-ed2/Chapter_06/2.0.0/scala-spark-app/src/main/scala/org/sparksamples/classification/stumbleupon/StumbleUponExecutor.scala) object can be used to choose and run the respective classification model; for example, to run `LogisiticRegression` and to execute the logistic regression pipeline, set program argument as LR. For other commands, refer to the following code snippet:

```
case "LR" =>
LogisticRegressionPipeline.logisticRegressionPipeline(vectorAssembler,
dataFrame)

case "DT" => DecisionTreePipeline.decisionTreePipeline(vectorAssembler,
dataFrame)

case "RF" => RandomForestPipeline.randomForestPipeline(vectorAssembler,
dataFrame)
```

```
case "GBT" =>
GradientBoostedTreePipeline.gradientBoostedTreePipeline(vectorAssembler,
dataFrame)

case "NB" => NaiveBayesPipeline.naiveBayesPipeline(vectorAssembler,
dataFrame)

case "SVM" => SVMPipeline.svmPipeline(sparkContext)
```

Let's train the StumbleUpon dataset by splitting it into 80% training and 20% testing; use `LogisticRegression` with `TrainValidationSplit` from Spark to build the model, and get the evaluation metrics around test data:

```
// create logisitic regression object
val lr = new LogisticRegression()
```

To create a pipeline object, we will use `ParamGridBuilder`. `ParamGridBuilder` is used to build the param grid, which is a list of parameters to choose from or search over by the estimator for best model selection. You can find more details about it at the following link: `https://spark.apache.org/docs/2.0.0/api/java/org/apache/spark/ml/tuning/ParamGridBuilder.html`

```
--------------------------------------------------------------------
----------------
org.apache.spark.ml.tuning
Class ParamGridBuilder
Builder for a param grid used in grid search-based model selection.
--------------------------------------------------------------------
----------------

// set params using ParamGrid builder
val paramGrid = new ParamGridBuilder()
  .addGrid(lr.regParam, Array(0.1, 0.01))
  .addGrid(lr.fitIntercept)
  .addGrid(lr.elasticNetParam, Array(0.0, 0.25, 0.5, 0.75, 1.0))
  .build()

// set pipeline to run the vector assembler and logistic regression //
estimator
val pipeline = new Pipeline().setStages(Array(vectorAssembler,
 lr))
```

We will use `TrainValidationSplit` for hyperparameter tuning. It evaluates each combination of parameters once as opposed to *k* times in the case of `CrossValidator`. It creates a single training, test dataset pair, and splits between the training and testing is done based on the `trainRatio` parameter.

Trainvalidationsplit **takes** Estimator, **a set of** ParamMaps **provided in the** estimatorParamMaps **parameter, and** Evaluator. **Refer to the following link for more information:**

```
http://spark.apache.org/docs/latest/api/scala/index.html#org.apache.spark.ml
.tuning.TrainValidationSplit
```

```
-------------------------------------------------------------------------
----------------
org.apache.spark.ml.tuning
Class TraiValidationSplit
Validation for hyper-parameter tuning. Randomly splits the input dataset
into train and validation sets.
-------------------------------------------------------------------------
----------------

// use train validation split and regression evaluator for //evaluation
val trainValidationSplit = new TrainValidationSplit()
  .setEstimator(pipeline)
  .setEvaluator(new RegressionEvaluator)
  .setEstimatorParamMaps(paramGrid)
  .setTrainRatio(0.8)

val Array(training, test) = dataFrame.randomSplit(Array(0.8, 0.2), seed =
12345)

// run the estimator
val model = trainValidationSplit.fit(training)

val holdout = model.transform(test).select("prediction","label")

// have to do a type conversion for RegressionMetrics
val rm = new RegressionMetrics(holdout.rdd.map(x =>
(x(0).asInstanceOf[Double], x(1).asInstanceOf[Double])))

logger.info("Test Metrics")
logger.info("Test Explained Variance:")
logger.info(rm.explainedVariance)
logger.info("Test R^2 Coef:")
logger.info(rm.r2)
logger.info("Test MSE:")
logger.info(rm.meanSquaredError)
logger.info("Test RMSE:")
logger.info(rm.rootMeanSquaredError)

val totalPoints = test.count()
val lrTotalCorrect = holdout.rdd.map(
  x => if (x(0).asInstanceOf[Double] == x(1).asInstanceOf[Double])
  1 else 0).sum()
```

```
val accuracy = lrTotalCorrect/totalPoints
println("Accuracy of LogisticRegression is: ", accuracy)
```

You will see the following output displayed:

```
Accuracy of LogisticRegression is: ,0.6374918354016982
Mean Squared Error:,0.3625081645983018
Root Mean Squared Error:,0.6020865092312747
```

The code listing can be found at this link: https://github.com/ml-resources/spark-ml/b
lob/branch-ed2/Chapter_06/2.0.0/scala-spark-app/src/main/scala/org/sparksampl
es/classification/stumbleupon/LogisticRegressionPipeline.scala

The visualization of predicted and actual data in a two-dimensional scatter plot is shown in
these two screenshots:

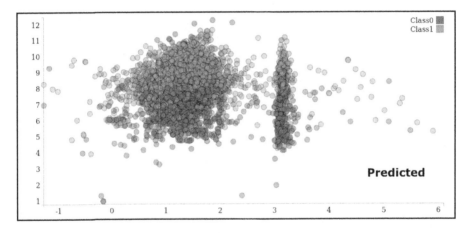

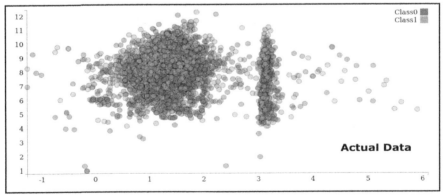

Linear support vector machines

SVM is a powerful and popular technique for regression and classification. Unlike logistic regression, it is not a probabilistic model but predicts classes based on whether the model evaluation is positive or negative.

The SVM link function is the identity link, so the predicted outcome is as follows:

$$y = w^T x$$

Hence, if the evaluation of wTx is greater than or equal to a threshold of 0, the SVM will assign the data point to class 1; otherwise, the SVM will assign it to class 0

(this threshold is a model parameter of SVM, and can be adjusted).

The loss function for SVM is known as the hinge loss and is defined as follows:

$$max(0, 1 - yw^T x)$$

SVM is a maximum margin classifier--it tries to find a weight vector such that the classes are separated as much as possible. It has been shown to perform well on many classification tasks, and the linear variant can scale to very large datasets.

> SVMs have a large amount of theory behind them, which is beyond the scope of this book, but you can visit http://en.wikipedia.org/wiki/Sup port_vector_machineand http://www.support-vector-machines.org/ for more details.

In the following figure, we have plotted the different decision functions for logistic regression (the blue line) and linear SVM (the red line) based on the simple binary classification example explained earlier.

You can see that the SVM effectively focuses on the points that lie closest to the decision function (the margin lines are shown with red dashes):

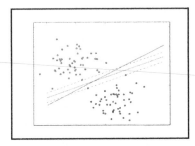

Decision functions for logistic regression and linear SVM for binary classification

Let's train the StumbleUpon dataset by splitting it into 80% training and 20% testing, use SVM from Spark to build the model, and get evaluation metrics around the test data:

```
// read stumble upon dataset as rdd
val records = sc.textFile("/home/ubuntu/work/ml-resources/spark-
ml/train_noheader.tsv").map(line => line.split("\t"))

// get features and label from the rdd
val data = records.map { r =>
    val trimmed = r.map(_.replaceAll("\"", ""))
    val label = trimmed(r.size - 1).toInt
    val features = trimmed.slice(4, r.size - 1).map(d => if (d == "?") 0.0
else d.toDouble)
    LabeledPoint(label, Vectors.dense(features))
  }

// params for SVM
val numIterations = 10

// Run training algorithm to build the model
val svmModel = SVMWithSGD.train(data, numIterations)

// Clear the default threshold.
svmModel.clearThreshold()

val svmTotalCorrect = data.map { point =>
  if(svmModel.predict(point.features) == point.label) 1 else 0
}.sum()

// calculate accuracy
val svmAccuracy = svmTotalCorrect / data.count()
println(svmAccuracy)
```

```
}
```

You will see the following output displayed:

```
Area under ROC = 1.0
```

The code listing is available at https://github.com/ml-resources/spark-ml/blob/branch-ed2/Chapter_06/2.0.0/scala-spark-app/src/main/scala/org/sparksamples/classification/stumbleupon/SVMPipeline.scala.

The naive Bayes model

Naive Bayes is a probabilistic model, which makes predictions by computing the probability of a data point that belongs to a given class. A naive Bayes model assumes that each feature makes an independent contribution to the probability assigned to a class (it assumes conditional independence between features).

Due to this assumption, the probability of each class becomes a function of the product of the probability of a feature occurring, given the class, as well as the probability of this class. This makes training the model tractable and relatively straightforward. The class prior probabilities and feature conditional probabilities are all estimated from the frequencies present in the dataset. Classification is performed by selecting the most probable class, given the features and class probabilities.

An assumption is also made about the feature distributions (the parameters of which are estimated from the data). Spark ML implements multinomial naive Bayes, which assumes that the feature distribution is a multinomial distribution that represents non-negative frequency counts of the features.

It is suitable for binary features (for example, 1-of-k encoded categorical features), and is commonly used for text and document classification (where, as we have seen in Chapter 4, *Obtaining, Processing, and Preparing Data with Spark,* the bag-of-words vector is a typical feature representation).

 Take a look at the *ML - Naive Bayes* section in the Spark documentation at http://spark.apache.org/docs/latest/ml-classification-regression.html#naive-bayes for more information.

 The Wikipedia page at http://en.wikipedia.org/wiki/Naive_Bayes_classifier has a more detailed explanation of the mathematical formulation.

In the following figure, we have shown the decision function of naive Bayes on our simple binary classification example:

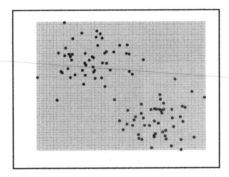

Decision function of naive Bayes for binary classification

Let's train the StumbleUpon dataset by splitting it into 80% training and 20% testing, use naive Bayes from Spark to build the model, and get evaluation metrics around the test data as follows:

```
// split data randomly into training and testing dataset
val Array(training, test) = dataFrame.randomSplit(Array(0.8, 0.2), seed =
12345)

// Set up Pipeline
val stages = new mutable.ArrayBuffer[PipelineStage]()

val labelIndexer = new StringIndexer()
  .setInputCol("label")
  .setOutputCol("indexedLabel")
stages += labelIndexer

// create naive bayes model
val nb = new NaiveBayes()

stages += vectorAssembler
stages += nb
val pipeline = new Pipeline().setStages(stages.toArray)

// Fit the Pipeline
val startTime = System.nanoTime()
val model = pipeline.fit(training)
val elapsedTime = (System.nanoTime() - startTime) / 1e9
println(s"Training time: $elapsedTime seconds")

val holdout = model.transform(test).select("prediction","label")
```

```
// Select (prediction, true label) and compute test error
val evaluator = new MulticlassClassificationEvaluator()
  .setLabelCol("label")
  .setPredictionCol("prediction")
  .setMetricName("accuracy")
val mAccuracy = evaluator.evaluate(holdout)
println("Test set accuracy = " + mAccuracy)
```

You will see the following output displayed:

```
Training time: 2.114725642 seconds
Accuracy: 0.5660377358490566
```

The complete code listing is available at `https://github.com/ml-resources/spark-ml/bl ob/branch-ed2/Chapter_06/2.0.0/scala-spark-app/src/main/scala/org/sparksample s/classification/stumbleupon/NaiveBayesPipeline.scala`.

The visualization of predicted and actual data in a two-dimensional scatter plot is shown here:

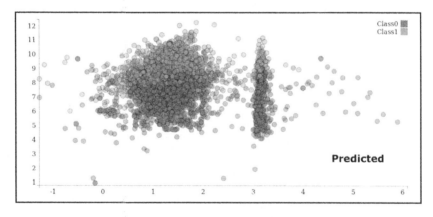

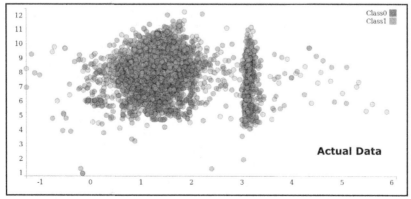

Decision trees

The Decision tree model is a powerful, non-probabilistic technique, which can capture more complex non-linear patterns and feature interactions. They have been shown to perform well on many tasks, are relatively easy to understand and interpret, can handle categorical and numerical features, and do not require input data to be scaled or standardized. They are well-suited to be included in ensemble methods (for example, ensembles of decision tree models, which are called decision forests).

The decision tree model constructs a tree, where the leaves represent a class assignment to class 0 or 1, and the branches are a set of features. In the following figure, we show a simple decision tree where the binary outcome is **Stay at home** or **Go to beach!**. The features are the weather outside.

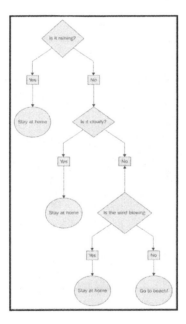

A simple decision tree

The decision tree algorithm is a top-down approach, which begins with a root node (or feature), and then selects a feature at each step that gives the best split of the dataset as measured by the information gain of this split. The information gain is computed from the node impurity (which is the extent to which the labels at the node are similar, or homogenous) minus the weighted sum of the impurities for the two child nodes that would be created by the split. For classification tasks, there are two measures that can be used to select the best split. These are Gini impurity and entropy.

See the *ML Library - Decision Tree* section in the *Spark Programming Guide* at `http://spark.apache.org/docs/latest/ml-classification-regressi on.html#decision-tree-classifier`for further details on the decision tree algorithm and impurity measures for classification.

In the following screenshot, we have plotted the decision boundary for the decision tree model, as we did for the other models earlier. We can see that the decision tree is able to fit complex, non-linear models:

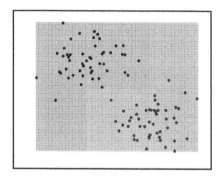

Decision function for a decision tree for binary classification

Let's train the StumbleUpon dataset by splitting it into 80% training and 20% testing, use decision trees from Spark to build the model, and get evaluation metrics around the test data as follows:

```
// split data randomly into training and testing dataset
val Array(training, test) = dataFrame.randomSplit(Array(0.8, 0.2), seed =
12345)

// Set up Pipeline
val stages = new mutable.ArrayBuffer[PipelineStage]()

val labelIndexer = new StringIndexer()
  .setInputCol("label")
  .setOutputCol("indexedLabel")
stages += labelIndexer

// create Decision Tree Model
val dt = new DecisionTreeClassifier()
  .setFeaturesCol(vectorAssembler.getOutputCol)
  .setLabelCol("indexedLabel")
  .setMaxDepth(5)
  .setMaxBins(32)
  .setMinInstancesPerNode(1)
```

```
    .setMinInfoGain(0.0)
    .setCacheNodeIds(false)
    .setCheckpointInterval(10)

stages += vectorAssembler
stages += dt
val pipeline = new Pipeline().setStages(stages.toArray)

// Fit the Pipeline
val startTime = System.nanoTime()
val model = pipeline.fit(training)
val elapsedTime = (System.nanoTime() - startTime) / 1e9
println(s"Training time: $elapsedTime seconds")

val holdout = model.transform(test).select("prediction","label")

// Select (prediction, true label) and compute test error
val evaluator = new MulticlassClassificationEvaluator()
    .setLabelCol("label")
    .setPredictionCol("prediction")
    .setMetricName("accuracy")
val mAccuracy = evaluator.evaluate(holdout)
println("Test set accuracy = " + mAccuracy)
```

You will see the following output displayed:

Accuracy: 0.3786163522012579

The code listing is available at https://github.com/ml-resources/spark-ml/blob/branch-ed2/Chapter_06/2.0.0/scala-spark-app/src/main/scala/org/sparksamples/classification/stumbleupon/DecisionTreePipeline.scala.

The visualization of predicted and actual data in a two-dimensional scatter plot is shown in the following figures:

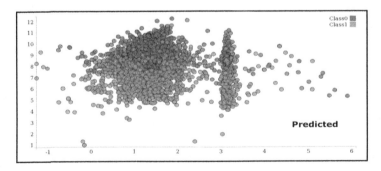

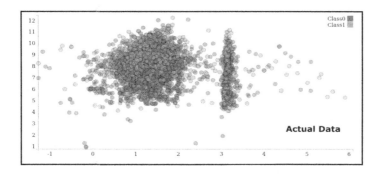

Ensembles of trees

The ensemble method is a machine learning algorithm that creates a model composed of a set of other base models. Spark machine learning supports two major ensemble algorithms: RandomForest and GradientBoostedTrees.

Random Forests

Random Forests are known as ensembles of decision trees, formed by combining many decision trees. Like decision trees, random forests can handle categorical features, support multiclass classification, and don't require feature scaling.

Spark ML supports random forests for both binary and multiclass classification and regression using both continuous and categorical features.

Let's train the sample lib SVM data by splitting it into 80% training and 20% testing, use Random Forest Classifier from Spark to build the model, and get evaluation metrics around the test data. The model can be persisted and loaded for later use.

Let's train the StumbleUpon dataset by splitting it into 80% training and 20% testing, use Random Forest Trees from Spark to build the model, and get evaluation metrics around the test data:

```
// split data randomly into training and testing dataset
val Array(training, test) = dataFrame.randomSplit(Array(0.8, 0.2), seed =
12345)

// Set up Pipeline
val stages = new mutable.ArrayBuffer[PipelineStage]()

val labelIndexer = new StringIndexer()
  .setInputCol("label")
```

```
    .setOutputCol("indexedLabel")
stages += labelIndexer

// create Random Forest Model
val rf = new RandomForestClassifier()
  .setFeaturesCol(vectorAssembler.getOutputCol)
  .setLabelCol("indexedLabel")
  .setNumTrees(20)
  .setMaxDepth(5)
  .setMaxBins(32)
  .setMinInstancesPerNode(1)
  .setMinInfoGain(0.0)
  .setCacheNodeIds(false)
  .setCheckpointInterval(10)

stages += vectorAssembler
stages += rf
val pipeline = new Pipeline().setStages(stages.toArray)

// Fit the Pipeline
val startTime = System.nanoTime()
val model = pipeline.fit(training)
val elapsedTime = (System.nanoTime() - startTime) / 1e9
println(s"Training time: $elapsedTime seconds")

val holdout = model.transform(test).select("prediction","label")

// Select (prediction, true label) and compute test error
val evaluator = new MulticlassClassificationEvaluator()
  .setLabelCol("label")
  .setPredictionCol("prediction")
  .setMetricName("accuracy")
val mAccuracy = evaluator.evaluate(holdout)
println("Test set accuracy = " + mAccuracy)
```

You will see the following output displayed:

```
Accuracy: 0.348
```

The complete code listing is available at https://github.com/ml-resources/spark-ml/blob/branch-ed2/Chapter_06/2.0.0/scala-spark-app/src/main/scala/org/sparksamples/classification/stumbleupon/RandomForestPipeline.scala.

The visualization of predicted and actual data in a two-dimensional scatter plot is shown here:

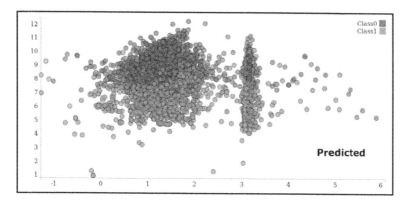

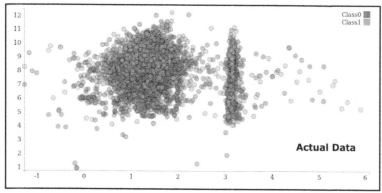

Gradient-Boosted Trees

Gradient-Boosted Trees are ensembles of decision trees. Gradient-Boosted Trees iteratively train decision trees to minimize loss function. Gradient-Boosted Trees handle categorical features, support multiclass classification, and don't require feature scaling.

Spark ML implements Gradient-Boosted Trees using the existing decision tree implementation. It supports both classification and regression.

Let's train the StumbleUpon dataset by splitting it into 80% training and 20% testing, use Gradient-Boosted Trees from Spark to build the model, and get evaluation metrics around the test data as follows:

```
// split data randomly into training and testing dataset
val Array(training, test) = dataFrame.randomSplit(Array(0.8, 0.2), seed =
12345)

// Set up Pipeline
```

```
val stages = new mutable.ArrayBuffer[PipelineStage]()

val labelIndexer = new StringIndexer()
  .setInputCol("label")
  .setOutputCol("indexedLabel")
stages += labelIndexer

// create GBT Model
val gbt = new GBTClassifier()
  .setFeaturesCol(vectorAssembler.getOutputCol)
  .setLabelCol("indexedLabel")
  .setMaxIter(10)

stages += vectorAssembler
stages += gbt
val pipeline = new Pipeline().setStages(stages.toArray)

// Fit the Pipeline
val startTime = System.nanoTime()
val model = pipeline.fit(training)
val elapsedTime = (System.nanoTime() - startTime) / 1e9
println(s"Training time: $elapsedTime seconds")

val holdout = model.transform(test).select("prediction","label")

// have to do a type conversion for RegressionMetrics
val rm = new RegressionMetrics(holdout.rdd.map(x =>
(x(0).asInstanceOf[Double], x(1).asInstanceOf[Double])))

logger.info("Test Metrics")
logger.info("Test Explained Variance:")
logger.info(rm.explainedVariance)
logger.info("Test R^2 Coef:")
logger.info(rm.r2)
logger.info("Test MSE:")
logger.info(rm.meanSquaredError)
logger.info("Test RMSE:")
logger.info(rm.rootMeanSquaredError)

val predictions =
model.transform(test).select("prediction").rdd.map(_.getDouble(0))
val labels = model.transform(test).select("label").rdd.map(_.getDouble(0))
val accuracy = new MulticlassMetrics(predictions.zip(labels)).precision
println(s"  Accuracy : $accuracy")
```

You will see the following output displayed:

```
Accuracy: 0.3647
```

The code listing can be found at `https://github.com/ml-resources/spark-ml/blob/bra nch-ed2/Chapter_06/2.0.0/scala-spark-app/src/main/scala/org/sparksamples/clas sification/stumbleupon/GradientBoostedTreePipeline.scala`.

The visualization of predictions in a two-dimensional scatter plot is shown in the following figures:

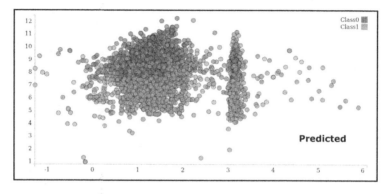

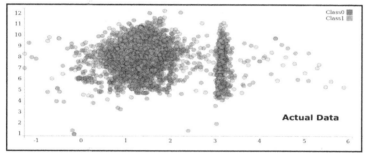

Multilayer perceptron classifier

The neural network is a complex adaptive system, which changes its internal structure based on the information flowing through it using weights. Optimizing the weights of a multilayered neural network is called **backpropagation**. Backpropagation is a bit beyond the scope of this book, and involves an activation function and basic calculus.

The multilayer perceptron classifier is based on a feed-forward artificial neural network. It consists of multiple layers. Each neural layer is completely connected to the next neural layer in the network, and nodes in the input layer denote the input data. All other nodes map inputs to the outputs by performing a linear combination of the inputs with the nodes' weights and bias, and by applying an activation or link function.

Let's train the sample `libsvm` data by splitting it into 80% training and 20% testing, use Multi Layer Perceptron classifier from Spark to build the model, and get evaluation metrics around the test data:

```scala
package org.sparksamples.classification.stumbleupon

import org.apache.spark.ml.classification.MultilayerPerceptronClassifier
import org.apache.spark.ml.evaluation.MulticlassClassificationEvaluator
import org.apache.spark.sql.SparkSession

// set VM Option as -Dspark.master=local[1]
object MultilayerPerceptronClassifierExample {

  def main(args: Array[String]): Unit = {
    val spark = SparkSession
      .builder
      .appName("MultilayerPerceptronClassifierExample")
      .getOrCreate()

    // Load the data stored in LIBSVM format as a DataFrame.
    val data = spark.read.format("libsvm")
.load("/Users/manpreet.singh/Sandbox/codehub/github/machinelearning/spark-
ml/Chapter_06/2.0.0/scala-spark-
app/src/main/scala/org/sparksamples/classification/dataset/spark-
data/sample_multiclass_classification_data.txt")

    // Split the data into train and test
    val splits = data.randomSplit(Array(0.8, 0.2), seed = 1234L)
    val train = splits(0)
    val test = splits(1)

    // specify layers for the neural network:
    // input layer of size 4 (features),
    //two intermediate of size 5 and 4
    // and output of size 3 (classes)
    val layers = Array[Int](4, 5, 4, 3)

    // create the trainer and set its parameters
    val trainer = new MultilayerPerceptronClassifier()
      .setLayers(layers)
      .setBlockSize(128)
      .setSeed(1234L)
      .setMaxIter(100)

    // train the model
    val model = trainer.fit(train)

    // compute accuracy on the test set
```

```
val result = model.transform(test)
val predictionAndLabels = result.select("prediction", "label")
val evaluator = new MulticlassClassificationEvaluator()
  .setMetricName("accuracy")

println("Test set accuracy = " +
  evaluator.evaluate(predictionAndLabels))

spark.stop()
  }
}
```

You will see the following output displayed:

```
Precision = 1.0
```

The code listing is available at https://github.com/ml-resources/spark-ml/blob/branc
h-ed2/Chapter_06/2.0.0/scala-spark-app/src/main/scala/org/sparksamples/classi
fication/stumbleupon/MultilayerPerceptronClassifierExample.scala.

 Before we proceed further, please note that the following examples for
Feature Extraction and Classification use the MLLib package from Spark
v1.6. Kindly follow the code listing mentioned earlier to use Spark v2.0
Dataframe-based APIs. As of Spark 2.0, RDD-based APIs have entered
maintenance mode.

Extracting the right features from your data

You might recall from Chapter 4, *Obtaining, Processing, and Preparing Data with Spark*, that
the majority of machine learning models operate on numerical data in the form of feature
vectors. In addition, for supervised learning methods such as classification and regression,
we need to provide the target variable (or variables in the case of multiclass situations)
together with the feature vector.

Classification models in MLlib operate on instances of LabeledPoint, which is a wrapper
around the target variable (called label) and the feature vector.

```
case class LabeledPoint(label: Double, features: Vector)
```

While in most examples of using classification, you will come across existing datasets that
are already in the vector format, in practice, you will usually start with raw data that needs
to be transformed into features. As we have already seen, this can involve preprocessing
and transformation such as binning numerical features, scaling and normalizing features,
and using 1-of-k encodings for categorical features.

Training classification models

Now that we have extracted some basic features from our dataset and created our input RDD, we are ready to train a number of models. To compare the performance and use of different models, we will train a model using logistic regression, SVM, naive Bayes, and a decision tree. You will notice that training each model looks nearly identical, although each has its own specific model parameters, which can be set. Spark ML sets sensible defaults in most cases, but in practice, the best parameter setting should be selected using evaluation techniques, which we will cover later in this chapter.

Training a classification model on the Kaggle/StumbleUpon evergreen classification dataset

We can now apply the models from Spark ML to our input data. First, we need to import the required classes, and set up some minimal input parameters for each model. For logistic regression and SVM, this is the number of iterations while, for the decision tree model, it is the maximum tree depth.

```
import
org.apache.spark.mllib.classification.LogisticRegressionWithSGD
import org.apache.spark.mllib.classification.SVMWithSGD
import org.apache.spark.mllib.classification.NaiveBayes
import org.apache.spark.mllib.tree.DecisionTree
import org.apache.spark.mllib.tree.configuration.Algo
import org.apache.spark.mllib.tree.impurity.Entropy
val numIterations = 10
val maxTreeDepth = 5
```

Now, train each model in turn. First, we will train logistic regression as follows:

```
val lrModel = LogisticRegressionWithSGD.train(data, numIterations)
```

You will see the following output:

```
. . .
14/12/06 13:41:47 INFO DAGScheduler: Job 81 finished: reduce at
RDDFunctions.scala:112, took 0.011968 s
14/12/06 13:41:47 INFO GradientDescent: GradientDescent.runMiniBatchSGD
finished. Last 10 stochastic losses 0.6931471805599474, 1196521.395699124,
Infinity, 1861127.002201189, Infinity, 2639638.049627607, Infinity,
Infinity, Infinity, Infinity
lrModel: org.apache.spark.mllib.classification.LogisticRegressionModel =
```

```
(weights=[-0.11372778986947886,-0.511619752777837,
...
```

Next up, we will train an SVM model like this:

```
val svmModel = SVMWithSGD.train(data, numIterations)
```

You will now see the following output:

```
...
14/12/06 13:43:08 INFO DAGScheduler: Job 94 finished: reduce at
RDDFunctions.scala:112, took 0.007192 s
14/12/06 13:43:08 INFO GradientDescent: GradientDescent.runMiniBatchSGD
finished. Last 10 stochastic losses 1.0, 2398226.619666797,
2196192.9647478117, 3057987.2024311484, 271452.9038284356,
3158131.191895948, 1041799.350498323, 1507522.941537049,
1754560.9909073508, 136866.76745605646
svmModel: org.apache.spark.mllib.classification.SVMModel =
(weights=[-0.12218838697834929,-0.5275107581589767,
...
```

Then, we will train the naive Bayes model; remember to use your special non-negative feature dataset:

```
val nbModel = NaiveBayes.train(nbData)
```

The following is the output:

```
...
14/12/06 13:44:48 INFO DAGScheduler: Job 95 finished: collect at
NaiveBayes.scala:120, took 0.441273 s
nbModel: org.apache.spark.mllib.classification.NaiveBayesModel =
org.apache.spark.mllib.classification.NaiveBayesModel@666ac612
...
```

Finally, we will train our decision tree.

```
val dtModel = DecisionTree.train(data, Algo.Classification, Entropy,
maxTreeDepth)
```

The output is as follows:

```
...
14/12/06 13:46:03 INFO DAGScheduler: Job 104 finished: collectAsMap at
DecisionTree.scala:653, took 0.031338 s
...
total: 0.343024
findSplitsBins: 0.119499
findBestSplits: 0.200352
```

```
chooseSplits: 0.199705
dtModel: org.apache.spark.mllib.tree.model.DecisionTreeModel =
DecisionTreeModel classifier of depth 5 with 61 nodes
...
```

Notice that we set the mode or Algo of the decision tree to `Classification`, and we used the `Entropy` impurity measure.

Using classification models

We now have four models trained on our input labels and features. We will now see how to use these models to make predictions on our dataset. For now, we will use the same training data to illustrate the predict method of each model.

Generating predictions for the Kaggle/StumbleUpon evergreen classification dataset

We will use our logistic regression model as an example (the other models are used in the same way):

```
val dataPoint = data.first
val prediction = lrModel.predict(dataPoint.features)
```

The following is the output:

prediction: Double = 1.0

We saw that, for the first data point in our training dataset, the model predicted a label of 1 (that is, evergreen). Let's examine the true label for this data point.

```
val trueLabel = dataPoint.label
```

You can see the following output:

trueLabel: Double = 0.0

So, in this case, our model got it wrong!

We can also make predictions in bulk by passing in an `RDD[Vector]` as input:

```
val predictions = lrModel.predict(data.map(lp => lp.features))
```

```
predictions.take(5)
```

The following is the output:

```
Array[Double] = Array(1.0, 1.0, 1.0, 1.0, 1.0)
```

Evaluating the performance of classification models

When we make predictions using our model, as we did earlier, how do we know whether the predictions are good or not? We need to be able to evaluate how well our model performs. Evaluation metrics commonly used in binary classification include prediction accuracy and error, precision and recall, the area under the precision-recall curve, the receiver operating characteristic (ROC) curve, the area under ROC curve (AUC), and the F-measure.

Accuracy and prediction error

The prediction error for binary classification is possibly the simplest measure available. It is the number of training examples that are misclassified, divided by the total number of examples. Similarly, accuracy is the number of correctly classified examples divided by the total examples.

We can calculate the accuracy of our models in our training data by making predictions on each input feature and comparing them to the true label. We will sum up the number of correctly classified instances, and divide this by the total number of data points to get the average classification accuracy.

```
val lrTotalCorrect = data.map { point =>
  if (lrModel.predict(point.features) == point.label) 1 else 0
}.sum
val lrAccuracy = lrTotalCorrect / data.count
```

The output is as follows:

```
lrAccuracy: Double = 0.5146720757268425
```

This gives us 51.5 percent accuracy, which doesn't look particularly impressive! Our model got only half of the training examples correct, which seems to be about as good as a random chance.

The predictions made by the model are not naturally exactly 1 or 0. The output is usually a real number that must be turned into a class prediction. This is done through the use of a threshold in the classifier's decision or scoring function.

For example, binary logistic regression is a probabilistic model, which returns the estimated probability of class 1 in its scoring function. Thus, a decision threshold of 0.5 is typical. That is, if the estimated probability of being in class 1 is higher than 50 percent, the model decides to classify the point as class 1; otherwise, it will be classified as class 0.

The threshold itself is effectively a model parameter that can be tuned in some models. It also plays a role in evaluation measures, as we will see now.

What about the other models? Let's compute the accuracy for the other three:

```
val svmTotalCorrect = data.map { point =>
  if (svmModel.predict(point.features) == point.label) 1 else 0
}.sum
val nbTotalCorrect = nbData.map { point =>
  if (nbModel.predict(point.features) == point.label) 1 else 0
}.sum
```

Note that the decision tree prediction threshold needs to be specified explicitly, as highlighted here:

```
val dtTotalCorrect = data.map { point =>
  val score = dtModel.predict(point.features)
  val predicted = if (score > 0.5) 1 else 0
  if (predicted == point.label) 1 else 0
}.sum
```

We can now inspect the accuracy for the other three models. First, the SVM model, which is as follows:

```
val svmAccuracy = svmTotalCorrect / numData
```

Here is the output for the SVM model:

svmAccuracy: Double = 0.5146720757268425

Next, is our naive Bayes model.

```
val nbAccuracy = nbTotalCorrect / numData
```

The output is as follows:

nbAccuracy: Double = 0.5803921568627451

Finally, we compute the accuracy for the decision tree:

```
val dtAccuracy = dtTotalCorrect / numData
```

The output is this:

dtAccuracy: Double = 0.6482758620689655

We can see that both SVM and naive Bayes also performed quite poorly. The decision tree model is better with 65% accuracy, but this is still not particularly high.

Precision and recall

In information retrieval, precision is a commonly used measure of the quality of the results, while recall is a measure of the completeness of the results.

In the binary classification context, precision is defined as the number of true positives (that is, the number of examples correctly predicted as class 1) divided by the sum of true positives and false positives (that is, the number of examples that were incorrectly predicted as class 1). Thus, we can see that a precision of 1.0 (or 100%) is achieved if every example predicted by the classifier to be class 1 is, in fact, in class 1 (that is, there are no false positives).

Recall is defined as the number of true positives divided by the sum of true positives and false negatives (that is, the number of examples that were in class 1, but were predicted as class 0 by the model). We can see that a recall of 1.0 (or 100%) is achieved if the model doesn't miss any examples that were in class 1 (that is, there are no false negatives).

Generally, precision and recall are inversely related; often, higher precision is related to lower recall and vice versa. To illustrate this, assume that we built a model that always predicted class 1. In this case, the model predictions would have no false negatives, because the model always predicts 1; it will not miss any of class 1. Thus, the recall will be 1.0 for this model. On the other hand, the false positive rate could be very high, meaning precision would be low (this depends on the exact distribution of the classes in the dataset).

Precision and recall are not particularly useful as standalone metrics, but are typically used together to form an aggregate or averaged metric. Precision and recall are also dependent on the threshold selected for the model.

Intuitively, the following are some threshold levels where a model will always predict class 1. Hence, it will have a recall of 1, but most likely, it will have low precision. At a high enough threshold, the model will always predict class 0. The model will then have a recall of 0, since it cannot achieve any true positives, and will likely have many false negatives. Furthermore, its precision score will be undefined, as it will achieve zero true positives and zero false positives.

The precision-recall (PR) curve shown in the following figure plots precision against the recall outcomes for a given model, as the decision threshold of the classifier is changed. The area under this PR curve is referred to as the average precision. Intuitively, an area under the PR curve of 1.0 will equate to a perfect classifier that will achieve 100 percent in both precision and recall.

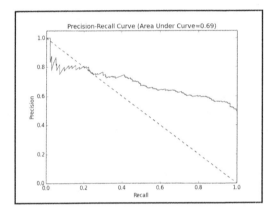

Precision-recall curve

 See http://en.wikipedia.org/wiki/Precision_and_recall and http://en.wikipedia.org/wiki/Average_precision#Average_precision for more details on precision, recall, and area under the PR curve.

ROC curve and AUC

The ROC curve is a concept similar to the PR curve. It is a graphical illustration of the true positive rate against the false positive rate for a classifier.

The true positive rate (TPR) is the number of true positives divided by the sum of true positives and false negatives. In other words, it is the ratio of true positives to all positive examples. This is the same as the recall we saw earlier, and is also commonly referred to as sensitivity.

The false positive rate (**FPR**) is the number of false positives divided by the sum of false positives and true negatives (that is, the number of examples correctly predicted as class 0). In other words, it is the ratio of false positives to all negative examples.

In a manner similar to precision and recall, the ROC curve (plotted in the following figure) represents the classifier's performance trade-off of TPR against FPR, for different decision thresholds. Each point on the curve represents a different threshold in the decision function for the classifier.

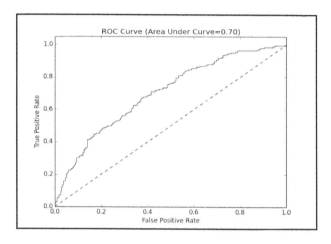

The ROC curve

The area under the ROC curve (commonly referred to as AUC) represents an average value. Again, an AUC of 1.0 will represent a perfect classifier. An area of 0.5 is referred to as the random score. Thus, a model that achieves an AUC of 0.5 is no better than guessing randomly.

As both, the area under the PR curve and the area under the ROC curve, are effectively normalized (with a minimum of 0 and maximum of 1), we can use these measures to compare models with differing parameter settings, and even compare completely different models. Thus, these metrics are popular for model evaluation and selection purposes.

MLlib comes with a set of built-in routines to compute the area under the PR and ROC curves for binary classification. Here, we will compute these metrics for each of our models:

```
import org.apache.spark.mllib.evaluation.BinaryClassificationMetrics
val metrics = Seq(lrModel, svmModel).map { model =>
  val scoreAndLabels = data.map { point =>
    (model.predict(point.features), point.label)
  }
```

```
    val metrics = new BinaryClassificationMetrics(scoreAndLabels)
    (model.getClass.getSimpleName, metrics.areaUnderPR, metrics.areaUnderROC)
}
```

As we did previously to train the naive Bayes model and computing accuracy, we need to use the special `nbData` version of the dataset that we created to compute the classification metrics.

```
val nbMetrics = Seq(nbModel).map{ model =>
  val scoreAndLabels = nbData.map { point =>
    val score = model.predict(point.features)
    (if (score > 0.5) 1.0 else 0.0, point.label)
  }
  val metrics = new BinaryClassificationMetrics(scoreAndLabels)
  (model.getClass.getSimpleName, metrics.areaUnderPR,
  metrics.areaUnderROC)
}
```

Note that because the `DecisionTreeModel` model does not implement the `ClassificationModel` interface that is implemented by the other three models, we need to compute the results separately for this model in the following code:

```
val dtMetrics = Seq(dtModel).map{ model =>
  val scoreAndLabels = data.map { point =>
    val score = model.predict(point.features)
    (if (score > 0.5) 1.0 else 0.0, point.label)
  }
  val metrics = new BinaryClassificationMetrics(scoreAndLabels)
  (model.getClass.getSimpleName, metrics.areaUnderPR,
  metrics.areaUnderROC)
}
val allMetrics = metrics ++ nbMetrics ++ dtMetrics
allMetrics.foreach{ case (m, pr, roc) =>
  println(f"$m, Area under PR: ${pr * 100.0}%2.4f%%, Area under
  ROC: ${roc * 100.0}%2.4f%%")
}
```

Your output will look similar to the one here:

```
LogisticRegressionModel, Area under PR: 75.6759%, Area under ROC: 50.1418%
SVMModel, Area under PR: 75.6759%, Area under ROC: 50.1418%
NaiveBayesModel, Area under PR: 68.0851%, Area under ROC: 58.3559%
DecisionTreeModel, Area under PR: 74.3081%, Area under ROC: 64.8837%
```

We can see that all models achieve broadly similar results for the average precision metric.

Logistic regression and SVM achieve results of around 0.5 for AUC. This indicates that they do no better than random chance! Our naive Bayes and decision tree models fare a little better, achieving an AUC of 0.58 and 0.65, respectively. Still, this is not a very good result in terms of binary classification performance.

> While we don't cover multiclass classification here, MLlib provides a similar evaluation class called `MulticlassMetrics`, which provides averaged versions of many common metrics.

Improving model performance and tuning parameters

So, what went wrong? Why have our sophisticated models achieved nothing better than random chance? Is there a problem with our models?

Recall that we started out by just throwing the data at our model. In fact, we didn't even throw all our data at the model, just the numeric columns that were easy to use. Furthermore, we didn't do a lot of analysis on these numeric features.

Feature standardization

Many models that we employ make inherent assumptions about the distribution or scale of input data. One of the most common forms of assumption is about normally-distributed features. Let's take a deeper look at the distribution of our features.

To do this, we can represent the feature vectors as a distributed matrix in MLlib, using the `RowMatrix` class. `RowMatrix` is an RDD made up of vectors, where each vector is a row of our matrix.

The `RowMatrix` class comes with some useful methods to operate on the matrix, one of which is a utility to compute statistics on the columns of the matrix.

```
import org.apache.spark.mllib.linalg.distributed.RowMatrix
val vectors = data.map(lp => lp.features)
val matrix = new RowMatrix(vectors)
val matrixSummary = matrix.computeColumnSummaryStatistics()
```

The following code statement will print the mean of the matrix:

```
println(matrixSummary.mean)
```

Here is the output:

```
[0.41225805299526636,2.761823191986623,0.46823047328614004, ...
```

The following code statement will print the minimum value of the matrix:

```
println(matrixSummary.min)
```

Here is the output:

```
[0.0,0.0,0.0,0.0,0.0,0.0,0.0,-1.0,0.0,0.0,0.0,0.045564223,-1.0, ...
```

The following code statement will print the maximum value of the matrix:

```
println(matrixSummary.max)
```

The output is as follows:

```
[0.999426,363.0,1.0,1.0,0.980392157,0.980392157,21.0,0.25,0.0,0.444444444,
...
```

The following code statement will print the variance of the matrix:

```
println(matrixSummary.variance)
```

The output of the variance is:

```
[0.1097424416755897,74.30082476809638,0.04126316989120246, ...
```

The following code statement will print the non-zero number of the matrix:

```
println(matrixSummary.numNonzeros)
```

Here is the output:

```
[5053.0,7354.0,7172.0,6821.0,6160.0,5128.0,7350.0,1257.0,0.0, ...
```

The `computeColumnSummaryStatistics` method computes a number of statistics over each column of features including the mean and variance, storing each of these in a vector with one entry per column (that is, one entry per feature in our case).

Looking at the preceding output for mean and variance, we can see quite clearly that the second feature has a much higher mean and variance than some of the other features (you will find a few other features that are similar, and a few others that are more extreme). So, our data definitely does not conform to a standard Gaussian distribution in its raw form. To get the data in a more suitable form for our models, we can standardize each feature such that it has zero mean and unit standard deviation. We can do this by subtracting the column mean from each feature value, and then scaling it by dividing it by the column standard deviation for the feature as follows:

$$(x - \mu) / sqrt(variance)$$

Practically, for each feature vector in our input dataset, we can simply perform an element-wise subtraction of the preceding mean vector from the feature vector, and then perform an element-wise division of the feature vector by the vector of feature standard deviations. The standard deviation vector itself can be obtained by performing an element-wise square root operation on the variance vector.

As we mentioned in Chapter 4, *Obtaining, Processing, and Preparing Data with Spark*, we fortunately have access to a convenience method from Spark's StandardScaler to accomplish this.

StandardScaler works in much the same way as the Normalizer feature we used in that chapter. We will instantiate it by passing in two arguments that tell it whether to subtract the mean from the data, and whether to apply standard deviation scaling. We will then fit StandardScaler on our input vectors. Finally, we will pass in an input vector to the transform function, which will then return a normalized vector. We will do this within the following map function to preserve the label from our dataset:

```
import org.apache.spark.mllib.feature.StandardScaler
val scaler = new StandardScaler(withMean = true, withStd =
true).fit(vectors)
val scaledData = data.map(lp => LabeledPoint(lp.label,
scaler.transform(lp.features)))
```

Our data should now be standardized. Let's inspect the first row of the original and standardized features.

```
println(data.first.features)
```

The output of the preceding line of code is as follows:

```
[0.789131,2.055555556,0.676470588,0.205882353,
```

The following code will be the first row of the standardized features:

```
println(scaledData.first.features)
```

The output is as follows:

```
[1.1376439023494747,-0.08193556218743517,1.025134766284205,-0.0558631837375
738,
```

As we can see, the first feature has been transformed by applying the standardization formula. We can check this by subtracting the mean (which we computed earlier) from the first feature, and dividing the result by the square root of the variance (which we computed earlier).

```
println((0.789131 - 0.41225805299526636)/ math.sqrt(0.1097424416755897))
```

The result should be equal to the first element of our scaled vector:

```
1.137647336497682
```

We can now retrain our model using the standardized data. We will use only the logistic regression model to illustrate the impact of feature standardization (since the decision tree and naive Bayes are not impacted by this).

```
val lrModelScaled = LogisticRegressionWithSGD.train(scaledData,
numIterations)
val lrTotalCorrectScaled = scaledData.map { point =>
  if (lrModelScaled.predict(point.features) == point.label) 1 else
  0
}.sum
val lrAccuracyScaled = lrTotalCorrectScaled / numData
val lrPredictionsVsTrue = scaledData.map { point =>
  (lrModelScaled.predict(point.features), point.label)
}
val lrMetricsScaled = new BinaryClassificationMetrics(lrPredictionsVsTrue)
val lrPr = lrMetricsScaled.areaUnderPR
val lrRoc = lrMetricsScaled.areaUnderROC
println(f"${lrModelScaled.getClass.getSimpleName}\nAccuracy:
${lrAccuracyScaled * 100}%2.4f%%\nArea under PR: ${lrPr *
100.0}%2.4f%%\nArea under ROC: ${lrRoc * 100.0}%2.4f%%")
```

The result should look similar to this:

```
LogisticRegressionModel
Accuracy: 62.0419%
Area under PR: 72.7254%
Area under ROC: 61.9663%
```

Simply through standardizing our features, we have improved the logistic regression performance for accuracy and AUC from 50%, no better than random, to 62%.

Additional features

We have seen that we need to be careful about standardizing and potentially normalizing our features, and the impact on model performance can be serious. In this case, we used only a portion of the features available. For example, we completely ignored the category variable and the textual content in the boilerplate variable column.

This was done for ease of illustration, but let's assess the impact of adding an additional feature such as the category feature.

First, we will inspect the categories, and form a mapping of index to category, which you might recognize as the basis for a 1-of-k encoding of this categorical feature:

```
val categories = records.map(r => r(3)).distinct.collect.zipWithIndex.toMap
val numCategories = categories.size
println(categories)
```

The output of the different categories is as follows:

```
Map("weather" -> 0, "sports" -> 6, "unknown" -> 4, "computer_internet" ->
12, "?" -> 11, "culture_politics" -> 3, "religion" -> 8, "recreation" -> 2,
"arts_entertainment" -> 9, "health" -> 5, "law_crime" -> 10, "gaming" ->
13, "business" -> 1, "science_technology" -> 7)
```

The following code will print the number of categories:

```
println(numCategories)
```

Here is the output:

14

So, we will need to create a vector of length 14 to represent this feature, and assign a value of 1 for the index of the relevant category for each data point. We can then prepend this new feature vector to the vector of other numerical features, as follows:

```
val dataCategories = records.map { r =>
  val trimmed = r.map(_.replaceAll("\"", ""))
  val label = trimmed(r.size - 1).toInt
  val categoryIdx = categories(r(3))
  val categoryFeatures = Array.ofDim[Double](numCategories)
  categoryFeatures(categoryIdx) = 1.0
```

```
  val otherFeatures = trimmed.slice(4, r.size - 1).map(d => if   (d == "?")
0.0 else d.toDouble)
  val features = categoryFeatures ++ otherFeatures
  LabeledPoint(label, Vectors.dense(features))
}
println(dataCategories.first)
```

You should see output similar to what is shown here. You can see that the first part of our feature vector is now a vector of length 14 with one nonzero entry at the relevant category index.

```
LabeledPoint(0.0[0.0,1.0,0.0,0.0,0.0,0.0,0.0,0.0,0.0,0.0,0.0,0.0,0.0,0.
789131,2.055555556,0.676470588,0.205882353,0.047058824,0.023529412,0.443783
175,0.0,0.0,0.09077381,0.0,0.245831182,0.003883495,1.0,1.0,24.0,0.0,5424.0,
170.0,8.0,0.152941176,0.079129575])
```

Again, since our raw features are not standardized, we should perform this transformation using the same StandardScaler approach that we used earlier before training a new model on this expanded dataset:

```
val scalerCats = new StandardScaler(withMean = true, withStd =
true).fit(dataCategories.map(lp => lp.features))
val scaledDataCats = dataCategories.map(lp => LabeledPoint(lp.label,
scalerCats.transform(lp.features)))
```

We can inspect the features before and after scaling as we did earlier.

```
println(dataCategories.first.features)
```

The output is as follows:

```
0.0,1.0,0.0,0.0,0.0,0.0,0.0,0.0,0.0,0.0,0.0,0.0,0.0,0.789131,2.05555555
6 ...
```

The following code will print the features after scaling:

```
println(scaledDataCats.first.features)
```

You will see the following on the screen:

```
[-0.023261105535492967,2.720728254208072,-0.4464200056407091,-0.22052583608
69135, ...
```

 While the original raw features were sparse (that is, there are many entries that are zero), if we subtract the mean from each entry, we would end up with a non-sparse (dense) representation, as can be seen in the preceding example. This is not a problem in this case as the data size is small, but often large-scale real-world problems have extremely sparse input data with many features (online advertising and text classification are good examples). In this case, it is not advisable to lose this sparsity, as the memory and processing requirements for the equivalent dense representation can quickly explode with many millions of features. We can use `StandardScaler` and set `withMean` to `false` to avoid this.

We're now ready to train a new logistic regression model with our expanded feature set, and then we will evaluate the performance.

```
val lrModelScaledCats = LogisticRegressionWithSGD.train(scaledDataCats,
numIterations)
val lrTotalCorrectScaledCats = scaledDataCats.map { point =>
  if (lrModelScaledCats.predict(point.features) == point.label) 1 else 0
}.sum
val lrAccuracyScaledCats = lrTotalCorrectScaledCats / numData
val lrPredictionsVsTrueCats = scaledDataCats.map { point =>
  (lrModelScaledCats.predict(point.features), point.label)
}
val lrMetricsScaledCats = new
BinaryClassificationMetrics(lrPredictionsVsTrueCats)
val lrPrCats = lrMetricsScaledCats.areaUnderPR
val lrRocCats = lrMetricsScaledCats.areaUnderROC
println(f"${lrModelScaledCats.getClass.getSimpleName}\nAccuracy:
${lrAccuracyScaledCats * 100}%2.4f%%\nArea under PR: ${lrPrCats *
100.0}%2.4f%%\nArea under ROC: ${lrRocCats * 100.0}%2.4f%%")
```

You should see output similar to this one:

```
LogisticRegressionModel
Accuracy: 66.5720%
Area under PR: 75.7964%
Area under ROC: 66.5483%
```

By applying a feature standardization transformation to our data, we improved both the accuracy and AUC measures from 50% to 62%, and then, we achieved a further boost to 66% by adding the category feature into our model (remember to apply the standardization to our new feature set).

The best model performance in the competition was an AUC of 0.88906 (see `http://www.kaggle.com/c/stumbleupon/leaderboard/private`). One approach to achieving performance almost as high is outlined at `http://www.kaggle.com/c/stumbleupon/forums/t/5680/beating-the-benchmark-leaderboard-auc-0-878`.

Notice that there are still features that we have not yet used; most notably, the text features in the boilerplate variable. The leading competition submissions predominantly use the boilerplate features and features based on the raw textual content to achieve their performance. As we saw earlier, while adding category-improved performance, it appears that most of the variables are not very useful as predictors, while the textual content turned out to be highly predictive.

Going through some of the best performing approaches for these competitions can give you a good idea as to how feature extraction and engineering play a critical role in model performance.

Using the correct form of data

Another critical aspect of model performance is using the correct form of data for each model. Previously, we saw that applying a naive Bayes model to our numerical features resulted in very poor performance. Is this because the model itself is deficient?

In this case, recall that MLlib implements a multinomial model. This model works on input in the form of non-zero count data. This can include a binary representation of categorical features (such as the 1-of-k encoding covered previously) or frequency data (such as the frequency of occurrences of words in a document). The numerical features we used initially do not conform to this assumed input distribution, so it is probably unsurprising that the model did so poorly.

To illustrate this, we'll use only the category feature, which, when 1-of-k encoded, is of the correct form for the model. We will create a new dataset as follows:

```
val dataNB = records.map { r =>
  val trimmed = r.map(_.replaceAll("\"", ""))
  val label = trimmed(r.size - 1).toInt
  val categoryIdx = categories(r(3))
  val categoryFeatures = Array.ofDim[Double](numCategories)
```

```
        categoryFeatures(categoryIdx) = 1.0
        LabeledPoint(label, Vectors.dense(categoryFeatures))
}
```

Next, we will train a new naïve Bayes model and evaluate its performance.

```
val nbModelCats = NaiveBayes.train(dataNB)
val nbTotalCorrectCats = dataNB.map { point =>
  if (nbModelCats.predict(point.features) == point.label) 1 else 0
}.sum
val nbAccuracyCats = nbTotalCorrectCats / numData
val nbPredictionsVsTrueCats = dataNB.map { point =>
  (nbModelCats.predict(point.features), point.label)
}
val nbMetricsCats = new
BinaryClassificationMetrics(nbPredictionsVsTrueCats)
val nbPrCats = nbMetricsCats.areaUnderPR
val nbRocCats = nbMetricsCats.areaUnderROC
println(f"${nbModelCats.getClass.getSimpleName}\nAccuracy: ${nbAccuracyCats
* 100}%2.4f%%\nArea under PR: ${nbPrCats * 100.0}%2.4f%%\nArea under ROC:
${nbRocCats * 100.0}%2.4f%%")
```

You should see the following output:

```
NaiveBayesModel
Accuracy: 60.9601%
Area under PR: 74.0522%
Area under ROC: 60.5138%
```

So, by ensuring that we use the correct form of input, we have improved the performance of the naïve Bayes model slightly from 58% to 60%.

Tuning model parameters

The previous section showed the impact of feature extraction and selection on model performance as well as the form of input data and a model's assumptions around data distributions. So far, we have discussed model parameters only in passing, but they also play a significant role in model performance.

MLlib's default train methods use default values for the parameters of each model. Let's take a deeper look at them.

Linear models

Both logistic regression and SVM share the same parameters, because they use the same underlying optimization technique of **stochastic gradient descent** (**SGD**). They differ only in the loss function applied. If we take a look at the class definition for logistic regression in MLlib, we will see the following definition:

```
class LogisticRegressionWithSGD private (
  private var stepSize: Double,
  private var numIterations: Int,
  private var regParam: Double,
  private var miniBatchFraction: Double)
  extends GeneralizedLinearAlgorithm[LogisticRegressionModel] ...
```

We can see that the arguments that can be passed to the constructor are `stepSize`, `numIterations`, `regParam`, and `miniBatchFraction`. Of these, all except `regParam` are related to the underlying optimization technique.

The instantiation code for logistic regression initializes the `gradient`, `updater`, and `optimizer`, and sets the relevant arguments for `optimizer` (`GradientDescent` in this case).

```
private val gradient = new LogisticGradient()
private val updater = new SimpleUpdater()
override val optimizer = new GradientDescent(gradient, updater)
  .setStepSize(stepSize)
  .setNumIterations(numIterations)
  .setRegParam(regParam)
  .setMiniBatchFraction(miniBatchFraction)
```

`LogisticGradient` sets up the logistic loss function that defines our logistic regression model.

While a detailed treatment of optimization techniques is beyond the scope of this book, MLlib provides two optimizers for linear models: SGD and L-BFGS. L-BFGS is often more accurate, and has fewer parameters to tune. SGD is the default, while L-BGFS can currently only be used directly for logistic regression via `LogisticRegressionWithLBFGS`. Try it out yourself, and compare the results to those found with SGD. See `http://spark.apache.org/docs/latest/mllib-optimization.html` for further details.

To investigate the impact of the remaining parameter settings, we will create a helper function, which will train a logistic regression model given a set of parameter inputs. First, we will import the required classes:

```
import org.apache.spark.rdd.RDD
import org.apache.spark.mllib.optimization.Updater
import org.apache.spark.mllib.optimization.SimpleUpdater
import org.apache.spark.mllib.optimization.L1Updater
import org.apache.spark.mllib.optimization.SquaredL2Updater
import org.apache.spark.mllib.classification.ClassificationModel
```

Next, we will define our helper function to train a model given a set of inputs:

```
def trainWithParams(input: RDD[LabeledPoint], regParam: Double,
numIterations: Int, updater: Updater, stepSize: Double) = {
  val lr = new LogisticRegressionWithSGD
  lr.optimizer.setNumIterations(numIterations).
  setUpdater(updater).setRegParam(regParam).setStepSize(stepSize)
  lr.run(input)
}
```

Finally, we will create a second helper function to take the input data and a classification model, and generate the relevant AUC metrics:

```
def createMetrics(label: String, data: RDD[LabeledPoint], model:
ClassificationModel) = {
  val scoreAndLabels = data.map { point =>
    (model.predict(point.features), point.label)
  }
  val metrics = new BinaryClassificationMetrics(scoreAndLabels)
  (label, metrics.areaUnderROC)
}
```

We will also cache our scaled dataset, including categories, to speed up the

multiple model training runs that we will be using to explore these different parameter settings, as follows:

```
scaledDataCats.cache
```

Iterations

Many machine learning methods are iterative in nature, converging to a solution (the optimal weight vector that minimizes the chosen loss function) over a number of iteration steps. SGD typically requires relatively few iterations to converge to a reasonable solution, but can be run for more iterations to improve the solution. We can see this by trying a few different settings for the numIterations parameter, and comparing the AUC results like this:

```
val iterResults = Seq(1, 5, 10, 50).map { param =>
  val model = trainWithParams(scaledDataCats, 0.0, param, new
```

```
SimpleUpdater, 1.0)
  createMetrics(s"$param iterations", scaledDataCats, model)
}
iterResults.foreach { case (param, auc) => println(f"$param, AUC =
${auc * 100}%2.2f%%") }
```

Your output should look like this:

```
1 iterations, AUC = 64.97%
5 iterations, AUC = 66.62%
10 iterations, AUC = 66.55%
50 iterations, AUC = 66.81%
```

So, we can see that the number of iterations has a minor impact on the results once a certain number of iterations have been completed.

Step size

In SGD, the step size parameter controls how far in the direction of the steepest gradient the algorithm takes a step when updating the model weight vector after each training example. A larger step size might speed up convergence, but a step size that is too large might cause problems with convergence, as good solutions are overshot. The learning rate determines the size of the steps we take to reach a (local or global) minimum. In other words, we follow the direction of the slope of the surface created by the objective function downhill until we reach a valley.

We can see the impact of changing the step size here:

```
val stepResults = Seq(0.001, 0.01, 0.1, 1.0, 10.0).map { param =>
  val model = trainWithParams(scaledDataCats, 0.0, numIterations, new
SimpleUpdater, param)
  createMetrics(s"$param step size", scaledDataCats, model)
}
stepResults.foreach { case (param, auc) => println(f"$param, AUC =
${auc * 100}%2.2f%%") }
```

This will give us the following results, which show that increasing the step size too much can begin to negatively impact performance:

```
0.001 step size, AUC = 64.95%
0.01 step size, AUC = 65.00%
0.1 step size, AUC = 65.52%
1.0 step size, AUC = 66.55%
10.0 step size, AUC = 61.92%
```

Regularization

We briefly touched on the Updater class in the preceding logistic regression code. An Updater class in MLlib implements regularization. Regularization can help avoid over-fitting of a model to training data by effectively penalizing model complexity. This can be done by adding a term to the loss function, which acts to increase the loss as a function of the model weight vector.

Regularization is almost always required in real use cases, but is of particular importance when the feature dimension is very high (that is, the effective number of variable weights that can be learned is high) relative to the number of training examples.

When regularization is absent or low, models can tend to overfit. Without regularization, most models will overfit on a training dataset. This is a key reason behind the use of cross-validation techniques for model fitting (which we will cover now).

Before we proceed further, let's define what it means to overfit and underfit data. Overfitting occurs when a model learns details and the noise in training data to an extent that negatively impacts the performance of the model on new data. The model should not follow the training dataset very rigorously, and in underfitting, a model can neither model the training data nor generalize to new data.

Conversely, since applying regularization encourages simpler models, model performance can suffer when regularization is high through underfitting the data.

The forms of regularization available in MLlib are the following:

- SimpleUpdater: This equates to no regularization, and is the default for logistic regression
- SquaredL2Updater: This implements a regularizer based on the squared L2-norm of the weight vector; this is the default for SVM models
- L1Updater: This applies a regularizer based on the L1-norm of the weight vector; this can lead to sparse solutions in the weight vector (as less important weights are pulled towards zero)

 Regularization and its relation to optimization is a broad and heavily researched area. Some more information is available from the following links:

- General regularization overview: http://en.wikipedia.org/wiki/Regularization_(mathematics)
- L2 regularization: http://en.wikipedia.org/wiki/Tikhonov_regularization

- Overfitting and underfitting: `http://en.wikipedia.org/wiki/Overfitting`
  Detailed overview of overfitting and L1 versus L2 regularization:
  `http://citeseerx.ist.psu.edu/viewdoc/download?doi=10.1.1.92.9860&rep=r ep1&type=pdf`

Let's explore the impact of a range of regularization parameters using `SquaredL2Updater`:

```
val regResults = Seq(0.001, 0.01, 0.1, 1.0, 10.0).map { param =>
  val model = trainWithParams(scaledDataCats, param, numIterations, new
SquaredL2Updater, 1.0)
  createMetrics(s"$param L2 regularization parameter",
scaledDataCats, model)
}
regResults.foreach { case (param, auc) => println(f"$param, AUC =
${auc * 100}%2.2f%%") }
```

Your output should look like this:

```
0.001 L2 regularization parameter, AUC = 66.55%
0.01 L2 regularization parameter, AUC = 66.55%
0.1 L2 regularization parameter, AUC = 66.63%
1.0 L2 regularization parameter, AUC = 66.04%
10.0 L2 regularization parameter, AUC = 35.33%
```

As we can see, at low levels of regularization, there is not much impact in model performance. However, as we increase regularization, we can see the impact of under-fitting on our model evaluation.

You will find similar results when using the L1 regularization. Give it a try by performing the same evaluation of regularization parameter against the AUC measure for `L1Updater`.

Decision trees

The decision trees, which controls the maximum depth of the tree and, thus, the complexity of the model. Deeper trees result in more complex models that will be able to fit the data better.

For classification problems, we can also select between two measures of impurity: `Gini` and `Entropy`.

Tuning tree depth and impurity

We will illustrate the impact of tree depth in a similar manner as we did for our logistic regression model.

First, we will need to create another helper function in the Spark shell as follows:

```
import org.apache.spark.mllib.tree.impurity.Impurity
import org.apache.spark.mllib.tree.impurity.Entropy
import org.apache.spark.mllib.tree.impurity.Gini

def trainDTWithParams(input: RDD[LabeledPoint], maxDepth: Int, impurity:
Impurity) = {
  DecisionTree.train(input, Algo.Classification, impurity, maxDepth)
}
```

Now, we're ready to compute our AUC metric for different settings of tree depth. We will simply use our original dataset in this example, since we do not need the data to be standardized.

> Note that decision tree models generally do not require features to be standardized or normalized, nor do they require categorical features to be binary-encoded.

First, train the model using the Entropy impurity measure and varying tree depths like this:

```
val dtResultsEntropy = Seq(1, 2, 3, 4, 5, 10, 20).map { param =>
  val model = trainDTWithParams(data, param, Entropy)
  val scoreAndLabels = data.map { point =>
    val score = model.predict(point.features)
    (if (score > 0.5) 1.0 else 0.0, point.label)
  }
  val metrics = new BinaryClassificationMetrics(scoreAndLabels)
  (s"$param tree depth", metrics.areaUnderROC)
}
dtResultsEntropy.foreach { case (param, auc) => println(f"$param, AUC =
${auc * 100}%2.2f%%") }
```

This preceding code should output the results shown here:

```
1 tree depth, AUC = 59.33%
2 tree depth, AUC = 61.68%
3 tree depth, AUC = 62.61%
4 tree depth, AUC = 63.63%
5 tree depth, AUC = 64.88%
```

```
10 tree depth, AUC = 76.26%
20 tree depth, AUC = 98.45%
```

Next, we will perform the same computation using the `Gini` impurity measure (we omitted the code as it is very similar, but it can be found in the code bundle). Your results should look something like this:

```
1 tree depth, AUC = 59.33%
2 tree depth, AUC = 61.68%
3 tree depth, AUC = 62.61%
4 tree depth, AUC = 63.63%
5 tree depth, AUC = 64.89%
10 tree depth, AUC = 78.37%
20 tree depth, AUC = 98.87%
```

As you can see from the preceding results, increasing the tree depth parameter results in a more accurate model (as expected, since the model is allowed to get more complex with greater tree depth). It is very likely that at higher tree depths, the model will overfit the dataset significantly. As the tree depth increases, the generalization capability reduces, where generalization is how the concepts learned by a machine learning model apply to an example which has not ever been seen by the model.

There is very little difference in performance between the two impurity measures.

The naive Bayes model

Finally, let's see the impact of changing the `lambda` parameter for naive Bayes. This parameter controls additive smoothing, which handles the case when a `class` and `feature` value do not occur together in the dataset.

 See `http://en.wikipedia.org/wiki/Additive_smoothing`for more details on additive smoothing.

We will take the same approach as we did earlier, first creating a convenience training function and training the model with varying levels of `lambda` as follows:

```
def trainNBWithParams(input: RDD[LabeledPoint], lambda: Double) = {
  val nb = new NaiveBayes
  nb.setLambda(lambda)
  nb.run(input)
}
val nbResults = Seq(0.001, 0.01, 0.1, 1.0, 10.0).map { param =>
  val model = trainNBWithParams(dataNB, param)
```

```
    val scoreAndLabels = dataNB.map { point =>
      (model.predict(point.features), point.label)
    }
    val metrics = new BinaryClassificationMetrics(scoreAndLabels)
    (s"$param lambda", metrics.areaUnderROC)
  }
  nbResults.foreach { case (param, auc) => println(f"$param, AUC = ${auc *
  100}%2.2f%%")
  }
```

The results of the training are as follows:

```
0.001 lambda, AUC = 60.51%
0.01 lambda, AUC = 60.51%
0.1 lambda, AUC = 60.51%
1.0 lambda, AUC = 60.51%
10.0 lambda, AUC = 60.51%
```

We can see that `lambda` has no impact in this case, since it will not be a problem if the combination of feature and class label do not occur together in the dataset.

Cross-validation

So far in this book, we have only briefly mentioned the idea of cross-validation and out-of-sample testing. Cross-validation is a critical part of real-world machine learning, and is central to many model selection and parameter tuning pipelines.

The general idea behind cross-validation is that we want to know how our model will perform on unseen data. Evaluating this on real, live data (for example, in a production system) is risky, because we don't really know whether the trained model is the best in the sense of being able to make accurate predictions on new data. As we saw previously with regard to regularization, our model might have overfit the training data, and be poor at making predictions on data it has not been trained on.

Cross-validation provides a mechanism where we use part of our available dataset to train our model, and another part to evaluate the performance of this model. As the model is tested on data that it has not seen during the training phase, its performance, when evaluated on this part of the dataset, gives us an estimate as to how well our model generalizes for the new data points.

Here, we will implement a simple cross-validation evaluation approach using a train-test split. We will divide our dataset into two non-overlapping parts. The first dataset is used to train our model, and is called the **training set**. The second dataset, called the **test set** or **hold-out set**, is used to evaluate the performance of our model using our chosen evaluation measure. Common splits used in practice include 50/50, 60/40, and 80/20 splits, but you can use any split as long as the training set is not too small for the model to learn (generally, at least 50% is a practical minimum).

In many cases, three sets are created: a training set, an evaluation set (which is used like the aforementioned test set to tune the model parameters such as lambda and step size), and a test set (which is never used to train a model or tune any parameters, but is only used to generate an estimated true performance on completely unseen data).

Here, we will explore a simple train-test split approach. There are many cross-validation techniques that are more exhaustive and complex. One popular example is the **K-fold cross-validation**, where the dataset is split into *K* non-overlapping folds. The model is trained on *K-1* folds of data, and tested on the remaining, held-out fold. This is repeated *K* times, and the results are averaged to give the cross-validation score. The train-test split is effectively like a two-fold cross-validation.

Other approaches include leave-one-out cross-validation and random sampling. See the article at `http://en.wikipedia.org/wiki/Cross-vali dation_(statistics)` for further details.

First, we will split our dataset into a 60% training set and a 40% test set (we will use a constant random seed of 123 here to ensure that we get the same results for ease of illustration).

```
val trainTestSplit = scaledDataCats.randomSplit(Array(0.6, 0.4), 123)
val train = trainTestSplit(0)
val test = trainTestSplit(1)
```

Next, we will compute the evaluation metric of interest (again, we will use AUC) for a range of regularization parameter settings. Note that here we will use a finer-grained step size between the evaluated regularization parameters to better illustrate the differences in AUC, which are very small in this case.

```
val regResultsTest = Seq(0.0, 0.001, 0.0025, 0.005, 0.01).map { param =>
  val model = trainWithParams(train, param, numIterations, new
SquaredL2Updater, 1.0)
  createMetrics(s"$param L2 regularization parameter", test, model)
}
regResultsTest.foreach { case (param, auc) => println(f"$param, AUC = ${auc
* 100}%2.6f%%")
```

```
}
```

This preceding code will compute the results of training on the training set, and the results of evaluating on the test set, as shown here:

```
0.0 L2 regularization parameter, AUC = 66.480874%
0.001 L2 regularization parameter, AUC = 66.480874%
0.0025 L2 regularization parameter, AUC = 66.515027%
0.005 L2 regularization parameter, AUC = 66.515027%
0.01 L2 regularization parameter, AUC = 66.549180%
```

Now, let's compare this to the results of training and testing on the training set

(this is what we were doing previously by training and testing on all data). Again, we will omit the code, as it is very similar (but it is available in the code bundle):

```
0.0 L2 regularization parameter, AUC = 66.260311%
0.001 L2 regularization parameter, AUC = 66.260311%
0.0025 L2 regularization parameter, AUC = 66.260311%
0.005 L2 regularization parameter, AUC = 66.238294%
0.01 L2 regularization parameter, AUC = 66.238294%
```

So, we can see that when we train and evaluate our model on the same dataset, we generally achieve the highest performance when regularization is lower. This is because our model has seen all the data points, and with low levels of regularization, it can overfit the data set and achieve higher performance.

In contrast, when we train on one dataset and test on another, we see that, generally, a slightly higher level of regularization results in better test set performance.

In cross-validation, we would typically find the parameter settings (including regularization as well as the various other parameters, such as step size and so on) that result in the best test set performance. We would then use these parameter settings to retrain the model on all of our data in order to use it to make predictions on new data.

> Recall from Chapter 5, *Building a Recommendation Engine with Spark* that we did not cover cross-validation. You can apply the same techniques we used earlier to split the ratings dataset from that chapter into a training and test dataset. You can then try out different parameter settings on the training set while evaluating the MSE and MAP performance metrics on the test set in a manner similar to what we did earlier. Give it a try!

Summary

In this chapter, we covered the various classification models available in Spark MLlib, and we saw how to train models on input data, and how to evaluate their performance using standard metrics and measures. We also explored how to apply some of the techniques previously introduced to transform our features. Finally, we investigated the impact of using the correct input data format or distribution on model performance, and we also saw the impact of adding more data to our model, tuning model parameters and implementing cross-validation.

In the next chapter, we will take a similar approach to delve into MLlib's regression models.

7
Building a Regression Model with Spark

In this chapter, we will build on what we covered in `Chapter 6`, *Building a Classification Model with Spark*. While classification models deal with outcomes that represent discrete classes, regression models are concerned with target variables that can take any real value. The underlying principle is very similar--we wish to find a model that maps input features to predicted target variables. Like classification, regression is also a form of supervised learning.

Regression models can be used to predict just about any variable of interest. A few examples include the following:

- Predicting stock returns and other economic variables
- Predicting loss amounts for loan defaults (this can be combined with a classification model that predicts the probability of default, while the regression model predicts the amount in the case of a default)
- Recommendations (the Alternating Least Squares factorization model from `Chapter 5`, *Building a Recommendation Engine with Spark*, uses linear regression in each iteration)
- Predicting **customer lifetime value** (**CLTV**) in a retail, mobile, or other business, based on user behavior and spending patterns

In the different sections of this chapter, we will do the following:

- Introduce the various types of regression models available in ML
- Explore feature extraction and target variable transformation for regression models
- Train a number of regression models using ML

- See how to make predictions using the trained models
- Investigate the impact on performance of various parameter settings for regression using cross-validation

Types of regression models

The core idea of linear models (or generalized linear models) is that we model the predicted outcome of interest (often called the target or dependent variable) as a function of a simple linear predictor applied to the input variables (also referred to as features or independent variables).

$$y = f(w^T x)$$

Here, y is the target variable, w is the vector of parameters (known as the weight vector), and x is the vector of input features.

$w^T x$ is the linear predictor (or vector dot product) of the weight vector w and feature vector x. To this linear predictor, we applied a function f (called the link function).

Linear models can, in fact, be used for both classification and regression simply by changing the link function. Standard linear regression uses an identity link (that is, $y = w^T x$ directly), while binary classification uses alternative link functions as discussed here.

Spark's ML library offers different regression models, which are as follows:

- Linear regression
- Generalized linear regression
- Logistical regression
- Decision trees
- Random forest regression
- Gradient boosted trees
- Survival regression
- Isotonic regression
- Ridge regression

Regression models define the relationship between a dependent variable and one or more independent variables. It builds the best model that fits the values of independent variables or features.

Linear regression unlike classification models such as support vector machines and logistic regression is used for predicting the value of a dependent variable with generalized value rather than predicting the exact class label.

Linear regression models are essentially the same as their classification counterparts, the only difference is that linear regression models use a different loss function, related link function, and decision function. Spark ML provides a standard least squares regression model (although other types of generalized linear models for regression are planned).

Least squares regression

You might recall from `Chapter 6`, *Building a Classification Model with Spark,* that there are a variety of loss functions that can be applied to generalized linear models. The loss function used for least squares is the squared loss, which is defined as follows:

$$\tfrac{1}{2} (w^T x - y)^2$$

Here, as for the classification setting, y is the target variable (this time, real valued), w is the weight vector, and x is the feature vector.

The related link function is the identity link, and the decision function is also the identity function, as generally, no thresholding is applied in regression. So, the model's prediction is simply $y = w^T x$.

The standard least squares regression in ML library does not use regularization. Regularization is used to solve the problem of overfitting. Looking at the squared loss function, we can see that the loss applied to incorrectly predicted points will be magnified since the loss is squared. This means that least squares regression is susceptible to outliers in the dataset, and also to over-fitting. Generally, as for classification, we should apply some level of regularization in practice.

Linear regression with L2 regularization is commonly referred to as ridge regression, while applying L1 regularization is called the lasso.

When the dataset is small, or the number of examples is fewer, the tendency of the model to over fit is very high, therefore, it is highly recommended to use regularizers like L1, L2, or elastic net.

See the section on linear least squares in the Spark MLlib documentation at `http://spark.apache.org/docs/latest/mllib-linear-methods.html#linear-least-squares-lasso-and-ridge-regression` for further information.

Decision trees for regression

Just like using linear models for regression tasks involves changing the loss function used, using decision trees for regression involves changing the measure of the node impurity used. The impurity metric is called **variance**, and is defined in the same way as the squared loss for least squares linear regression.

> See the *MLlib - Decision Tree* section in the Spark documentation at `http://spark.apache.org/docs/latest/mllib-decision-tree.html` for further details on the decision tree algorithm and impurity measure for regression.

Now, we will plot a simple example of a regression problem with only one input variable shown on the *x* axis and the target variable on the *y* axis. The linear model prediction function is shown by a red-dashed line, while the decision tree prediction function is shown by a green-dashed line. We can see that the decision tree allows a more complex, nonlinear model to be fitted to the data:

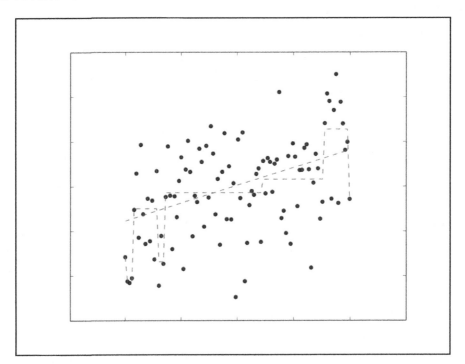

Evaluating the performance of regression models

We saw in `Chapter 6`, *Building a Classification Model with Spark*, that evaluation methods for classification models typically focus on measurements related to predicted class memberships relative to the actual class memberships. These are binary outcomes (either the predicted class is correct or incorrect), and it is less important whether the model just barely predicted correctly or not; what we care most about is the number of correct and incorrect predictions.

When dealing with regression models, it is very unlikely that our model will precisely predict the target variable, because the target variable can take on any real value. However, we would naturally like to understand how far away our predicted values are from the true values, so will we utilize a metric that takes into account the overall deviation.

Some of the standard evaluation metrics used to measure the performance of regression models include the **Mean Squared Error** (**MSE**) and **Root Mean Squared Error** (**RMSE**), the **Mean Absolute Error** (**MAE**), the R-squared coefficient, and many others.

Mean Squared Error and Root Mean Squared Error

MSE is the average of the squared error that is used as the loss function for least squares regression:

$$\sum_{i=1}^{n} \frac{\left(w^{T}x(i) - y(i)\right)^{2}}{n}$$

It is the sum, over all the data points, of the square of the difference between the predicted and actual target variables, divided by the number of data points.

RMSE is the square root of MSE. MSE is measured in units that are the square of the target variable, while RMSE is measured in the same units as the target variable. Due to its formulation, MSE, just like the squared loss function that it derives from, effectively penalizes larger errors more severely.

In order to evaluate our predictions based on the mean of an error metric, we will first make predictions for each input feature vector in an RDD of `LabeledPoint` instances by computing the error for each record using a function that takes the prediction and true target value as inputs. This will return a `[Double]` RDD that contains the error values. We can then find the average using the mean method of RDDs that contain double values.

Let's define our squared error function as follows:

```Scala
def squaredError(actual:Double, pred : Double) : Double = {
  return Math.pow( (pred - actual), 2.0)
}
```

Mean Absolute Error

MAE is the average of the absolute differences between the predicted and actual targets and is given as follows:

$$\sum_{i=1}^{n} \frac{\left| w^T x(i) - y(i) \right|}{n}$$

MAE is similar in principle to MSE, but it does not punish large deviations as much.

Our function to compute MAE is as follows:

```Scala
def absError(actual:Double, pred: Double) : Double = {
  return Math.abs( (pred - actual))
}
```

Root Mean Squared Log Error

This measurement is not as widely used as MSE and MAE, but it is used as the metric for the Kaggle competition that uses the bike-sharing dataset. It is, effectively, the RMSE of the log-transformed predicted and target values. This measurement is useful when there is a wide range in the target variable, and you do not necessarily want to penalize large errors when the predicted and target values are themselves high. It is also effective when you care about percentage errors rather than the absolute value of errors.

The Kaggle competition evaluation page can be found at
`https://www.kaggle.com/c/bike-sharing-demand/details/evaluation`.

The function to compute RMSLE is shown here:

```Scala
def squaredLogError(actual:Double, pred : Double) : Double = {
  return Math.pow( (Math.log(pred +1) - Math.log(actual +1)), 2.0)
}
```

The R-squared coefficient

The R-squared coefficient, also known as the coefficient of determination, is a measure of how well a model fits a dataset. It is commonly used in statistics. It measures the degree of variation in the target variable; this is explained by the variation in the input features. An R-squared coefficient generally takes a value between 0 and 1, where 1 equates to a perfect fit of the model.

Extracting the right features from your data

As the underlying models for regression are the same as those for the classification case, we can use the same approach to create input features. The only practical difference is that the target is now a real-valued variable as opposed to a categorical one. The `LabeledPoint` class in ML library already takes this into account, as the `label` field is of the `Double` type, so it can handle both cases.

Extracting features from the bike sharing dataset

To illustrate the concepts in this chapter, we will be using the bike sharing dataset. This dataset contains hourly records of the number of bicycle rentals in the capital bike sharing system. It also contains variables related to date, time, weather, seasonal, and holiday information.

The dataset is available at
`http://archive.ics.uci.edu/ml/datasets/Bike+Sharing+Dataset`.
Click on the **Data Folder** link, and then download the `Bike-Sharing-Dataset.zip` file.

The bike sharing data was enriched with weather and seasonal data by Hadi Fanaee-T at the University of Porto and used in the following paper: Fanaee-T, Hadi and Gama Joao, Event labeling combining ensemble detectors and background knowledge, *Progress in Artificial Intelligence*, pp. 1-15, Springer Berlin Heidelberg, 2013.
The paper is available at
`http://link.springer.com/article/10.1007%2Fs13748-013-0040-3.`

Once you have downloaded the `Bike-Sharing-Dataset.zip` file, unzip it. This will create a directory called `Bike-Sharing-Dataset`, which contains the `day.csv`, `hour.csv`, and the `Readme.txt` files.

The `Readme.txt` file contains information on the dataset, including the variable names and descriptions. Take a look at the file, and you will see that we have the following variables available:

- `instant`: This is the record ID
- `dteday`: This is the raw date
- `season`: This refers to the different seasons such as spring, summer, winter, and fall
- `yr`: This is the year (2011 or 2012)
- `mnth`: This is the month of the year
- `hr`: This is the hour of the day
- `holiday`: This shows whether the day was a holiday or not
- `weekday`: This is the day of the week
- `workingday`: This refers to whether the day was a working day or not
- `weathersit`: This is a categorical variable that describes the weather at a particular time
- `temp`: This is the normalized temperature
- `atemp`: This is the normalized apparent temperature
- `hum`: This is the normalized humidity
- `windspeed`: This is the normalized wind speed
- `cnt`: This is the target variable, that is, the count of bike rentals for that hour

We will work with the hourly data contained in `hour.csv`. If you look at the first line of the dataset, you will see that it contains the column names as header. The following code snippet prints the header and the top 20 records:

```
val spark = SparkSession
  .builder
  .appName("BikeSharing")
  .master("local[1]")
  .getOrCreate()

// read from csv
val df = spark.read.format("csv").option("header",
    "true").load("/dataset/BikeSharing/hour.csv")
df.cache()

df.registerTempTable("BikeSharing")
print(df.count())

spark.sql("SELECT * FROM BikeSharing").show()
```

The preceding code snippet should output the following result:

```
root
 |-- instant: integer (nullable = true)
 |-- dteday: timestamp (nullable = true)
 |-- season: integer (nullable = true)
 |-- yr: integer (nullable = true)
 |-- mnth: integer (nullable = true)
 |-- hr: integer (nullable = true)
 |-- holiday: integer (nullable = true)
 |-- weekday: integer (nullable = true)
 |-- workingday: integer (nullable = true)
 |-- weathersit: integer (nullable = true)
 |-- temp: double (nullable = true)
 |-- atemp: double (nullable = true)
 |-- hum: double (nullable = true)
 |-- windspeed: double (nullable = true)
 |-- casual: integer (nullable = true)
 |-- registered: integer (nullable = true)
 |-- cnt: integer (nullable = true)
```

instant	dteday	season	yr	mnth	hr	holiday	weekday	workingday	weathersit	temp	atemp	hum	windspeed	casual	registered	cnt
1	2011-01-01 00:00:...	1	0	1	0	0	6	0	1	0.24	0.2879	0.81	0.0	3	13	16
2	2011-01-01 00:00:...	1	0	1	1	0	6	0	1	0.22	0.2727	0.8	0.0	8	32	40
3	2011-01-01 00:00:...	1	0	1	2	0	6	0	1	0.22	0.2727	0.8	0.0	5	27	32
4	2011-01-01 00:00:...	1	0	1	3	0	6	0	1	0.24	0.2879	0.75	0.0	3	10	13
5	2011-01-01 00:00:...	1	0	1	4	0	6	0	1	0.24	0.2879	0.75	0.0	0	1	1
6	2011-01-01 00:00:...	1	0	1	5	0	6	0	2	0.24	0.2576	0.75	0.0896	0	1	1
7	2011-01-01 00:00:...	1	0	1	6	0	6	0	1	0.22	0.2727	0.8	0.0	2	0	2
8	2011-01-01 00:00:...	1	0	1	7	0	6	0	1	0.2	0.2576	0.86	0.0	1	2	3
9	2011-01-01 00:00:...	1	0	1	8	0	6	0	1	0.24	0.2879	0.75	0.0	1	7	8
10	2011-01-01 00:0:...	1	0	1	9	0	6	0	1	0.32	0.3485	0.76	0.0	8	6	14
11	2011-01-01 00:00:...	1	0	1	10	0	6	0	1	0.38	0.3939	0.76	0.2537	12	24	36
12	2011-01-01 00:00:...	1	0	1	11	0	6	0	1	0.36	0.3333	0.81	0.2836	26	30	56
13	2011-01-01 00:00:...	1	0	1	12	0	6	0	1	0.42	0.4242	0.77	0.2836	29	55	84
14	2011-01-01 00:00:...	1	0	1	13	0	6	0	2	0.46	0.4545	0.72	0.2985	47	47	94
15	2011-01-01 00:00:...	1	0	1	14	0	6	0	2	0.46	0.4545	0.72	0.2836	35	71	106
16	2011-01-01 00:00:...	1	0	1	15	0	6	0	2	0.44	0.4394	0.77	0.2985	40	70	110
17	2011-01-01 00:00:...	1	0	1	16	0	6	0	2	0.42	0.4242	0.82	0.2985	41	52	93
18	2011-01-01 00:00:...	1	0	1	17	0	6	0	2	0.44	0.4394	0.82	0.2836	15	52	67
19	2011-01-01 00:00:...	1	0	1	18	0	6	0	3	0.42	0.4242	0.88	0.2537	9	26	35
20	2011-01-01 00:00:...	1	0	1	19	0	6	0	3	0.42	0.4242	0.88	0.2537	6	31	37

only showing top 20 rows

We will be using Scala to demonstrate the examples in this chapter. The source code for the chapter can be found at the location

`https://github.com/ml-resources/spark-ml/tree/branch-ed2/Chapter_07`.

We'll start as usual by loading the dataset and inspecting it; from the previous dataframe, get the record count as follows:

```
print(df.count())
```

This should output the following result:

```
17,379
```

So, we have `17,379` hourly records in our dataset. We have inspected the column names already. We will ignore the record ID and raw date columns. We will also ignore the `casual` and `registered` count target variables, and focus on the overall count variable, `cnt` (which is the sum of the other two counts). We are left with 12 variables. The first eight are categorical, while the last four are normalized real-valued variables.

```
// drop record id, date, casual and registered columns
val df1 =
    df.drop("instant").drop("dteday").drop("casual")
    .drop("registered")
df1.printSchema()
```

This last bit of code should output the following result:

```
root
|-- season: integer (nullable = true)
|-- yr: integer (nullable = true)
|-- mnth: integer (nullable = true)
|-- hr: integer (nullable = true)
```

```
|-- holiday: integer (nullable = true)
|-- weekday: integer (nullable = true)
|-- workingday: integer (nullable = true)
|-- weathersit: integer (nullable = true)
|-- temp: double (nullable = true)
|-- atemp: double (nullable = true)
|-- hum: double (nullable = true)
|-- windspeed: double (nullable = true)
|-- cnt: integer (nullable = true)
```

All the columns are casted to double; the following snippet shows how this is done:

```
// convert to double:
season,yr,mnth,hr,holiday,weekday,workingday,weathersit,temp,atemp,hum,wind
speed,casual,registered,cnt
val df2 = df1.withColumn("season",
   df1("season").cast("double")).withColumn("yr",
   df1("yr").cast("double"))
 .withColumn("mnth", df1("mnth").cast("double")).withColumn("hr",
   df1("hr").cast("double")).withColumn("holiday",
   df1("holiday").cast("double"))
 .withColumn("weekday",
   df1("weekday").cast("double")).withColumn("workingday",
   df1("workingday").cast("double")).withColumn("weathersit",
   df1("weathersit").cast("double"))
 .withColumn("temp",
   df1("temp").cast("double")).withColumn("atemp",
   df1("atemp").cast("double")).withColumn("hum",
   df1("hum").cast("double"))
 .withColumn("windspeed",
   df1("windspeed").cast("double")).withColumn("label",
   df1("label").cast("double"))

df2.printSchema()
```

The preceding code should output the following result:

```
root
|-- season: double (nullable = true)
|-- yr: double (nullable = true)
|-- mnth: double (nullable = true)
|-- hr: double (nullable = true)
|-- holiday: double (nullable = true)
|-- weekday: double (nullable = true)
|-- workingday: double (nullable = true)
|-- weathersit: double (nullable = true)
|-- temp: double (nullable = true)
|-- atemp: double (nullable = true)
```

```
|-- hum: double (nullable = true)
|-- windspeed: double (nullable = true)
|-- label: double (nullable = true)
```

The bike sharing dataset is categorical in nature, and needs to be processed using **Vector Assembler** and **Vector Indexer** as described next:

- Vector Assembler is a transformer that combines a list of columns into a single vector column. It combines raw features into a feature vector in order to train ML models like linear regression and decision trees.
- Vector Indexer indexes categorical features, passed from Vector Assembler in this case. It automatically decides which features are categorical, and converts actual values to category indices.

In our case, all the columns in df2 except `label` are converted by `VectorAssembler` into `rawFeatures`.

Given an input column of type `Vector` and a `param` called `maxCategories`, it decides which features should be categorical based on distinct values, where features with at most `maxCategories` are declared categorical.

```
// drop label and create feature vector
val df3 = df2.drop("label")
val featureCols = df3.columns

val vectorAssembler = new
    VectorAssembler().setInputCols(featureCols)
    .setOutputCol("rawFeatures")
val vectorIndexer = new
    VectorIndexer().setInputCol("rawFeatures")
    .setOutputCol("features").setMaxCategories(4)
```

 The complete code-listing is available at `https://github.com/ml-resour ces/spark-ml/blob/branch-ed2/Chapter_07/scala/2.0.0/scala-spar k-app/src/main/scala/org/sparksamples/regression/bikesharing/B ikeSharingExecutor.scala`.

Training and using regression models

Training for regression models follows the same procedure as for classification models. We simply pass the training data to the relevant train method.

BikeSharingExecutor

The BikeSharingExecutor object can be used to choose and run the respective regression model, for example, to run LinearRegression and execute the linear regression pipeline, set the program argument as LR_<type>, where type is the data format; for other commands, refer to the following code snippet:

```
def executeCommand(arg: String, vectorAssembler: VectorAssembler,
    vectorIndexer: VectorIndexer, dataFrame: DataFrame, spark:
    SparkSession) = arg match {
    case "LR_Vectors" =>
     LinearRegressionPipeline.linearRegressionWithVectorFormat
     (vectorAssembler, vectorIndexer, dataFrame)
    case "LR_SVM" =>
     LinearRegressionPipeline.linearRegressionWithSVMFormat(spark)

    case "GLR_Vectors" =>
     GeneralizedLinearRegressionPipeline
     .genLinearRegressionWithVectorFormat(vectorAssembler,
      vectorIndexer, dataFrame)
    case "GLR_SVM"=>
     GeneralizedLinearRegressionPipeline
     .genLinearRegressionWithSVMFormat(spark)

    case "DT_Vectors" => DecisionTreeRegressionPipeline
     .decTreeRegressionWithVectorFormat(vectorAssembler,
     vectorIndexer, dataFrame)
    case "DT_SVM"=>
     GeneralizedLinearRegressionPipeline
     .genLinearRegressionWithSVMFormat(spark)

    case "RF_Vectors" =>
     RandomForestRegressionPipeline
     .randForestRegressionWithVectorFormat(vectorAssembler,
     vectorIndexer, dataFrame)
    case "RF_SVM"=>
     RandomForestRegressionPipeline
     .randForestRegressionWithSVMFormat(spark)

    case "GBT_Vectors" =>
     GradientBoostedTreeRegressorPipeline
     .gbtRegressionWithVectorFormat(vectorAssembler, vectorIndexer,
     dataFrame)
    case "GBT_SVM"=>
     GradientBoostedTreeRegressorPipeline
     .gbtRegressionWithSVMFormat(spark)
```

```
}
```

The code-listing can be found at this link:
https://github.com/ml-resources/spark-ml/blob/branch-ed2/Chapter
_07/scala/2.0.0/scala-spark-
app/src/main/scala/org/sparksamples/regression/bikesharing/BikeS
haringExecutor.scala

Training a regression model on the bike sharing dataset

Linear regression

Linear regression is the most commonly used algorithm. At the core of the regression analysis is the task of fitting a single line through a data plot. Linear equation is described by $y = c + b*x$, where y = estimated dependent, c = constant, b = regression coefficients, and x = independent variable.

Let's train the bike sharing dataset by splitting it into 80% training and 20% testing, use `LinearRegression` with the regression evaluator from Spark to build the model, and get evaluation metrics around the test data. The `linearRegressionWithVectorFormat` method uses categorical data, whereas `linearRegressionWithSVMFormat` uses the `libsvm` format of the `Bike-sharing` dataset.

```
def linearRegressionWithVectorFormat(vectorAssembler:
  VectorAssembler, vectorIndexer: VectorIndexer, dataFrame:
  DataFrame) = {
val lr = new LinearRegression()
  .setFeaturesCol("features")
  .setLabelCol("label")
  .setRegParam(0.1)
  .setElasticNetParam(1.0)
  .setMaxIter(10)

val pipeline = new Pipeline().setStages(Array(vectorAssembler,
  vectorIndexer, lr))

val Array(training, test) = dataFrame.randomSplit(Array(0.8,
  0.2), seed = 12345)

val model = pipeline.fit(training)

val fullPredictions = model.transform(test).cache()
```

```
    val predictions =
      fullPredictions.select("prediction").rdd.map(_.getDouble(0))
    val labels =
      fullPredictions.select("label").rdd.map(_.getDouble(0))
    val RMSE = new
      RegressionMetrics(predictions.zip(labels)).rootMeanSquaredError
    println(s"  Root mean squared error (RMSE): $RMSE")
  }

  def linearRegressionWithSVMFormat(spark: SparkSession) = {
    // Load training data
    val training = spark.read.format("libsvm")
      .load("/dataset/BikeSharing/lsvmHours.txt")

    val lr = new LinearRegression()
      .setMaxIter(10)
      .setRegParam(0.3)
      .setElasticNetParam(0.8)

    // Fit the model
    val lrModel = lr.fit(training)

    // Print the coefficients and intercept for linear regression
    println(s"Coefficients: ${lrModel.coefficients} Intercept:
      ${lrModel.intercept}")

    // Summarize the model over the training set and print out some
      metrics
    val trainingSummary = lrModel.summary
    println(s"numIterations: ${trainingSummary.totalIterations}")
    println(s"objectiveHistory:
      ${trainingSummary.objectiveHistory.toList}")
    trainingSummary.residuals.show()
    println(s"RMSE: ${trainingSummary.rootMeanSquaredError}")
    println(s"r2: ${trainingSummary.r2}")
  }
```

This preceding code should show the following output. Please note that residual stands for the expression Residuals: (label-predicted value)

```
+-------------------+
|          residuals|
+-------------------+
|  32.92325797801143|
|  59.97614044359903|
|  35.80737062786482|
|-12.509886468051075|
|-25.979774633117792|
```

```
|-29.352862474201224|
|-5.9517346926691435|
| 18.453701019500947|
|-24.859327293384787|
| -47.14282080103287|
| -27.50652100848832|
| 21.865309097336535|
|   4.037722798853395|
|-25.691348213368343|
| -13.59830538387368|
|  9.336691727080336|
| 12.83461983259582|
|  -20.5026155752185|
| -34.83240621318937|
| -34.30229437825615|
+-------------------+
only showing top 20 rows
RMSE: 149.54567868651284
r2: 0.3202369690447968
```

The code-listing can be found at `https://github.com/ml-resources/spa rk-ml/blob/branch-ed2/Chapter_07/scala/2.0.0/scala-spark-app/s rc/main/scala/org/sparksamples/regression/bikesharing/LinearRe gressionPipeline.scala`.

Generalized linear regression

Linear regression follows a Gaussian distribution, whereas, **generalized linear models (GLMs)** are specifications of linear models where the response variable Y follows some distribution from the exponential family of distributions.

Let's train the bike sharing dataset by splitting it into 80 % training and 20% testing, use `GeneralizedLinearRegression` with regression evaluator from Spark to build the model, and get evaluation metrics around the test data.

```scala
@transient lazy val logger = Logger.getLogger(getClass.getName)

def genLinearRegressionWithVectorFormat(vectorAssembler:
  VectorAssembler, vectorIndexer: VectorIndexer, dataFrame:
  DataFrame) = {
  val lr = new GeneralizedLinearRegression()
   .setFeaturesCol("features")
   .setLabelCol("label")
   .setFamily("gaussian")
   .setLink("identity")
   .setMaxIter(10)
```

```scala
      .setRegParam(0.3)

    val pipeline = new Pipeline().setStages(Array(vectorAssembler,
      vectorIndexer, lr))

    val Array(training, test) = dataFrame.randomSplit(Array(0.8,
      0.2), seed = 12345)

    val model = pipeline.fit(training)

    val fullPredictions = model.transform(test).cache()
    val predictions =
      fullPredictions.select("prediction").rdd.map(_.getDouble(0))
    val labels =
      fullPredictions.select("label").rdd.map(_.getDouble(0))
    val RMSE = new
      RegressionMetrics(predictions.zip(labels)).rootMeanSquaredError
    println(s"  Root mean squared error (RMSE): $RMSE")
}

def genLinearRegressionWithSVMFormat(spark: SparkSession) = {
  // Load training data
  val training = spark.read.format("libsvm")
    .load("/dataset/BikeSharing/lsvmHours.txt")

  val lr = new GeneralizedLinearRegression()
    .setFamily("gaussian")
    .setLink("identity")
    .setMaxIter(10)
    .setRegParam(0.3)

  // Fit the model
  val model = lr.fit(training)

  // Print the coefficients and intercept for generalized linear
    regression model
  println(s"Coefficients: ${model.coefficients}")
  println(s"Intercept: ${model.intercept}")

  // Summarize the model over the training set and print out some
    metrics
  val summary = model.summary
  println(s"Coefficient Standard Errors:
    ${summary.coefficientStandardErrors.mkString(",")}")
  println(s"T Values: ${summary.tValues.mkString(",")}")
  println(s"P Values: ${summary.pValues.mkString(",")}")
  println(s"Dispersion: ${summary.dispersion}")
  println(s"Null Deviance: ${summary.nullDeviance}")
```

```
println(s"Residual Degree Of Freedom Null:
  ${summary.residualDegreeOfFreedomNull}")
println(s"Deviance: ${summary.deviance}")
println(s"Residual Degree Of Freedom:
  ${summary.residualDegreeOfFreedom}")
println(s"AIC: ${summary.aic}")
println("Deviance Residuals: ")
summary.residuals().show()
}
```

This should output the following result:

Standard error of estimated coefficients and intercept.

If [GeneralizedLinearRegression.fitIntercept] is set to true, then the last element returned corresponds to the intercept.

Coefficient Standard Errors in the previous code are as follows:

```
1.1353970394903834,2.2827202289405677,0.5060828045490352,0.1735367945
  7103457,7.062338310890969,0.5694233355369813,2.5250738792716176,
2.0099641224706573,0.7596421898012983,0.6228803024758551,0.0735818071
  8894239,0.30550603737503224,12.369537640641184
```

T-statistic of estimated coefficients and intercept is as follows:

```
T Values: 15.186791802016964,33.26578339676457,-
  11.27632316133038,8.658129103690262,-
  3.8034120518318013,2.6451862430890807,0.9799958329796699,
3.731755243874297,4.957582264860384,6.02053185645345,-
  39.290272209592864,5.5283417898112726,-0.7966500413552742
```

The two-sided p-value of estimated coefficients and intercept is as follows:

```
P Values: 0.0,0.0,0.0,0.0,1.4320532622846827E-
  4,0.008171946193283652,0.3271018275330657,1.907562616410008E-
  4,7.204877614519489E-7,
1.773422964035376E-9,0.0,3.2792739856901676E-8,0.42566519676340153
```

The dispersion is as follows:

```
Dispersion: 22378.414478769333
```

 The dispersion of the fitted model is taken as 1.0 for the "binomial" and "poisson" families, and otherwise estimated by the residual Pearson's Chi-Squared statistic (which is defined as the sum of the squares of the Pearson residuals) divided by the residual degrees of freedom.

The Null deviance output of the preceding code is as follows:

```
Null Deviance: 5.717615910707208E8
```

Residual degree of freedom is as follows:

```
Residual Degree Of Freedom Null: 17378
```

In logistic regression analysis, deviance is used in lieu of the sum of squares calculations. Deviance is analogous to the sum of squares calculations in linear regression, and is a measure of the lack of fit to the data in a logistic regression model. When a "saturated" model is available (a model with a theoretically perfect fit), deviance is calculated by comparing a given model with the saturated model.

Deviance: 3.886235458383082E8

 Reference: https://en.wikipedia.org/wiki/Logistic_regression

Degrees of freedom:

The concept of degrees of freedom is central to the principle of estimating statistics of populations from samples of them. "Degrees of freedom" is commonly abbreviated to df.

Think of df as a mathematical restriction that needs to be put in place when estimating one statistic from an estimate of another. The preceding code will give the following output:

```
Residual Degree Of Freedom: 17366
```

The **Akaike information criterion** (**AIC**) is a measure of the relative quality of statistical models for a given set of data. Given a collection of models for the data, AIC estimates the quality of each model relative to each of the other models. Hence, AIC provides a means for model selection.

 Reference : https://en.wikipedia.org/wiki/Akaike_information_cri terion

AIC for the fitted model output will be as follows:

```
AIC: 223399.95490762248
+-------------------+
|  devianceResiduals|
```

```
+------------------+
| 32.385412453563546|
|  59.5079185994115|
|  34.98037491140896|
|-13.503450469022432|
|-27.005954440659032|
|-30.197952952158246|
|  -7.039656861683778|
|  17.320193923055445|
|    -26.0159703272054|
|  -48.69166247116218|
|  -29.50984967584955|
|  20.520222192742004|
|  1.6551311183207815|
|-28.524373674665213|
|-16.337935852841838|
|   6.441923904310045|
|    9.91072545492193|
|-23.418896074866524|
|-37.870797650696346|
|-37.373301622332946|
+------------------+
only showing top 20 rows
```

The complete code listing is available at this link:

https://github.com/ml-resources/spark-ml/blob/branch-ed2/Chapter
_07/scala/2.0.0/scala-spark-
app/src/main/scala/org/sparksamples/regression/bikesharing/Gener
alizedLinearRegressionPipeline.scala

Decision tree regression

The decision tree model is a powerful, non-probabilistic technique, which can capture more complex nonlinear patterns and feature interactions. They have been shown to perform well on many tasks, are relatively easy to understand and interpret, can handle categorical and numerical features, and do not require input data to be scaled or standardized. They are well-suited to be included in ensemble methods (for example, ensembles of decision tree models, which are called decision forests).

The decision tree algorithm is a top-down approach, which begins at a root node (or feature), and then selects a feature at each step that gives the best split of the dataset, as measured by the information gain of this split. The information gain is computed from the node impurity (which is the extent to which the labels at the node are similar, or homogenous) minus the weighted sum of the impurities for the two child nodes that would be created by the split.

Let's train the bike sharing dataset by splitting it into 80 % training and 20% testing, use `DecisionTreeRegression` with regression evaluator from Spark to build the model, and get evaluation metrics around the test data.

```scala
@transient lazy val logger = Logger.getLogger(getClass.getName)

def decTreeRegressionWithVectorFormat(vectorAssembler:
  VectorAssembler, vectorIndexer: VectorIndexer, dataFrame:
  DataFrame) = {
 val lr = new DecisionTreeRegressor()
   .setFeaturesCol("features")
   .setLabelCol("label")

 val pipeline = new Pipeline().setStages(Array(vectorAssembler,
  vectorIndexer, lr))

 val Array(training, test) = dataFrame.randomSplit(Array(0.8,
  0.2), seed = 12345)

 val model = pipeline.fit(training)

 // Make predictions.
 val predictions = model.transform(test)

 // Select example rows to display.
 predictions.select("prediction", "label", "features").show(5)

 // Select (prediction, true label) and compute test error.
 val evaluator = new RegressionEvaluator()
   .setLabelCol("label")
   .setPredictionCol("prediction")
   .setMetricName("rmse")
 val rmse = evaluator.evaluate(predictions)
 println("Root Mean Squared Error (RMSE) on test data = " + rmse)

 val treeModel =
  model.stages(1).asInstanceOf[DecisionTreeRegressionModel]
 println("Learned regression tree model:\n" +
  treeModel.toDebugString)   }

def decTreeRegressionWithSVMFormat(spark: SparkSession) = {
 // Load training data
 val training = spark.read.format("libsvm")
   .load("/dataset/BikeSharing/lsvmHours.txt")

 // Automatically identify categorical features, and index them.
 // Here, we treat features with > 4 distinct values as
  continuous.
```

```
val featureIndexer = new VectorIndexer()
  .setInputCol("features")
  .setOutputCol("indexedFeatures")
  .setMaxCategories(4)
  .fit(training)

// Split the data into training and test sets (30% held out for
  testing).
val Array(trainingData, testData) =
  training.randomSplit(Array(0.7, 0.3))

// Train a DecisionTree model.
val dt = new DecisionTreeRegressor()
  .setLabelCol("label")
  .setFeaturesCol("indexedFeatures")

// Chain indexer and tree in a Pipeline.
val pipeline = new Pipeline()
  .setStages(Array(featureIndexer, dt))

// Train model. This also runs the indexer.
val model = pipeline.fit(trainingData)

// Make predictions.
val predictions = model.transform(testData)

// Select example rows to display.
predictions.select("prediction", "label", "features").show(5)

// Select (prediction, true label) and compute test error.
val evaluator = new RegressionEvaluator()
  .setLabelCol("label")
  .setPredictionCol("prediction")
  .setMetricName("rmse")
val rmse = evaluator.evaluate(predictions)
println("Root Mean Squared Error (RMSE) on test data = " + rmse)

val treeModel =
  model.stages(1).asInstanceOf[DecisionTreeRegressionModel]
println("Learned regression tree model:\n" +
  treeModel.toDebugString)
}
```

This should output the following result:

```
Coefficients:
[17.243038451366886,75.93647669134975,-5.7067532504873215,1.502503971636592
7,-26.86098264575616,1.5062307736563205,2.4745618796519953,7.50069415402907
```

5,3.7659886477986215,3.7500707038132464,-2.8910492341273235,1.6889417934600
353]
Intercept: -9.85419267296242

Coefficient Standard Errors:
1.1353970394903834,2.2827202289405677,0.5060828045490352,0.1735367945710345
7,7.062338310890969,0.5694233355369813,2.5250738792716176,2.009964122470657
3,0.7596421898012983,0.6228803024758551,0.07358180718894239,0.3055060373750
3224,12.369537640641184
T Values:
15.186791802016964,33.26578339676457,-11.27632316133038,8.658129103690262,-
3.8034120518318013,2.6451862430890807,0.9799958329796699,3.731755243874297,
4.957582264860384,6.02053185645345,-39.290272209592864,5.5283417898112726,-
0.7966500413552742
P Values:
0.0,0.0,0.0,0.0,1.4320532622846827E-4,0.008171946193283652,0.32710182753306
57,1.907562616410008E-4,7.204877614519489E-7,1.773422964035376E-9,0.0,3.279
2739856901676E-8,0.42566519676340153
Dispersion: 22378.414478769333

Null Deviance: 5.717615910707208E8
Residual Degree Of Freedom Null: 17378
Deviance: 3.886235458383082E8
Residual Degree Of Freedom: 17366

AIC: 223399.95490762248
Deviance Residuals:
```
+--------------------+
|  devianceResiduals|
+--------------------+
|  32.385412453563546|
|    59.5079185994115|
|   34.98037491140896|
|-13.503450469022432|
|-27.005954440659032|
|-30.197952952158246|
|  -7.039656861683778|
|  17.320193923055445|
|   -26.0159703272054|
|  -48.69166247116218|
|  -29.50984967584955|
|  20.520222192742004|
|  1.6551311183207815|
|-28.524373674665213|
|-16.337935852841838|
|   6.441923904310045|
|    9.91072545492193|
|-23.418896074866524|
```

```
|-37.870797650696346|
|-37.373301622332946|
+-------------------+
only showing top 20 rows
```

Please refer to the previous section (Generalized Linear Regression) to learn how to interpret the results.

The code listing is available at `https://github.com/ml-resources/spar k-ml/blob/branch-ed2/Chapter_07/scala/2.0.0/scala-spark-app/sr c/main/scala/org/sparksamples/regression/bikesharing/DecisionT reeRegressionPipeline.scala`.

Ensembles of trees

The ensemble method is a machine learning algorithm, which creates a model composed of a set of other base models. Spark machine learning supports two major ensemble algorithms: `RandomForest` and `GradientBoostedTrees`.

Random forest regression

Random forests are known as ensembles of decision trees formed by combining many decision trees. Like decision trees, random forests can handle categorical features, support multiclass, and don't require feature scaling.

Let's train the bike sharing dataset by splitting it into 80 % training and 20% testing, use `RandomForestRegressor` with Regression Evaluator from Spark to build the model, and get evaluation metrics around the test data.

```
@transient lazy val logger = Logger.getLogger(getClass.getName)

def randForestRegressionWithVectorFormat(vectorAssembler:
  VectorAssembler, vectorIndexer: VectorIndexer, dataFrame:
  DataFrame) = {
  val lr = new RandomForestRegressor()
    .setFeaturesCol("features")
    .setLabelCol("label")

  val pipeline = new Pipeline().setStages(Array(vectorAssembler,
  vectorIndexer, lr))

  val Array(training, test) = dataFrame.randomSplit(Array(0.8,
  0.2), seed = 12345)
```

```
    val model = pipeline.fit(training)

    // Make predictions.
    val predictions = model.transform(test)

    // Select example rows to display.
    predictions.select("prediction", "label", "features").show(5)

    // Select (prediction, true label) and compute test error.
    val evaluator = new RegressionEvaluator()
      .setLabelCol("label")
      .setPredictionCol("prediction")
      .setMetricName("rmse")
    val rmse = evaluator.evaluate(predictions)
    println("Root Mean Squared Error (RMSE) on test data = " + rmse)

    val treeModel =
     model.stages(1).asInstanceOf[RandomForestRegressionModel]
    println("Learned regression tree model:\n" + treeModel.toDebugString)   }

def randForestRegressionWithSVMFormat(spark: SparkSession) = {
  // Load training data
  val training = spark.read.format("libsvm")
    .load("/dataset/BikeSharing/lsvmHours.txt")

  // Automatically identify categorical features, and index them.
  // Set maxCategories so features with > 4 distinct values are
   treated as continuous.
  val featureIndexer = new VectorIndexer()
    .setInputCol("features")
    .setOutputCol("indexedFeatures")
    .setMaxCategories(4)
    .fit(training)

  // Split the data into training and test sets (30% held out for
   testing).
  val Array(trainingData, testData) =
   training.randomSplit(Array(0.7, 0.3))

  // Train a RandomForest model.
  val rf = new RandomForestRegressor()
    .setLabelCol("label")
    .setFeaturesCol("indexedFeatures")

  // Chain indexer and forest in a Pipeline.
  val pipeline = new Pipeline()
    .setStages(Array(featureIndexer, rf))
```

```
// Train model. This also runs the indexer.
val model = pipeline.fit(trainingData)

// Make predictions.
val predictions = model.transform(testData)

// Select example rows to display.
predictions.select("prediction", "label", "features").show(5)

// Select (prediction, true label) and compute test error.
val evaluator = new RegressionEvaluator()
  .setLabelCol("label")
  .setPredictionCol("prediction")
  .setMetricName("rmse")
val rmse = evaluator.evaluate(predictions)
println("Root Mean Squared Error (RMSE) on test data = " + rmse)

val rfModel =
  model.stages(1).asInstanceOf[RandomForestRegressionModel]
println("Learned regression forest model:\n" +
  rfModel.toDebugString)
}
```

This should output the following result:

```
RandomForest:    init: 2.114590873
total: 3.343042855
findSplits: 1.387490192
findBestSplits: 1.191715923
chooseSplits: 1.176991821


+------------------+-----+--------------------+
|        prediction|label|            features|
+------------------+-----+--------------------+
| 70.75171441904584|  1.0|(12,[0,1,2,3,4,5,...|
| 53.43733657257549|  1.0|(12,[0,1,2,3,4,5,...|
| 57.18242812368521|  1.0|(12,[0,1,2,3,4,5,...|
| 49.73744636247659|  1.0|(12,[0,1,2,3,4,5,...|
|56.433579398691144|  1.0|(12,[0,1,2,3,4,5,...|

Root Mean Squared Error (RMSE) on test data = 123.03866156451954
Learned regression forest model:
RandomForestRegressionModel (uid=rfr_bd974271ffe6) with 20 trees
  Tree 0 (weight 1.0):
    If (feature 9 <= 40.0)
     If (feature 9 <= 22.0)
      If (feature 8 <= 13.0)
       If (feature 6 in {0.0})
```

```
       If (feature 1 in {0.0})
        Predict: 35.0945945945946
       Else (feature 1 not in {0.0})
        Predict: 63.3921568627451
      Else (feature 6 not in {0.0})
       If (feature 0 in {0.0,1.0})
        Predict: 83.05714285714286
       Else (feature 0 not in {0.0,1.0})
        Predict: 120.76608187134502
     Else (feature 8 > 13.0)
      If (feature 3 <= 21.0)
       If (feature 3 <= 12.0)
        Predict: 149.56363636363636
       Else (feature 3 > 12.0)
        Predict: 54.73593073593074
      Else (feature 3 > 21.0)
       If (feature 6 in {0.0})
        Predict: 89.63333333333334
       Else (feature 6 not in {0.0})
        Predict: 305.6588235294118
```

The preceding code uses various features and their values to create a decision tree.

The code listing can be found at `https://github.com/ml-resources/spark-ml/blob/branch-ed2/Chapter_07/scala/2.0.0/scala-spark-app/src/main/scala/org/sparksamples/regression/bikesharing/RandomForestRegressionPipeline.scala`.

Gradient boosted tree regression

Gradient boosted trees are ensembles of decision trees. Gradient boosted trees iteratively train decision trees to minimize the loss function. Gradient boosted trees handle categorical features, support multiclass, and don't require feature scaling.

Spark ML implements gradient boosted trees using the existing decision tree implementation. It supports both classification and regression.

Let's train the bike sharing dataset by splitting it into 80% training and 20% testing, use GBTRegressor with regression evaluator from Spark to build the model, and get evaluation metrics around the test data.

```
@transient lazy val logger = Logger.getLogger(getClass.getName)

def gbtRegressionWithVectorFormat(vectorAssembler:
   VectorAssembler, vectorIndexer: VectorIndexer, dataFrame:
   DataFrame) = {
```

```
val lr = new GBTRegressor()
  .setFeaturesCol("features")
  .setLabelCol("label")
  .setMaxIter(10)

val pipeline = new Pipeline().setStages(Array(vectorAssembler,
  vectorIndexer, lr))

val Array(training, test) = dataFrame.randomSplit(Array(0.8,
  0.2), seed = 12345)

val model = pipeline.fit(training)

// Make predictions.
val predictions = model.transform(test)

// Select example rows to display.
predictions.select("prediction", "label", "features").show(5)

// Select (prediction, true label) and compute test error.
val evaluator = new RegressionEvaluator()
  .setLabelCol("label")
  .setPredictionCol("prediction")
  .setMetricName("rmse")
val rmse = evaluator.evaluate(predictions)
println("Root Mean Squared Error (RMSE) on test data = " + rmse)

val treeModel = model.stages(1).asInstanceOf[GBTRegressionModel]
println("Learned regression tree model:\n" +
  treeModel.toDebugString)   }

def gbtRegressionWithSVMFormat(spark: SparkSession) = {
  // Load training data
  val training = spark.read.format("libsvm")
    .load("/dataset/BikeSharing/lsvmHours.txt")

  // Automatically identify categorical features, and index them.
  // Set maxCategories so features with > 4 distinct values are
    treated as continuous.
  val featureIndexer = new VectorIndexer()
    .setInputCol("features")
    .setOutputCol("indexedFeatures")
    .setMaxCategories(4)
    .fit(training)

  // Split the data into training and test sets (30% held out for
    testing).
  val Array(trainingData, testData) =
```

```
    training.randomSplit(Array(0.7, 0.3))

// Train a GBT model.
val gbt = new GBTRegressor()
  .setLabelCol("label")
  .setFeaturesCol("indexedFeatures")
  .setMaxIter(10)

// Chain indexer and GBT in a Pipeline.
val pipeline = new Pipeline()
  .setStages(Array(featureIndexer, gbt))

// Train model. This also runs the indexer.
val model = pipeline.fit(trainingData)

// Make predictions
val predictions = model.transform(testData)

// Select example rows to display.
 predictions.select("prediction", "label", "features").show(5)

// Select (prediction, true label) and compute test error.
val evaluator = new RegressionEvaluator()
  .setLabelCol("label")
  .setPredictionCol("prediction")
  .setMetricName("rmse")
val rmse = evaluator.evaluate(predictions)
println("Root Mean Squared Error (RMSE) on test data = " + rmse)

val gbtModel = model.stages(1).asInstanceOf[GBTRegressionModel]
println("Learned regression GBT model:\n" +
  gbtModel.toDebugString)
}
```

This should output the following result:

```
RandomForest:   init: 1.366356823
total: 1.883186039
findSplits: 1.0378687
findBestSplits: 0.501171071
chooseSplits: 0.495084674


+-------------------+-----+--------------------+
|         prediction|label|            features|
+-------------------+-----+--------------------+
|-20.753742348814352|  1.0|(12,[0,1,2,3,4,5,...|
|-20.760717579684087|  1.0|(12,[0,1,2,3,4,5,...|
| -17.73182527714976|  1.0|(12,[0,1,2,3,4,5,...|
```

```
|  -17.73182527714976|   1.0|(12,[0,1,2,3,4,5,...|
|   -21.397094071362|   1.0|(12,[0,1,2,3,4,5,...|
+--------------------+-----+--------------------+
only showing top 5 rows

Root Mean Squared Error (RMSE) on test data = 73.62468541448783
Learned regression GBT model:
GBTRegressionModel (uid=gbtr_24c6ef8f52a7) with 10 trees
  Tree 0 (weight 1.0):
    If (feature 9 <= 41.0)
     If (feature 3 <= 12.0)
      If (feature 3 <= 3.0)
       If (feature 3 <= 2.0)
        If (feature 6 in {1.0})
         Predict: 24.50709219858156
        Else (feature 6 not in {1.0})
         Predict: 74.94945848375451
       Else (feature 3 > 2.0)
        If (feature 6 in {1.0})
         Predict: 122.1732283464567
        Else (feature 6 not in {1.0})
         Predict: 206.3304347826087
      Else (feature 3 > 3.0)
       If (feature 8 <= 18.0)
        If (feature 0 in {0.0,1.0})
         Predict: 137.29818181818183
        Else (feature 0 not in {0.0,1.0})
         Predict: 257.90157480314963
```

The code listing is available at https://github.com/ml-resources/spar
k-ml/blob/branch-ed2/Chapter_07/scala/2.0.0/scala-spark-app/sr
c/main/scala/org/sparksamples/regression/bikesharing/GradientB
oostedTreeRegressorPipeline.scala.

Improving model performance and tuning parameters

In Chapter 6, *Building a Classification Model with Spark*, we showed how feature transformation and selection can make a large difference to the performance of a model. In this chapter, we will focus on another type of transformation that can be applied to a dataset: transforming the target variable itself.

Transforming the target variable

Recall that many machine learning models, including linear models, make assumptions regarding the distribution of the input data as well as target variables. In particular, linear regression assumes a normal distribution.

In many real-world cases, the distributional assumptions of linear regression do not hold. In this case, for example, we know that the number of bike rentals can never be negative. This alone should indicate that the assumption of normality might be problematic. To get a better idea of the target distribution, it is often a good idea to plot a histogram of the target values.

We will now create a plot of the target variable distribution in the following piece of code:

Scala

 The code for plotting raw data can be found at https://github.com/ml-r esources/spark-ml/blob/branch-ed2/Chapter_07/scala/1.6.2/scala -spark-app/src/main/scala/org/sparksamples/PlotRawData.scala.

```scala
object PlotRawData {

  def main(args: Array[String]) {
    val records = Util.getRecords()._1
    val records_x = records.map(r => r(r.length -1))
    var records_int = new Array[Int](records_x.collect().length)
    print(records_x.first())
    val records_collect = records_x.collect()

    for (i <- 0 until records_collect.length){
      records_int(i) = records_collect(i).toInt
    }
    val min_1 = records_int.min
    val max_1 = records_int.max
```

```
    val min = min_1
    val max = max_1
    val bins = 40
    val step = (max/bins).toInt

    var mx = Map(0 -> 0)
    for (i <- step until (max + step) by step) {
      mx += (i -> 0);
    }

    for(i <- 0 until records_collect.length){
      for (j <- 0 until (max + step) by step) {
        if(records_int(i) >= (j) && records_int(i) < (j + step)){
          mx = mx + (j -> (mx(j) + 1))
        }
      }
    }
    val mx_sorted = ListMap(mx.toSeq.sortBy(_._1):_*)
    val ds = new org.jfree.data.category.DefaultCategoryDataset
    var i = 0
    mx_sorted.foreach{ case (k,v) => ds.addValue(v,"", k)}

    val chart = ChartFactories.BarChart(ds)
    val font = new Font("Dialog", Font.PLAIN,4);

    chart.peer.getCategoryPlot.getDomainAxis().
      setCategoryLabelPositions(CategoryLabelPositions.UP_90);
    chart.peer.getCategoryPlot.getDomainAxis.setLabelFont(font)
    chart.show()
    Util.sc.stop()
  }
}
```

The plot for the preceding output is shown as follows:

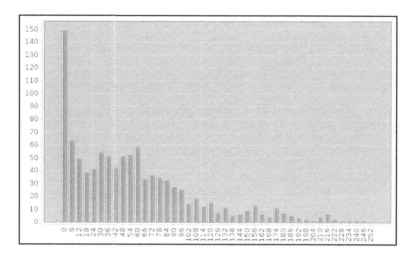

One way in which we might deal with this situation is by applying a transformation to the target variable such that we take the logarithm of the target value instead of the raw value. This is often referred to as log-transforming the target variable (this transformation can also be applied to feature values).

We will apply a log transformation to the following target variable, and plot a histogram of the log-transformed values using the following code:

Scala

```
object PlotLogData {

  def main(args: Array[String]) {
    val records = Util.getRecords()._1
    val records_x = records.map(
      r => Math.log(r(r.length -1).toDouble))
    var records_int = new Array[Int](records_x.collect().length)
    print(records_x.first())
    val records_collect = records_x.collect()

    for (i <- 0 until records_collect.length){
      records_int(i) = records_collect(i).toInt
    }
    val min_1 = records_int.min
    val max_1 = records_int.max

    val min = min_1.toFloat
    val max = max_1.toFloat
    val bins = 10
    val step = (max/bins).toFloat
```

```
var mx = Map(0.0.toString -> 0)
for (i <- step until (max + step) by step) {
  mx += (i.toString -> 0);
}

for(i <- 0 until records_collect.length){
  for (j <- 0.0 until (max + step) by step) {
    if(records_int(i) >= (j) && records_int(i) < (j + step)){
      mx = mx + (j.toString -> (mx(j.toString) + 1))
    }
  }
}
val mx_sorted = ListMap(mx.toSeq.sortBy(_._1.toFloat):_*)
val ds = new org.jfree.data.category.DefaultCategoryDataset
var i = 0
mx_sorted.foreach{ case (k,v) => ds.addValue(v,"", k)}

val chart = ChartFactories.BarChart(ds)
val font = new Font("Dialog", Font.PLAIN,4);

chart.peer.getCategoryPlot.getDomainAxis().
  setCategoryLabelPositions(CategoryLabelPositions.UP_90);
chart.peer.getCategoryPlot.getDomainAxis.setLabelFont(font)
chart.show()
Util.sc.stop()
  }
}
```

The plot for the preceding output is shown as follows:

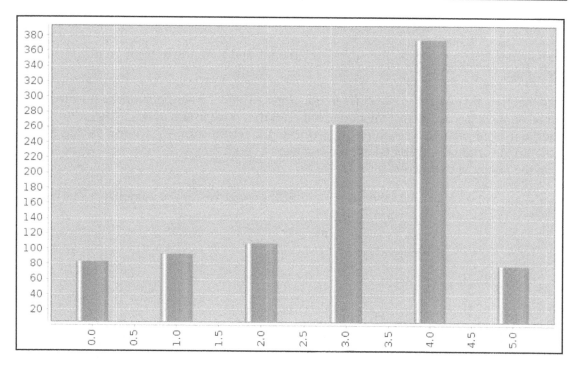

A second type of transformation that is useful in the case of target values that do not take on negative values, and, in addition, might take on a very wide range of values, is to take the square root of the variable.

We will apply the square root transform in the following code, once more plotting the resulting target variable distribution:

From the plots of the log and square root transformations, we can see that both result in a more even distribution relative to the raw values. While they are still not normally distributed, they are a lot closer to a normal distribution when compared to the original target variable.

Impact of training on log-transformed targets

So, does applying these transformations have any impact on model performance? Let's evaluate the various metrics we used previously on the log-transformed data as an example.

We will do this first for the linear model by applying the log function to the `label` field of each `LabeledPoint` RDD. Here, we will only transform the target variable, and we will not apply any transformations to the features.

We will then train a model on this transformed data, and form the RDD of predicted versus true values.

Note that now that we have transformed the target variable, the predictions of the model will be on the log scale, as will the target values of the transformed dataset. Therefore, in order to use our model and evaluate its performance, we must first transform the log data back into the original scale by taking the exponent of both the predicted and true values using the numpy exp function.

Finally, we will compute the MSE, MAE, and RMSLE metrics for the model:

Scala

```scala
object LinearRegressionWithLog{

  def main(args: Array[String]) {

    val recordsArray = Util.getRecords()
    val records = recordsArray._1
    val first = records.first()
    val numData = recordsArray._2

    println(numData.toString())
    records.cache()
     print("Mapping of first categorical feature column: " +
       Util.get_mapping(records, 2))
    var list = new ListBuffer[Map[String, Long]]()
    for( i <- 2 to 9){
      val m =  Util.get_mapping(records, i)
      list += m
    }
    val mappings = list.toList
    var catLen = 0
    mappings.foreach( m => (catLen +=m.size))

    val numLen = records.first().slice(11, 15).size
    val totalLen = catLen + numLen
    print("Feature vector length for categorical features:"+
        catLen)
     print("Feature vector length for numerical features:" +
       numLen)
     print("Total feature vector length: " + totalLen)

    val data = {
      records.map(r => LabeledPoint(Math.log(Util.extractLabel(r)),
```

```
                Util.extractFeatures(r, catLen, mappings)))
        }
    val first_point = data.first()
    println("Linear Model feature vector:" +
        first_point.features.toString)
    println("Linear Model feature vector length: " +
        first_point.features.size)


    val iterations = 10
    val step = 0.025
    val intercept =true
    val linear_model = LinearRegressionWithSGD.train(data,
        iterations, step)
    val x = linear_model.predict(data.first().features)
    val true_vs_predicted = data.map(p => (Math.exp(p.label),
        Math.exp(linear_model.predict(p.features))))
    val true_vs_predicted_csv = data.map(p => p.label + " ," +
        linear_model.predict(p.features))
    val format = new java.text.SimpleDateFormat(
        "dd-MM-yyyy-hh-mm-ss")
    val date = format.format(new java.util.Date())
    val save = false
    if (save){
            true_vs_predicted_csv.saveAsTextFile(
                "./output/linear_model_" + date + ".csv")
    }
    val true_vs_predicted_take5 = true_vs_predicted.take(5)
    for(i <- 0 until 5) {
      println("True vs Predicted: " + "i :" +
            true_vs_predicted_take5(i))
    }

    Util.calculatePrintMetrics(true_vs_predicted,
        "LinearRegressioWithSGD Log")
  }
}
```

The output of the preceding code will be similar to the following:

```
LinearRegressioWithSGD Log - Mean Squared Error: 5055.089410453301
LinearRegressioWithSGD Log - Mean Absolute Error: 51.56719871511336
LinearRegressioWithSGD Log - Root Mean Squared Log
    Error:1.7785399629180894
```

The code listing is available at this link:

- https://github.com/ml-resources/spark-ml/tree/branch-ed
  2/Chapter_07/scala/2.0.0/scala-spark-
  app/src/main/scala/org/sparksamples/regression/
  linearregression/LinearRegressionWithLog.scala
- https://github.com/ml-resources/spark-ml/tree/branch-ed
  2/Chapter_07/scala/2.0.0/scala-spark-
  app/src/main/scala/org/sparksamples/regression/
  linearregression/LinearRegression.scala

If we compare these preceding results to the results on the raw target variable, we see that all three values became worse.

```
LinearRegressioWithSGD - Mean Squared Error: 35817.9777663029
LinearRegressioWithSGD - Mean Absolute Error: 136.94887209426008
LinearRegressioWithSGD - Root Mean Squared Log Error:
    1.4482391780194306
LinearRegressioWithSGD Log - Mean Squared Error: 60192.54096079104
LinearRegressioWithSGD Log - Mean Absolute Error:
    170.82191606911752
LinearRegressioWithSGD Log - Root Mean Squared Log Error:
    1.9587586971094555
```

Tuning model parameters

So far in this chapter, we have illustrated the concepts of model training and evaluation for MLlib's regression models by training and testing on the same dataset. We will now use a cross-validation approach similar to what we used previously to evaluate the effect of different parameter settings on the performance of our models.

Creating training and testing sets to evaluate parameters

The first step is to create a test and training set for cross-validation purposes.

In Scala, the split is easier to implement, and the randomSplit function is available:

```
val splits = data.randomSplit(Array(0.8, 0.2), seed = 11L)
val training = splits(0).cache()
val test = splits(1)
```

Splitting data for Decision tree

The final step is to apply the same approach to the features extracted for the decision tree model.

Scala

```
val splits = data_dt.randomSplit(Array(0.8, 0.2), seed = 11L)
val training = splits(0).cache()
val test = splits(1)
```

The impact of parameter settings for linear models

Now that we have prepared our training and test sets, we are ready to investigate the impact of the different parameter settings on model performance. We will first carry out this evaluation for the linear model. We will create a convenience function to evaluate the relevant performance metric by training the model on the training set, and evaluating it on the test set for different parameter settings.

We will use the RMSLE evaluation metric, as it is the one used in the Kaggle competition with this dataset, and this allows us to compare our model results against the competition leaderboard to see how we perform.

The evaluation function is defined here:

Scala

```
def evaluate(train: RDD[LabeledPoint],test: RDD[LabeledPoint],
  iterations:Int,step:Double,
  intercept:Boolean): Double ={
  val linReg =
    new LinearRegressionWithSGD().setIntercept(intercept)
```

```
linReg.optimizer.setNumIterations(iterations).setStepSize(step)
val linear_model = linReg.run(train)

val true_vs_predicted = test.map(p => (p.label,
   linear_model.predict(p.features)))
val rmsle = Math.sqrt(true_vs_predicted.map{
   case(t, p) => Util.squaredLogError(t, p)}.mean())
return rmsle
}
```

Note that in the following sections, you might get slightly different results due to some random initialization for SGD. However, your results will be comparable.

Iterations

As we saw when evaluating our classification models, we generally expect that a model trained with SGD will achieve better performance as the number of iterations increases, although the increase in performance will slow down as the number of iterations goes above some minimum number. Note that here, we will set the step size to 0.01 to better illustrate the impact at higher iteration numbers.

We implemented the same in Scala with different values of iterations, as follows:

```
val data = LinearRegressionUtil.getTrainTestData()
val train_data = data._1
val test_data = data._2
val iterations = 10
//LinearRegressionCrossValidationStep$
//params = [1, 5, 10, 20, 50, 100, 200]
val iterations_param = Array(1, 5, 10, 20, 50, 100, 200)
val step =0.01
//val steps_param = Array(0.01, 0.025, 0.05, 0.1, 1.0)
val intercept =false

val i = 0
val results = new Array[String](5)
val resultsMap = new scala.collection.mutable.HashMap[String,
   String]
val dataset = new DefaultCategoryDataset()
for(i <- 0 until iterations_param.length) {
  val iteration = iterations_param(i)
  val rmsle = LinearRegressionUtil.evaluate(train_data,
  test_data,iteration,step,intercept)
  //results(i) = step + ":" + rmsle
```

```
resultsMap.put(iteration.toString,rmsle.toString)
dataset.addValue(rmsle, "RMSLE", iteration)
}
```

For the scala implementation, we use JfreeChart's scala version. Implementation reaches minimum RMSLE at 20 iterations:

```
Map(5 -> 0.8403179051522236, 200 -> 0.35682322830872604, 50 ->
0.07224447567763903, 1 -> 1.6381266770967882, 20 ->
0.23992956602621263, 100 -> 0.2525579338412989, 10 ->
0.5236271681647611)
```

The plot for the preceding output is shown as follows:

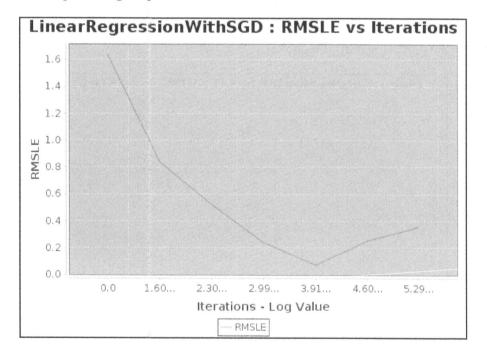

Step size

We will perform a similar analysis for step size in the following code:

Scala

```
val steps_param = Array(0.01, 0.025, 0.05, 0.1, 1.0)
val intercept =false

val i = 0
```

```scala
val results = new Array[String](5)
val resultsMap = new scala.collection.mutable.HashMap[String, String]
val dataset = new DefaultCategoryDataset()
for(i <- 0 until steps_param.length) {
  val step = steps_param(i)
  val rmsle = LinearRegressionUtil.evaluate(train_data,
        test_data,iterations,step,intercept)
  resultsMap.put(step.toString,rmsle.toString)
  dataset.addValue(rmsle, "RMSLE", step)
}
```

Output for the previous code is as follows:

```
[1.7904244862988534, 1.4241062778987466, 1.3840130355866163,
1.4560061007109475, nan]
```

The plot for the preceding output is shown as follows:

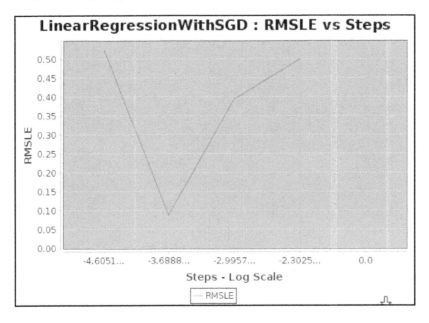

Now we can see why we avoided using the default step size when training the linear model originally. The default is set to *1.0*, which, in this case, results in a nan output for the RMSLE metric. This typically means that the SGD model has converged to a very poor local minimum in the error function that it is optimizing. This can happen when the step size is relatively large, as it is easier for the optimization algorithm to overshoot good solutions.

We can also see that for low step sizes and a relatively low number of iterations (we used 10 here), the model performance is slightly poorer. However, in the preceding *Iterations* section, we saw that for the lower step-size setting, a higher number of iterations will generally converge to a better solution.

Generally speaking, setting step size and number of iterations involves a trade-off. A lower step size means that convergence is slower, but slightly more assured. However, it requires a higher number of iterations, which is more costly in terms of computation and time, particularly, at a very large scale.

Selecting the best parameter settings can be an intensive process, which involves training a model on many combinations of parameter settings and selecting the best outcome. Each instance of model training involves a number of iterations, so this process can be very expensive and time consuming when performed on very large datasets. Model initialization also has an impact on the results, both on reaching global minima, or reaching a sub-optimal local minima in the gradient descent graph.

L2 regularization

In Chapter 6, *Building a Classification Model with Spark*, we saw that regularization has the effect of penalizing model complexity in the form of an additional loss term that is a function of the model weight vector. L2 regularization penalizes the L2-norm of the weight vector, while L1 regularization penalizes the L1-norm.

We expect training set performance to deteriorate with increasing regularization, as the model cannot fit the dataset well. However, we would also expect some amount of regularization that will result in optimal generalization performance as evidenced by the best performance on the test set.

L1 regularization

We can apply the same approach for differing levels of L1 regularization, as follows:

```
params = [0.0, 0.01, 0.1, 1.0, 10.0, 100.0, 1000.0]
metrics = [evaluate(train_data, test_data, 10, 0.1, param, 'l1',
    False) for param in params]
print params
print metrics
plot(params, metrics)
fig = matplotlib.pyplot.gcf()
pyplot.xscale('log')
```

Again, the results are more clearly seen when plotted in the following graph. We see that there is a much more subtle decline in RMSLE, and it takes a very high value to cause a jump back up. Here, the level of L1 regularization required is much higher than that for the L2 form; however, the overall performance is poorer:

```
[0.0, 0.01, 0.1, 1.0, 10.0, 100.0, 1000.0]
[1.5384660954019971, 1.5384518080419873, 1.5383237472930684,
    1.5372017600929164, 1.5303809928601677, 1.4352494587433793,
    4.7551250073268614]
```

Using L1 regularization can encourage sparse weight vectors. Does this hold true in this case? We can find out by examining the number of entries in the weight vector that are zero, with increasing levels of regularization.

```
model_l1 = LinearRegressionWithSGD.train(train_data, 10, 0.1,
    regParam=1.0, regType='l1', intercept=False)
model_l1_10 = LinearRegressionWithSGD.train(train_data, 10, 0.1,
    regParam=10.0, regType='l1', intercept=False)
model_l1_100 = LinearRegressionWithSGD.train(train_data, 10, 0.1,
    regParam=100.0, regType='l1', intercept=False)
print "L1 (1.0) number of zero weights: " +
    str(sum(model_l1.weights.array == 0))
print "L1 (10.0) number of zeros weights: " +
    str(sum(model_l1_10.weights.array == 0))
print "L1 (100.0) number of zeros weights: " +
    str(sum(model_l1_100.weights.array == 0))
```

We can see from the results that, as we might expect, the number of zero feature weights in the model weight vector increases as greater levels of L1 regularization are applied.

```
L1 (1.0) number of zero weights: 4
L1 (10.0) number of zeros weights: 20
L1 (100.0) number of zeros weights: 55
```

Intercept

The final parameter option for the linear model is whether to use an intercept or not. An intercept is a constant term that is added to the weight vector, and effectively accounts for the mean value of the target variable. If the data is already centered or normalized, an intercept is not necessary; however, it often does not hurt to use one in any case.

We will evaluate the effect of adding an intercept term to the model here:

Scala

```scala
object LinearRegressionCrossValidationIntercept{
  def main(args: Array[String]) {
    val data = LinearRegressionUtil.getTrainTestData()
    val train_data = data._1
    val test_data = data._2

    val iterations = 10
    val step = 0.1
    val paramsArray = new Array[Boolean](2)
    paramsArray(0) = true
    paramsArray(1) = false
    val i = 0
    val results = new Array[String](2)
    val resultsMap = new scala.collection.mutable.HashMap[
    String, String]
    val dataset = new DefaultCategoryDataset()
    for(i <- 0 until 2) {
      val intercept = paramsArray(i)
      val rmsle = LinearRegressionUtil.evaluate(train_data,
        test_data,iterations,step,intercept)
      results(i) = intercept + ":" + rmsle
      resultsMap.put(intercept.toString, rmsle.toString)
      dataset.addValue(rmsle, "RMSLE", intercept.toString)
    }
    val chart = new LineChart(
      "Steps" ,
      "LinearRegressionWithSGD : RMSLE vs Intercept")
    chart.exec("Steps","RMSLE",dataset)
    chart.lineChart.getCategoryPlot().getRangeAxis().setRange(
    1.56, 1.57)
    chart.pack( )
    RefineryUtilities.centerFrameOnScreen( chart )
    chart.setVisible( true )
    println(results)
  }
}
```

The plot for the preceding output is shown as follows:

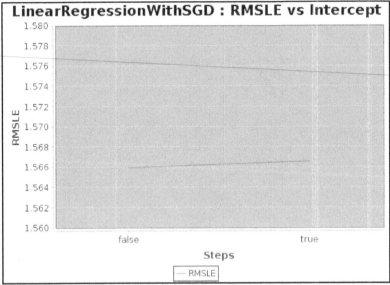

As can be seen in the preceding image, the RMSLE value for intercept=true is slightly higher as compared to intercept=false.

The impact of parameter settings for the decision tree

Decision trees provide two main parameters: maximum tree depth and maximum number of bins. We will now perform the same evaluation of the effect of parameter settings for the decision tree model. Our starting point is to create an evaluation function for the model, similar to the one used for the linear regression earlier. This function is provided here:

Scala

```scala
def evaluate(train: RDD[LabeledPoint],test: RDD[LabeledPoint],
  categoricalFeaturesInfo: scala.Predef.Map[Int, Int],
  maxDepth :Int, maxBins: Int): Double = {
    val impurity = "variance"
    val decisionTreeModel = DecisionTree.trainRegressor(train,
      categoricalFeaturesInfo,
      impurity, maxDepth, maxBins)
    val true_vs_predicted = test.map(p => (p.label,
      decisionTreeModel.predict(p.features)))
    val rmsle = Math.sqrt(true_vs_predicted.map{
      case(t, p) => Util.squaredLogError(t, p)}.mean())
```

```
        return rmsle
    }
```

Tree depth

We would generally expect performance to increase with more complex trees (that is, trees of greater depth). Having a lower tree depth acts as a form of regularization, and it might be the case that as with L2 or L1 regularization in linear models, there is a tree depth that is optimal with respect to the test set performance.

Here, we will try to increase the depth of trees to see what impact they have on the test set RMSLE, keeping the number of bins at the default level of 32:

Scala

```scala
val data = DecisionTreeUtil.getTrainTestData()
  val train_data = data._1
  val test_data = data._2
  val iterations = 10
  val bins_param = Array(2, 4, 8, 16, 32, 64, 100)
  val depth_param = Array(1, 2, 3, 4, 5, 10, 20)
  val bin = 32
  val categoricalFeaturesInfo = scala.Predef.Map[Int, Int]()
  val i = 0
  val results = new Array[String](7)
  val resultsMap = new scala.collection.mutable.HashMap[
    String, String]
  val dataset = new DefaultCategoryDataset()
  for(i <- 0 until depth_param.length) {
    val depth = depth_param(i)
    val rmsle = DecisionTreeUtil.evaluate(
    train_data, test_data, categoricalFeaturesInfo, depth, bin)

    resultsMap.put(depth.toString,rmsle.toString)
    dataset.addValue(rmsle, "RMSLE", depth)
  }
  val chart = new LineChart(
    "MaxDepth" ,
    "DecisionTree : RMSLE vs MaxDepth")
  chart.exec("MaxDepth","RMSLE",dataset)
  chart.pack()
  RefineryUtilities.centerFrameOnScreen( chart )
  chart.setVisible( true )
  print(resultsMap)
}
```

The plot for the preceding output is shown as follows:

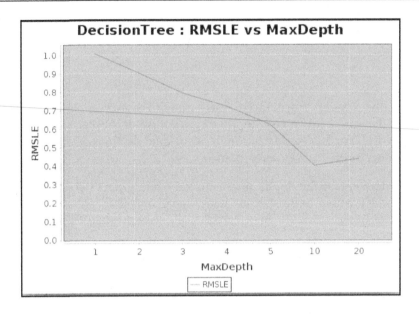

Maximum bins

Finally, we will perform our evaluation on the impact of setting the number of bins for the decision tree. As with the tree depth, a larger number of bins should allow the model to become more complex, and might help performance with larger feature dimensions. After a certain point, it is unlikely that it will help any more, and might, in fact, hinder performance on the test set due to over-fitting.

Scala

```scala
object DecisionTreeMaxBins{
  def main(args: Array[String]) {
    val data = DecisionTreeUtil.getTrainTestData()
    val train_data = data._1
    val test_data = data._2
    val iterations = 10
    val bins_param = Array(2, 4, 8, 16, 32, 64, 100)
    val maxDepth = 5
    val categoricalFeaturesInfo = scala.Predef.Map[Int, Int]()
    val i = 0
    val results = new Array[String](5)
    val resultsMap = new scala.collection.mutable.HashMap[
      String, String]
    val dataset = new DefaultCategoryDataset()
    for(i <- 0 until bins_param.length) {
      val bin = bins_param(i)
```

```
val rmsle = {
  DecisionTreeUtil.evaluate(train_data, test_data,
    categoricalFeaturesInfo, 5, bin)
}
resultsMap.put(bin.toString,rmsle.toString)
dataset.addValue(rmsle, "RMSLE", bin)
}
val chart = new LineChart(
  "MaxBins" ,
  "DecisionTree : RMSLE vs MaxBins")
chart.exec("MaxBins","RMSLE",dataset)
chart.pack( )
RefineryUtilities.centerFrameOnScreen( chart )
chart.setVisible( true )
print(resultsMap)
}
```

The plot for the preceding output is shown as follows:

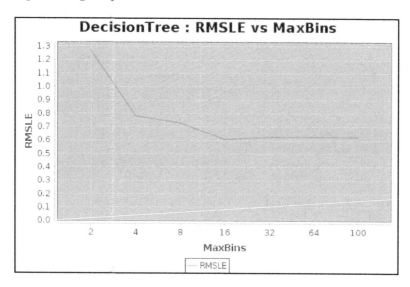

The impact of parameter settings for the Gradient Boosted Trees

Gradient boosted trees have two main parameter iterations and maximum depth. We are going to make variations in these and see the effects.

Iterations

Scala

```scala
object GradientBoostedTreesIterations{

  def main(args: Array[String]) {
    val data = GradientBoostedTreesUtil.getTrainTestData()
    val train_data = data._1
    val test_data = data._2

    val iterations_param = Array(1, 5, 10, 15, 18)

    val i = 0
    val resultsMap = new scala.collection.mutable.HashMap[
        String, String]
    val dataset = new DefaultCategoryDataset()
    for(i <- 0 until iterations_param.length) {
      val iteration = iterations_param(i)
      val rmsle = GradientBoostedTreesUtil.evaluate(train_data,
        test_data,iteration,maxDepth)
      resultsMap.put(iteration.toString,rmsle.toString)
      dataset.addValue(rmsle, "RMSLE", iteration)
    }
    val chart = new LineChart(
      "Iterations" ,
      "GradientBoostedTrees : RMSLE vs Iterations")
    chart.exec("Iterations","RMSLE",dataset)
    chart.pack( )
    chart.lineChart.getCategoryPlot().
      getRangeAxis().setRange(1.32, 1.37)
    RefineryUtilities.centerFrameOnScreen( chart )
    chart.setVisible( true )
    print(resultsMap)
  }
}
```

The plot for the preceding output is shown as follows:

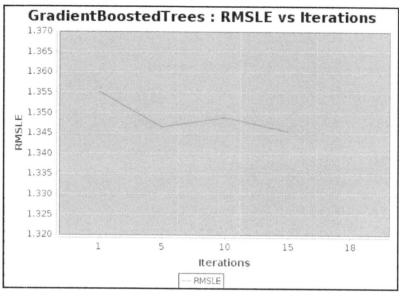

MaxBins

Next we look at how changing the maximum number of bins affects the RMSLE values.

Scala

Let us look at the sample implementation in Scala. We will calculate the RMSLE value for maximum number of bins: 10, 16, 32, and 64.

```scala
object GradientBoostedTreesMaxBins{

  def main(args: Array[String]) {
    val data = GradientBoostedTreesUtil.getTrainTestData()
    val train_data = data._1
    val test_data = data._2

    val maxBins_param = Array(10,16,32,64)
    val iteration = 10
    val maxDepth = 3

    val i = 0
    val resultsMap =
    new scala.collection.mutable.HashMap[String, String]
    val dataset = new DefaultCategoryDataset()
```

```
for(i <- 0 until maxBins_param.length) {
  val maxBin = maxBins_param(i)
  val rmsle = GradientBoostedTreesUtil.evaluate(train_data,
    test_data,iteration,maxDepth, maxBin)

  resultsMap.put(maxBin.toString,rmsle.toString)
  dataset.addValue(rmsle, "RMSLE", maxBin)
}
val chart = new LineChart(
  "Max Bin" ,
  "GradientBoostedTrees : RMSLE vs MaxBin")
chart.exec("MaxBins","RMSLE",dataset)
chart.pack( )
chart.lineChart.getCategoryPlot().
    getRangeAxis().setRange(1.35, 1.37)
RefineryUtilities.centerFrameOnScreen( chart )
chart.setVisible(true)
print(resultsMap)
}
```

The plot for the preceding output is shown as follows:

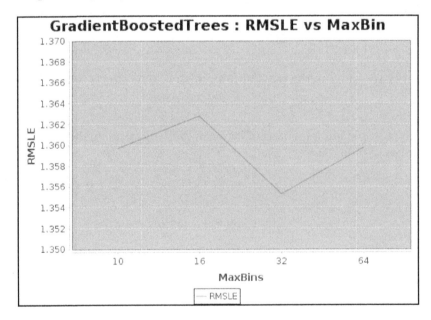

Summary

In this chapter, you saw how to use ML Library's linear model, decision tree, gradient boosted trees, Ridge Regression, and the isotonic regression functionality in Scala within the context of regression models. We explored categorical feature extraction, and the impact of applying transformations to the target variable in a regression problem. Finally, we implemented various performance-evaluation metrics, and used them to implement a cross-validation exercise that explores the impact of the various parameter settings available in both linear models and decision trees on test set model performance.

In the next chapter, we will cover a different approach to machine learning, that is, unsupervised learning, specifically in clustering models.

8
Building a Clustering Model with Spark

In the last few chapters, we covered supervised learning methods, where the training data is labeled with the true outcome that we would like to predict (for example, a rating for recommendations and class assignment for classification or a real target variable in the case of regression).

Next, we will consider the case where we do not have labeled data available. This is called **unsupervised learning**, as the model is not supervised with the true target label. The unsupervised case is very common in practice, since obtaining labeled training data can be very difficult or expensive in many real-world scenarios (for example, having humans label training data with class labels for classification). However, we would still like to learn some underlying structure in the data and use these to make predictions.

This is where unsupervised learning approaches can be useful. Unsupervised learning models are also often combined with supervised models; for example, applying unsupervised techniques to create new input features for supervised models.

Clustering models are, in many ways, the unsupervised equivalent of classification models. With classification, we tried to learn a model that would predict which class a given training example belonged to. The model was essentially a mapping from a set of features to the class.

In clustering, we would like to segment the data such that each training example is assigned to a segment called a **cluster**. The clusters act much like classes, except that the true class assignments are unknown.

Clustering models have many use cases that are the same as classification; these include the following:

- Segmenting users or customers into different groups based on behavior characteristics and metadata
- Grouping content on a website or products in a retail business
- Finding clusters of similar genes
- Segmenting communities in ecology
- Creating image segments for use in image analysis applications such as object detection

In this chapter, we will:

- Briefly explore a few types of clustering models
- Extract features from the data specifically using the output of one model as input features for our clustering model
- Train a clustering model and use it to make predictions
- Apply performance-evaluation and parameter-selection techniques to select the optimal number of clusters to use

Types of clustering models

There are many different forms of clustering models available, ranging from simple to extremely complex ones. The Spark MLlib currently provides k-means clustering, which is among the simplest approaches available. However, it is often very effective, and its simplicity means it is relatively easy to understand and is scalable.

k-means clustering

k-means attempts to partition a set of data points into K distinct clusters (where K is an input parameter for the model).

More formally, k-means tries to find clusters so as to minimize the sum of squared errors (or distances) within each cluster. This objective function is known as the **within cluster sum of squared errors (WCSS)**.

$$\sum_{i=1}^{n}\sum_{j=1}^{n}(x(j)-u(i))^{2}$$

It is the sum, over each cluster, of the squared errors between each point and the cluster center.

Starting with a set of K initial cluster centers (which are computed as the mean vector for all data points in the cluster), the standard method for K-means iterates between two steps:

1. Assign each data point to the cluster that minimizes the WCSS. The sum of squares is equivalent to the squared Euclidean distance; therefore, this equates to assigning each point to the **closest** cluster center as measured by the Euclidean distance metric.
2. Compute the new cluster centers based on the cluster assignments from the first step.

The algorithm proceeds until either a maximum number of iterations has been reached or convergence has been achieved. **Convergence** means that the cluster assignments no longer change during the first step; therefore, the value of the WCSS objective function does not change either.

> For more details, refer to Spark's documentation on clustering at `http://s park.apache.org/docs/latest/mllib-clustering.html`or refer to `http ://en.wikipedia.org/wiki/K-means_clustering`.

To illustrate the basics of K-means, we will use the simple dataset we showed in our multiclass classification example in Chapter 6, *Building a Classification Model with Spark*. Recall that we have five classes, which are shown in the following figure:

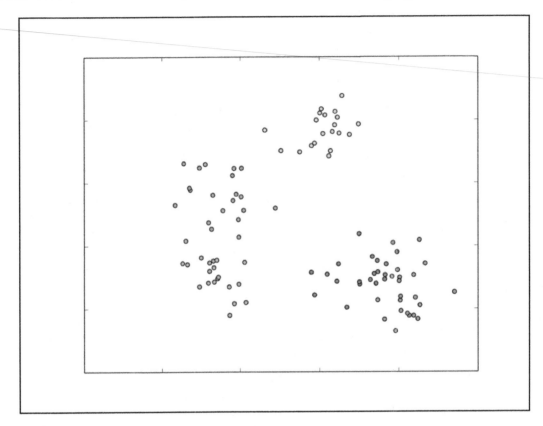

Multiclass dataset

However, assume that we don't actually know the true classes. If we use k-means with five clusters, then after the first step, the model's cluster assignments might look like this:

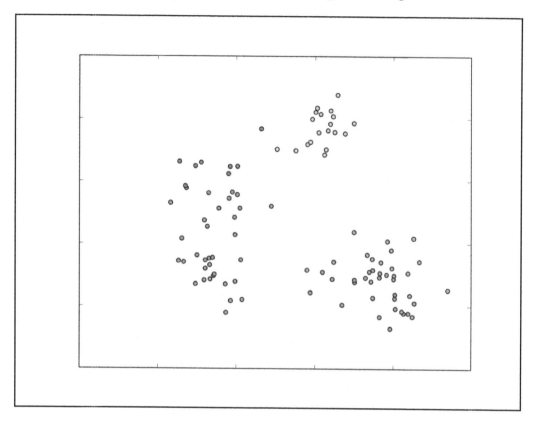

Cluster assignments after the first K-means iteration

We can see that k-means has already picked out the centers of each cluster fairly well. After the next iteration, the assignments might look like those shown in the following figure:

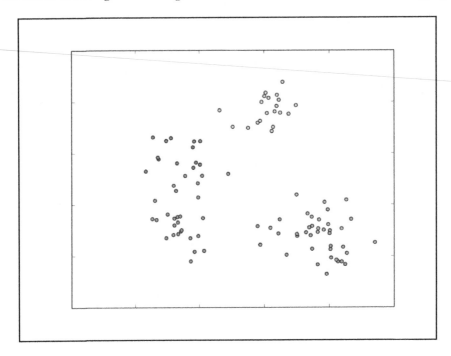

Cluster assignments after the second K-means iteration

Things are starting to stabilize, but the overall cluster assignments are broadly the same as they were after the first iteration. Once the model has converged, the final assignments could look like this:

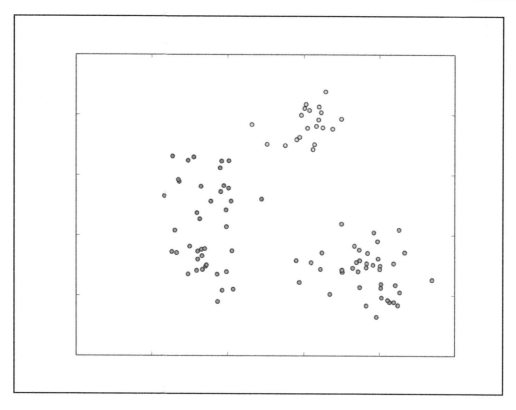

Final cluster assignments for K-means

As we can see, the model has done a decent job of separating the five clusters. The leftmost three are fairly accurate (with a few incorrect points). However, the two clusters in the bottom-right corner are less accurate.

This illustrates:

- The iterative nature of K-means
- The model's dependency on the method of initially selecting clusters' centers (here, we will use a random approach)
- That the final cluster assignments can be very good for well-separated data but can be poor for data that is more difficult

Initialization methods

The standard initialization method for k-means, usually simply referred to as the random method, starts by randomly assigning each data point to a cluster before proceeding with the first update step.

Spark ML provides a parallel variant for this initialization method, called **K-means ++**, which is the default initialization method used.

 See `http://en.wikipedia.org/wiki/K-means_clustering#Initializat ion_methods` and `http://en.wikipedia.org/wiki/K-means%2B%2B` for more information.

The results of using K-means++ are shown here. Note that this time, the difficult lower-right points have been mostly correctly clustered:

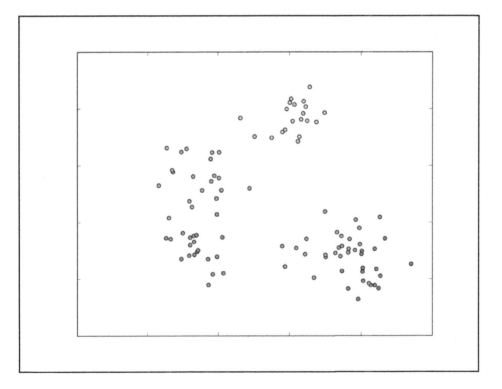

Final cluster assignments for K-means++

There are many other variants of K-means; they focus on initialization methods or the core model. One of the more common variants is **fuzzy K-means**. This model does not assign each point to one cluster as K-means does (a so-called hard assignment). Instead, it is a soft version of K-means, where each point can belong to many clusters, and is represented by the relative membership to each cluster. So, for *K* clusters, each point is represented as a K-dimensional membership vector, with each entry in this vector indicating the membership proportion in each cluster.

Mixture models

A **mixture model** is essentially an extension of the idea behind fuzzy K-means; however, it makes an assumption that there is an underlying probability distribution that generates the data. For example, we might assume that the data points are drawn from a set of K-independent Gaussian (normal) probability distributions. The cluster assignments are also soft, so each point is represented by *K* membership weights in each of the *K* underlying probability distributions.

See `http://en.wikipedia.org/wiki/Mixture_model`for further details and for a mathematical treatment of mixture models.

Hierarchical clustering

Hierarchical clustering is a structured clustering approach that results in a multilevel hierarchy of clusters, where each cluster might contain many subclusters (or child clusters). Each child cluster is, thus, linked to the parent cluster. This form of clustering is often also called **tree clustering**.

Agglomerative clustering is a bottom-up approach where:

- Each data point begins in its own cluster
- The similarity (or distance) between each pair of clusters is evaluated
- The pair of clusters that are most similar are found; this pair is then merged to form a new cluster
- The process is repeated until only one top-level cluster remains

Divisive clustering is a top-down approach that works in reverse, starting with one cluster and at each stage, splitting a cluster into two, until all data points are allocated to their own bottom-level cluster.

Top-down clustering is more complex than bottom-up clustering since a second, flat clustering algorithm is needed as a "subroutine". Top-down clustering has the advantage of being more efficient if we do not generate a complete hierarchy to individual document leaves.

> You can find more information at
> http://en.wikipedia.org/wiki/Hierarchical_clustering.

Extracting the right features from your data

Like most of the machine learning models we have encountered so far, k-means clustering requires numerical vectors as input. The same feature extraction and transformation approaches that we have seen for classification and regression are applicable for clustering.

As k-means, like least squares regression, uses a squared error function as the optimization objective, it tends to be impacted by outliers and features with large variance.

Clustering could be leveraged to detect outliers as they can cause a lot of problems.

As for regression and classification cases, input data can be normalized and standardized to overcome this, which might improve accuracy. In some cases, however, it might be desirable not to standardize data, if, for example, the objective is to find segmentations according to certain specific features.

Extracting features from the MovieLens dataset

We will use the ALS algorithm to get numerical features for users and items (movies) in this case before we can use the clustering algorithm on the data:

1. First we load the data u.data into a DataFrame:

```
val ratings = spark.sparkContext
.textFile(DATA_PATH + "/u.data")
.map(_.split("\t"))
.map(lineSplit => Rating(lineSplit(0).toInt,
```

```
lineSplit(1).toInt, lineSplit(2).toFloat,
lineSplit(3).toLong))
.toDF()
```

2. Then we split it into a 80:20 ratio to get the training and test data:

```
val Array(training, test) =
    ratings.randomSplit(Array(0.8, 0.2))
```

3. We instantiate the ALS class, set the maximum iterations at 5, and the regularization parameter at 0.01:

```
val als = new ALS()
    .setMaxIter(5)
    .setRegParam(0.01)
    .setUserCol("userId")
    .setItemCol("movieId")
    .setRatingCol("rating")
```

4. Then we create a model, followed by calculating predictions:

```
val model = als.fit(training)
val predictions = model.transform(test)
```

5. This is followed by calculating userFactors and itemFactors:

```
val itemFactors = model.itemFactors
itemFactors.show()

val userFactors = model.userFactors
userFactors.show()
```

6. We convert them into libsvmformat and persist them in a file. Notice that we are persisting all the features as well two features:

```
val itemFactorsOrdererd = itemFactors.orderBy("id")
val itemFactorLibSVMFormat =
    itemFactorsOrdererd.rdd.map(x => x(0) + " " +
    getDetails(x(1).asInstanceOf
        [scala.collection.mutable.WrappedArray[Float]]))
println("itemFactorLibSVMFormat.count() : " +
    itemFactorLibSVMFormat.count())
print("itemFactorLibSVMFormat.first() : " +
    itemFactorLibSVMFormat.first())

itemFactorLibSVMFormat.coalesce(1)
    .saveAsTextFile(output + "/" + date_time +
```

```
"/movie_lens_items_libsvm")
```

The output of `movie_lens_items_libsvm` will look like the following listing:

```
1 1:0.44353345 2:-0.7453435 3:-0.55146646 4:-0.40894786
5:-0.9921601 6:1.2012635 7:0.50330496 8:-0.23256435
9:0.55483425 10:-1.4781344
2 1:0.34384087 2:-1.0242497 3:-0.20907198 4:-0.102892995
5:-1.0616653 6:1.1338154 7:0.5742042 8:-0.46505615
9:0.3823278 10:-1.0695107 3 1:-0.04743084 2:-0.6035447
3:-0.7999673 4:0.16897096
5:-1.0216197 6:0.3304353 7:1.5495727 8:0.2972699
9:-0.6855238
10:-1.5391738
4 1:0.24745995 2:-0.33971268 3:0.025664425 4:0.16798466
5:-0.8462472 6:0.6734541 7:0.7537076 8:-0.7119413
9:0.7475001
10:-1.965572
5 1:0.30903652 2:-0.8523586 3:-0.54090345 4:-0.7004097
5:-1.0383878 6:1.1784278 7:0.5125761 8:0.2566347
9:-0.020201845
10:-1.118083
. . . .
1681 1:-0.14603947 2:-0.4475343 3:-0.50514024 4:-0.7221697
5:-0.7997808 6:0.21069092 7:0.22631708 8:-0.32458723
9:0.20187362 10:-1.2734087
1682 1:0.21975909 2:0.45303428 3:-0.73912954 4:-0.40584692
5:-0.5299451 6:0.79586357 7:0.5154468 8:-0.4033669
9:0.2220822
10:-0.70235217
```

7. Next, we persist the top two features (with maximum variation) and persist them in a file:

```
var itemFactorsXY = itemFactorsOrdererd.rdd.map(
  x => getXY(x(1).asInstanceOf
  [scala.collection.mutable.WrappedArray[Float]]))
itemFactorsXY.first()
itemFactorsXY.coalesce(1).saveAsTextFile(output + "/" +
  date_time + "/movie_lens_items_xy")
```

The output of `movie_lens_items_xy` will look like this:

```
2.254384458065033, 0.5487040132284164
-2.0540390759706497, 0.5557805597782135
-2.303591560572386, -0.047419726848602295
-0.7448508385568857, -0.5028514862060547
```

```
-2.8230229914188385, 0.8093537855893373
-1.4274845123291016, 1.4835840165615082
-1.3214656114578247, 0.09438827633857727
-2.028286747634411, 1.0806758720427752
-0.798517256975174, 0.8371041417121887
-1.556841880083084, -0.8985426127910614
-1.0867036543786526, 1.7443277575075626
-1.4234793484210968, 0.624072947978973
-0.04958712309598923, 0.14585793018341064
```

8. Next we calculate the libsvm format for `userFactors`:

```
val userFactorsOrdererd = userFactors.orderBy("id")
val userFactorLibSVMFormat =
  userFactorsOrdererd.rdd.map(x => x(0) + " " +
  getDetails(x(1).asInstanceOf
    [scala.collection.mutable.WrappedArray[Float]]))
println("userFactorLibSVMFormat.count() : " +
  userFactorLibSVMFormat.count())
print("userFactorLibSVMFormat.first() : " +
  userFactorLibSVMFormat.first())

userFactorLibSVMFormat.coalesce(1)
  .saveAsTextFile(output + "/" + date_time +
  "/movie_lens_users_libsvm")
```

The output of `movie_lens_users_libsvm` will look like the following listing:

```
1 1:0.75239724 2:0.31830165 3:0.031550772 4:-0.63495475
5:-0.719721 6:0.5437525 7:0.59800273 8:-0.4264512
9:0.6661331
10:-0.9702077
2 1:-0.053673547 2:-0.24080916 3:-0.6896337 4:-0.3918436
5:-0.4108574 6:0.663401 7:0.1975566 8:0.43086317 9:1.0833738
10:-0.9398713
3 1:0.6261427 2:0.58282375 3:-0.48752788 4:-0.36584544
5:-1.1869227 6:0.14955235 7:-0.17821303 8:0.3922112
9:0.5596394 10:-0.83293504
4 1:1.0485783 2:0.2569924 3:-0.48094323 4:-1.8882223
5:-1.4912299 6:0.50734115 7:1.2781366 8:0.028034585
9:1.1323715 10:0.4267411
5 1:0.31982875 2:0.13479441 3:0.5392742 4:0.33915272
5:-1.1892766 6:0.33669636 7:0.38314193 8:-0.9331541
9:0.531006 10:-1.0546529
6 1:-0.5351592 2:0.1995535 3:-0.9234565 4:-0.5741345
5:-0.4506062 6:0.35505387 7:0.41615438 8:-0.32665777
9:0.22966743 10:-1.1040379
```

```
7 1:0.41014928 2:-0.32102737 3:-0.73221415 4:-0.4017513
5:-0.87815255 6:0.3717881 7:-0.070220165 8:-0.5443932
9:0.24361002 10:-1.2957898
8 1:0.2991327 2:0.3574251 3:-0.03855041 4:-0.1719838
5:-0.840421 6:0.89891523 7:0.024321048 8:-0.9811069
9:0.57676667 10:-1.2015694
9 1:-1.4988179 2:0.42335498 3:0.5973782 4:-0.11305857
5:-1.3311529 6:0.91228217 7:1.461522 8:1.4502159 9:0.5554214
10:-1.5014526
10 1:0.5876411 2:-0.26684982 3:-0.30273324 4:-0.78348076
5:-0.61448336 6:0.5506227 7:0.2809167 8:-0.08864456
9:0.57811487 10:-1.1085391
```

9. Next we extract the top two features and persist them in a file:

```
var userFactorsXY = userFactorsOrdererd.rdd.map(
  x => getXY(x(1).asInstanceOf
  [scala.collection.mutable.WrappedArray[Float]]))
userFactorsXY.first()
userFactorsXY.coalesce(1).saveAsTextFile(output + "/" +
  date_time + "/movie_lens_user_xy")
```

The output of `movie_lens_user_xy` will look like this:
```
-0.2524261102080345, 0.4112294316291809
-1.7868174277245998, 1.435323253273964
-0.8313295543193817, 0.09025487303733826
-2.55482479929924, 3.3726249802857637
0.14377352595329285, -0.736962765455246
-2.283802881836891, -0.4298199713230133
-1.9229961037635803, -1.2950050458312035
-0.39439742639660835, -0.682673366740346
-1.9222962260246277, 2.8779889345169067
-1.3799060583114624, 0.21247059851884842
```

We will need *xy* features to do clustering for two features so that we can create a two-dimensional plot.

K-means - training a clustering model

Training for K-means in Spark ML takes an approach similar to the other models -- we pass a DataFrame that contains our training data to the fit method of the KMeans object.

Here we use the libsvm data format.

Training a clustering model on the MovieLens dataset

We will train a model for both the movie and user factors that we generated by running our recommendation model.

We need to pass in the number of clusters K and the maximum number of iterations for the algorithm to run. Model training might run for less than the maximum number of iterations if the change in the objective function from one iteration to the next is less than the tolerance level (the default for this tolerance is 0.0001).

Spark ML's k-means provides random and K-means || initialization, with the default being K-means ||. As both of these initialization methods are based on random selection to some extent, each model training run will return a different result.

K-means does not generally converge to a global optimum model, so performing multiple training runs and selecting the most optimal model from these runs is a common practice. MLlib's training methods expose an option to complete multiple model training runs. The best training run, as measured by the evaluation of the loss function, is selected as the final model.

1. First we create a `SparkSession` instance and use it to load the `movie_lens_users_libsvm` data:

```
val spConfig = (new
  SparkConf).setMaster("local[1]").setAppName("SparkApp").
  set("spark.driver.allowMultipleContexts", "true")

val spark = SparkSession
  .builder()
  .appName("Spark SQL Example")
  .config(spConfig)
  .getOrCreate()

val datasetUsers = spark.read.format("libsvm").load(
  "./OUTPUT/11_10_2016_10_28_56/movie_lens_users_libsvm/part-
  00000")
datasetUsers.show(3)
```

The output is:

```
+-----+--------------------+
|label|            features|
+-----+--------------------+
|  1.0|(10,[0,1,2,3,4,5,...|
|  2.0|(10,[0,1,2,3,4,5,...|
|  3.0|(10,[0,1,2,3,4,5,...|
+-----+--------------------+
only showing top 3 rows
```

2. Then we create a model:

```
val kmeans = new KMeans().setK(5).setSeed(1L)
val modelUsers = kmeans.fit(datasetUsers)
```

3. Finally, we train a K-means model using a dataset of user vectors:

```
val modelUsers = kmeans.fit(datasetUsers)
```

K-means: Making predictions using a clustering model.

Using the trained K-means model is straightforward and similar to the other models we have encountered so far, such as classification and regression.

We can make predictions for multiple inputs by passing a DataFrame to the transform method of the model:

```
val predictedUserClusters = modelUsers.transform(datasetUsers)
predictedUserClusters.show(5)
```

The resulting output is a cluster assignment for each data point in the prediction column:

```
+-----+--------------------+----------+
|label|            features|prediction|
+-----+--------------------+----------+
|  1.0|(10,[0,1,2,3,4,5,...|         2|
|  2.0|(10,[0,1,2,3,4,5,...|         0|
|  3.0|(10,[0,1,2,3,4,5,...|         0|
|  4.0|(10,[0,1,2,3,4,5,...|         2|
|  5.0|(10,[0,1,2,3,4,5,...|         2|
+-----+--------------------+----------+
only showing top 5 rows
```

Due to random initialization, the cluster assignments might change from one run of the model to another, so your results might differ from those shown earlier. The cluster IDs themselves have no inherent meaning; they are simply arbitrarily labeled, starting from 0.

K-means - interpreting cluster predictions on the MovieLens dataset

We have covered how to make predictions for a set of input vectors, but how do we evaluate how good the predictions are? We will cover performance metrics a little later; however, here, we will see how to manually inspect and interpret the cluster assignments made by our k-means model.

While unsupervised techniques have the advantage that they do not require us to provide labeled data for training, the disadvantage is that, often, the results need to be manually interpreted. Often, we would like to further examine the clusters that are found and possibly try to interpret them and assign some sort of labeling or categorization to them.

For example, we can examine the clustering of movies we have found to try to see whether there is some meaningful interpretation of each cluster, such as a common genre or theme among the movies in the cluster. There are many approaches we can use, but we will start by taking a few movies in each cluster that are closest to the center of the cluster. These movies, we assume, would be the ones that are least likely to be marginal in terms of their cluster assignment, and so, they should be among the most representative of the movies in the cluster. By examining these sets of movies, we can see what attributes are shared by the movies in each cluster.

Interpreting the movie clusters

We will try to list the movie associated with each cluster by joining the dataset with the movie name with the prediction output dataset:

```
Cluster : 0
------------------------
+--------------------+
|                name|
+--------------------+
|    GoldenEye (1995)|
|    Four Rooms (1995)|
|Shanghai Triad (Y...|
|Twelve Monkeys (1...|
```

```
|Dead Man Walking ...|
|Usual Suspects, T...|
|Mighty Aphrodite ...|
|Antonia's Line (1...|
|   Braveheart (1995)|
|   Taxi Driver (1976)|
+--------------------+
only showing top 10 rows


Cluster : 1
---------------------------
+--------------------+
|                name|
+--------------------+
|      Bad Boys (1995)|
|Free Willy 2: The...|
|         Nadja (1994)|
|      Net, The (1995)|
|        Priest (1994)|
|While You Were Sl...|
|Ace Ventura: Pet ...|
|    Free Willy (1993)|
|Remains of the Da...|
|Sleepless in Seat...|
+--------------------+
only showing top 10 rows


Cluster : 2
---------------------------
+--------------------+
|                name|
+--------------------+
|     Toy Story (1995)|
|    Get Shorty (1995)|
|       Copycat (1995)|
|   Richard III (1995)|
|Seven (Se7en) (1995)|
|Mr. Holland's Opu...|
|From Dusk Till Da...|
|Brothers McMullen...|
|Batman Forever (1...|
|    Disclosure (1994)|
+--------------------+
only showing top 10 rows
```

```
Cluster : 3
-------------------------
+-------------------+
|               name|
+-------------------+
|         Babe (1995)|
|   Postino, Il (1994)|
|White Balloon, Th...|
|Muppet Treasure I...|
|Rumble in the Bro...|
|Birdcage, The (1996)|
|       Apollo 13 (1995)|
|Belle de jour (1967)|
| Crimson Tide (1995)|
|To Wong Foo, Than...|
+-------------------+
only showing top 10 rows
```

Interpreting the movie clusters

In this section, we review the code where we get the predictions for each label and save them in a text file and draw a two-dimensional scatter plot.

We will create two scatter plots, one for users and the other for items (which is movies in this case):

```
object MovieLensKMeansPersist {

  val BASE= "./data/movie_lens_libsvm_2f"
  val time = System.currentTimeMillis()
  val formatter = new SimpleDateFormat("dd_MM_yyyy_hh_mm_ss")

  import java.util.Calendar
  val calendar = Calendar.getInstance()
  calendar.setTimeInMillis(time)
  val date_time = formatter.format(calendar.getTime())


  def main(args: Array[String]): Unit = {

    val spConfig = (
    new SparkConf).setMaster("local[1]").
    setAppName("SparkApp").
      set("spark.driver.allowMultipleContexts", "true")

    val spark = SparkSession
      .builder()
```

```
.appName("Spark SQL Example")
.config(spConfig)
.getOrCreate()


val datasetUsers = spark.read.format("libsvm").load(
  BASE + "/movie_lens_2f_users_libsvm/part-00000")
datasetUsers.show(3)

val kmeans = new KMeans().setK(5).setSeed(1L)
val modelUsers = kmeans.fit(datasetUsers)

// Evaluate clustering by computing Within
//Set Sum of Squared Errors.

val predictedDataSetUsers = modelUsers.transform(datasetUsers)
print(predictedDataSetUsers.first())
print(predictedDataSetUsers.count())
val predictionsUsers =
predictedDataSetUsers.select("prediction").
rdd.map(x=> x(0))
predictionsUsers.saveAsTextFile(
BASE + "/prediction/" + date_time + "/users")


val datasetItems = spark.read.format("libsvm").load(
  BASE + "/movie_lens_2f_items_libsvm/part-00000")
datasetItems.show(3)

val kmeansItems = new KMeans().setK(5).setSeed(1L)
val modelItems = kmeansItems.fit(datasetItems)
// Evaluate clustering by computing Within
//Set Sum of Squared Errors.
val WSSSEItems = modelItems.computeCost(datasetItems)
println(s"Items :  Within Set Sum of Squared Errors =
  $WSSSEItems")

// Shows the result.
println("Items - Cluster Centers: ")
modelUsers.clusterCenters.foreach(println)
val predictedDataSetItems = modelItems.transform(datasetItems)
val predictionsItems = predictedDataSetItems.
  select("prediction").rdd.map(x=> x(0))
predictionsItems.saveAsTextFile(BASE + "/prediction/" +
  date_time + "/items")
spark.stop()
}
```

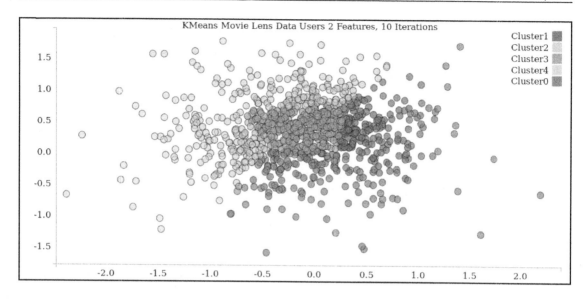

K-means clustering with user data

The preceding figure shows K-means clusters for user data.

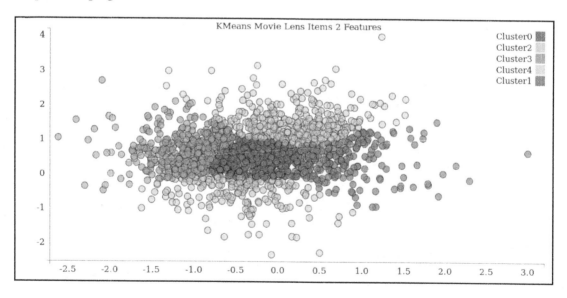

K-means clustering plot with item data

The preceding figure shows K-means clusters for item data.

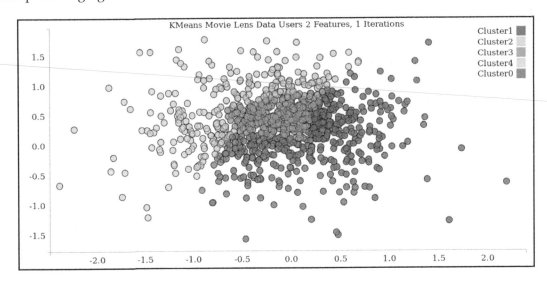

K-means plotting effect of number of clusters

The preceding figure shows K-means clusters for user data with two features and one iteration.

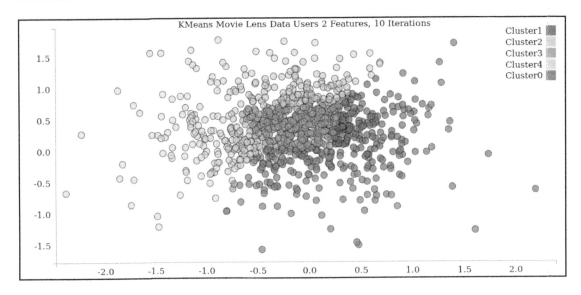

The preceding figure shows K-means clusters for user data with two features and 10 iterations. Notice how the cluster boundaries are moving.

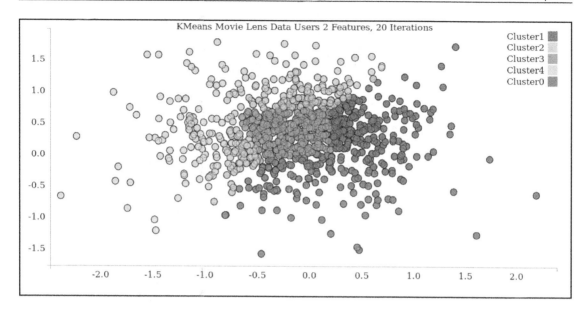

KMeans Movie Lens Data Users 2 Features, 20 Iterations

The preceding figure shows K-means clusters for user data with two features and 10 iterations. Notice how cluster boundaries are moving.

K-means - evaluating the performance of clustering models

With models such as regression, classification, and recommendation engines, there are many evaluation metrics that can be applied to clustering models to analyze their performance and the goodness of the clustering of the data points. Clustering evaluation is generally divided into either internal or external evaluation. Internal evaluation refers to the case where the same data used to train the model is used for evaluation. External evaluation refers to using data external to the training data for evaluation purposes.

Internal evaluation metrics

Common internal evaluation metrics include the WCSS we covered earlier (which is exactly the k-means objective function), the Davies-Bouldin Index, the Dunn Index, and the silhouette coefficient. All these measures tend to reward clusters where elements within a cluster are relatively close together, while elements in different clusters are relatively far away from each other.

The Wikipedia page on clustering evaluation at `http://en.wikipedia.or g/wiki/Cluster_analysis#Internal_evaluation`has more details.

External evaluation metrics

Since clustering can be thought of as unsupervised classification, if we have some form of labeled (or partially labeled) data available, we could use these labels to evaluate a clustering model. We can make predictions of clusters (that is, the class labels) using the model and evaluate the predictions against the true labels using metrics similar to some that we saw for classification evaluation (that is, based on true positive and negative and false positive and negative rates).

These include the Rand measure, F-measure, Jaccard index, and others.

See `http://en.wikipedia.org/wiki/Cluster_analysis#External_evaluatio n` for more information on external evaluation for clustering.

Computing performance metrics on the MovieLens dataset

Spark ML provides a convenient `computeCost` function to compute the WSSS objective function given a DataFrame. We will compute this metric for the following item and user training data:

```
val WSSSEUsers = modelUsers.computeCost(datasetUsers)
println(s"Users :  Within Set Sum of Squared Errors = $WSSSEUsers")
val WSSSEItems = modelItems.computeCost(datasetItems)
println(s"Items :  Within Set Sum of Squared Errors = $WSSSEItems")
```

This should output the result similar to the following one:

```
Users :  Within Set Sum of Squared Errors = 2261.3086181660324
Items :  Within Set Sum of Squared Errors = 5647.825222497311
```

The best way to measure effectiveness of WSSSE is to plot against iterations as shown in the next section.

Effect of iterations on WSSSE

Let us find out the effect of iterations on WSSSE for the MovieLens dataset. We will calculate WSSSE for various values of iterations and plot the output.

The code listing is:

```scala
object MovieLensKMeansMetrics {
  case class RatingX(userId: Int, movieId: Int, rating: Float,
    timestamp: Long)
  val DATA_PATH= "../../../data/ml-100k"
  val PATH_MOVIES = DATA_PATH + "/u.item"
  val dataSetUsers = null

  def main(args: Array[String]): Unit = {

    val spConfig = (new
      SparkConf).setMaster("local[1]").setAppName("SparkApp").
      set("spark.driver.allowMultipleContexts", "true")

    val spark = SparkSession
      .builder()
      .appName("Spark SQL Example")
      .config(spConfig)
      .getOrCreate()

    val datasetUsers = spark.read.format("libsvm").load(
      "./data/movie_lens_libsvm/movie_lens_users_libsvm/part-
      00000")
    datasetUsers.show(3)

    val k = 5
    val itr = Array(1,10,20,50,75,100)
    val result = new Array[String](itr.length)
    for(i <- 0 until itr.length){
      val w = calculateWSSSE(spark,datasetUsers,itr(i),5,1L)
      result(i) = itr(i) + "," + w
    }
    println("----------Users----------")
    for(j <- 0 until itr.length) {
      println(result(j))
    }
    println("--------------------------")

    val datasetItems = spark.read.format("libsvm").load(
      "./data/movie_lens_libsvm/movie_lens_items_libsvm/"+
      "part-00000")
```

```
    val resultItems = new Array[String](itr.length)
    for(i <- 0 until itr.length){
      val w = calculateWSSSE(spark,datasetItems,itr(i),5,1L)
      resultItems(i) = itr(i) + "," + w
    }

    println("----------Items ---------")
    for(j <- 0 until itr.length) {
      println(resultItems(j))
    }
    println("-----------------------")


    spark.stop()
  }

import org.apache.spark.sql.DataFrame

def calculateWSSSE(spark : SparkSession, dataset : DataFrame,
    iterations : Int, k : Int, seed : Long) : Double = {
  val x = dataset.columns

  val kmeans =
    new KMeans().setK(k).setSeed(seed).setMaxIter(iterations)

  val model = kmeans.fit(dataset)
  val WSSSEUsers = model.computeCost(dataset)
  return WSSSEUsers

}
```

The output is:

```
----------Users----------
1,2429.214784372865
10,2274.362593105573
20,2261.3086181660324
50,2261.015660051977
75,2261.015660051977
100,2261.015660051977
-----------------------

----------Items----------
1,5851.444935665099
10,5720.505597821477
20,5647.825222497311
50,5637.7439669472005
75,5637.7439669472005
```

```
100,5637.7439669472005
```

Let us plot these numbers to get a better idea:

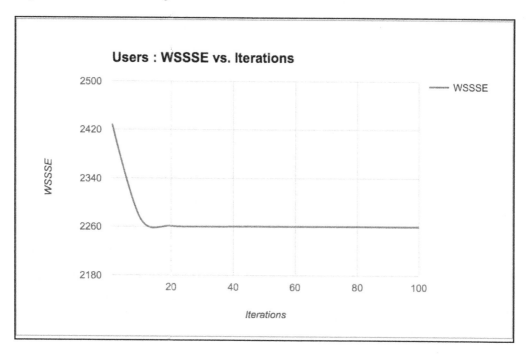

Users WSSSE versus iterations

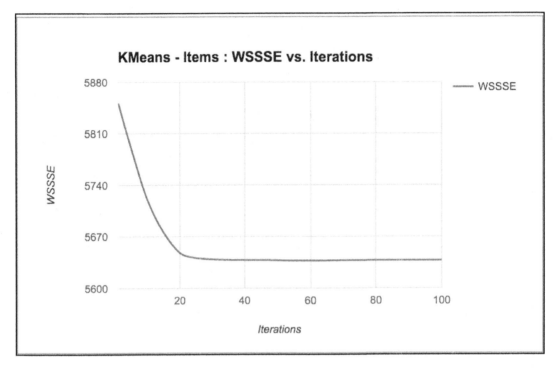

KMeans - Items : WSSSE vs. Iterations

Items WSSSE versus iterations

Bisecting KMeans

It is a variation of generic KMeans.

Reference: http://www.siam.org/meetings/sdm01/pdf/sdm01_05.pdf

The steps of the algorithm are:

1. Initialize by randomly selecting a point, say $c_R \in \Re^p$ then compute the centroid w of M and compute:

$$c_R \in \Re^p \text{ as } c_R = w - (c_L - w)$$

The **centroid** is the center of the cluster. A centroid is a vector containing one number for each variable, where each number is the mean of a variable for the observations in that cluster.

2. Divide $M =[x1, x2, ... xn]$ into two, sub-clusters M_L and M_R, according to the following rule:

$$\begin{cases} x_i \in M_L & if \quad \|x_i - c_L\| \le \|x_i - c_R\| \\ x_i \in M_R & if \quad \|x_i - c_L\| > \|x_i - c_R\| \end{cases}$$

3. Compute the centroids of M_L and M_R, w_L and w_R, as in step 2.

4. If $w_L = c_L$ and $w_R = c_R$, stop.

Otherwise, let $c_L = w_L$ $c_R = w_R$, go to step 2.

Bisecting K-means - training a clustering model

Training for bisecting K-means in Spark ML involves taking an approach similar to the other models -- we pass a DataFrame that contains our training data to the fit method of the KMeans object. Note that here we use the libsvm data format:

1. Instantiate the cluster object:

```
val spConfig = (new
SparkConf).setMaster("local[1]").setAppName("SparkApp").
set("spark.driver.allowMultipleContexts", "true")

val spark = SparkSession
  .builder()
  .appName("Spark SQL Example")
  .config(spConfig)
  .getOrCreate()

val datasetUsers = spark.read.format("libsvm").load(
  BASE + "/movie_lens_2f_users_libsvm/part-00000")
datasetUsers.show(3)
```

The output of the command `show(3)` is shown here:

```
+-----+--------------------+
|label|            features|
+-----+--------------------+
|  1.0|(2,[0,1],[0.37140...|
|  2.0|(2,[0,1],[-0.2131...|
|  3.0|(2,[0,1],[0.28579...|
+-----+--------------------+
only showing top 3 rows
```

Create the `BisectingKMeans` object and set the parameters:

```
val bKMeansUsers = new BisectingKMeans()
bKMeansUsers.setMaxIter(10)
bKMeansUsers.setMinDivisibleClusterSize(5)
```

2. Train the data:

```
val modelUsers = bKMeansUsers.fit(datasetUsers)

val movieDF = Util.getMovieDataDF(spark)
val predictedUserClusters =
  modelUsers.transform(datasetUsers)
predictedUserClusters.show(5)
```

The output is:

```
+-----+--------------------+----------+
|label|            features|prediction|
+-----+--------------------+----------+
|  1.0|(2,[0,1],[0.37140...|        3|
|  2.0|(2,[0,1],[-0.2131...|        3|
|  3.0|(2,[0,1],[0.28579...|        3|
|  4.0|(2,[0,1],[-0.6541...|        1|
|  5.0|(2,[0,1],[0.90333...|        2|
+-----+--------------------+----------+
only showing top 5 rows
```

3. Show movies by cluster:

```
val joinedMovieDFAndPredictedCluster =
  movieDF.join(predictedUserClusters,predictedUserClusters
  ("label") === movieDF("id"))
print(joinedMovieDFAndPredictedCluster.first())
joinedMovieDFAndPredictedCluster.show(5)
```

The output is:

```
+--+---------------+-----------+-----+--------------------+----------+
|id|           name|       date|label|            features|prediction|
+--+---------------+-----------+-----+--------------------+----------+
| 1|  Toy Story (1995)  |01-Jan-1995|  1.0|(2,[0,1],[0.37140...|3|
| 2|  GoldenEye (1995)  |01-Jan-1995|  2.0|(2,[0,1],[-0.2131...|3|
| 3|Four Rooms (1995)  |01-Jan-1995|  3.0|(2,[0,1],[0.28579...|3|
| 4|  Get Shorty (1995) |01-Jan-1995|  4.0|(2,[0,1],[-0.6541...|1|
| 5|  Copycat (1995)    |01-Jan-1995|  5.0|(2,[0,1],[0.90333...|2|
+--+---------------+-----------+-----+--------------------+----------
+
```

only showing top 5 rows

Let us print the movies segregated by cluster number:

```
for(i <- 0 until 5) {
val prediction0 =
joinedMovieDFAndPredictedCluster.filter("prediction == " + i)
println("Cluster : " + i)
println("------------------------")
prediction0.select("name").show(10)
}
```

The output is:
```
Cluster : 0
+--------------------+
|                name|
+--------------------+
|Antonia's Line (1...|
|Angels and Insect...|
|Rumble in the Bro...|
|Doom Generation, ...|
|      Mad Love (1995)|
| Strange Days (1995)|
|        Clerks (1994)|
|   Hoop Dreams (1994)|
|Legends of the Fa...|
|Professional, The...|
+--------------------+
only showing top 10 rows


Cluster : 1
------------------------

+--------------------+
|                name|
```

```
+--------------------+
|   Get Shorty (1995)|
|Dead Man Walking ...|
|   Richard III (1995)|
|Seven (Se7en) (1995)|
|Usual Suspects, T...|
|Mighty Aphrodite ...|
|French Twist (Gaz...|
|Birdcage, The (1996)|
|    Desperado (1995)|
|Free Willy 2: The...|
+--------------------+
only showing top 10 rows


Cluster : 2
--------------------------
+--------------------+
|                name|
+--------------------+
|     Copycat (1995)|
|Shanghai Triad (Y...|
|   Postino, Il (1994)|
|From Dusk Till Da...|
|    Braveheart (1995)|
|Batman Forever (1...|
|        Crumb (1994)|
|To Wong Foo, Than...|
|Billy Madison (1995)|
|Dolores Claiborne...|
+--------------------+
only showing top 10 rows


Cluster : 3
--------------------------
+--------------------+
|                name|
+--------------------+
|    Toy Story (1995)|
|    GoldenEye (1995)|
|    Four Rooms (1995)|
|Twelve Monkeys (1...|
|         Babe (1995)|
|Mr. Holland's Opu...|
|White Balloon, Th...|
|Muppet Treasure I...|
|   Taxi Driver (1976)|
```

```
|Brothers McMullen...|
+--------------------+
only showing top 10 rows
```

Let us calculate the WSSSE:

```
val WSSSEUsers = modelUsers.computeCost(datasetUsers)
println(s"Users : Within Set Sum of Squared Errors =
$WSSSEUsers")

println("Users : Cluster Centers: ")
modelUsers.clusterCenters.foreach(println)
```

The output is:

```
Users : Within Set Sum of Squared Errors = 220.213984126387
Users : Cluster Centers:
[-0.5152650631965345,-0.17908608684257435]
[-0.7330009110582011,0.5699292831746033]
[0.4657482296168242,0.07541218866995708]
[0.07297392612510972,0.7292946749843259]
```

Next we run the predictions for the items:

```
val datasetItems = spark.read.format("libsvm").load(
  BASE + "/movie_lens_2f_items_libsvm/part-00000")
datasetItems.show(3)

val kmeansItems = new BisectingKMeans().setK(5).setSeed(1L)
val modelItems = kmeansItems.fit(datasetItems)

// Evaluate clustering by computing Within Set
// Sum of Squared Errors.
val WSSSEItems = modelItems.computeCost(datasetItems)
println(s"Items : Within Set Sum of Squared Errors =
  $WSSSEItems")

// Shows the result.
println("Items - Cluster Centers: ")
modelUsers.clusterCenters.foreach(println)

Items: within Set Sum of Squared Errors = 538.4272487824393
Items - Cluster Centers:
  [-0.5152650631965345,-0.17908608684257435]
  [-0.7330009110582011,0.5699292831746033]
  [0.4657482296168242,0.07541218866995708]
  [0.07297392612510972,0.7292946749843259]
```

Source code:
https://github.com/ml-resources/spark-ml/blob/branch-ed
2/Chapter_08/scala/2.0.0/src/main/scala/org/sparksample
s/kmeans/BisectingKMeans.scala

4. Plot the user and item clusters.

As a next step, let us take two features and plot the user and item clusters with their respective clusters:

```scala
object BisectingKMeansPersist {
  val PATH = "/home/ubuntu/work/spark-2.0.0-bin-hadoop2.7/"
  val BASE = "./data/movie_lens_libsvm_2f"

  val time = System.currentTimeMillis()
  val formatter = new
    SimpleDateFormat("dd_MM_yyyy_hh_mm_ss")

  import java.util.Calendar
  val calendar = Calendar.getInstance()
  calendar.setTimeInMillis(time)
  val date_time = formatter.format(calendar.getTime())

  def main(args: Array[String]): Unit = {

    val spConfig = (new
      SparkConf).setMaster("local[1]")
      .setAppName("SparkApp").
    set("spark.driver.allowMultipleContexts", "true")

    val spark = SparkSession
      .builder()
      .appName("Spark SQL Example")
      .config(spConfig)
      .getOrCreate()

    val datasetUsers = spark.read.format("libsvm").load(
      BASE + "/movie_lens_2f_users_libsvm/part-00000")

    val bKMeansUsers = new BisectingKMeans()
    bKMeansUsers.setMaxIter(10)
    bKMeansUsers.setMinDivisibleClusterSize(5)

    val modelUsers = bKMeansUsers.fit(datasetUsers)
    val predictedUserClusters =
      modelUsers.transform(datasetUsers)
```

```
modelUsers.clusterCenters.foreach(println)
val predictedDataSetUsers =
  modelUsers.transform(datasetUsers)
val predictionsUsers =
  predictedDataSetUsers.select("prediction")
  .rdd.map(x=> x(0))
predictionsUsers.saveAsTextFile(BASE +
  "/prediction/" +
date_time + "/bkmeans_2f_users")

val datasetItems =
  spark.read.format("libsvm").load(BASE +
  "/movie_lens_2f_items_libsvm/part-00000")


val kmeansItems = new
  BisectingKMeans().setK(5).setSeed(1L)
val modelItems = kmeansItems.fit(datasetItems)


val predictedDataSetItems =
  modelItems.transform(datasetItems)
val predictionsItems =
  predictedDataSetItems.select("prediction")
  .rdd.map(x=> x(0))
  predictionsItems.saveAsTextFile(BASE +
  "/prediction/" +
date_time + "/bkmeans_2f_items")
spark.stop()
  }
}
```

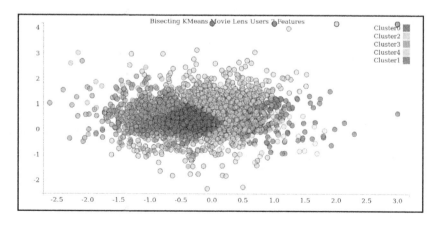

Plotting of MovieLens user data with clusters

The preceding plot shows what user clusters look like for two features.

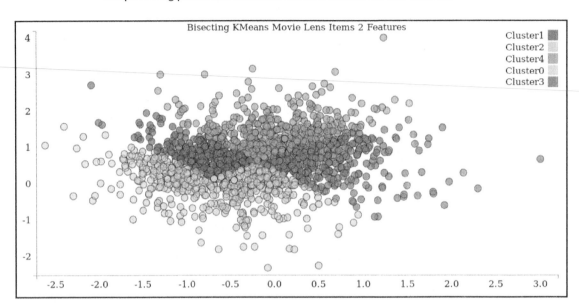

Plotting of MovieLens item (movies) data with clusters

The preceding plot shows what item clusters look like for two features.

WSSSE and iterations

In this section, we evaluate the effect or iterations on WSSSE for bisecting the K-means algorithm.

The source code is:

```
object BisectingKMeansMetrics {
  case class RatingX(userId: Int, movieId: Int,
    rating: Float, timestamp: Long)
  val DATA_PATH= "../../../data/ml-100k"
  val PATH_MOVIES = DATA_PATH + "/u.item"
  val dataSetUsers = null

  def main(args: Array[String]): Unit = {

    val spConfig = (
      new SparkConf).setMaster("local[1]").setAppName("SparkApp").
      set("spark.driver.allowMultipleContexts", "true")

    val spark = SparkSession
```

```scala
    .builder()
    .appName("Spark SQL Example")
    .config(spConfig)
    .getOrCreate()

  val datasetUsers = spark.read.format("libsvm").load(
    "./data/movie_lens_libsvm/movie_lens_users_libsvm/part-
    00000")
  datasetUsers.show(3)

  val k = 5
  val itr = Array(1,10,20,50,75,100)
  val result = new Array[String](itr.length)
  for(i <- 0 until itr.length){
    val w = calculateWSSSE(spark,datasetUsers,itr(i),5)
    result(i) = itr(i) + "," + w
  }
  println("----------Users----------")
  for(j <- 0 until itr.length) {
    println(result(j))
  }
  println("------------------------")

  val datasetItems = spark.read.format("libsvm").load(
    "./data/movie_lens_libsvm/movie_lens_items_libsvm/part-
    00000")
  val resultItems = new Array[String](itr.length)
  for(i <- 0 until itr.length){
    val w = calculateWSSSE(spark,datasetItems,itr(i),5)
    resultItems(i) = itr(i) + "," + w
  }

  println("----------Items----------")
  for(j <- 0 until itr.length) {
    println(resultItems(j))
  }
  println("------------------------")


  spark.stop()
}

import org.apache.spark.sql.DataFrame

def calculateWSSSE(spark : SparkSession, dataset : DataFrame,
  iterations : Int, k : Int) : Double =
{
  val x = dataset.columns
```

```
val bKMeans = new BisectingKMeans()
bKMeans.setMaxIter(iterations)
bKMeans.setMinDivisibleClusterSize(k)

val model = bKMeans.fit(dataset)
val WSSSE = model.computeCost(dataset)
return WSSSE
```

    }
}

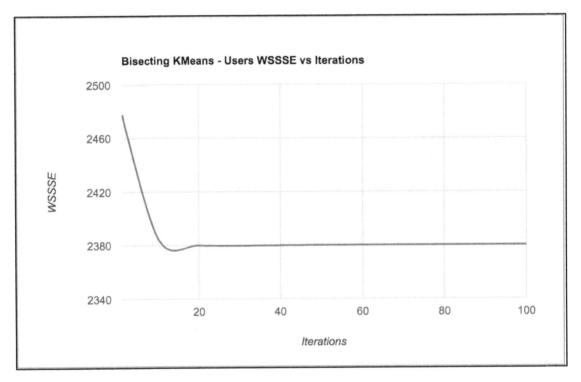

Plot: WSSSE versus iterations for users

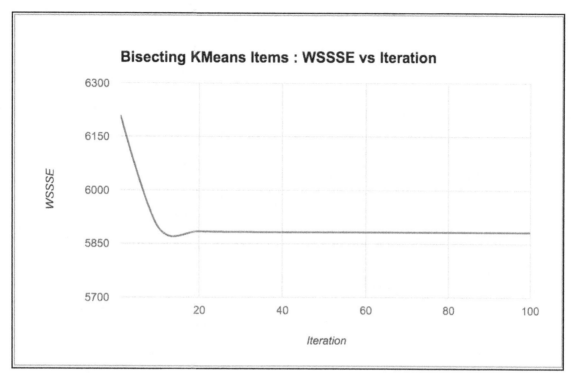

Plot: WSSSE versus iterations for items in the case of bisecting K-means

It is clear that the algorithm reaches optimal WSSSE by 20 iterations for both users and items.

Gaussian Mixture Model

A mixture model is a probabilistic model of a sub-population within a population. These models are used to make statistical inferences about a sub-population, given the observations of pooled populations.

A **Gaussian Mixture Model (GMM)** is a mixture model represented as a weighted sum of Gaussian component densities. Its model coefficients are estimated from training data using the iterative **Expectation-Maximization (EM)** algorithm or **Maximum A Posteriori (MAP)** estimation from a trained model.

The `spark.ml` implementation uses the EM algorithm.

It has the following parameters:

- **k**: Number of desired clusters
- **convergenceTol**: Maximum change in log-likelihood at which one considers convergence achieved
- **maxIterations**: Maximum number of iterations to perform without reaching convergence
- **initialModel**: Optional starting point from which to start the EM algorithm

  (if this parameter is omitted, a random starting point will be constructed from the data)

Clustering using GMM

We will create clusters for both users and items (movies in this case) to get a better understanding of how the algorithm groups users and items.

Perform the following steps:

1. Load the `libsvm` file for users.
2. Create a Gaussian Mixture instance. The instance has the following parameters which can be configured:

```
final val featuresCol: Param[String]
Param for features column name.
final val k: IntParam
Number of independent Gaussians in the mixture model.
final val
maxIter: IntParam
Param for maximum number of iterations (>= 0).
final val predictionCol: Param[String]
Param for prediction column name.
final val probabilityCol: Param[String]
Param for Column name for predicted class conditional
probabilities.
final val seed: LongParam
Param for random seed.
final val tol: DoubleParam
```

3. In our case, we will be setting only the number of Gaussian distributions and seed number:

```
val gmmUsers = new GaussianMixture().setK(5).setSeed(1L)
```

4. Create a user model:

```
Print Covariance and Mean
for (i <- 0 until modelUsers.gaussians.length) {
  println("Users: weight=%f\ncov=%s\nmean=\n%s\n" format
    (modelUsers.weights(i), modelUsers.gaussians(i).cov,
    modelUsers.gaussians(i).mean))
}
```

The full code listing is:

```
object GMMClustering {
  def main(args: Array[String]): Unit = {
    val spConfig = (new SparkConf).setMaster("local[1]").
      setAppName("SparkApp").
      set("spark.driver.allowMultipleContexts", "true")

    val spark = SparkSession
      .builder()
      .appName("Spark SQL Example")
      .config(spConfig)
      .getOrCreate()

    val datasetUsers = spark.read.format("libsvm").
      load("./data/movie_lens_libsvm/movie_lens_users_libsvm/"
      + "part-00000")
    datasetUsers.show(3)

    val gmmUsers = new GaussianMixture().setK(5).setSeed(1L)
    val modelUsers = gmmUsers.fit(datasetUsers)

    for (i <- 0 until modelUsers.gaussians.length) {
      println("Users : weight=%f\ncov=%s\nmean=\n%s\n"
        format (modelUsers.weights(i),
        modelUsers.gaussians(i).cov,
        modelUsers.gaussians(i).mean))
    }

    val dataSetItems = spark.read.format("libsvm").load(
      "./data/movie_lens_libsvm/movie_lens_items_libsvm/" +
      "part-00000")

    val gmmItems = new
```

```
        GaussianMixture().setK(5).setSeed(1L)
val modelItems = gmmItems.fit(dataSetItems)

for (i <- 0 until modelItems.gaussians.length) {
  println("Items : weight=%f\ncov=%s\nmean=\n%s\n"
    format (modelUsers.weights(i),
    modelUsers.gaussians(i).cov,
    modelUsers.gaussians(i).mean))
}
spark.stop()
}
```

Plotting the user and item data with GMM clustering

In this section, we look at how GMM-based cluster boundaries move as the number of iterations increase:

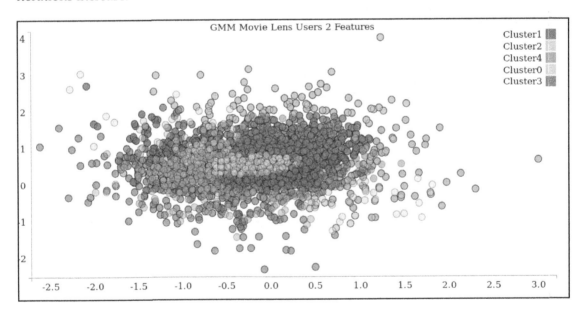

Plot of MovieLens user data clusters assigned by GMM

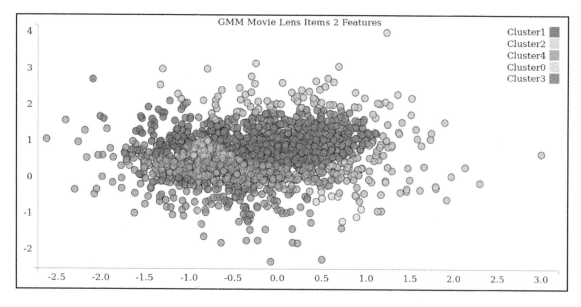

Plot of MovieLens item data clusters assigned by GMM

GMM - effect of iterations on cluster boundaries

Let us look at how cluster boundaries change as the number of iterations increase for GMM:

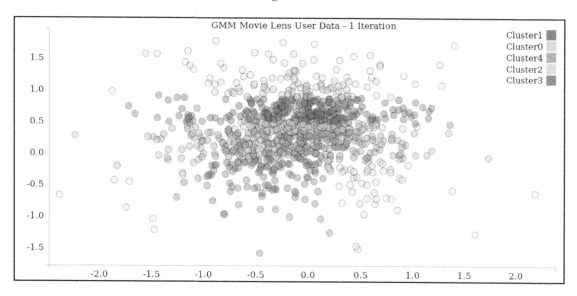

Cluster plot for GMM for user data with one iteration

The preceding figure plots GMM clusters for user data with one iteration.

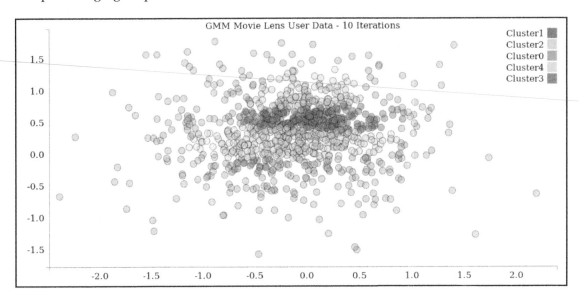

Cluster plot for GMM for user data with 10 iterations

The preceding figure plots GMM clusters for user data with 10 iterations.

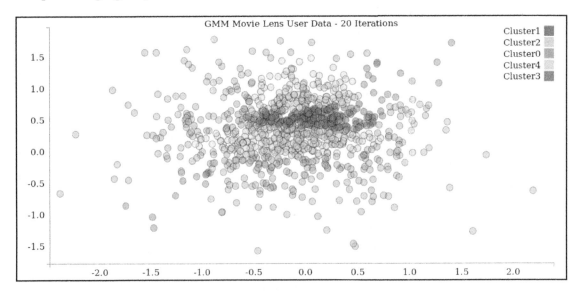

Cluster plot for GMM for user data with 20 iterations

The preceding figure plots GMM clusters for user data with 20 iterations.

Summary

In this chapter, we explored a new class of model that learns structures from unlabeled data -- unsupervised learning. We worked through the required input data and feature extraction, and saw how to use the output of one model (a recommendation model in our example) as the input to another model (our k-means clustering model). Finally, we evaluated the performance of the clustering model, using both manual interpretation of the cluster assignments and using mathematical performance metrics.

In the next chapter, we will cover another type of unsupervised learning used to reduce our data down to its most important features or components -- dimensionality reduction models.

9
Dimensionality Reduction with Spark

Over the course of this chapter, we will continue our exploration of unsupervised learning models in the form of **dimensionality reduction**.

Unlike the models we have covered so far, such as regression, classification, and clustering, dimensionality reduction does not focus on making predictions. Instead, it tries to take a set of input data with a feature dimension D (that is, the length of our feature vector), and extracts a representation of the data of dimension k, where k is usually significantly smaller than D. It is, therefore, a form of preprocessing or feature transformation rather than a predictive model in its own right.

It is important that the representation that is extracted should still be able to capture a large proportion of the variability or structure of the original data. The idea behind this is that most data sources will contain some form of underlying structure. This structure is typically unknown (often called latent features or latent factors), but if we can uncover some of this structure, our models could learn this structure, and make predictions from it rather than from the data in its raw form, which might be noisy or contain many irrelevant features. In other words, dimensionality reduction throws away some of the noise in the data, and keeps the hidden structure that is present.

In some cases, the dimensionality of the raw data is far higher than the number of data points we have, so, without dimensionality reduction, it would be difficult for other machine learning models, such as classification and regression, to learn anything, as they need to fit a number of parameters that is far larger than the number of training examples (in this sense, these methods bear some similarity to the regularization approaches that we have seen being used in classification and regression).

A few use cases of dimensionality reduction techniques include the following:

- Exploratory data analysis
- Extracting features to train other machine learning models
- Reducing storage and computation requirements for very large models in the prediction phase (for example, a production system that makes predictions)
- Reducing a large group of text documents down to a set of hidden topics or concepts
- Making learning and generalization of models easier when our data has a very large number of features (for example, when working with text, sound, images, or video data, which tends to be very high-dimensional)

In this chapter, we will do the following:

- Introduce the types of dimensionality reduction models available in MLlib
- Work with images of faces to extract features suitable for dimensionality reduction
- Train a dimensionality reduction model using MLlib
- Visualize and evaluate the results
- Perform parameter selection for our dimensionality reduction model

Types of dimensionality reduction

MLlib provides two models for dimensionality reduction; these models are closely related to each other. These models are **Principal Components Analysis (PCA)** and **Singular Value Decomposition (SVD)**.

Principal components analysis

PCA operates on a data matrix X, and seeks to extract a set of k principal components from X. The principal components are each uncorrelated to each other, and are computed such that the first principal component accounts for the largest variation in the input data. Each subsequent principal component is, in turn, computed such that it accounts for the largest variation, provided that it is independent of the principal components computed so far.

In this way, the *k* principal components returned are guaranteed to account for the highest amount of variation in the input data possible. Each principal component, in fact, has the same feature dimensionality as the original data matrix. Hence, a projection step is required in order to actually perform dimensionality reduction, where the original data is projected into the *k*-dimensional space represented by the principal components.

Singular value decomposition

SVD seeks to decompose a matrix X of dimension *m x n* into these three component matrices:

- U of dimension *m x m*
- S, a diagonal matrix of size *m x n*; the entries of S are referred to as the **singular values**
- VT of dimension *n x n*

$$X = U * S * V^T$$

Looking at the preceding formula, it appears that we have not reduced the dimensionality of the problem at all, as by multiplying U, S, and V, we reconstruct the original matrix. In practice, the truncated SVD is usually computed. That is, only the top k singular values, which represent the most variation in the data, are kept, while the rest are discarded. The formula to reconstruct X based on the component matrices is then approximate, and is given as follows:

$$X \sim U_k * S_k * V_{kT}$$

An illustration of the truncated SVD is shown in this diagram:

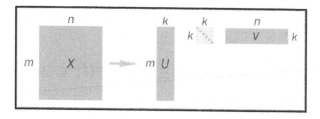

The truncated singular value decomposition

Keeping the top k singular values is similar to keeping the top k principal components in PCA. In fact, SVD and PCA are directly related, as we will see a little later in this chapter.

A detailed mathematical treatment of both PCA and SVD is beyond the scope of this book.

An overview of dimensionality reduction can be found in the Spark documentation at `http://spark.apache.org/docs/latest/mllib-dimen sionality-reduction.html`.

The following links contain a more in-depth mathematical overview of PCA and SVD respectively: `http://en.wikipedia.org/wiki/Principal_ component_analysis`and `http://en.wikipedia.org/wiki/Singular_va lue_decomposition`.

Relationship with matrix factorization

PCA and SVD are both matrix factorization techniques, in the sense that they decompose a data matrix into subcomponent matrices, each of which has a lower dimension (or rank) than the original matrix. Many other dimensionality reduction techniques are based on matrix factorization.

You might remember another example of matrix factorization, that is, collaborative filtering, which we have already seen in `Chapter 6`, *Building a Classification Model with Spark*. Matrix factorization approaches to collaborative filtering work by factorizing the ratings matrix into two components: the user factor matrix and the item factor matrix. Each of these has a lower dimension than the original data, so these methods also act as dimensionality reduction models.

Many of the best performing approaches to collaborative filtering include models based on SVD. Simon Funk's approach to the Netflix prize is a famous example. You can look it up at `http://sifter.org/~simon/journal/20061211.html`.

Clustering as dimensionality reduction

The clustering models we covered in the previous chapter can also be used for a form of dimensionality reduction. This works in the following way:

- Assume that we cluster our high-dimensional feature vectors using a K-means clustering model, with k clusters. The result is a set of k cluster centers.

- We can represent each of our original data points in terms of how far it is from each of these cluster centers. That is, we can compute the distance of a data point to each cluster center. The result is a set of k distances for each data point.

- These k distances can form a new vector of dimension k. We can now represent our original data as a new vector of lower dimension relative to the original feature dimension.

Depending on the distance metric used, this can result in both dimensionality reduction and a form of nonlinear transformation of the data, allowing us to learn a more complex model, while still benefiting from the speed and scalability of a linear model. For example, using a Gaussian or exponential distance function can approximate a very complex nonlinear feature transformation.

Extracting the right features from your data

As with all machine learning models we have explored so far, dimensionality reduction models also operate on a feature vector representation of our data.

For this chapter, we will dive into the world of image processing, using the **Labeled Faces in the Wild (LFW)** dataset of facial images. This dataset contains over 13,000 images of faces generally taken from the Internet, and belonging to well-known public figures. The faces are labeled with the person's name.

Extracting features from the LFW dataset

In order to avoid having to download and process a very large dataset, we will work with a subset of the images, using people who have names that start with an A. This dataset can be downloaded from `http://vis-www.cs.umass.edu/lfw/lfw-a.tgz`.

For more details and other variants of the data, visit `http://vis-www.cs.umass.edu/lfw/`.
The original research paper reference is:
Gary B. Huang, Manu Ramesh, Tamara Berg, and *Erik Learned-Miller. Labeled Faces in the Wild: A Database for Studying Face Recognition in Unconstrained Environments*. University of Massachusetts, Amherst, Technical Report 07-49, October, 2007.
It can be downloaded from `http://vis-www.cs.umass.edu/lfw/lfw.pdf`.

Unzip the data using the following command:

```
>tar xfvz lfw-a.tgz
```

This will create a folder called `lfw`, which contains a number of subfolders, one for each person.

Exploring the face data

We will use the Spark application to analyze the data. Make sure the data is unzipped into the `data` folder as follows:

```
Chapter_09
|-- 2.0.x
|    |-- python
|    |-- scala
|-- data
```

The actual code is in the `scala` folder, except a few graphs, which are in the `python` folder:

```
scala
|-- src
|    |-- main
|    |    |-- java
|    |    |-- resources
|    |    |-- scala
|    |    |    |-- org
|    |    |    |    |-- sparksamples
|    |    |    |         |-- ImageProcessing.scala
|    |    |    |         |-- Util.scala
|    |    |-- scala-2.11
|    |-- test
```

Now that we've unzipped the data, we face a small challenge. Spark provides us with a way to read text files and custom Hadoop input data sources. However, there is no built-in functionality to allow us to read images.

Spark provides a method called `wholeTextFiles`, which allows us to operate on entire files at once, compared to the `textFile` method that we have been using so far, which operates on the individual lines within a text file (or multiple files).

We will use the `wholeTextFiles` method to access the location of each file. Using these file paths, we will write custom code to load and process the images. In the following example code, we will use PATH to refer to the directory in which you extracted the `lfw` subdirectory.

We can use a wildcard path specification (using the * character highlighted in the following code snippet) to tell Spark to look for files in each directory under the `lfw` directory:

```
val spConfig = (new SparkConf).setMaster("local[1]")
  .setAppName("SparkApp")
  .set("spark.driver.allowMultipleContexts", "true")
val sc = new SparkContext(spConfig)
val path = PATH +  "/lfw/*"
val rdd = sc.wholeTextFiles(path)
val first = rdd.first
println(first)
```

Running the `first` command might take a little time, as Spark first scans the specified directory structure for all available files. Once completed, you should see an output similar to the one shown here:

```
first: (String, String) =  (file:/PATH/lfw/Aaron_Eckhart
/Aaron_Eckhart_0001.jpg,??JFIF????? ...
```

You will see that `wholeTextFiles` returns an RDD that contains key-value pairs, where the key is the file location, while the value is the content of the entire text file. For our purposes, we only care about the file path, as we cannot work directly with the image data as a string (notice that it is displayed as "binary nonsense" in the shell output).

Let's extract the file paths from the RDD. Note that earlier, the file path starts with the `file:` text. This is used by Spark when reading files in order to differentiate between different filesystems (for example, `file://` for the local filesystem, `hdfs://` for HDFS, `s3n://` for Amazon S3, and so on).

In our case, we will use custom code to read the images, so we don't need this part of the path. Thus, we will remove it with the following `map` function:

```
val files = rdd.map { case (fileName, content) =>
  fileName.replace("file:", "") }
```

The preceding function will display the file location with the `file:` prefix removed:

```
/PATH/lfw/Aaron_Eckhart/Aaron_Eckhart_0001.jpg
```

Next, we will see how many files we are dealing with:

```
println(files.count)
```

Running these commands creates a lot of noisy output in Spark, as it outputs all the file paths that are read to the console. Ignore this part, but after the command has completed, the output should look something like this:

```
..., /PATH/lfw/Azra_Akin/Azra_Akin_0003.jpg:0+19927,
   /PATH/lfw/Azra_Akin/Azra_Akin_0004.jpg:0+16030
...
14/09/18 20:36:25 INFO SparkContext: Job finished:
   count at  <console>:19, took 1.151955 s
1055
```

So, we can see that we have 1055 images to work with.

Visualizing the face data

Although there are a few tools available in Scala or Java to display images, this is one area where Python and the matplotlib library shine. We will use Scala to process and extract the images and run our models, and IPython to display the actual images.

You can run a separate IPython Notebook by opening a new terminal window and launching a new notebook as follows:

```
>ipython notebook
```

 If using Python Notebook, you should first execute the following code snippet to ensure that the images are displayed inline after each notebook cell (including the % character): %pylab inline

Alternatively, you can launch a plain IPython console without the web notebook, enabling the pylab plotting functionality using the following command:

```
>ipython --pylab
```

The dimensionality reduction techniques in MLlib are only available in Scala or Java at the time of writing this book, so we will continue to use the Scala Spark shell to run the models. Therefore, you won't need to run a PySpark console.

We have provided the full Python code with this chapter as a Python script as well as in the IPython Notebook format. For instructions on installing IPython, see the code bundle.

Let's display the image given by the first path, which we extracted earlier using PIL's image library:

```
from PIL import Image, ImageFilter
path = PATH + "/lfw/Aaron_Eckhart/Aaron_Eckhart_0001.jpg"
im = Image.open(path)
im.show()
```

You should see the screenshot displayed as follows:

```
def main():

    path = PATH + "/lfw/Aaron_Eckhart/Aaron_Eckhart_0001.jpg"

    im = Image.open(path)
    im.show()

    tmp_path = PATH + "/aeGray.jpg"
    ae_gary = Image.open(tmp_path)
    ae_gary.show()

    pc = np.loadtxt(PATH + "/pc.csv", delimiter=",")
    print(pc.shape)
    # (2500, 10)


    plot_gallery(pc, 50, 50)
```

Extracting facial images as vectors

While a full treatment of image processing is beyond the scope of this book, you will need to know a few basics to proceed. Each color image can be represented as a three-dimensional array, or matrix, of pixels. The first two dimensions, that is the x and y axes, represent the position of each pixel, while the third dimension represents the **Red**, **Blue**, and **Green** (**RGB**) color values for each pixel.

A grayscale image only requires one value per pixel (there are no RGB values), so it can be represented as a plain two-dimensional matrix. For many image processing and machine learning tasks related to images, it is common to operate on grayscale images. We will do this here by converting the color images to grayscale first.

It is also a common practice in machine learning tasks to represent an image as a vector instead of a matrix. We do this by concatenating each row (or, alternatively, each column) of the matrix to form a long vector (this is known as `reshaping`). In this way, each raw, grayscale image matrix is transformed into a feature vector, which is usable as input to a machine learning model.

Fortunately, for us, the built-in Java **Abstract Window Toolkit** (**AWT**) contains various basic image-processing functions. We will define a few utility functions to perform this processing using the `java.awt` classes.

Loading images

The first of these is a function to read an image from a file.

```
import java.awt.image.BufferedImage
def loadImageFromFile(path: String): BufferedImage = {
  ImageIO.read(new File(path))
}
```

This preceding code is available in `Util.scala`.

This returns an instance of a `java.awt.image.BufferedImage` class, which stores the image data, and provides a number of useful methods. Let's test it out by loading the first image into our Spark shell, as follows:

```
val aePath = "/PATH/lfw/Aaron_Eckhart/Aaron_Eckhart_0001.jpg"
val aeImage = loadImageFromFile(aePath)
```

You should see the image details displayed in the shell.

```
aeImage: java.awt.image.BufferedImage = BufferedImage@f41266e:
type =  5 ColorModel: #pixelBits = 24 numComponents = 3 color space =
java.awt.color.ICC_ColorSpace@7e420794 transparency = 1 has
alpha =  false isAlphaPre = false ByteInterleavedRaster:
width = 250 height =  250 #numDataElements 3 dataOff[0] = 2
```

There is quite a lot of information here. Of particular interest to us is that the image width and height are 250 pixels, and as we can see, there are three components (that is, the RGB values) that are highlighted in the preceding output.

Converting to grayscale and resizing the images

The next function we will define will take the image that we have loaded with our preceding function, convert the image from color to grayscale, and resize the image's width and height.

These steps are not strictly necessary, but both steps are done in many cases for efficiency purposes. Using RGB color images instead of grayscale increases the amount of data to be processed by a factor of three. Similarly, larger images increase the processing and storage overhead significantly. Our raw 250 x 250 images represent 187,500 data points per image using three color components. For a set of 1055 images, this is 197,812,500 data points. Even if stored as integer values, each value stored takes 4 bytes of memory, so just 1055 images represent around 800 MB of memory! As you can see, image-processing tasks can quickly become extremely memory intensive.

If we convert to grayscale and resize the images to, say, 50 x 50 pixels, we only require 2500 data points per image. For our 1055 images, this equates to 10 MB of memory, which is far more manageable for illustrative purposes.

Let's define our processing function. We will do the grayscale conversion and resizing in one step, using the `java.awt.image` package:

```
def processImage(image: BufferedImage, width: Int, height: Int):
  BufferedImage = {
    val bwImage = new BufferedImage(width, height,
    BufferedImage.TYPE_BYTE_GRAY)
    val g = bwImage.getGraphics()
    g.drawImage(image, 0, 0, width, height, null)
    g.dispose()
    bwImage
  }
```

The first line of the function creates a new image of the desired width and height, and specifies a grayscale color model. The third line draws the original image onto this newly created image. The `drawImage` method takes care of the color conversion and resizing for us! Finally, we return the new, processed image.

Let's test this out on our sample image. We will convert it to grayscale, and resize it to 100 x 100 pixels:

```
val grayImage = processImage(aeImage, 100, 100)
```

You should see the following output on the console:

```
grayImage: java.awt.image.BufferedImage = BufferedImage@21f8ea3b:
type = 10 ColorModel: #pixelBits = 8 numComponents = 1 color space =
java.awt.color.ICC_ColorSpace@5cd9d8e9 transparency = 1 has
alpha =  false isAlphaPre = false ByteInterleavedRaster:
width = 100 height =  100 #numDataElements 1 dataOff[0] = 0
```

As you can see from the highlighted output, the image's width and height are indeed `100`, and the number of color components is `1`.

Next, we will save the processed image to a temporary location so that we can read it back and display it using the Python application.

```
import javax.imageio.ImageIO
import java.io.File
ImageIO.write(grayImage, "jpg", new File("/tmp/aeGray.jpg"))
```

You should see a result of `true` displayed on your console, indicating that you've successfully saved the image to the `aeGray.jpg` file in your `/tmp` directory.

Finally, we will read the image in Python, and use matplotlib to display the image. Type the following code into your IPython Notebook or shell (remember that this should be open in a new terminal window):

```
tmp_path = PATH + "/aeGray.jpg"
ae_gary = Image.open(tmp_path)
ae_gary.show()
```

This should display the image (note again, we haven't shown the image here). You will see that it is grayscale, and of slightly worse quality as compared to the original image. Furthermore, you will notice that the scale of the axes is different, representing the new 100 x 100 dimension instead of the original 250 x 250 size.

```
def main():

    path = PATH + "/lfw/Aaron_Eckhart/Aaron_Eckhart_0001.jpg"

    im = Image.open(path)
    im.show()

    tmp_path = PATH + "/aeGray.jpg"
    ae_gary = Image.open(tmp_path)
    ae_gary.show()

    pc = np.loadtxt(PATH + "/pc.csv", delimiter=",")
    print(pc.shape)
    # (2500, 10)


    plot_gallery(pc, 50, 50)
```

Extracting feature vectors

The final step in the processing pipeline is to extract the actual feature vectors that will be the input to our dimensionality reduction model. As we mentioned earlier, the raw grayscale pixel data will be our features. We will form the vectors by flattening out the two-dimensional pixel matrix. The BufferedImage class provides a utility method to do just this, which we will use in our function as follows:

```
def getPixelsFromImage(image: BufferedImage): Array[Double] = {
  val width = image.getWidth
  val height = image.getHeight
  val pixels = Array.ofDim[Double](width * height)
  image.getData.getPixels(0, 0, width, height, pixels)
}
```

We can then combine these three functions into one utility function, which takes a file location together with the desired image's width and height, and returns the raw Array[Double] value that contains the pixel data.

```
def extractPixels(path: String, width: Int, height: Int):
  Array[Double] = {
    val raw = loadImageFromFile(path)
    val processed = processImage(raw, width, height)
    getPixelsFromImage(processed)
  }
```

Applying this preceding function to each element of the RDD that contains all the image file paths will give us a new RDD that contains the pixel data for each image. Let's do this and inspect the first few elements as follows:

```
val pixels = files.map(f => extractPixels(f, 50, 50))
println(pixels.take(10).map(_.take(10).mkString  ("", ",", ",
  ...")).mkString("n"))
```

You should see output similar to this:

```
0.0,0.0,0.0,0.0,0.0,0.0,1.0,1.0,0.0,0.0, ...
241.0,243.0,245.0,244.0,231.0,205.0,177.0,160.0,150.0,147.0, ...
253.0,253.0,253.0,253.0,253.0,253.0,254.0,254.0,253.0,253.0, ...
244.0,244.0,243.0,242.0,241.0,240.0,239.0,239.0,237.0,236.0, ...
44.0,47.0,47.0,49.0,62.0,116.0,173.0,223.0,232.0,233.0, ...
0.0,0.0,0.0,0.0,0.0,0.0,0.0,0.0,0.0,0.0, ...
1.0,1.0,1.0,1.0,1.0,1.0,1.0,1.0,0.0,0.0, ...
26.0,26.0,27.0,26.0,24.0,24.0,25.0,26.0,27.0,27.0, ...
240.0,240.0,240.0,240.0,240.0,240.0,240.0,240.0,240.0,240.0, ...
0.0,0.0,0.0,0.0,0.0,0.0,0.0,0.0,0.0,0.0, ...
```

The final step is to create an MLlib `vector` instance for each image. We will cache the RDD to speed up our later computations:

```
import org.apache.spark.mllib.linalg.Vectors
val vectors = pixels.map(p => Vectors.dense(p))
// the setName method create a human-readable name that is
// displayed in the Spark Web UI
vectors.setName("image-vectors")
// remember to cache the vectors to speed up computation
vectors.cache
```

> We used the `setName` function earlier to assign an RDD a name. In this case, we called it `image-vectors`. This is so that we can later identify it more easily when looking at the Spark web interface.

Normalization

It is a common practice to standardize input data prior to running dimensionality reduction models, particularly, for PCA. As we did in Chapter 6, *Building a Classification Model with Spark*, we will do this using the built-in `StandardScaler` provided by MLlib's `feature` package. We will only subtract the mean from the data in this case.

```
import org.apache.spark.mllib.linalg.Matrix
import org.apache.spark.mllib.linalg.distributed.RowMatrix
import org.apache.spark.mllib.feature.StandardScaler
val scaler = new StandardScaler(withMean = true, withStd = false)
  .fit(vectors)
```

> **Standard Scalar**: It standardizes features by removing the mean, and scaling to unit standard using column summary statistics on the samples in the training set.
>
> `@paramwithMean`: `False` by default. This centers the data with the mean before scaling. It builds a dense output, so this does not work on sparse input, and raises an exception.
>
> `@param withStd`: `True` by default. This scales the data to unit standard deviation.

Calling `fit` triggers a computation on our `RDD[Vector]`. You should see an output similar to the one shown here:

```
. . .
14/09/21 11:46:58 INFO SparkContext: Job finished: reduce at
RDDFunctions.scala:111, took 0.495859 s
scaler: org.apache.spark.mllib.feature.StandardScalerModel =
org.apache.spark.mllib.feature.StandardScalerModel@6bb1a1a1
```

Note that subtracting the mean works for dense input data. In Image processing, we always have dense input data, because each pixel has a value. However, for sparse vectors, subtracting the mean vector from each input will transform the sparse data into dense data. For very high-dimensional input, this will likely exhaust the available memory resources, so it is not advisable.

Finally, we will use the returned `scaler` to transform the raw image vectors to vectors with the column means subtracted.

```
val scaledVectors = vectors.map(v => scaler.transform(v))
```

We mentioned earlier that the resized grayscale images would take up around 10 MB of memory. Indeed, you can take a look at the memory usage in the Spark application monitor storage page by going to `http://localhost:4040/storage/` in your web browser.

Since we gave our RDD of image vectors a friendly name of `image-vectors`, you should see something like the following screenshot (note that, as we are using `Vector[Double]`, each element takes up 8 bytes instead of 4 bytes; hence, we actually use 20 MB of memory):

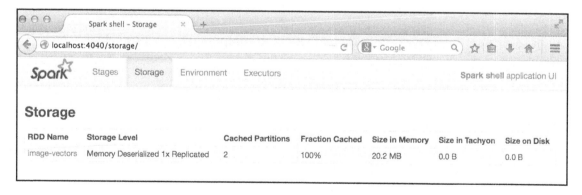

Size of image vectors in memory

Training a dimensionality reduction model

Dimensionality reduction models in MLlib require vectors as inputs. However, unlike clustering that operated on an `RDD[Vector]`, PCA and SVD computations are provided as methods on a distributed `RowMatrix` (this difference is largely down to syntax, as a `RowMatrix` is simply a wrapper around an `RDD[Vector]`).

Running PCA on the LFW dataset

Now that we have extracted our image pixel data into vectors, we can instantiate a new `RowMatrix`.

def computePrincipalComponents(k: Int): Matrix
Computes the top k principal components. Rows correspond to observations, and columns correspond to variables. The principal components are stored as a local matrix of size n-by-k. Each column corresponds for one principal component, and the columns are in descending order of component variance. The row data do not need to be "centered" first; it is not necessary for the mean of each column to be 0. Note that this cannot be computed on matrices with more than 65535 columns.
K is the number of top principal components.
It returns a matrix of size n-by-k, whose columns are principal components
Annotations
@Since("1.0.0")

Call the `computePrincipalComponents` method to compute the top K principal components of our distributed matrix:

```
import org.apache.spark.mllib.linalg.Matrix
import org.apache.spark.mllib.linalg.distributed.RowMatrix
val matrix = new RowMatrix(scaledVectors)
val K = 10
val pc = matrix.computePrincipalComponents(K)
```

You will likely see quite a lot of output on your console while the model runs.

If you see warnings such as **WARN LAPACK: Failed to load implementation from: com.github.fommil.netlib.NativeSystemLAPACK or WARN LAPACK: Failed to load implementation from: com.github.fommil.netlib.NativeRefLAPACK**, you can safely ignore

TIP

these.

This means that the underlying linear algebra libraries used by MLlib could not load the native routines. In this case, a Java-based fallback will be used, which is slower, but there is nothing to worry about for the purposes of this example.

Once the model training is complete, you should see a result that looks similar to the following one displayed on the console:

```
pc: org.apache.spark.mllib.linalg.Matrix =
-0.023183157256614906   -0.010622723054037303  ... (10 total)
-0.023960537953442107   -0.011495966728461177  ...
-0.024397470862198022   -0.013512219690177352  ...
-0.02463158818330343    -0.014758658113862178  ...
-0.024941633606137027   -0.014878858729655142  ...
-0.02525998879466241    -0.014602750644394844  ...
-0.025494722450369593   -0.014678013626511024  ...
-0.02604194423255582    -0.01439561589951032   ...
-0.025942214214865228   -0.013907665261197633  ...
-0.026151551334429365   -0.014707035797934148  ...
-0.026106572186134578   -0.016701471378568943  ...
-0.026242986173995755   -0.016254664123732318  ...
-0.02573628754284022    -0.017185663918352894  ...
-0.02545319635905169    -0.01653357295561698   ...
-0.025325893980995124   -0.0157082218373399...
```

Visualizing the Eigenfaces

Now that we have trained our PCA model, what is the result? Let's inspect the dimensions of the resulting matrix:

```
val rows = pc.numRows
val cols = pc.numCols
println(rows, cols)
```

As you should see from your console output, the matrix of the principal components has 2500 rows and 10 columns.

```
(2500,10)
```

Recall that the dimension of each image is 50 x 50, so here, we have the top 10 principal components, each with a dimension identical to that of the input images. These principal components can be thought of as the set of latent (or hidden) features that capture the greatest variation in the original data.

In facial recognition and image processing, these principal components are often referred to as **Eigenfaces**, as PCA is closely related to the eigenvalue decomposition of the covariance matrix of the original data. See `http://en.wikipedia.org/wiki/Eigenface` for more details.

Since each principal component is of the same dimension as the original images, each component can itself be thought of and represented as an image, making it possible to visualize the Eigenfaces as we would the input images.

As we have often done in this book, we will use functionality from the Breeze linear algebra library as well as Python's numpy and matplotlib to visualize the Eigenfaces.

First, we will extract the pc variable (an MLlib matrix) into a Breeze `DenseMatrix` as follows:

```
import breeze.linalg.DenseMatrix
val pcBreeze = new DenseMatrix(rows, cols, pc.toArray)
```

Breeze provides a useful function within the `linalg` package to write the matrix out as a CSV file. We will use this to save the principal components to a temporary CSV file.

```
import breeze.linalg.csvwrite
csvwrite(new File("/tmp/pc.csv"), pcBreeze)
```

Next, we will load the matrix in IPython, and visualize the principal components as images. Fortunately, numpy provides a utility function to read the matrix from the CSV file we created.

```
pcs = np.loadtxt(PATH + "/pc.csv", delimiter=",")
print(pcs.shape)
```

You should see the following output, confirming that the matrix we read has the same dimensions as the one we saved:

```
(2500, 10)
```

We will need a utility function to display the images, which we define here:

```
def plot_gallery(images, h, w, n_row=2, n_col=5):
    """Helper function to plot a gallery of portraits"""
    plt.figure(figsize=(1.8 * n_col, 2.4 * n_row))
    plt.subplots_adjust(bottom=0, left=.01, right=.99, top=.90,
        hspace=.35)
    for i in range(n_row * n_col):
        plt.subplot(n_row, n_col, i + 1)
        plt.imshow(images[:, i].reshape((h, w)),
            cmap=plt.cm.gray)
```

```
plt.title("Eigenface %d" % (i + 1), size=12)
plt.xticks(())
plt.yticks(())

plt.show()
```

This preceding function is adapted from the LFW dataset example code in the **scikit-learn** documentation available at `http://scikit-learn.org/stable/auto_examples/applications/face_r ecognition.html`.

We will now use this function to plot the top 10 Eigenfaces as follows:

```
plot_gallery(pcs, 50, 50)
```

This last command should display the following plot:

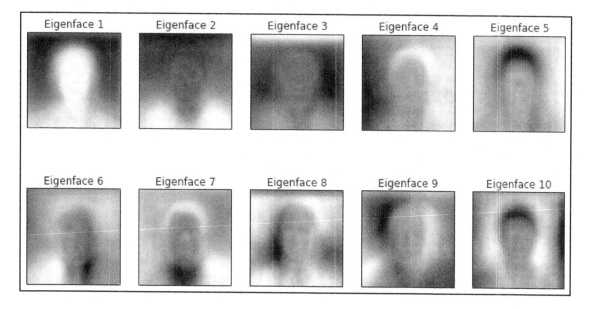

Top 10 Eigenfaces

Interpreting the Eigenfaces

Looking at the preceding images, we can see that the PCA model has effectively extracted recurring patterns of variation, which represent various features of the facial images. Each principal component can, as with clustering models, be interpreted.

Again, like clustering, it is not always straightforward to interpret precisely what each principal component represents.

We can see from these images that there appear to be some images that pick up directional factors (for example, images 6 and 9), some hone in on hair patterns (such as images 4, 5, 7, and 10), while others seem to be somewhat more related to facial features such as eyes, nose, and mouth (images 1, 7, and 9).

Using a dimensionality reduction model

It is interesting to be able to visualize the outcome of a model in this way; however, the overall purpose of using dimensionality reduction is to create a more compact representation of the data that still captures the important features and variability in the raw dataset. To do this, we need to use a trained model to transform our raw data by projecting it into the new, lower-dimensional space represented by the principal components.

Projecting data using PCA on the LFW dataset

We will illustrate this concept by projecting each LFW image into a ten-dimensional vector. This is done through a matrix multiplication of the image matrix with the matrix of principal components. As the image matrix is a distributed MLlib `RowMatrix`, Spark takes care of distributing this computation for us through the `multiply` function.

```
val projected = matrix.multiply(pc)
println(projected.numRows, projected.numCols)
```

This preceding function will give you the following output:

```
(1055,10)
```

Observe that each image that had a dimension of 2500, has been transformed into a vector of size 10. Let's take a look at the first few vectors:

```
println(projected.rows.take(5).mkString("n"))
```

Here is the output:

```
[2648.9455749636277,1340.3713412351376,443.67380716760965,
-353.0021423043161,52.53102289832631,423.39861446944354,
413.8429065865399,-484.18122999722294,87.98862070273545,
-104.62720604921965]
```

```
[172.67735747311974,663.9154866829355,261.0575622447282,
-711.4857925259682,462.7663154755333,167.3082231097332,
-71.44832640530836,624.4911488194524,892.3209964031695, -528.0056327351435]
[-1063.4562028554978,388.3510869550539,1508.2535609357597,
361.2485590837186,282.08588829583596,-554.3804376922453,
604.6680021092125,-224.16600191143075,-228.0771984153961,
-110.21539201855907]
[-4690.549692385103,241.83448841252638,-153.58903325799685,
-28.26215061165965,521.8908276360171,-442.0430200747375,
-490.1602309367725,-456.78026845649435,-78.79837478503592,
70.62925170688868]
[-2766.7960144161225,612.8408888724891,-405.76374113178616,
-468.56458995613974,863.1136863614743,-925.0935452709143,
69.24586949009642,-777.3348492244131,504.54033662376435, 257.0263568009851]
```

As the projected data is in the form of vectors, we can use the projection as an input to another machine learning model. For example, we could use these projected inputs together with a set of input data generated from various images without faces to train a facial recognition model. Alternatively, we could train a multiclass classifier, where each person is a class, thus creating a model that learns to identify the particular person that a face belongs to.

The relationship between PCA and SVD

We mentioned earlier that there is a close relationship between PCA and SVD. In fact, we can recover the same principal components, and also apply the same projection into the space of principal components using SVD.

In our example, the right singular vectors derived from computing the SVD will be equivalent to the principal components we have calculated. We can see that this is the case by first computing the SVD on our image matrix and comparing the right singular vectors to the result of PCA. As was the case with PCA, SVD computation is provided as a function on a distributed RowMatrix:

```
val svd = matrix.computeSVD(10, computeU = true)
println(s"U dimension: (${svd.U.numRows}, ${svd.U.numCols})")
println(s"S dimension: (${svd.s.size}, )")
println(s"V dimension: (${svd.V.numRows}, ${svd.V.numCols})")
```

We can see that SVD returns a matrix U of dimension 1055 x 10, a vector S of the singular values of length 10, and a matrix V of the right singular vectors of dimension 2500 x 10.

```
U dimension: (1055, 10)
S dimension: (10, )
```

```
V dimension: (2500, 10)
```

The matrix V is exactly equivalent to the result of PCA (ignoring the sign of the values and floating point tolerance). We can verify this with this next utility function to compare the two by approximately comparing the data arrays of each matrix:

```
def approxEqual(array1: Array[Double], array2: Array[Double],
tolerance: Double = 1e-6): Boolean = {
  // note we ignore sign of the principal component /
  // singular vector elements
  val bools = array1.zip(array2).map { case (v1, v2) => if
    (math.abs(math.abs(v1) - math.abs(v2)) > 1e-6) false else true }
  bools.fold(true)(_ & _)
}
```

We will test the function on some test data, as follows:

```
println(approxEqual(Array(1.0, 2.0, 3.0), Array(1.0, 2.0, 3.0)))
```

This will give you the following output:

```
true
```

Let's try another test data:

```
println(approxEqual(Array(1.0, 2.0, 3.0), Array(3.0, 2.0, 1.0)))
```

This will give you the following output:

```
false
```

Finally, we can apply our equality function as follows:

```
println(approxEqual(svd.V.toArray, pc.toArray))
```

Here is the output:

```
true
```

Both SVD and PCA can be used to calculate the principal components and corresponding Eigen/Singular values; the extra step of calculating the covariance matrix can lead to numerical rounding off errors while calculating Eigen vectors. SVD summarizes the ways in which the data deviates from zero, and PCA summarizes the ways in which the data deviates from the mean data sample.

The other relationship that holds is that the multiplication of the matrix U and vector S (or, strictly speaking, the diagonal matrix S) is equivalent to the PCA projection of our original image data into the space of the top 10 principal components.

We will now show that this is indeed the case. We will first use Breeze to multiply each vector in U by S, element-wise. We will then compare each vector in our PCA-projected vectors with the equivalent vector in our SVD projection, and sum up the number of equal cases, as follows:

```
val breezeS = breeze.linalg.DenseVector(svd.s.toArray)
val projectedSVD = svd.U.rows.map { v =>
  val breezeV = breeze.linalg.DenseVector(v.toArray)
  val multV = breezeV :* breezeS
  Vectors.dense(multV.data)
}
projected.rows.zip(projectedSVD).map { case (v1, v2) =>
  approxEqual(v1.toArray, v2.toArray) }.filter(b => true).count
```

This preceding code should display a result of 1055, as we would expect, confirming that each row of projected PCA is equal to each row of `projectedSVD`.

 Note that the :* operator, highlighted in the preceding code, represents element-wise multiplication of the vectors.

Evaluating dimensionality reduction models

Both PCA and SVD are deterministic models. That is, given a certain input dataset, they will always produce the same result. This is in contrast to many of the models we have seen so far, which depend on some random element (most often for the initialization of model weight vectors, and so on).

Both models are also guaranteed to return the top principal components or singular values, and hence, the only parameter is k. Like clustering models, increasing k always improves the model performance (for clustering, the relevant error function, while for PCA and SVD, the total amount of variability explained by the k components). Therefore, selecting a value for k is a trade-off between capturing as much structure of the data as possible while keeping the dimensionality of projected data low.

Evaluating k for SVD on the LFW dataset

We will examine the singular values obtained from computing the SVD on our image data. We can verify that the singular values are the same for each run, and that they are returned in a decreasing order, as follows:

```
val sValues = (1 to 5).map {
  i => matrix.computeSVD(i,  computeU = false).s
}
sValues.foreach(println)
```

This last code should generate an output similar to the following:

```
[54091.00997110354]
[54091.00997110358,33757.702867982436]
[54091.00997110357,33757.70286798241,24541.193694775946]
[54091.00997110358,33757.70286798242,24541.19369477593,  23309.58418888302]
[54091.00997110358,33757.70286798242,24541.19369477593,
23309.584188882982,21803.09841158358]
```

Singular values

Singular values lets us understand the trade-off between space and time for fidelity of the reduction.

As with evaluating values of *k* for clustering, in the case of SVD (and PCA), it is often useful to plot the singular values for a larger range of *k*, and see where the point on the graph is where the amount of additional variance accounted for by each additional singular value starts to flatten out considerably.

We will do this by first computing the top 300 singular values, as shown next:

```
val svd300 = matrix.computeSVD(300, computeU = false)
val sMatrix = new DenseMatrix(1, 300, svd300.s.toArray)
println(sMatrix)
csvwrite(new File("/home/ubuntu/work/ml-resources/
  spark-ml/Chapter_09/data/s.csv"), sMatrix)
```

We will write out the vector S of singular values to a temporary CSV file (as we did for our matrix of Eigenfaces previously), and then read it back in our IPython console, plotting the singular values for each *k*.

```
file_name = '/home/ubuntu/work/ml-resources/spark-ml/Chapter_09/data/s.csv'
data = np.genfromtxt(file_name, delimiter=',')
plt.plot(data)
plt.suptitle('Variation 300 Singular Values ')
```

```
plt.xlabel('Singular Value No')
plt.ylabel('Variation')
plt.show()
```

You should see an image displayed similar to the one shown here:

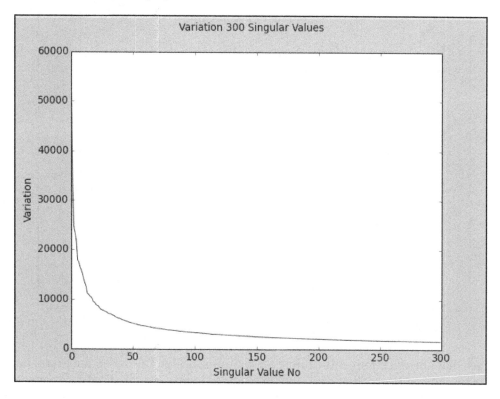

Top 300 singular values

A similar pattern is seen in the cumulative variation accounted for by the top 300 singular values (which we will plot on a log scale for the *y* axis).

```
plt.plot(cumsum(data))
plt.yscale('log')
plt.suptitle('Cumulative Variation 300 Singular Values ')
plt.xlabel('Singular Value No')
plt.ylabel('Cumulative Variation')
plt.show()
```

Full Source code for Python plots can be found at the following link: `https://github.com` `/ml-resources/spark-ml/tree/branch-ed2/Chapter_09/data/python`

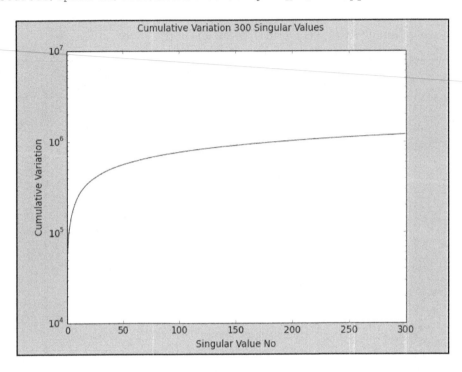

Cumulative sum of top 300 singular values

We can see that after a certain value range for *k* (around 100 in this case), the graph flattens considerably. This indicates that a number of singular values (or principal components) equivalent to this value of *k* probably explains enough of the variation of the original data.

Of course, if we are using dimensionality reduction to help improve the performance of another model, we could use the same evaluation methods used for that model to help us choose a value for *k*.

For example, we could use the AUC metric, together with cross-validation, to choose both the model parameters for a classification model as well as the value of *k* for our dimensionality reduction model. This does come at the expense of higher computation cost, however, as we would have to recompute the full model training and testing pipeline.

Summary

In this chapter, we explored two new unsupervised learning methods, PCA and SVD, for dimensionality reduction. We saw how to extract features for, and train, these models using facial image data. We visualized the results of the model in the form of Eigenfaces, saw how to apply the models to transform our original data into a reduced dimensionality representation, and investigated the close link between PCA and SVD.

In the next chapter, we will delve more deeply into techniques for text processing and analysis with Spark.

10

Advanced Text Processing with Spark

In Chapter 4, *Obtaining, Processing, and Preparing Data with Spark*, we covered various topics related to feature extraction and data processing, including the basics of extracting features from text data. In this chapter, we will introduce more advanced text processing techniques available in Spark ML to work with large-scale text datasets.

In this chapter, we will:

- Work through detailed examples that illustrate data processing, feature extraction, and the modeling pipeline, as they relate to text data
- Evaluate the similarity between two documents based on the words in the documents
- Use the extracted text features as inputs for a classification model
- Cover a recent development in natural language processing to model words themselves as vectors and illustrate the use of Spark's Word2Vec model to evaluate the similarity between two words, based on their meaning

We will look at how to use Spark's MLlib as well as Spark ML for text processing examples as well clustering of documents.

What's so special about text data?

Text data can be complex to work with for two main reasons. First, text and language have an inherent structure that is not easily captured using the raw words as is (for example, meaning, context, different types of words, sentence structure, and different languages, to highlight a few). Therefore, naive feature extraction is usually relatively ineffective.

Second, the effective dimensionality of text data is extremely large and potentially limitless. Think about the number of words in the English language alone and add all kinds of special words, characters, slang, and so on to this. Then, throw in other languages and all the types of text one might find across the Internet. The dimension of text data can easily exceed tens or even hundreds of millions of words, even in relatively small datasets. For example, the Common Crawl dataset of billions of websites contains over 840 billion individual words.

To deal with these issues, we need ways of extracting more structured features and methods to handle the huge dimensionality of text data.

Extracting the right features from your data

The field of **Natural Language Processing** (**NLP**) covers a wide range of techniques to work with text, from text processing and feature extraction through to modeling and machine learning. In this chapter, we will focus on two feature extraction techniques available within Spark MLlib and Spark ML: the **term frequency-inverse document frequency** (**tf-idf**) term weighting scheme and feature hashing.

Working through an example of tf-idf, we will also explore the ways in which processing, tokenization, and filtering during feature extraction can help reduce the dimensionality of our input data as well as improve the information content and usefulness of the features we extract.

Term weighting schemes

In `Chapter 4`, *Obtaining, Processing, and Preparing Data with Spark*, we looked at vector representation, where text features are mapped to a simple binary vector called the **bag-of-words** model. Another representation used commonly in practice is called Term Frequency-Inverse Document Frequency.

tf-idf weights each term in a piece of text (referred to as a **document**) based on its frequency in the document (the **term frequency**). A global normalization, called the **inverse document frequency**, is then applied based on the frequency of this term among all documents (the set of documents in a dataset is commonly referred to as a **corpus**). The standard definition of tf-idf is shown here:

$$tf\text{-}idf(t,d) = tf(t,d) \times idf(t)$$

Here, $tf(t,d)$ is the frequency (number of occurrences) of term t in document d and $idf(t)$ is the inverse document frequency of term t in the corpus; this is defined as follows:

$$idf(t) = log(N / d)$$

Here, N is the total number of documents, and d is the number of documents in which the term t occurs.

The tf-idf formulation means that terms occurring many times in a document receive a higher weighting in the vector representation relative to those that occur few times in the document. However, the IDF normalization has the effect of reducing the weight of terms that are very common across all documents. The end result is that truly rare or important terms should be assigned higher weighting, while more common terms (which are assumed to have less importance) should have less impact in terms of weighting.

> A good resource to learn more about the bag-of-words model (or vector space model) is the book Introduction to Information Retrieval, Christopher D. Manning, Prabhakar Raghavan and Hinrich Schütze, Cambridge University Press (available in HTML form at `http://nlp.stan ford.edu/IR-book/html/htmledition/irbook.html`).
>
> It contains sections on text processing techniques, including tokenization, stop word removal, stemming, and the vector space model, as well as weighting schemes such as tf-idf.
>
> An overview can also be found at `http://en.wikipedia.org/wiki/Tf%E 2%80%93idf`.

Feature hashing

Feature hashing is a technique to deal with high-dimensional data and is often used with text and categorical datasets where the features can take on many unique values (often many millions of values). In the previous chapters, we often used the *1-of-K* encoding approach for categorical features, including text. While this approach is simple and effective, it can break down in the face of extremely high-dimensional data.

Building and using *1-of-K* feature encoding requires us to keep a mapping of each possible feature value to an index in a vector. Furthermore, the process of creating the mapping itself requires at least one additional pass through the dataset and can be tricky to do in parallel scenarios. Up until now, we have often used a simple approach of collecting the distinct feature values and zipping this collection with a set of indices to create a map of feature value to index. This mapping is then broadcast (either explicitly in our code or implicitly by Spark) to each worker.

However, when dealing with huge feature dimensions in the tens of millions or more that are common when working with text, this approach can be slow and can require significant memory and network resources, both on the Spark master (to collect the unique values) and workers (to broadcast the resulting mapping to each worker, which keeps it in memory to allow it to apply the feature encoding to its local piece of the input data).

Feature hashing works by assigning the vector index for a feature based on the value obtained by hashing this feature to a number (usually, an integer value) using a hash function. For example, let's say the hash value of a categorical feature for the geolocation of United States is 342. We will use the hashed value as the vector index, and the value at this index will be 1.0 to indicate the presence of the United States feature. The hash function used must be consistent (that is, for a given input, it returns the same output each time).

This encoding works the same way as mapping-based encoding, except that we choose a size for our feature vector upfront. As the most common hash functions return values in the entire range of integers, we will use a *modulo* operation to restrict the index values to the size of our vector, which is typically much smaller (a few tens of thousands to a few million, depending on our requirements).

Feature hashing has the advantage that we do not need to build a mapping and keep it in memory. It is also easy to implement, very fast, and can be done online and in real time, thus not requiring a pass through our dataset first. Finally, because we selected a feature vector dimension that is significantly smaller than the raw dimensionality of our dataset, we bound the memory usage of our model both in training and production; hence, memory usage does not scale with the size and dimensionality of our data.

However, there are two important drawbacks, which are as follows:

- As we don't create a mapping of features to index values, we also cannot do the reverse mapping of feature index to value. This makes it harder to, for example, determine which features are most informative in our models.
- As we are restricting the size of our feature vectors, we might experience **hash collisions**. This happens when two different features are hashed into the same index in our feature vector. Surprisingly, this doesn't seem to have a severe impact on model performance as long as we choose a reasonable feature vector dimension relative to the dimension of the input data. If the Hashed vector is large the affect of collision is minimal but the gain is still significant. Please refer to this paper for more details : http://www.cs.jhu.edu/~mdredze/publication s/mobile_nlp_feature_mixing.pdf

Further information on hashing can be found at
`http://en.wikipedia.org/wiki/Hash_function`.

A key paper that introduced the use of hashing for feature extraction and machine learning is:

Kilian Weinberger, Anirban Dasgupta, John Langford, Alex Smola, and *Josh Attenberg. Feature Hashing for Large Scale Multitask Learning. Proc. ICML 2009*, which is available at
`http://alex.smola.org/papers/2009/Weinbergeretal09.pdf`.

Extracting the tf-idf features from the 20 Newsgroups dataset

To illustrate the concepts in this chapter, we will use a well-known text dataset called **20 Newsgroups**; this dataset is commonly used for text-classification tasks. This is a collection of newsgroup messages posted across 20 different topics. There are various forms of data available. For our purposes, we will use the `bydate` version of the dataset, which is available at `http://qwone.com/~jason/20Newsgroups`.

This dataset splits up the available data into training and test sets that comprise 60 percent and 40 percent of the original data, respectively. Here, the messages in the test set occur after those in the training set. This dataset also excludes some of the message headers that identify the actual newsgroup; hence, it is an appropriate dataset to test the real-world performance of classification models.

Further information on the original dataset can be found in the *UCI Machine Learning Repository* page at
`http://kdd.ics.uci.edu/databases/20newsgroups/20newsgroups.data.html`.

To get started, download the data and unzip the file using the following command:

```
>tar xfvz 20news-bydate.tar.gz
```

This will create two folders: one called `20news-bydate-train` and another one called `20news-bydate-test`. Let's take a look at the directory structure under the training dataset folder:

```
>cd 20news-bydate-train/
>ls
```

You will see that it contains a number of subfolders, one for each newsgroup:

```
alt.atheism              comp.windows.x          rec.sport.hockey
   soc.religion.christian
comp.graphics            misc.forsale            sci.crypt
   talk.politics.guns
comp.os.ms-windows.misc  rec.autos               sci.electronics
   talk.politics.mideast
comp.sys.ibm.pc.hardware rec.motorcycles         sci.med
   talk.politics.misc
comp.sys.mac.hardware    rec.sport.baseball      sci.space
   talk.religion.misc
```

There are a number of files under each newsgroup folder; each file contains an individual message posting:

```
> ls rec.sport.hockey
52550 52580 52610 52640 53468 53550 53580 53610 53640 53670 53700
53731 53761 53791
...
```

We can take a look at a part of one of these messages to see the format:

```
> head -20 rec.sport.hockey/52550
From: dchhabra@stpl.ists.ca (Deepak Chhabra)
Subject: Superstars and attendance (was Teemu Selanne, was +/-
   leaders)
Nntp-Posting-Host: stpl.ists.ca
Organization: Solar Terresterial Physics Laboratory, ISTS
Distribution: na
Lines: 115


Dean J. Falcione (posting from jrmst+8@pitt.edu) writes:
[I wrote:]

>>When the Pens got Mario, granted there was big publicity,etc, etc,
>>and interest was immediately generated. Gretzky did the same thing for
>>LA.
>>However, imnsho, neither team would have seen a marked improvement in
>>attendance if the team record did not improve. In the year before Lemieux
>>came, Pittsburgh finished with 38 points. Following his arrival, the Pens
>>finished with 53, 76, 72, 81, 87, 72, 88, and 87 points, with a couple of
                              ^^
>>Stanley Cups thrown in.
...
```

As we can see, each message contains some header fields that contain the sender, subject, and other metadata, followed by the raw content of the message.

Exploring the 20 Newsgroups data

We will use a Spark Program to load and analyze the dataset.

```
object TFIDFExtraction {

  def main(args: Array[String]) {

  }
}
```

Looking at the directory structure, you might recognize that once again, we have data contained in individual text files (one text file per message). Therefore, we will again use Spark's `wholeTextFiles` method to read the content of each file into a record in our RDD.

In the code that follows, `PATH` refers to the directory in which you extracted the `20news-bydate` ZIP file:

```
val sc = new SparkContext("local[2]", "First Spark App")

val path = "../data/20news-bydate-train/*"
val rdd = sc.wholeTextFiles(path)
// count the number of records in the dataset
println(rdd.count)
```

If you put a breakpoint, you will see the following line displayed, indicating the total number of files that Spark has detected:

```
...
INFO FileInputFormat: Total input paths to process : 11314
...
```

After the command has finished running, you will see the total record count, which should be the same as the preceding `Total input paths to process` screen output:

```
11314
```

Let us now print first element of the `rdd` into which data has been loaded:

```
16/12/30 20:42:02 INFO DAGScheduler: Job 1 finished: first at
TFIDFExtraction.scala:27, took 0.067414 s
(file:/home/ubuntu/work/ml-resources/spark-
ml/Chapter_10/data/20news- bydate-train/alt.atheism/53186,From:
ednclark@kraken.itc.gu.edu.au (Jeffrey Clark)
Subject: Re: some thoughts.
Keywords: Dan Bissell
Nntp-Posting-Host: kraken.itc.gu.edu.au
Organization: ITC, Griffith University, Brisbane, Australia
Lines: 70
....
```

Next, we will take a look at the newsgroup topics available:

```
val newsgroups = rdd.map { case (file, text) =>
  file.split("/").takeRight(2).head }
println(newsgroups.first())
val countByGroup = newsgroups.map(n => (n, 1)).reduceByKey(_ +
  _).collect.sortBy(-_._2).mkString("n")
println(countByGroup)
```

This will display the following result:

```
(rec.sport.hockey,600)
(soc.religion.christian,599)
(rec.motorcycles,598)
(rec.sport.baseball,597)
(sci.crypt,595)
(rec.autos,594)
(sci.med,594)
(comp.windows.x,593)
(sci.space,593)
(sci.electronics,591)
(comp.os.ms-windows.misc,591)
(comp.sys.ibm.pc.hardware,590)
(misc.forsale,585)
(comp.graphics,584)
(comp.sys.mac.hardware,578)
(talk.politics.mideast,564)
(talk.politics.guns,546)
(alt.atheism,480)
(talk.politics.misc,465)
(talk.religion.misc,377)
```

We can see that the number of messages is roughly even between the topics.

Applying basic tokenization

The first step in our text processing pipeline is to split up the raw text content in each document into a collection of terms (also referred to as **tokens**). This is known as **tokenization**. We will start by applying a simple **whitespace** tokenization, together with converting each token to lowercase for each document:

```
val text = rdd.map { case (file, text) => text }
val whiteSpaceSplit = text.flatMap(t => t.split("
  ").map(_.toLowerCase))
println(whiteSpaceSplit.distinct.count)
```

In the preceding code, we used the `flatMap` function instead of `map`, as for now, we want to inspect all the tokens together for exploratory analysis. Later in this chapter, we will apply our tokenization scheme on a per-document basis, so we will use the `map` function.

After running this code snippet, you will see the total number of unique tokens after applying our tokenization:

402978

As you can see, for even a relatively small amount of text, the number of raw tokens (and, therefore, the dimensionality of our feature vectors) can be very high.

Let's take a look at a randomly selected document. We will use the sample method of RDD:

```
def sample(
      withReplacement: Boolean,
      fraction: Double,
      seed: Long = Utils.random.nextLong): RDD[T]

Return a sampled subset of this RDD.
@param withReplacement can elements be sampled multiple times
  (replaced when sampled out)
@param fraction expected size of the sample as a fraction of this
  RDD's size without replacement: probability that each element is
  chosen; fraction must be [0, 1] with replacement: expected number
  of times each element is chosen; fraction must be >= 0
@param seed seed for the random number generator

      println(nonWordSplit.distinct.sample(
      true, 0.3, 42).take(100).mkString(","))
```

Note that we set the third parameter to the `sample` function, which is the random seed. We set this function to `42` so that we get the same results from each call to `sample` so that your results match those in this chapter.

This will display the following result:

```
atheist,resources
summary:,addresses,,to,atheism
keywords:,music,,thu,,11:57:19,11:57:19,gmt
distribution:,cambridge.,290

archive-name:,atheism/resources
alt-atheism-archive-
name:,december,,,,,,,,,,,,,,,,,,,,,addresses,addresses,,,,,,,
religion,to:,to:,,p.o.,53701.
telephone:,sell,the,,fish,on,their,cars,,with,and,written

inside.,3d,plastic,plastic,,evolution,evolution,7119,,,,,san,san,
san,mailing,net,who,to,atheist,press

aap,various,bible,,and,on.,,,,one,book,is:

"the,w.p.,american,pp.,,,1986.,bible,contains,ball,,based,based,
james,of
```

Improving our tokenization

The preceding simple approach results in a lot of tokens and does not filter out many nonword characters (such as punctuation). Most tokenization schemes will remove these characters. We can do this by splitting each raw document on nonword characters using a regular expression pattern:

```
val nonWordSplit = text.flatMap(t =>
  t.split("""\W+""").map(_.toLowerCase))
println(nonWordSplit.distinct.count)
```

This reduces the number of unique tokens significantly:

```
130126
```

If we inspect the first few tokens, we will see that we have eliminated most of the less useful characters in the text:

```
println(
nonWordSplit.distinct.sample(true, 0.3,
```

```
50).take(100).mkString(","))
```

You will see the following result displayed:

```
jejones,ml5,w1w3s1,k29p,nothin,42b,beleive,robin,believiing,749,
steaminess,tohc4,fzbv1u,ao,
instantaneous,nonmeasurable,3465,tiems,tiems,tiems,eur,3050,pgva4,
animating,10011100b,413,randall_clark,
mswin,cannibal,cannibal,congresswoman,congresswoman,theoreticians,
34ij,logically,kxo,contoler,
contoler,13963,13963,ets,sask,sask,sask,uninjured,930420,pws,vfj,
jesuit,kocharian,6192,1tbs,octopi,
012537,012537,yc0,dmitriev,icbz,cj1v,bowdoin,computational,
jkis_ltd,
caramate,cfsmo,springer,springer,
005117,shutdown,makewindow,nowadays,mtearle,discernible,
discernible,qnh1,hindenburg,hindenburg,umaxc,
njn2e5,njn2e5,njn2e5,x4_i,x4_i,monger,rjs002c,rjs002c,rjs002c,
warms,ndallen,g45,herod,6w8rg,mqh0,suspects,
floor,flq1r,io21087,phoniest,funded,ncmh,c4uzus
```

While our nonword pattern to split text works fairly well, we are still left with numbers and tokens that contain numeric characters. In some cases, numbers can be an important part of a corpus. For our purposes, the next step in our pipeline will be to filter out numbers and tokens that are words mixed with numbers.

We can do this by applying another regular expression pattern and use this to filter out tokens that do not match the pattern, `val regex = """[^0-9]*""".r`.

```
val regex = """[^0-9]*""".r
val filterNumbers = nonWordSplit.filter(token =>
  regex.pattern.matcher(token).matches)
println(filterNumbers.distinct.count)
```

This further reduces the size of the token set:

84912

```
println(filterNumbers.distinct.sample(true, 0.3,
50).take(100).mkString(","))
```

Let's take a look at another random sample of the filtered tokens.

You will see output like the following:

```
jejones,silikian,reunion,schwabam,nothin,singen,husky,tenex,
eventuality,beleive,goofed,robin,upsets,aces,nondiscriminatory,
underscored,bxl,believiing,believiing,believiing,historians,
```

```
nauseam,kielbasa,collins,noport,wargame,isv,bellevue,seetex,seetex,
negotiable,negotiable,viewed,rolled,unforeseen,dlr,museum,museum,
wakaluk,wakaluk,dcbq,beekeeper,beekeeper,beekeeper,wales,mop,win,
ja_jp,relatifs,dolphin,strut,worshippers,wertheimer,jaze,jaze,
logically,kxo,nonnemacher,sunprops,sask,bbzx,jesuit,logos,aichi,
remailing,remailing,winsor,dtn,astonished,butterfield,miserable,
icbz,icbz,poking,sml,sml,makeing,deterministic,deterministic,
deterministic,rockefeller,rockefeller,explorers,bombardments,
bombardments,bombardments,ray_bourque,hour,cfsmo,mishandles,
scramblers,alchoholic,shutdown,almanac_,bruncati,karmann,hfd,
makewindow,perptration,mtearle
```

We can see that we have removed all the numeric characters. This still leaves us with a few strange *words*, but we will not worry about these too much here.

Removing stop words

Stop words refer to common words that occur many times across almost all documents in a corpus (and across most corpuses). Examples of typical English stop words include and, but, the, of, and so on. It is a standard practice in text feature extraction to exclude stop words from the extracted tokens.

When using tf-idf weighting, the weighting scheme actually takes care of this for us. As stop words have a very low idf score, they will tend to have very low tf-idf weightings and thus less importance. In some cases, for information retrieval and search tasks, it might be desirable to include stop words. However, it can still be beneficial to exclude stop words during feature extraction, as it reduces the dimensionality of the final feature vectors as well as the size of the training data.

We can take a look at some of the tokens in our corpus that have the highest occurrence across all documents to get an idea about some other stop words to exclude:

```
val tokenCounts = filterNumbers.map(t => (t, 1)).reduceByKey(_ +
  _)
val oreringDesc = Ordering.by[(String, Int), Int](_._2)
println(tokenCounts.top(20)(oreringDesc).mkString("n"))
```

In the preceding code, we took the tokens after filtering out numeric characters and generated a count of the occurrence of each token across the corpus. We can now use Spark's top function to retrieve the top 20 tokens by count. Notice that we need to provide the top function with an ordering that tells Spark how to order the elements of our RDD. In this case, we want to order by the count, so we will specify the second element of our key-value pair.

Running the preceding code snippet will result in the following top tokens:

```
(the,146532)
(to,75064)
(of,69034)
(a,64195)
(ax,62406)
(and,57957)
(i,53036)
(in,49402)
(is,43480)
(that,39264)
(it,33638)
(for,28600)
(you,26682)
(from,22670)
(s,22337)
(edu,21321)
(on,20493)
(this,20121)
(be,19285)
(t,18728)
```

As we might expect, there are a lot of common words in this list that we could potentially label as stop words. Let's create a set of stop words with some of these as well as other common words. We will then look at the tokens after filtering out these stop words:

```
val stopwords = Set(
    "the","a","an","of","or","in","for","by","on","but", "is",
    "not", "with", "as", "was", "if",
    "they", "are", "this", "and", "it", "have", "from", "at", "my",
    "be", "that", "to"
val tokenCountsFilteredStopwords = tokenCounts.filter {
    case (k, v) => !stopwords.contains(k)
    }

println(tokenCountsFilteredStopwords.top(20)
    (oreringDesc).mkString("n"))
```

You will see the following output:

```
(ax,62406)
(i,53036)
(you,26682)
(s,22337)
(edu,21321)
(t,18728)
```

```
(m,12756)
(subject,12264)
(com,12133)
(lines,11835)
(can,11355)
(organization,11233)
(re,10534)
(what,9861)
(there,9689)
(x,9332)
(all,9310)
(will,9279)
(we,9227)
(one,9008)
```

You might notice that there are still quite a few common words in this top list. In practice, we might have a much larger set of stop words. However, we will keep a few (partly to illustrate the impact of common words when using tf-idf weighting a little later).

You can find list of common stop words here : `http://xpo6.com/list-of-english-stop-words/`

One other filtering step that we will use is removing any tokens that are only one character in length. The reasoning behind this is similar to removing stop words-these single-character tokens are unlikely to be informative in our text model and can further reduce the feature dimension and model size. We will do this with another filtering step:

```
val tokenCountsFilteredSize =
  tokenCountsFilteredStopwords.filter {
    case (k, v) => k.size >= 2
  }
println(tokenCountsFilteredSize.top(20)
  (oreringDesc).mkString("n"))
```

Again, we will examine the tokens remaining after this filtering step:

```
(ax,62406)
(you,26682)
(edu,21321)
(subject,12264)
(com,12133)
(lines,11835)
(can,11355)
(organization,11233)
(re,10534)
(what,9861)
(there,9689)
(all,9310)
```

```
(will,9279)
(we,9227)
(one,9008)
(would,8905)
(do,8674)
(he,8441)
(about,8336)
(writes,7844)
```

Apart from some of the common words that we have not excluded, we see that a few, potentially more informative words are starting to appear.

Excluding terms based on frequency

It is also a common practice to exclude terms during tokenization when their overall occurrence in the corpus is very low. For example, let's examine the least occurring terms in the corpus (notice the different ordering we use here to return the results sorted in ascending order):

```
val oreringAsc = Ordering.by[(String, Int), Int](-_._2)
println(tokenCountsFilteredSize.top(20)(oreringAsc)
   .mkString("n"))
```

You will get the following results:

```
(lennips,1)
(bluffing,1)
(preload,1)
(altina,1)
(dan_jacobson,1)
(vno,1)
(actu,1)
(donnalyn,1)
(ydag,1)
(mirosoft,1)
(xiconfiywindow,1)
(harger,1)
(feh,1)
(bankruptcies,1)
(uncompression,1)
(d_nibby,1)
(bunuel,1)
(odf,1)
(swith,1)
(lantastic,1)
```

As we can see, there are many terms that only occur once in the entire corpus. Since typically, we want to use our extracted features for other tasks such as document similarity or machine learning models, tokens that only occur once are not useful to learn from, as we will not have enough training data relative to these tokens. We can apply another filter to exclude these rare tokens:

```scala
val rareTokens = tokenCounts.filter{ case (k, v) => v < 2 }.map {
    case (k, v) => k }.collect.toSet
val tokenCountsFilteredAll = tokenCountsFilteredSize.filter {
    case (k, v) => !rareTokens.contains(k) }
println(tokenCountsFilteredAll.top(20)
    (oreringAsc).mkString("n"))
```

We can see that we are left with tokens that occur at least twice in the corpus:

```
(sina,2)
(akachhy,2)
(mvd,2)
(hizbolah,2)
(wendel_clark,2)
(sarkis,2)
(purposeful,2)
(feagans,2)
(wout,2)
(uneven,2)
(senna,2)
(multimeters,2)
(bushy,2)
(subdivided,2)
(coretest,2)
(oww,2)
(historicity,2)
(mmg,2)
(margitan,2)
(defiance,2)
```

Now, let's count the number of unique tokens:

```scala
println(tokenCountsFilteredAll.count)
```

You will see the following output:

```
51801
```

As we can see, by applying all the filtering steps in our tokenization pipeline, we have reduced the feature dimension from $402,978$ to $51,801$.

We can now combine all our filtering logic into one function, which we can apply to each document in our RDD:

```
def tokenize(line: String): Seq[String] = {
  line.split("""\W+""")
    .map(_.toLowerCase)
    .filter(token => regex.pattern.matcher(token).matches)
    .filterNot(token => stopwords.contains(token))
    .filterNot(token => rareTokens.contains(token))
    .filter(token => token.size >= 2)
    .toSeq
}
```

We can check whether this function gives us the same result with the following code snippet:

```
println(text.flatMap(doc => tokenize(doc)).distinct.count)
```

This will output 51801, giving us the same unique token count as our step-by-step pipeline.

We can tokenize each document in our RDD as follows:

```
val tokens = text.map(doc => tokenize(doc))
println(tokens.first.take(20))
```

You will see output similar to the following, showing the first part of the tokenized version of our first document:

```
WrappedArray(mathew, mantis, co, uk, subject, alt, atheism,
faq, atheist, resources, summary, books, addresses, music,
anything, related, atheism, keywords, faq)
```

A note about stemming

A common step in text processing and tokenization is **stemming**. This is the conversion of whole words to a **base form** (called a **word stem**). For example, plurals might be converted to singular (*dogs* becomes *dog*), and forms such as *walking* and *walker* might become walk. Stemming can become quite complex and is typically handled with specialized NLP or search engine software (such as NLTK, OpenNLP, and Lucene, for example). We will ignore stemming for the purpose of our example here.

A full treatment of stemming is beyond the scope of this book. You can find more details at http://en.wikipedia.org/wiki/Stemming.

Feature Hashing

First we explain what is feature hashing so that it becomes easier to understand the tf-idf model in the next section.

Feature hashing converts a String or a word into a fixed length vector which makes it easy to process text.

Spark currently uses Austin Appleby's MurmurHash 3 algorithm (MurmurHash3_x86_32) for hashing text into numbers.

You can find the implementation here

```
private[spark] def murmur3Hash(term: Any): Int = {
  term match {
  case null => seed
  case b: Boolean => hashInt(if (b) 1 else 0, seed)
  case b: Byte => hashInt(b, seed)
  case s: Short => hashInt(s, seed)
  case i: Int => hashInt(i, seed)
  case l: Long => hashLong(l, seed)
  case f: Float => hashInt(java.lang.Float
    .floatToIntBits(f), seed)
  case d: Double => hashLong(java.lang.Double.
    doubleToLongBits(d), seed)
  case s: String => val utf8 = UTF8String.fromString(s)
    hashUnsafeBytes(utf8.getBaseObject, utf8.getBaseOffset,
    utf8.numBytes(), seed)
  case _ => throw new SparkException(
    "HashingTF with murmur3 algorithm does not " +
    s"support type ${term.getClass.getCanonicalName} of input
    data.")
  }
}
```

Please note functions hashInt, hasnLong etc are called from Util.scala

Building a tf-idf model

We will now use Spark ML to transform each document, in the form of processed tokens, into a vector representation. The first step will be to use the HashingTF implementation, which makes use of feature hashing to map each token in the input text to an index in the vector of term frequencies. Then, we will compute the global IDF and use it to transform the term frequency vectors into tf-idf vectors.

For each token, the index will thus be the hash of the token (mapped in turn onto the dimension of the feature vector). The value for each token will be the tf-idf weighting for that token (that is, the term frequency multiplied by the inverse document frequency).

First, we will import the classes we need and create our `HashingTF` instance, passing in a `dim` dimension parameter. While the default feature dimension is 2^{20} (or around 1 million), we will choose 2^{18} (or around 260,000), since with about 50,000 tokens, we should not experience a significant number of hash collisions, and a smaller dimension will be more memory and processing friendly for illustrative purposes:

```
import org.apache.spark.mllib.linalg.{ SparseVector => SV }
import org.apache.spark.mllib.feature.HashingTF
import org.apache.spark.mllib.feature.IDF
val dim = math.pow(2, 18).toInt
val hashingTF = new HashingTF(dim)
val tf = hashingTF.transform(tokens)
tf.cache
```

Note that we imported MLlib's `SparseVector` using an alias of `SV`. This is because later, we will use Breeze's `linalg` module, which itself also imports `SparseVector`. This way, we will avoid namespace collisions.

The `transform` function of `HashingTF` maps each input document (that is, a sequence of tokens) to an MLlib `Vector`. We will also call `cache` to pin the data in memory to speed up subsequent operations.

Let's inspect the first element of our transformed dataset:

Note that `HashingTF.transform` returns an `RDD[Vector]`, so we will cast the result returned to an instance of an MLlib `SparseVector`.

The `transform` method can also work on an individual document by taking an `Iterable` argument (for example, a document as a `Seq[String]`). This returns a single vector.

```
val v = tf.first.asInstanceOf[SV]
println(v.size)
println(v.values.size)
println(v.values.take(10).toSeq)
println(v.indices.take(10).toSeq)
```

You will see the following output displayed:

```
262144
706
WrappedArray(1.0, 1.0, 1.0, 1.0, 2.0, 1.0, 1.0, 2.0, 1.0, 1.0)
WrappedArray(313, 713, 871, 1202, 1203, 1209, 1795, 1862, 3115,
3166)
```

We can see that the dimension of each sparse vector of term frequencies is 262,144 (or 2^{18} as we specified). However, the number on non-zero entries in the vector is only 706. The last two lines of the output show the frequency counts and vector indexes for the first few entries in the vector.

We will now compute the inverse document frequency for each term in the corpus by creating a new IDF instance and calling fit with our RDD of term frequency vectors as the input. We will then transform our term frequency vectors to tf-idf vectors through the transform function of IDF:

```
val idf = new IDF().fit(tf)
val tfidf = idf.transform(tf)
val v2 = tfidf.first.asInstanceOf[SV]
println(v2.values.size)
println(v2.values.take(10).toSeq)
println(v2.indices.take(10).toSeq)
```

When you examine the first element in the RDD of tf-idf transformed vectors, you will see output similar to the one shown here:

```
706
WrappedArray(2.3869085659322193, 4.670445463955571,
6.561295835827856, 4.597686109673142,  ...
WrappedArray(313, 713, 871, 1202, 1203, 1209, 1795, 1862, 3115,
3166)
```

We can see that the number of non-zero entries hasn't changed (at 706), nor have the vector indices for the terms. What has changed are the values for each term. Earlier, these represented the frequency of each term in the document, but now, the new values represent the frequencies weighted by the IDF.

IDF weightage came into picture when we executed the following two lines

```
val idf = new IDF().fit(tf)
val tfidf = idf.transform(tf)
```

Analyzing the tf-idf weightings

Next, let's investigate the tf-idf weighting for a few terms to illustrate the impact of the commonality or rarity of a term.

First, we can compute the minimum and maximum tf-idf weights across the entire corpus:

```
val minMaxVals = tfidf.map { v =>
  val sv = v.asInstanceOf[SV]
  (sv.values.min, sv.values.max)
}
val globalMinMax = minMaxVals.reduce { case ((min1, max1),
  (min2, max2)) =>
  (math.min(min1, min2), math.max(max1, max2))
}
println(globalMinMax)
```

As we can see, the minimum tf-idf is zero, while the maximum is significantly larger:

```
(0.0,66155.39470409753)
```

We will now explore the tf-idf weight attached to various terms. In the previous section on stop words, we filtered out many common terms that occur frequently. Recall that we did not remove all such potential stop words. Instead, we kept a few in the corpus so that we could illustrate the impact of applying the tf-idf weighting scheme on these terms.

Tf-idf weighting will tend to assign a lower weighting to common terms. To see this, we can compute the tf-idf representation for a few of the terms that appear in the list of top occurrences that we previously computed, such as you, do, and we:

```
val common = sc.parallelize(Seq(Seq("you", "do", "we")))
val tfCommon = hashingTF.transform(common)
val tfidfCommon = idf.transform(tfCommon)
val commonVector = tfidfCommon.first.asInstanceOf[SV]
println(commonVector.values.toSeq)
```

If we form a tf-idf vector representation of this document, we would see the following values assigned to each term. Note that because of feature hashing, we are not sure exactly which term represents what. However, the values illustrate that the weighting applied to these terms is relatively low:

```
WrappedArray(0.9965359935704624, 1.3348773448236835,
0.5457486182039175)
```

Now, let's apply the same transformation to a few less common terms that we might intuitively associate with being more linked to specific topics or concepts:

```
val uncommon = sc.parallelize(Seq(Seq("telescope",
  "legislation", "investment")))
val tfUncommon = hashingTF.transform(uncommon)
val tfidfUncommon = idf.transform(tfUncommon)
val uncommonVector = tfidfUncommon.first.asInstanceOf[SV]
println(uncommonVector.values.toSeq)
```

We can see from the following results that the tf-idf weightings are indeed significantly higher than for the more common terms:

```
WrappedArray(5.3265513728351666, 5.308532867332488,
5.483736956357579)
```

Using a tf-idf model

While we often refer to training a tf-idf model, it is actually a feature extraction process or transformation rather than a machine learning model. Tf-idf weighting is often used as a preprocessing step for other models, such as dimensionality reduction, classification, or regression.

To illustrate the potential uses of tf-idf weighting, we will explore two examples. The first is using the tf-idf vectors to compute document similarity, while the second involves training a multilabel classification model with the tf-idf vectors as input features.

Document similarity with the 20 Newsgroups dataset and tf-idf features

You might recall from Chapter 5, *Building a Recommendation Engine with Spark*, that the similarity between two vectors can be computed using a distance metric. The closer two vectors are (that is, the lower the distance metric), the more similar they are. One such metric that we used to compute similarity between movies is cosine similarity.

Just like we did for movies, we can also compute the similarity between two documents. Using tf-idf, we have transformed each document into a vector representation. Hence, we can use the same techniques as we used for movie vectors to compare two documents.

Intuitively, we might expect two documents to be more similar to each other if they share many terms. Conversely, we might expect two documents to be less similar if they each contain many terms that are different from each other. As we compute cosine similarity by computing a dot product of the two vectors and each vector is made up of the terms in each document, we can see that documents with a high overlap of terms will tend to have a higher cosine similarity.

Now, we can see tf-idf at work. We might reasonably expect that even very different documents might contain many overlapping terms that are relatively common (for example, our stop words). However, due to a low tf-idf weighting, these terms will not have a significant impact on the dot product and, therefore, will not have much impact on the similarity computed.

For example, we might expect two randomly chosen messages from the `hockey` newsgroup to be relatively similar to each other. Let's see if this is the case:

```
val hockeyText = rdd.filter { case (file, text) =>
  file.contains("hockey") }
val hockeyTF = hockeyText.mapValues(doc =>
  hashingTF.transform(tokenize(doc)))
val hockeyTfIdf = idf.transform(hockeyTF.map(_._2))
```

In the preceding code, we first filtered our raw input RDD to keep only the messages within the hockey topic. We then applied our tokenization and term frequency transformation functions. Note that the `transform` method used is the version that works on a single document (in the form of a `Seq[String]`) rather than the version that works on an RDD of documents.

Finally, we applied the `IDF` transform (note that we use the same IDF that we have already computed on the whole corpus).

Once we have our `hockey` document vectors, we can select two of these vectors at random and compute the cosine similarity between them (as we did earlier, we will use Breeze for the linear algebra functionality, in particular converting our MLlib vectors to Breeze `SparseVector` instances first):

```
import breeze.linalg._
val hockey1 = hockeyTfIdf.sample(
  true, 0.1, 42).first.asInstanceOf[SV]
val breeze1 = new SparseVector(hockey1.indices,
  hockey1.values, hockey1.size)
val hockey2 = hockeyTfIdf.sample(true, 0.1,
  43).first.asInstanceOf[SV]
val breeze2 = new SparseVector(hockey2.indices,
  hockey2.values, hockey2.size)
```

```
val cosineSim = breeze1.dot(breeze2) /
  (norm(breeze1) * norm(breeze2))
println(cosineSim)
```

We can see that the cosine similarity between the documents is around 0.06:

```
0.06700095047242809
```

While this might seem quite low, recall that the effective dimensionality of our features is high due to the large number of unique terms that is typical when dealing with text data. Hence, we can expect that any two documents might have a relatively low overlap of terms even if they are about the same topic, and therefore would have a lower absolute similarity score.

By contrast, we can compare this similarity score to the one computed between one of our `hockey` documents and another document chosen randomly from the `comp.graphics` newsgroup, using the same methodology:

```
val graphicsText = rdd.filter { case (file, text) =>
  file.contains("comp.graphics") }
val graphicsTF = graphicsText.mapValues(doc =>
  hashingTF.transform(tokenize(doc)))
val graphicsTfIdf = idf.transform(graphicsTF.map(_._2))
val graphics = graphicsTfIdf.sample(true, 0.1,
  42).first.asInstanceOf[SV]
val breezeGraphics = new SparseVector(graphics.indices,
  graphics.values, graphics.size)
val cosineSim2 = breeze1.dot(breezeGraphics) / (norm(breeze1) *
  norm(breezeGraphics))
println(cosineSim2)
```

The cosine similarity is significantly lower at 0.0047:

```
0.001950124251275256
```

Finally, it is likely that a document from another sports-related topic might be more similar to our `hockey` document than one from a computer-related topic. However, we would probably expect a `baseball` document to not be as similar as our `hockey` document. Let's see whether this is the case by computing the similarity between a random message from the `baseball` newsgroup and our `hockey` document:

```
// compare to sport.baseball topic
val baseballText = rdd.filter { case (file, text) =>
  file.contains("baseball") }
val baseballTF = baseballText.mapValues(doc =>
  hashingTF.transform(tokenize(doc)))
val baseballTfIdf = idf.transform(baseballTF.map(_._2))
```

```
val baseball = baseballTfIdf.sample(true, 0.1,
  42).first.asInstanceOf[SV]
val breezeBaseball = new SparseVector(baseball.indices,
  baseball.values, baseball.size)
val cosineSim3 = breeze1.dot(breezeBaseball) / (norm(breeze1) *
  norm(breezeBaseball))
println(cosineSim3)
```

Indeed, as we expected, we found that the `baseball` and `hockey` documents have a cosine similarity of 0.05, which is significantly higher than the `comp.graphics` document, but also somewhat lower than the other `hockey` document:

```
0.05047395039466008
```

Source Code:

```
https://github.com/ml-resources/spark-ml/blob/branch-ed2/Chapter_10/scala-2.0.x
/src/main/scala/TFIDFExtraction.scala
```

Training a text classifier on the 20 Newsgroups dataset using tf-idf

When using tf-idf vectors, we expected that the cosine similarity measure would capture the similarity between documents, based on the overlap of terms between them. In a similar way, we would expect that a machine learning model, such as a classifier, would be able to learn weightings for individual terms; this would allow it to distinguish between documents from different classes. That is, it should be possible to learn a mapping between the presence (and weighting) of certain terms and a specific topic.

In the 20 Newsgroups example, each newsgroup topic is a class, and we can train a classifier using our tf-idf transformed vectors as input.

Since we are dealing with a multiclass classification problem, we will use the naive Bayes model in MLlib, which supports multiple classes. As the first step, we will import the Spark classes that we will be using:

```
import org.apache.spark.mllib.regression.LabeledPoint
import org.apache.spark.mllib.classification.NaiveBayes
import org.apache.spark.mllib.evaluation.MulticlassMetrics.
```

We will keep our clustering code in an object called `Document clustering`

```
object DocumentClassification {

  def main(args: Array[String]) {
    val sc = new SparkContext("local[2]", "")
    ...
  }
}
```

Next, we will need to extract the 20 topics and convert them to class mappings. We can do this in exactly the same way as we might for *1-of-K* feature encoding, by assigning a numeric index to each class:

```
val newsgroupsMap =
  newsgroups.distinct.collect().zipWithIndex.toMap
val zipped = newsgroups.zip(tfidf)
val train = zipped.map { case (topic, vector) =>
  LabeledPoint(newsgroupsMap(topic), vector) }
train.cache
```

In the preceding code snippet, we took the `newsgroups` RDD, where each element is the topic, and used the `zip` function to combine it with each element in our `tfidf` RDD of tf-idf vectors. We then mapped over each key-value element in our new zipped RDD and created a `LabeledPoint` instance, where `label` is the class index and `features` is the tf-idf vector.

Note that the `zip` operator assumes that each RDD has the same number of partitions as well as the same number of elements in each partition. It will fail if this is not the case. We can make this assumption here because we have effectively created both our `tfidf` RDD and `newsgroups` RDD from a series of `map` transformations on the same original RDD that preserved the partitioning structure.

Now that we have an input RDD in the correct form, we can simply pass it to the naive Bayes `train` function:

```
val model = NaiveBayes.train(train, lambda = 0.1)
```

Let's evaluate the performance of the model on the test dataset. We will load the raw test data from the `20news-bydate-test` directory, again using `wholeTextFiles` to read each message into an RDD element. We will then extract the class labels from the file paths in the same way as we did for the `newsgroups` RDD:

```
val testPath = "/PATH/20news-bydate-test/*"
val testRDD = sc.wholeTextFiles(testPath)
val testLabels = testRDD.map { case (file, text) =>
  val topic = file.split("/").takeRight(2).head
```

```
    newsgroupsMap(topic)
}
```

Transforming the text in the test dataset follows the same procedure as for the training data-we will apply our `tokenize` function followed by the term frequency transformation, and we will again use the same IDF computed from the training data to transform the TF vectors into tf-idf vectors. Finally, we will zip the test class labels with the tf-idf vectors and create our test RDD [LabeledPoint]:

```
val testTf = testRDD.map { case (file, text) =>
  hashingTF.transform(tokenize(text)) }
val testTfIdf = idf.transform(testTf)
val zippedTest = testLabels.zip(testTfIdf)
val test = zippedTest.map { case (topic, vector) =>
  LabeledPoint(topic, vector) }
```

Note that it is important that we use the training set IDF to transform the test data, as this creates a more realistic estimation of model performance on new data, which might potentially contain terms that the model has not yet been trained on. It would be "cheating" to recompute the IDF vector based on the test dataset and, more importantly, would potentially lead to incorrect estimates of optimal model parameters selected through cross-validation.

Now, we're ready to compute the predictions and true class labels for our model. We will use this RDD to compute accuracy and the multiclass weighted F-measure for our model:

```
val predictionAndLabel = test.map(p =>
  (model.predict(p.features),   p.label))
val accuracy = 1.0 * predictionAndLabel.filter
  (x => x._1 == x._2).count() / test.count()
val metrics = new MulticlassMetrics(predictionAndLabel)
println(accuracy)
println(metrics.weightedFMeasure)
```

The weighted F-measure is an overall measure of precision and recall performance (where, like area under an ROC curve, values closer to 1.0 indicate better performance), which is then combined through a weighted averaged across the classes.

We can see that our simple multiclass naive Bayes model has achieved close to 80 percent for both accuracy and F-measure:

```
0.7928836962294211
0.7822644376431702
```

Evaluating the impact of text processing

Text processing and tf-idf weighting are examples of feature extraction techniques designed to both reduce the dimensionality of, and extract some structure from, raw text data. We can see the impact of applying these processing techniques by comparing the performance of a model trained on raw text data with one trained on processed and tf-idf weighted text data.

Comparing raw features with processed tf-idf features on the 20 Newsgroups dataset

In this example, we will simply apply the hashing term frequency transformation to the raw text tokens obtained using a simple whitespace splitting of the document text. We will train a model on this data and evaluate the performance on the test set as we did for the model trained with tf-idf features:

```
val rawTokens = rdd.map { case (file, text) => text.split(" ") }
val rawTF = texrawTokenst.map(doc => hashingTF.transform(doc))
val rawTrain = newsgroups.zip(rawTF).map { case (topic, vector)
  => LabeledPoint(newsgroupsMap(topic), vector) }
val rawModel = NaiveBayes.train(rawTrain, lambda = 0.1)
val rawTestTF = testRDD.map { case (file, text) =>
  hashingTF.transform(text.split(" ")) }
val rawZippedTest = testLabels.zip(rawTestTF)
val rawTest = rawZippedTest.map { case (topic, vector) =>
  LabeledPoint(topic, vector) }
val rawPredictionAndLabel = rawTest.map(p =>
  (rawModel.predict(p.features), p.label))
val rawAccuracy = 1.0 * rawPredictionAndLabel.filter(x => x._1
  == x._2).count() / rawTest.count()
println(rawAccuracy)
val rawMetrics = new MulticlassMetrics(rawPredictionAndLabel)
println(rawMetrics.weightedFMeasure)
```

Perhaps surprisingly, the raw model does quite well, although both accuracy and F-measure are a few percentage points lower than those of the tf-idf model. This is also partly a reflection of the fact that the naive Bayes model is well suited to data in the form of raw frequency counts:

```
0.7661975570897503
0.7653320418573546
```

Text classification with Spark 2.0

In this section, we will use the libsvm version of *20newsgroup* data to use the Spark DataFrame-based APIs to classify the text documents. In the current version of Spark libsvm version 3.22 is supported (https://www.csie.ntu.edu.tw/~cjlin/libsvmtools/datasets/)

Download the libsvm formatted data from the following link and copy output folder under Spark-2.0.x.

Visit the following link for the *20newsgroup libsvm* data:
https://1drv.ms/f/s!Av6fk5nQi2j-iF84quUlDnJc6G6D

Import the appropriate packages from `org.apache.spark.ml` and create Wrapper Scala:

```
package org.apache.spark.examples.ml

import org.apache.spark.SparkConf
import org.apache.spark.ml.classification.NaiveBayes
import
org.apache.spark.ml.evaluation.MulticlassClassificationEvaluator

import org.apache.spark.sql.SparkSession

object DocumentClassificationLibSVM {
  def main(args: Array[String]): Unit = {

  }
}
```

Next, we will load the `libsvm` data into a Spark DataFrame:

```
val spConfig = (new SparkConf).setMaster("local")
  .setAppName("SparkApp")
val spark = SparkSession
  .builder()
  .appName("SparkRatingData").config(spConfig)
  .getOrCreate()

val data = spark.read.format("libsvm").load("./output/20news-by-
  date-train-libsvm/part-combined")

val Array(trainingData, testData) = data.randomSplit(Array(0.7,
  0.3), seed = 1L)
```

Instantiate the `NaiveBayes` model from the
`org.apache.spark.ml.classification.NaiveBayes` class and train the model:

```
val model = new NaiveBayes().fit(trainingData)
val predictions = model.transform(testData)
predictions.show()
```

The following table is the output of the predictions DataFrame `.show()` command:

```
|label|      features      |    rawPrediction    |    probability    |
|prediction|
+-----+--------------------+---------------------+-------------------+----------
+
|0.0|(262141,[14,63,64...|[-8972.9535882773...|[1.0,0.0,1.009147...| 0.0|
|0.0|(262141,[14,329,6...|[-5078.5468878602...|[1.0,0.0,0.0,0.0,...| 0.0|
|0.0|(262141,[14,448,5...|[-3376.8302696656...|[1.0,0.0,2.138643...| 0.0|
|0.0|(262141,[14,448,5...|[-3574.2782864683...|[1.0,2.8958758424...| 0.0|
|0.0|(262141,[14,535,3...|[-5001.8808481928...|[8.85311976855360...| 12.0|
|0.0|(262141,[14,573,8...|[-5950.1635030844...|[1.0,0.0,1.757049...| 0.0|
|0.0|(262141,[14,836,5...|[-8795.2012408412...|[1.0,0.0,0.0,0.0,...| 0.0|
|0.0|(262141,[14,991,2...|[-1892.8829282793...|[0.99999999999999...| 0.0|
|0.0|(262141,[14,1176,...|[-4746.2275710890...|[1.0,5.8201E-319,...| 0.0|
|0.0|(262141,[14,1379,...|[-7104.8373572933...|[1.0,8.9577444139...| 0.0|
|0.0|(262141,[14,1582,...|[-5473.6206675848...|[1.0,5.3185120345...| 0.0|
|0.0|(262141,[14,1836,...|[-11289.582479676...|[1.0,0.0,0.0,0.0,...| 0.0|
|0.0|(262141,[14,2325,...|[-3957.9187837274...|[1.0,2.1880375223...| 0.0|
|0.0|(262141,[14,2325,...|[-7131.2028421844...|[1.0,2.6110663778...| 0.0|
|0.0|(262141,[14,3033,...|[-3014.6430319605...|[1.0,2.6341580467...| 0.0|
|0.0|(262141,[14,4335,...|[-8283.7207917560...|[1.0,8.9559011053...| 0.0|
|0.0|(262141,[14,5173,...|[-6811.3466537480...|[1.0,7.2593916980...| 0.0|
|0.0|(262141,[14,5232,...|[-2752.8846541292...|[1.0,1.8619374091...| 0.0|
|0.0|(262141,[15,5173,...|[-8741.7756643949...|[1.0,0.0,2.606005...| 0.0|
|0.0|(262141,[168,170,...|[-41636.025208445...|[1.0,0.0,0.0,0.0,...| 0.0|
+----+--------------------+--------------------+-------------------+--------
+
```

Test the accuracy of the model:

```
val accuracy = evaluator.evaluate(predictions)
println("Test set accuracy = " + accuracy)
spark.stop()
```

Accuracy of this model is above `0.8` as shown in the following output:

Test set accuracy = 0.8768458357944477
Accuracy is better as the Naive Bayes implementation has improved
from Spark 1.6 to Spark 2.0

Word2Vec models

Until now, we have used a bag-of-words vector, optionally with some weighting scheme such as tf-idf to represent the text in a document. Another recent class of models that has become popular is related to representing individual words as vectors.

These are generally based in some way on the co-occurrence statistics between the words in a corpus. Once the vector representation is computed, we can use these vectors in ways similar to how we might use tf-idf vectors (such as using them as features for other machine learning models). One such common use case is computing the similarity between two words with respect to their meanings, based on their vector representations.

Word2Vec refers to a specific implementation of one of these models, often referred to as **distributed vector representations**. The MLlib model uses a **skip-gram** model, which seeks to learn vector representations that take into account the contexts in which words occur.

> While a detailed treatment of Word2Vec is beyond the scope of this book, Spark's documentation at `http://spark.apache.org/docs/latest/mllib-feature-extraction.html#word2vec` contains some further details on the algorithm as well as links to the reference implementation.

> One of the main academic papers underlying Word2Vec is *Tomas Mikolov, Kai Chen, Greg Corrado,* and *Jeffrey Dean. Efficient Estimation of Word Representations in Vector Space. In Proceedings of Workshop at ICLR, 2013.*
>
> It is available at `http://arxiv.org/pdf/1301.3781.pdf`.
>
> Another recent model in the area of word vector representations is GloVe at `http://www-nlp.stanford.edu/projects/glove/`.

You can also leverage third party libraries to do Parts of Speech tagging. For example Stanford NLP library could be hooked into scala code. Please refer to this discussion thread (`http://stackoverflow.com/questions/18416561/pos-tagging-in-scala`) for more details on how to do it.

Word2Vec with Spark MLlib on the 20 Newsgroups dataset

Training a Word2Vec model in Spark is relatively simple. We will pass in an RDD where each element is a sequence of terms. We can use the RDD of tokenized documents we have already created as input to the model.

```scala
object Word2VecMllib {
  def main(args: Array[String]) {
    val sc = new SparkContext("local[2]", "Word2Vector App")
    val path = "./data/20news-bydate-train/alt.atheism/*"
    val rdd = sc.wholeTextFiles(path)
    val text = rdd.map { case (file, text) => text }
    val newsgroups = rdd.map { case (file, text) =>
      file.split("/").takeRight(2).head }
    val newsgroupsMap =
      newsgroups.distinct.collect().zipWithIndex.toMap
    val dim = math.pow(2, 18).toInt
    var tokens = text.map(doc => TFIDFExtraction.tokenize(doc))
    import org.apache.spark.mllib.feature.Word2Vec
    val word2vec = new Word2Vec()
    val word2vecModel = word2vec.fit(tokens)
      word2vecModel.findSynonyms("philosophers", 5).foreach(println)
    sc.stop()
  }
}
```

Our code is in the Scala object `Word2VecMllib`:

```scala
import org.apache.spark.SparkContext
import org.apache.spark.mllib.linalg.{SparseVector => SV}
object Word2VecMllib {
  def main(args: Array[String]) {
  }
}
```

Let us start by loading the text file:

```scala
val sc = new SparkContext("local[2]", "Word2Vector App")
val path = "./data/20news-bydate-train/alt.atheism/*"
val rdd = sc.wholeTextFiles(path)
val text = rdd.map { case (file, text) => text }
val newsgroups = rdd.map { case (file, text) =>
  file.split("/").takeRight(2).head }
val newsgroupsMap =
  newsgroups.distinct.collect().zipWithIndex.toMap
val dim = math.pow(2, 18).toInt
```

```
var tokens = text.map(doc => TFIDFExtraction.tokenize(doc))
```

We use the tokens created by tf-idf as the starting point for Word2Vec. Let us first initialize the object and set a seed:

```
import org.apache.spark.mllib.feature.Word2Vec
  val word2vec = new Word2Vec()
```

Now, let's create the model by calling `word2vec.fit()` on the tf-idf tokens:.

```
val word2vecModel = word2vec.fit(tokens)
```

You will see some output while the model is being trained.

Once trained, we can easily find the top 20 synonyms for a given term (that is, the most similar term to the input term, computed by cosine similarity between the word vectors). For example, to find the 20 most similar terms to `philosopher`, use the following lines of code:

```
word2vecModel.findSynonyms(philosophers", 5).foreach(println)
sc.stop()
```

As we can see from the following output, most of the terms relate to hockey or others:

```
(year,0.8417112940969042)
(motivations,0.833017707021745)
(solution,0.8284719617235932)
(whereas,0.8242997325042509)
(formed,0.8042383351975712)
```

Word2Vec with Spark ML on the 20 Newsgroups dataset

In this section, we look at how to use the Spark ML DataFrame and newer implementations from Spark 2.0.X to create a Word2Vector model.

We will create a DataFrame from the dataSet:

```
val spConfig = (new
  SparkConf).setMaster("local").setAppName("SparkApp")
val spark = SparkSession
  .builder
  .appName("Word2Vec Sample").config(spConfig)
  .getOrCreate()
import spark.implicits._
```

```
val rawDF = spark.sparkContext
  .wholeTextFiles("./data/20news-bydate-train/alt.atheism/*")
  val temp = rawDF.map( x => {
    (x._2.filter(_ >= ' ').filter(! _.toString.startsWith("(")) )
    })
  val textDF = temp.map(x => x.split(" ")).map(Tuple1.apply)
    .toDF("text")
```

This will be followed by creating the `Word2Vec` class and training the model on the DataFrame `textDF` created above:

```
val word2Vec = new Word2Vec()
  .setInputCol("text")
  .setOutputCol("result")
  .setVectorSize(3)
  .setMinCount(0)
val model = word2Vec.fit(textDF)
val result = model.transform(textDF)
  result.select("result").take(3).foreach(println)
)
```

Now let us try to find some synonyms for `hockey`:
The following

```
val ds = model.findSynonyms("philosophers", 5).select("word")
  ds.rdd.saveAsTextFile("./output/philiosphers-synonyms" +
System.nanoTime())
  ds.show(
```

Following output will be generated:

```
+--------------+
| word         |
+--------------+
| Fess         |
| guide        |
|validinference|
| problems.    |
| paperback    |
+--------------+
```

As you can see, the results are quite different from the results we got using RDD. This is because the two implementations differ for Word2Vector conversion in Spark 1.6 and Spark 2.0/2.1.

Summary

In this chapter, we took a deeper look into more complex text processing and explored MLlib's text feature extraction capabilities, in particular the tf-idf term weighting schemes. We covered examples of using the resulting tf-idf feature vectors to compute document similarity and train a newsgroup topic classification model. Finally, you learned how to use MLlib's cutting-edge Word2Vec model to compute a vector representation of words in a corpus of text and use the trained model to find words with contextual meaning that is similar to a given word. We also looked at using Word2Vec with Spark ML

In the next chapter, we will take a look at online learning, and you will learn how Spark Streaming relates to online learning models.

11
Real-Time Machine Learning with Spark Streaming

So far in this book, we have focused on batch data processing. That is, all our analysis, feature extraction, and model training has been applied to a fixed set of data that does not change. This fits neatly into Spark's core abstraction of RDDs, which are immutable distributed datasets. Once created, the data underlying the RDD does not change, although we might create new RDDs from the original RDD through Spark's transformation and action operators.

Our attention has also been on batch machine learning models where we train a model on a fixed batch of training data that is usually represented as an RDD of feature vectors (and labels, in the case of supervised learning models).

In this chapter, we will:

- Introduce the concept of online learning, where models are trained and updated on new data as it becomes available
- Explore stream processing using Spark Streaming
- See how Spark Streaming fits together with the online learning approach

- Introduce the concept of Structured Streaming

The following sections use RDD as the distributed dataset. In a similar way, we can use DataFrame or SQL operations on streaming data.

 See
https://spark.apache.org/docs/2.0.0-preview/sql-programming-guid
e.html for more details on DataFrame and SQL operations.

Online learning

The batch machine learning methods that we have applied in this book focus on processing an existing fixed set of training data. Typically, these techniques are also iterative, and we have performed multiple passes over our training data in order to converge to an optimal model.

By contrast, online learning is based on performing only one sequential pass through the training data in a fully incremental fashion (that is, one training example at a time). After seeing each training example, the model makes a prediction for this example and then receives the true outcome (for example, the label for classification or real target for regression). The idea behind online learning is that the model continually updates as new information is received, instead of being retrained periodically in batch training.

In some settings, when the data volume is very large or the process that generates the data is changing rapidly, online learning methods can adapt more quickly and in near real time, without needing to be retrained in an expensive batch process.

However, online learning methods do not have to be used in a purely online manner. In fact, we have already seen an example of using an online learning model in the batch setting when we used **Stochastic gradient descent (SGD)** optimization to train our classification and regression models. SGD updates the model after each training example. However, we still made use of multiple passes over the training data in order to converge to a better result.

In the pure online setting, we do not (or perhaps cannot) make multiple passes over the training data; hence, we need to process each input as it arrives. Online methods also include mini-batch methods where, instead of processing one input at a time, we process a small batch of training data.

Online and batch methods can also be combined in real-world situations. For example, we can periodically retrain our models offline (say, every day) using batch methods. We can then deploy the trained model to production and update it using online methods in real time (that is, during the day, in between batch retraining) to adapt to any changes in the environment. This is very similar to lambda architecture which is a data processing architecture supporting both batch and streaming methods.

As we will see in this chapter, the online learning setting can fit neatly into stream processing and the Spark Streaming framework.

See http://en.wikipedia.org/wiki/Online_machine_learning for more details on online machine learning.

Stream processing

Before covering online learning with Spark, we will first explore the basics of stream processing and introduce the Spark Streaming library.

In addition to the core Spark API and functionality, the Spark project contains another major library (in the same way as MLlib is a major project library) called **Spark Streaming**, which focuses on processing data streams in real time.

A data stream is a continuous sequence of records. Common examples include activity stream data from a web or mobile application, time-stamped log data, transactional data, and event streams from sensor or device networks.

The batch processing approach typically involves saving the data stream to an intermediate storage system (for example, HDFS or a database) and running a batch process on the saved data. In order to generate up-to-date results, the batch process must be run periodically (for example, daily, hourly, or even every few minutes) on the latest data available.

By contrast, the stream-based approach applies processing to the data stream as it is generated. This allows near real-time processing (of the order of a subsecond to a few tenths of a second time-frames rather than minutes, hours, days, or even weeks with typical batch processing).

An introduction to Spark Streaming

There are a few different general techniques to deal with stream processing. Two of the most common ones are as follows:

- Treat each record individually and process it as soon as it is seen.
- Combine multiple records into **mini-batches**. These mini-batches can be delineated either by time or by the number of records in a batch.

Spark Streaming takes the second approach. The core primitive in Spark Streaming is the **discretized stream**, or **DStream**. A DStream is a sequence of mini-batches, where each mini-batch is represented as a Spark RDD:

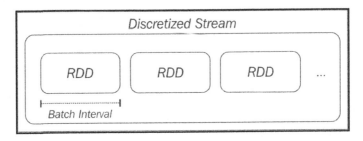

The discretized stream abstraction

A DStream is defined by its input source and a time window called the **batch interval**. The stream is broken up into time periods equal to the batch interval (beginning from the starting time of the application). Each RDD in the stream will contain the records that are received by the Spark Streaming application during a given batch interval. If no data is present in a given interval, the RDD will simply be empty.

Input sources

Spark Streaming **receivers** are responsible for receiving data from an **input source** and converting the raw data into a DStream made up of Spark RDDs.

Spark Streaming supports various input sources, including file-based sources (where the receiver watches for new files arriving at the input location and creates the DStream from the contents read from each new file) and network-based sources (such as receivers that communicate with socket-based sources, the Twitter API stream, Akka actors, or message queues and distributed stream and log transfer frameworks, such as Flume, Kafka, and Amazon Kinesis).

See the documentation on input sources at `http://spark.apache.org/docs/latest/streaming-programming-guide.html#input-dstreams` for more details and for links to various advanced sources.

Transformations

As we saw in `Chapter 1`, *Getting Up and Running with Spark*, and throughout this book, Spark allows us to apply powerful transformations to RDDs.

As DStreams are made up of RDDs, Spark Streaming provides a set of transformations available on DStreams; these transformations are similar to those available on RDDs. These include `map`, `flatMap`, `filter`, `join`, and `reduceByKey`.

Spark Streaming transformations, such as those applicable to RDDs, operate on each element of a DStream's underlying data. That is, the transformations are effectively applied to each RDD in the DStream, which, in turn, applies the transformation to the elements of the RDD.

Spark Streaming also provides operators such as reduce and count. These operators return a DStream made up of a single element (for example, the count value for each batch). Unlike the equivalent operators on RDDs, these do not trigger computation on DStreams directly. That is, they are not actions, but they are still transformations, as they return another DStream.

Keeping track of state

When we were dealing with batch processing of RDDs, keeping and updating a state variable was relatively straightforward. We could start with a certain state (for example, a count or sum of values) and then use broadcast variables or accumulators to update this state in parallel. Usually, we would then use an RDD action to collect the updated state to the driver and, in turn, update the global state.

With DStreams, this is a little more complex, as we need to keep track of states across batches in a fault-tolerant manner. Conveniently, Spark Streaming provides the `updateStateByKey` function on a DStream of key-value pairs, which takes care of this for us, allowing us to create a stream of arbitrary state information and update it with each batch of data seen. For example, the state could be a global count of the number of times each key has been seen. The state could, thus, represent the number of visits per web page, clicks per advert, tweets per user, or purchases per product, for example.

General transformations

The Spark Streaming API also exposes a general `transform` function that gives us access to the underlying RDD for each batch in the stream. That is, where the higher-level functions such as `map` transform a DStream to another DStream, `transform` allows us to apply functions from an RDD to another RDD. For example, we can use the RDD `join` operator to join each batch of the stream to an existing RDD that we computed separately from our streaming application (perhaps, in Spark or some other system).

The full list of transformations and further information on each of them is provided in the Spark documentation at `http://spark.apache.org/docs/latest/streaming-programming-guide.html#transformations-on-dstreams`.

Actions

While some of the operators we have seen in Spark Streaming, such as count, are not actions as in the batch RDD case, Spark Streaming has the concept of actions on DStreams. Actions are output operators that, when invoked, trigger computation on the DStream. They are as follows:

- `print`: This prints the first 10 elements of each batch to the console and is typically used for debugging and testing.
- `saveAsObjectFile`, `saveAsTextFiles`, and `saveAsHadoopFiles`: These functions output each batch to a Hadoop-compatible filesystem with a filename (if applicable) derived from the batch start timestamp.
- `forEachRDD`: This operator is the most generic and allows us to apply any arbitrary processing to the RDDs within each batch of a DStream. It is used to apply side effects, such as saving data to an external system, printing it for testing, exporting it to a dashboard, and so on.

 Note that, like batch processing with Spark, DStream operators are **lazy**. In the same way in which we need to call an action, such as count, on an RDD to ensure that processing takes place, we need to call one of the preceding action operators in order to trigger computation on a DStream. Otherwise, our streaming application will not actually perform any computation.

Window operators

As Spark Streaming operates on time-ordered batched streams of data, it introduces a new concept, which is that of **windowing**. A `window` function computes a transformation over a sliding window applied to the stream.

A window is defined by the length of the window and the sliding interval. For example, with a 10-second window and a 5-second sliding interval, we will compute results every 5 seconds, based on the latest 10 seconds of data in the DStream. For example, we might wish to calculate the top websites by page view numbers over the last 10 seconds and recompute this metric every 5 seconds using a sliding window.

The following figure illustrates a windowed DStream:

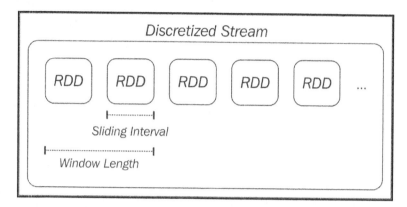

A windowed DStream

Caching and fault tolerance with Spark Streaming

Like Spark RDDs, DStreams can be cached in memory. The use cases for caching are similar to those for RDDs-if we expect to access the data in a DStream multiple times (perhaps performing multiple types of analysis or aggregation or outputting to multiple external systems), we will benefit from caching the data. Stateful operators, which include `window` functions and `updateStateByKey`, do this automatically for efficiency.

Recall that RDDs are immutable datasets and are defined by their input data source and **lineage**-that is, the set of transformations and actions that are applied to the RDD. Fault tolerance in RDDs works by recreating the RDD (or partition of an RDD) that is lost due to the failure of a worker node.

As DStreams are themselves batches of RDDs, they can also be recomputed as required to deal with worker node failure. However, this depends on the input data still being available. If the data source itself is fault-tolerant and persistent (such as HDFS or some other fault-tolerant data store), then the DStream can be recomputed.

If data stream sources are delivered over a network (which is a common case with stream processing), Spark Streaming's default persistence behavior is to replicate data to two worker nodes. This allows network DStreams to be recomputed in the case of failure. Note, however, that any data received by a node but *not yet replicated* might be lost when a node fails.

Spark Streaming also supports recovery of the driver node in the event of failure. However, currently, for network-based sources, data in the memory of worker nodes will be lost in this case. Hence, Spark Streaming is not fully fault-tolerant in the face of failure of the driver node or application. Instead lambda architecture can be used here. For example, nightly batch can come through and correct things in the case of a failure.

> See
> `http://spark.apache.org/docs/latest/streaming-programming-guide.html#caching-persistence` and
> `http://spark.apache.org/docs/latest/streaming-programming-guide.html#fault-tolerance-properties` for more details.

Creating a basic streaming application

We will now work through creating our first Spark Streaming application to illustrate some of the basic concepts around Spark Streaming that we introduced earlier.

We will expand on the example applications used in Chapter 1, *Getting Up and Running with Spark*, where we used a small example dataset of product purchase events. For this example, instead of using a static set of data, we will create a simple producer application that will randomly generate events and send them over a network connection. We will then create a few Spark Streaming consumer applications that will process this event stream.

The sample project for this chapter contains the code you will need. It is called `scala-spark-streaming-app`. It consists of a Scala SBT project definition file, the example application source code, and a `srcmainresources` directory that contains a file called `names.csv`.

The `build.sbt` file for the project contains the following project definition:

```
name := "scala-spark-streaming-app"
version := "1.0"
scalaVersion := "2.11.7"
val sparkVersion = "2.0.0"

libraryDependencies ++= Seq(
  "org.apache.spark" %% "spark-core" % sparkVersion,
  "org.apache.spark" %% "spark-mllib" % sparkVersion,
  "org.jfree" % "jfreechart" % "1.0.14",
  "com.github.wookietreiber" % "scala-chart_2.11" % "0.5.0",
  "org.apache.spark" %% "spark-streaming" % sparkVersion
)
```

Note that we added a dependency on Spark MLlib and Spark Streaming, which includes the dependency on the Spark core.

The `names.csv` file contains a set of 20 randomly generated user names. We will use these names as part of our data generation function in our producer application:

```
Miguel,Eric,James,Juan,Shawn,James,Doug,Gary,Frank,Janet,Michael,
James,Malinda,Mike,Elaine,Kevin,Janet,Richard,Saul,Manuela
```

The producer application

Our producer needs to create a network connection and generate some random purchase event data to send over this connection. First, we will define our object and main method definition. We will then read the random names from the `names.csv` resource and create a set of products with prices, from which we will generate our random product events:

```
/**
 * A producer application that generates random "product
 * events", up to 5 per second, and sends them over a network
 * connection
 */
object StreamingProducer {

  def main(args: Array[String]) {

    val random = new Random()

    // Maximum number of events per second
    val MaxEvents = 6

    // Read the list of possible names
    val namesResource =
      this.getClass.getResourceAsStream("/names.csv")
    val names = scala.io.Source.fromInputStream(namesResource)
      .getLines()
      .toList
      .head
      .split(",")
      .toSeq

    // Generate a sequence of possible products
    val products = Seq(
      "iPhone Cover" -> 9.99,
      "Headphones" -> 5.49,
      "Samsung Galaxy Cover" -> 8.95,
      "iPad Cover" -> 7.49
```

```
        )
```

Using the list of names and map of product name to price, we will create a function that will randomly pick a product and name from these sources, generating a specified number of product events:

```
/** Generate a number of random product events */
def generateProductEvents(n: Int) = {
  (1 to n).map { i =>
    val (product, price) =
      products(random.nextInt(products.size))
    val user = random.shuffle(names).head
      (user, product, price)
  }
}
```

Finally, we will create a network socket and set our producer to listen on this socket. As soon as a connection is made (which will come from our consumer streaming application), the producer will start generating random events at a random rate between 0 and 5 per second:

```
// create a network producer
val listener = new ServerSocket(9999)
println("Listening on port: 9999")

while (true) {
  val socket = listener.accept()
  new Thread() {
    override def run = {
      println("Got client connected from: " +
        socket.getInetAddress)
      val out = new PrintWriter(socket.getOutputStream(), true)

      while (true) {
        Thread.sleep(1000)
        val num = random.nextInt(MaxEvents)
        val productEvents = generateProductEvents(num)
        productEvents.foreach{ event =>
          out.write(event.productIterator.mkString(","))
          out.write("n")
        }
        out.flush()
        println(s"Created $num events...")
      }
      socket.close()
    }
  }.start()
}
```

This producer example is based on the `PageViewGenerator` example in the Spark Streaming examples.

The producer can be run by changing into the base directory of `scala-spark-streaming-app` and using SBT to run the application, as we did in `Chapter 1`, *Getting Up and Running with Spark*:

```
>cd scala-spark-streaming-app
>sbt
[info] ...
>
```

Use the `run` command to execute the application:

```
>run
```

You should see output similar to the following:

```
...
Multiple main classes detected, select one to run:

[1] StreamingProducer
[2] SimpleStreamingApp
[3] StreamingAnalyticsApp
[4] StreamingStateApp
[5] StreamingModelProducer
[6] SimpleStreamingModel
[7] MonitoringStreamingModel

Enter number:
```

Select the `StreamingProducer` option. The application will start running, and you should see the following output:

```
[info] Running StreamingProducer
Listening on port: 9999
```

We can see that the producer is listening on port `9999`, waiting for our consumer application to connect.

Creating a basic streaming application

Next, we will create our first streaming program. We will simply connect to the producer and print out the contents of each batch. Our streaming code looks like this:

```scala
/**
 * A simple Spark Streaming app in Scala
 **/
object SimpleStreamingApp {
  def main(args: Array[String]) {
    val ssc = new StreamingContext("local[2]", "First Streaming
      App", Seconds(10))
    val stream = ssc.socketTextStream("localhost", 9999)

    // here we simply print out the first few elements of each batch
    stream.print()
    ssc.start()
    ssc.awaitTermination()
  }
}
```

It looks fairly simple, and it is mostly due to the fact that Spark Streaming takes care of all the complexity for us. First, we initialized a `StreamingContext` (which is the streaming equivalent of the `SparkContext` we have used so far), specifying similar configuration options that are used to create a `SparkContext`. Notice, however, that here we are required to provide the batch interval, which we set to 10 seconds.

We then created our data stream using a predefined streaming source, `socketTextStream`, which reads text from a socket host and port and creates a `DStream[String]`. We then called the `print` function on the DStream; this function prints out the first few elements of each batch.

> Calling `print` on a DStream is similar to calling `take` on an RDD. It displays only the first few elements.

We can run this program using SBT. Open a second terminal window, leaving the producer program running, and run `sbt`:

```
>sbt
[info] ...
>run
```

Again, you should see a few options to select:

```
Multiple main classes detected, select one to run:

[1] StreamingProducer
[2] SimpleStreamingApp
[3] StreamingAnalyticsApp
[4] StreamingStateApp
[5] StreamingModelProducer
[6] SimpleStreamingModel
[7] MonitoringStreamingModel
```

Run the `SimpleStreamingApp` main class. You should see the streaming program start up, displaying output similar to the one shown here:

```
. . .
14/11/15 21:02:23 INFO scheduler.ReceiverTracker: ReceiverTracker
started
14/11/15 21:02:23 INFO dstream.ForEachDStream:
metadataCleanupDelay
=  -1
14/11/15 21:02:23 INFO dstream.SocketInputDStream:
metadataCleanupDelay = -1
14/11/15 21:02:23 INFO dstream.SocketInputDStream: Slide time =
10000 ms
14/11/15 21:02:23 INFO dstream.SocketInputDStream: Storage level =
StorageLevel(false, false, false, false, 1)
14/11/15 21:02:23 INFO dstream.SocketInputDStream: Checkpoint
interval = null
14/11/15 21:02:23 INFO dstream.SocketInputDStream: Remember
duration = 10000 ms
14/11/15 21:02:23 INFO dstream.SocketInputDStream: Initialized and
validated
org.apache.spark.streaming.dstream.SocketInputDStream@ff3436d
14/11/15 21:02:23 INFO dstream.ForEachDStream: Slide time =
10000
ms
14/11/15 21:02:23 INFO dstream.ForEachDStream: Storage level =
StorageLevel(false, false, false, false, 1)
14/11/15 21:02:23 INFO dstream.ForEachDStream: Checkpoint
interval
=  null
14/11/15 21:02:23 INFO dstream.ForEachDStream: Remember duration =
10000 ms
14/11/15 21:02:23 INFO dstream.ForEachDStream: Initialized and
validated
org.apache.spark.streaming.dstream.ForEachDStream@5a10b6e8
14/11/15 21:02:23 INFO scheduler.ReceiverTracker: Starting 1
receivers
14/11/15 21:02:23 INFO spark.SparkContext: Starting job: runJob at
```

```
ReceiverTracker.scala:275
. . .
```

At the same time, you should see that the terminal window running the producer displays something like the following:

```
. . .
Got client connected from: /127.0.0.1
Created 2 events...
Created 2 events...
Created 3 events...
Created 1 events...
Created 5 events...
. . .
```

After about 10 seconds, which is the time of our streaming batch interval, Spark Streaming will trigger a computation on the stream due to our use of the `print` operator. This should display the first few events in the batch, which will look something like the following output:

```
. . .
14/11/15 21:02:30 INFO spark.SparkContext: Job finished: take at
DStream.scala:608, took 0.05596 s
-------------------------------------------
Time: 1416078150000 ms
-------------------------------------------
Michael,Headphones,5.49
Frank,Samsung Galaxy Cover,8.95
Eric,Headphones,5.49
Malinda,iPad Cover,7.49
James,iPhone Cover,9.99
James,Headphones,5.49
Doug,iPhone Cover,9.99
Juan,Headphones,5.49
James,iPhone Cover,9.99
Richard,iPad Cover,7.49
. . .
```

 Note that you might see different results, as the producer generates a random number of random events each second.

You can terminate the streaming app by pressing *Ctrl + C*. If you want to, you can also terminate the producer (if you do, you will need to restart it again before starting the next streaming programs that we will create).

Streaming analytics

Next, we will create a slightly more complex streaming program. In Chapter 1, *Getting Up and Running with Spark,* we calculated a few metrics on our dataset of product purchases. These included the total number of purchases, the number of unique users, the total revenue, and the most popular product (together with its number of purchases and total revenue).

In this example, we will compute the same metrics on our stream of purchase events. The key difference is that these metrics will be computed per batch and printed out.

We will define our streaming application code here:

```
/**
 * A more complex Streaming app, which computes statistics and
   prints the results for each batch in a DStream
 */
object StreamingAnalyticsApp {

  def main(args: Array[String]) {

    val ssc = new StreamingContext("local[2]", "First Streaming
      App", Seconds(10))
    val stream = ssc.socketTextStream("localhost", 9999)

    // create stream of events from raw text elements
    val events = stream.map { record =>
      val event = record.split(",")
      (event(0), event(1), event(2))
    }
```

First, we created exactly the same StreamingContext and socket stream as we did earlier. Our next step is to apply a map transformation to the raw text, where each record is a comma-separated string representing the purchase event. The map function splits the text and creates a tuple of (user, product, price). This illustrates the use of map on a DStream and how it is the same as if we had been operating on an RDD.

Next, we will use foreachRDD to apply arbitrary processing on each RDD in the stream to compute our desired metrics and print them to the console:

```
/*
   We compute and print out stats for each batch.
   Since each batch is an RDD, we call forEeachRDD on the
   DStream, and apply the usual RDD functions
   we used in Chapter 1.
 */
```

```
events.foreachRDD { (rdd, time) =>
  val numPurchases = rdd.count()
  val uniqueUsers = rdd.map { case (user, _, _) => user
    }.distinct().count()
  val totalRevenue = rdd.map { case (_, _, price) =>
    price.toDouble }.sum()
  val productsByPopularity = rdd
    .map { case (user, product, price) => (product, 1) }
    .reduceByKey(_ + _)
    .collect()
    .sortBy(-_._2)
  val mostPopular = productsByPopularity(0)

  val formatter = new SimpleDateFormat
  val dateStr = formatter.format(new
    Date(time.milliseconds))
  println(s"== Batch start time: $dateStr ==")
  println("Total purchases: " + numPurchases)
  println("Unique users: " + uniqueUsers)
  println("Total revenue: " + totalRevenue)
  println("Most popular product: %s with %d
    purchases".format(mostPopular._1, mostPopular._2))
}

// start the context
ssc.start()
ssc.awaitTermination()
}

}
```

If you compare the code operating on the RDDs inside the preceding `foreachRDD` block with that used in Chapter 1, *Getting Up and Running with Spark,* you will notice that it is virtually the same code. This shows that we can apply any RDD-related processing we wish within the streaming setting by operating on the underlying RDDs, as well as using the built-in higher level streaming operations.

Let's run the streaming program again by calling `sbt run` and selecting `StreamingAnalyticsApp`.

> Remember that you might also need to restart the producer if you previously terminated the program. This should be done before starting the streaming application.

After about 10 seconds, you should see output from the streaming program similar to the following:

```
...
14/11/15 21:27:30 INFO spark.SparkContext: Job finished: collect
at
Streaming.scala:125, took 0.071145 s
== Batch start time: 2014/11/15 9:27 PM ==
Total purchases: 16
Unique users: 10
Total revenue: 123.72
Most popular product: iPad Cover with 6 purchases
...
```

You can again terminate the streaming program using *Ctrl + C*.

Stateful streaming

As a final example, we will apply the concept of **stateful** streaming using the `updateStateByKey` function to compute a global state of revenue and number of purchases per user, which will be updated with new data from each 10-second batch. Our `StreamingStateApp` app is shown here:

```
object StreamingStateApp {
    import org.apache.spark.streaming.StreamingContext
```

We will first define an `updateState` function that will compute the new state from the running state value and the new data in the current batch. Our state, in this case, is a tuple of `(number of products, revenue)` pairs, which we will keep for each user. We will compute the new state given the set of `(product, revenue)` pairs for the current batch and the accumulated state at the current time.

Notice that we will deal with an `Option` value for the current state, as it might be empty (which will be the case for the first batch), and we need to define a default value, which we will do using `getOrElse` as shown here:

```
def updateState(prices: Seq[(String, Double)], currentTotal:
  Option[(Int, Double)]) = {
  val currentRevenue = prices.map(_._2).sum
  val currentNumberPurchases = prices.size
  val state = currentTotal.getOrElse((0, 0.0))
  Some((currentNumberPurchases + state._1, currentRevenue +
    state._2))
}
```

```scala
def main(args: Array[String]) {

  val ssc = new StreamingContext("local[2]", "First Streaming
    App", Seconds(10))
  // for stateful operations, we need to set a checkpoint location
  ssc.checkpoint("/tmp/sparkstreaming/")
  val stream = ssc.socketTextStream("localhost", 9999)

  // create stream of events from raw text elements
  val events = stream.map { record =>
    val event = record.split(",")
    (event(0), event(1), event(2).toDouble)
  }

  val users = events.map{ case (user, product, price) =>
    (user, (product, price)) }
  val revenuePerUser = users.updateStateByKey(updateState)
  revenuePerUser.print()

  // start the context
  ssc.start()
  ssc.awaitTermination()

  }
}
```

After applying the same string split transformation we used in our previous example, we called updateStateByKey on our DStream, passing in our defined updateState function. We then printed the results to the console.

Start the streaming example using sbt run and by selecting [4] StreamingStateApp (also restart the producer program if necessary).

After around 10 seconds, you will start to see the first set of state outputs. We will wait another 10 seconds to see the next set of outputs. You will see the overall global state being updated:

```
. . .
-------------------------------------------
Time: 1416080440000 ms
-------------------------------------------
(Janet, (2,10.98))
(Frank, (1,5.49))
(James, (2,12.98))
(Malinda, (1,9.99))
(Elaine, (3,29.97))
(Gary, (2,12.98))
```

```
(Miguel, (3,20.47))
(Saul, (1,5.49))
(Manuela, (2,18.939999999999998))
(Eric, (2,18.939999999999998))
...
------------------------------------------------
Time: 1416080441000 ms
------------------------------------------------
(Janet, (6,34.94))
(Juan, (4,33.92))
(Frank, (2,14.44))
(James, (7,48.93000000000001))
(Malinda, (1,9.99))
(Elaine, (7,61.89))
(Gary, (4,28.46))
(Michael, (1,8.95))
(Richard, (2,16.439999999999998))
(Miguel, (5,35.95))
...
```

We can see that the number of purchases and revenue totals for each user are added to with each batch of data.

> Now, see if you can adapt this example to use Spark Streaming's `window` functions. For example, you can compute similar statistics per user over the past minute, sliding every 30 seconds.

Online learning with Spark Streaming

As we have seen, Spark Streaming makes it easy to work with data streams in a way that should be familiar to us from working with RDDs. Using Spark's stream processing primitives combined with the online learning capabilities of ML Library SGD-based methods, we can create real-time machine learning models that we can update on new data in the stream as it arrives.

Streaming regression

Spark provides a built-in streaming machine learning model in the `StreamingLinearAlgorithm` class. Currently, only a linear regression implementation is available-`StreamingLinearRegressionWithSGD`-but future versions will include classification.

The streaming regression model provides two methods for usage:

- `trainOn`: This takes `DStream[LabeledPoint]` as its argument. This tells the model to train on every batch in the input DStream. It can be called multiple times to train on different streams.
- `predictOn`: This also takes `DStream[LabeledPoint]`. This tells the model to make predictions on the input DStream, returning a new `DStream[Double]` that contains the model predictions.

Under the hood, the streaming regression model uses `foreachRDD` and `map` to accomplish this. It also updates the model variable after each batch and exposes the latest trained model, which allows us to use this model in other applications or save it to an external location.

The streaming regression model can be configured with parameters for step size and number of iterations in the same way as standard batch regression-the model class used is the same. We can also set the initial model weight vector.

When we first start training a model, we can set the initial weights to a zero vector, or a random vector, or perhaps load the latest model from the result of an offline batch process. We can also decide to save the model periodically to an external system and use the latest model state as the starting point (for example, in the case of a restart after a node or application failure).

A simple streaming regression program

To illustrate the use of streaming regression, we will create a simple example similar to the preceding one, which uses simulated data. We will write a producer program that generates random feature vectors and target variables, given a fixed, known weight vector, and writes each training example to a network stream.

Our consumer application will run a streaming regression model, training and then testing on our simulated data stream. Our first example consumer will simply print its predictions to the console.

Creating a streaming data producer

The data producer operates in a manner similar to our product event producer example. Recall from Chapter 5, *Building a Recommendation Engine with Spark*, that a linear model is a linear combination (or vector dot product) of a weight vector, w, and a feature vector, x (that is, wTx). Our producer will generate synthetic data using a fixed, known weight vector and randomly generated feature vectors. This data fits the linear model formulation exactly, so we will expect our regression model to learn the true weight vector fairly easily.

First, we will set up a maximum number of events per second (say, 100) and the number of features in our feature vector (also 100 in this example):

```
/**
 * A producer application that generates random linear
 regression data.
 */
object StreamingModelProducer {
  import breeze.linalg._

  def main(args: Array[String]) {

    // Maximum number of events per second
    val MaxEvents = 100
    val NumFeatures = 100

    val random = new Random()
```

The generateRandomArray function creates an array of the specified size where the entries are randomly generated from a normal distribution. We will use this function initially to generate our known weight vector, w, which will be fixed throughout the life of the producer. We will also create a random intercept value that will also be fixed. The weight vector and intercept will be used to generate each data point in our stream:

```
/** Function to generate a normally distributed dense vector */
def generateRandomArray(n: Int) = Array.tabulate(n)(_ =>
  random.nextGaussian())

// Generate a fixed random model weight vector
val w = new DenseVector(generateRandomArray(NumFeatures))
val intercept = random.nextGaussian() * 10
```

We will also need a function to generate a specified number of random data points. Each event is made up of a random feature vector and the target that we get from computing the dot product of our known weight vector with the random feature vector and adding the `intercept` value:

```scala
/** Generate a number of random product events */
def generateNoisyData(n: Int) = {
  (1 to n).map { i =>
    val x = new DenseVector(generateRandomArray(NumFeatures))
    val y: Double = w.dot(x)
    val noisy = y + intercept //+ 0.1 * random.nextGaussian()
    (noisy, x)
  }
}
```

Finally, we will use code similar to our previous producer to instantiate a network connection and send a random number of data points (between 0 and 100) in text format over the network each second:

```scala
// create a network producer
  val listener = new ServerSocket(9999)
  println("Listening on port: 9999")

  while (true) {
    val socket = listener.accept()
    new Thread() {
      override def run = {
        println("Got client connected from: " +
          socket.getInetAddress)
        val out = new PrintWriter(socket.getOutputStream(),
          true)

        while (true) {
          Thread.sleep(1000)
          val num = random.nextInt(MaxEvents)
          val data = generateNoisyData(num)
          data.foreach { case (y, x) =>
            val xStr = x.data.mkString(",")
            val eventStr = s"$yt$xStr"
            out.write(eventStr)
            out.write("n")
          }
          out.flush()
          println(s"Created $num events...")
        }
        socket.close()
      }
```

```
        }.start()
    }
  }
}
```

You can start the producer using `sbt run`, followed by choosing to execute the `StreamingModelProducer` main method. This should result in the following output, thus indicating that the producer program is waiting for connections from our streaming regression application:

```
[info] Running StreamingModelProducer
Listening on port: 9999
```

Creating a streaming regression model

In the next step in our example, we will create a streaming regression program. The basic layout and setup is the same as our previous streaming analytics examples:

```
/**
  * A simple streaming linear regression that prints out predicted
    value for each batch
  */
object SimpleStreamingModel {

  def main(args: Array[String]) {

    val ssc = new StreamingContext("local[2]", "First Streaming
      App", Seconds(10))
    val stream = ssc.socketTextStream("localhost", 9999)
```

Here, we will set up the number of features to match the records in our input data stream. We will then create a zero vector to use as the initial weight vector of our streaming regression model. Finally, we will select the number of iterations and step size:

```
val NumFeatures = 100
val zeroVector = DenseVector.zeros[Double](NumFeatures)
val model = new StreamingLinearRegressionWithSGD()
  .setInitialWeights(Vectors.dense(zeroVector.data))
  .setNumIterations(1)
  .setStepSize(0.01)
```

Next, we will again use the `map` function to transform the input DStream, where each record is a string representation of our input data, into a `LabeledPoint` instance that contains the target value and feature vector:

```
// create a stream of labeled points
```

```
val labeledStream = stream.map { event =>
  val split = event.split("t")
  val y = split(0).toDouble
  val features = split(1).split(",").map(_.toDouble)
  LabeledPoint(label = y, features = Vectors.dense(features))
}
```

The final step is to tell the model to train and test on our transformed DStream and also to print out the first few elements of each batch in the DStream of predicted values:

```
// train and test model on the stream, and print predictions
// for illustrative purposes
    model.trainOn(labeledStream)
    //model.predictOn(labeledStream).print()
    model.predictOnValues(labeledStream.map(lp => (lp.label,
    lp.features))).print()

    ssc.start()
    ssc.awaitTermination()

  }
}
```

Note that because we are using the same MLlib model classes for streaming as we did for batch processing, we can, if we choose, perform multiple iterations over the training data in each batch (which is just an RDD of `LabeledPoint` instances).

Here, we will set the number of iterations to 1 to simulate purely online learning. In practice, you can set the number of iterations higher, but note that the training time per batch will go up. If the training time per batch is much higher than the batch interval, the streaming model will start to lag behind the velocity of the data stream.

This can be handled by decreasing the number of iterations, increasing the batch interval, or increasing the parallelism of our streaming program by adding more Spark workers.

Now, we're ready to run `SimpleStreamingModel` in our second terminal window using `sbt run` in the same way as we did for the producer (remember to select the correct main method for SBT to execute). Once the streaming program starts running, you should see the following output in the producer console:

```
Got client connected from: /127.0.0.1
...
```

```
Created 10 events...
Created 83 events...
Created 75 events...
...
```

After about 10 seconds, you should start seeing the model predictions being printed to the streaming application console, similar to those shown here:

```
14/11/16 14:54:00 INFO StreamingLinearRegressionWithSGD: Model
updated at time 1416142440000 ms
14/11/16 14:54:00 INFO StreamingLinearRegressionWithSGD: Current
model: weights, [0.05160959387864821,0.05122747155689144,-
0.17224086785756998,0.05822993392274008,0.07848094246845688,-
0.1298315806501979,0.006059323642394124, ...
...
14/11/16 14:54:00 INFO JobScheduler: Finished job streaming job
1416142440000 ms.0 from job set of time 1416142440000 ms
14/11/16 14:54:00 INFO JobScheduler: Starting job streaming job
1416142440000 ms.1 from job set of time 1416142440000 ms
14/11/16 14:54:00 INFO SparkContext: Starting job: take at
DStream.scala:608
14/11/16 14:54:00 INFO DAGScheduler: Got job 3 (take at
DStream.scala:608) with 1 output partitions (allowLocal=true)
14/11/16 14:54:00 INFO DAGScheduler: Final stage: Stage 3(take at
DStream.scala:608)
14/11/16 14:54:00 INFO DAGScheduler: Parents of final stage: List()
14/11/16 14:54:00 INFO DAGScheduler: Missing parents: List()
14/11/16 14:54:00 INFO DAGScheduler: Computing the requested
partition locally
14/11/16 14:54:00 INFO SparkContext: Job finished: take at
DStream.scala:608, took 0.014064 s
----------------------------------------------
Time: 1416142440000 ms
----------------------------------------------
-2.0851430248312526
4.609405228401022
2.817934589675725
3.3526557917118813
4.624236379848475
-2.3509098272485156
-0.7228551577759544
2.914231548990703
0.896926579927631
1.1968162940541283
...
```

Congratulations! You've created your first streaming online learning model!

You can shut down the streaming application (and, optionally, the producer) by pressing *Ctrl + C* in each terminal window.

Streaming K-means

MLlib also includes a streaming version of K-means clustering; this is called `StreamingKMeans`. This model is an extension of the mini-batch K-means algorithm where the model is updated with each batch based on a combination between the cluster centers computed from the previous batches and the cluster centers computed for the current batch.

`StreamingKMeans` supports a *forgetfulness* parameter *alpha* (set using the `setDecayFactor` method); this controls how aggressive the model is in giving weight to newer data. An alpha value of 0 means the model will only use new data, while with an alpha value of 1, all data since the beginning of the streaming application will be used.

We will not cover streaming K-means further here (the Spark documentation at `http://spark.apache.org/docs/latest/mllib-clustering.html#streaming-clustering` contains further detail and an example). However, perhaps you could try to adapt the preceding streaming regression data producer to generate input data for a `StreamingKMeans` model. You could also adapt the streaming regression application to use `StreamingKMeans`.

You can create the clustering data producer by first selecting a number of clusters, *K*, and then generating each data point by:

- Randomly selecting a cluster index.
- Generating a random vector using specific normal distribution parameters for each cluster. That is, each of the *K* clusters will have a mean and variance parameter, from which the random vectors will be generated using an approach similar to our preceding `generateRandomArray` function.

In this way, each data point that belongs to the same cluster will be drawn from the same distribution, so our streaming clustering model should be able to learn the correct cluster centers over time.

Online model evaluation

Combining machine learning with Spark Streaming has many potential applications and use cases, including keeping a model or set of models up to date on new training data as it arrives, thus enabling them to adapt quickly to changing situations or contexts.

Another useful application is to track and compare the performance of multiple models in an online manner and, possibly, also perform model selection in real time so that the best performing model is always used to generate predictions on live data.

This can be used to do real-time "A/B testing" of models, or combined with more advanced online selection and learning techniques, such as Bayesian update approaches and bandit algorithms. It can also be used simply to monitor model performance in real time, thus being able to respond or adapt if performance degrades for some reason.

In this section, we will walk through a simple extension to our streaming regression example. In this example, we will compare the evolving error rate of two models with different parameters as they see more and more data in our input stream.

Comparing model performance with Spark Streaming

As we have used a known weight vector and intercept to generate the training data in our producer application, we would expect our model to eventually learn this underlying weight vector (in the absence of random noise, which we do not add for this example).

Therefore, we should see the model's error rate decrease over time, as it sees more and more data. We can also use standard regression error metrics to compare the performance of multiple models.

In this example, we will create two models with different learning rates, training them both on the same data stream. We will then make predictions for each model and measure the **mean-squared error** (MSE) and **root mean-squared error** (RMSE) metrics for each batch.

Our new monitored streaming model code is shown here:

```
/**
 * A streaming regression model that compares the model
 * performance of two models, printing out metrics for
 * each batch
 */
object MonitoringStreamingModel {
  import org.apache.spark.SparkContext._

  def main(args: Array[String]) {

    val ssc = new StreamingContext("local[2]", "First Streaming
      App", Seconds(10))
    val stream = ssc.socketTextStream("localhost", 9999)
```

```
val NumFeatures = 100
val zeroVector = DenseVector.zeros[Double](NumFeatures)
val model1 = new StreamingLinearRegressionWithSGD()
  .setInitialWeights(Vectors.dense(zeroVector.data))
  .setNumIterations(1)
  .setStepSize(0.01)

val model2 = new StreamingLinearRegressionWithSGD()
  .setInitialWeights(Vectors.dense(zeroVector.data))
  .setNumIterations(1)
  .setStepSize(1.0)

// create a stream of labeled points
val labeledStream = stream.map { event =>
val split = event.split("t")
val y = split(0).toDouble
val features = split(1).split(",").map(_.toDouble)
LabeledPoint(label = y, features =
  Vectors.dense(features))
}
```

Note that most of the preceding setup code is the same as our simple streaming model example. However, we created two instances of StreamingLinearRegressionWithSGD: one with a learning rate of 0.01 and one with the learning rate set to 1.0.

Next, we will train each model on our input stream, and using Spark Streaming's transform function, we will create a new DStream that contains the error rates for each model:

```
// train both models on the same stream
model1.trainOn(labeledStream)
model2.trainOn(labeledStream)

// use transform to create a stream with model error rates
val predsAndTrue = labeledStream.transform { rdd =>
  val latest1 = model1.latestModel()
  val latest2 = model2.latestModel()
  rdd.map { point =>
    val pred1 = latest1.predict(point.features)
    val pred2 = latest2.predict(point.features)
    (pred1 - point.label, pred2 - point.label)
  }
}
```

Finally, we will use foreachRDD to compute the MSE and RMSE metrics for each model and print them to the console:

```
// print out the MSE and RMSE metrics for each model per batch
predsAndTrue.foreachRDD { (rdd, time) =>
  val mse1 = rdd.map { case (err1, err2) => err1 * err1
  }.mean()
  val rmse1 = math.sqrt(mse1)
  val mse2 = rdd.map { case (err1, err2) => err2 * err2
  }.mean()
  val rmse2 = math.sqrt(mse2)
  println(
    s"""
      |--------------------------------------------
      |Time: $time
      |--------------------------------------------
    """.stripMargin)
  println(s"MSE current batch: Model 1: $mse1; Model 2:
    $mse2")
  println(s"RMSE current batch: Model 1: $rmse1; Model 2:
    $rmse2")
  println("...n")
}

ssc.start()
ssc.awaitTermination()

  }
}
```

If you terminated the producer earlier, start it again by executing sbt run and selecting StreamingModelProducer. Once the producer is running again, in your second terminal window, execute sbt run and choose the main class for MonitoringStreamingModel.

You should see the streaming program startup, and after about 10 seconds, the first batch will be processed, printing output similar to the following:

```
...
14/11/16 14:56:11 INFO SparkContext: Job finished: mean at
StreamingModel.scala:159, took 0.09122 s

--------------------------------------------
Time: 1416142570000 ms
--------------------------------------------

MSE current batch: Model 1: 97.9475827857361; Model 2:
97.9475827857361
RMSE current batch: Model 1: 9.896847113385965; Model 2:
9.896847113385965
...
```

Since both models start with the same initial weight vector, we see that they both make the same predictions on this first batch and, therefore, have the same error.

If we leave the streaming program running for a few minutes, we should eventually see that one of the models has started converging, leading to a lower and lower error, while the other model has tended to diverge to a poorer model due to the overly high learning rate:

```
. . .
14/11/16 14:57:30 INFO SparkContext: Job finished: mean at
StreamingModel.scala:159, took 0.069175 s

------------------------------------------------
Time: 1416142650000 ms
------------------------------------------------

MSE current batch: Model 1: 75.54543031658632; Model 2:
10318.213926882852
RMSE current batch: Model 1: 8.691687426304878; Model 2:
101.57860959317593
. . .
```

If you leave the program running for a number of minutes, you should eventually see the first model's error rate becoming quite small:

```
. . .
14/11/16 17:27:00 INFO SparkContext: Job finished: mean at
StreamingModel.scala:159, took 0.037856 s

------------------------------------------------
Time: 1416151620000 ms
------------------------------------------------

MSE current batch: Model 1: 6.551475362521364; Model 2:
1.057088005456417E26
RMSE current batch: Model 1: 2.559584998104451; Model 2:
1.0281478519436867E13
. . .
```

Note again, that due to random data generation, you might see different results, but the overall result should be the same-in the first batch, the models will have the same error, and subsequently, the first model should start to generate to a smaller and smaller error.

Structured Streaming

With Spark version 2.0 we have structured streaming which states that the output of the application is equal to executing a batch job on a prefix of the data. Structured Streaming handles consistency and reliability within the engine and in interactions with external systems. Structured Stream is a simple data frame and dataset API.

Users provide the query they want to run along with the input and output locations. The system then executes the query incrementally, maintaining enough state to recover from failure, keeping the results consistent in external storage, and so on.

Structured Streaming promises a much simpler model for building real-time applications, built on the features that work best in Spark Streaming. However Structured Streaming is in alpha for Spark 2.0.

Summary

In this chapter, we connected some of the dots between online machine learning and streaming data analysis. We introduced the Spark Streaming library and API for continuous processing of data streams based on familiar RDD functionality and we worked through examples of streaming analytics applications that illustrate this functionality.

Finally, we used ML Library's streaming regression model in a streaming application that involves computing and comparing model performance on a stream of input feature vectors.

12
Pipeline APIs for Spark ML

In this chapter, you will learn the basics of ML pipelines and how they can be used in a variety of contexts. The pipeline is made up of several components. ML pipelines leverage the Spark platform and machine learning to provide key features for making the construction of large-scale learning pipelines simple.

Introduction to pipelines

The pipeline API was introduced in Spark 1.2 and is inspired by scikit-learn. The concept of pipelines is to facilitate the creation, tuning, and inspection of ML workflows.

ML pipelines provide a set of high-level APIs built on top of DataFrames that help users create and tune practical machine learning pipelines. Multiple algorithms from Spark machine learning can be combined into a single pipeline.

An ML pipeline normally involves a sequence of data pre-processing, feature extraction, model fitting, and validation stages.

Let's take an example of text classification, where documents go through preprocessing stages, such as tokenization, segmentation and cleaning, extraction of feature vectors, and training a classification model with cross-validation. Many steps involving pre-processing and algorithms can be tied together using the pipeline. The pipeline typically sits above the ML library, orchestrating the workflow.

DataFrames

The Spark pipeline is defined by a sequence of stages where each stage is either a transformer or an estimator. These stages are run in order, and the input DataFrame is transformed as it passes through each stage.

A DataFrame is a basic data structure or tensor that flows through the pipeline. A DataFrame is represented by a dataset of rows, and supports many types, such as numeric, string, binary, boolean, datetime, and so on.

Pipeline components

An ML pipeline or an ML workflow is a sequence of transformers and estimators arranged to fit a pipeline model to an input dataset.

Transformers

A transformer is an abstraction that includes feature transformers and learned models. The transformer implements the `transform()` method, which converts one DataFrame to another.

A feature transformer takes a DataFrame, reads the text, maps it to a new column, and outputs a new DataFrame.

A learning model takes a DataFrame, reads the column containing feature vectors, predicts the label for each feature vector, and outputs a new DataFrame with the predicted labels.

Custom transformers are required to follow the following steps:

1. Implement the `transform` method.
2. Specify inputCol and outputCol.
3. Accept `DataFrame` as input and return `DataFrame` as output.

In nutshell, the **transformer:** `DataFrame =[transform]=> DataFrame`.

Estimators

An estimator is an abstraction of a learning algorithm that fits a model on a dataset.

An estimator implements a `fit()` method that takes a DataFrame and produces a model.
An example of a learning algorithm is `LogisticRegression`.

In a nutshell, the **estimator** is: `DataFrame =[fit]=> Model`.

In the following example, `PipelineComponentExample` introduces the concepts of
transformers and estimators:

```
import org.apache.spark.ml.classification.LogisticRegression
import org.apache.spark.ml.linalg.{Vector, Vectors}
import org.apache.spark.ml.param.ParamMap
import org.apache.spark.sql.Row
import org.utils.StandaloneSpark

object PipelineComponentExample {

  def main(args: Array[String]): Unit = {
    val spark = StandaloneSpark.getSparkInstance()

    // Prepare training data from a list of (label, features) tuples.
    val training = spark.createDataFrame(Seq(
      (1.0, Vectors.dense(0.0, 1.1, 0.1)),
      (0.0, Vectors.dense(2.0, 1.0, -1.0)),
      (0.0, Vectors.dense(2.0, 1.3, 1.0)),
      (1.0, Vectors.dense(0.0, 1.2, -0.5))
    )).toDF("label", "features")

    // Create a LogisticRegression instance. This instance is an Estimator.
    val lr = new LogisticRegression()
    // Print out the parameters, documentation, and any default values.
    println("LogisticRegression parameters:n" + lr.explainParams() + "n")

    // We may set parameters using setter methods.
    lr.setMaxIter(10)
      .setRegParam(0.01)

    // Learn a LogisticRegression model.
    // This uses the parameters stored in lr.
    val model1 = lr.fit(training)
    // Since model1 is a Model (i.e., a Transformer produced by an
Estimator),
    // we can view the parameters it used during fit().
    // This prints the parameter (name: value) pairs,
    // where names are unique IDs for this
    // LogisticRegression instance.
    println("Model 1 was fit using parameters: " +
    model1.parent.extractParamMap)
```

```scala
    // We may alternatively specify parameters using a ParamMap,
    // which supports several methods for specifying parameters.
    val paramMap = ParamMap(lr.maxIter -> 20)
    .put(lr.maxIter, 30) // Specify 1 Param.
    // This overwrites the original maxIter.
    .put(lr.regParam -> 0.1, lr.threshold -> 0.55) // Specify multiple
Params.

    // One can also combine ParamMaps.
    val paramMap2 = ParamMap(lr.probabilityCol ->
      "myProbability")
    // Change output column name.
    val paramMapCombined = paramMap ++ paramMap2

    // Now learn a new model using the paramMapCombined parameters.
    lr.set* methods.
    val model2 = lr.fit(training, paramMapCombined)
    println("Model 2 was fit using parameters: " +
      model2.parent.extractParamMap)

    // Prepare test data.
    val test = spark.createDataFrame(Seq(
      (1.0, Vectors.dense(-1.0, 1.5, 1.3)),
      (0.0, Vectors.dense(3.0, 2.0, -0.1)),
      (1.0, Vectors.dense(0.0, 2.2, -1.5))
        )).toDF("label", "features")

    // Make predictions on test data using the
    // Transformer.transform() method.
    // LogisticRegression.transform will only use the 'features'
    // column.
    // Note that model2.transform() outputs a 'myProbability'
    // column instead of the usual
    // 'probability' column since we renamed the
    lr.probabilityCol
    parameter previously.
    model2.transform(test)
      .select("features", "label", "myProbability",
      "prediction")
      .collect()
      .foreach { case Row(features: Vector, label: Double, prob:
        Vector, prediction: Double) =>
        println(s"($features, $label) -> prob=$prob,
        prediction=$prediction")
      }
  }
}
```

You will see the following output:

```
Model 2 was fit using parameters: {
logreg_158888baeffa-elasticNetParam: 0.0,
logreg_158888baeffa-featuresCol: features,
logreg_158888baeffa-fitIntercept: true,
logreg_158888baeffa-labelCol: label,
logreg_158888baeffa-maxIter: 30,
logreg_158888baeffa-predictionCol: prediction,
logreg_158888baeffa-probabilityCol: myProbability,
logreg_158888baeffa-rawPredictionCol: rawPrediction,
logreg_158888baeffa-regParam: 0.1,
logreg_158888baeffa-standardization: true,
logreg_158888baeffa-threshold: 0.55,
logreg_158888baeffa-tol: 1.0E-6
}
17/02/12 12:32:49 INFO Instrumentation: LogisticRegression-
logreg_158888baeffa-268961738-2: training finished
17/02/12 12:32:49 INFO CodeGenerator: Code generated in 26.525405
ms
17/02/12 12:32:49 INFO CodeGenerator: Code generated in 11.387162
ms
17/02/12 12:32:49 INFO SparkContext: Invoking stop() from shutdown
hook
([-1.0,1.5,1.3], 1.0) ->
prob=[0.05707304171033984,0.9429269582896601], prediction=1.0
([3.0,2.0,-0.1], 0.0) ->
prob=[0.9238522311704088,0.0761477688295912], prediction=0.0
([0.0,2.2,-1.5], 1.0) ->
prob=[0.10972776114779145,0.8902722388522085], prediction=1.0
```

Code listing:
https://github.com/ml-resources/spark-ml/blob/branch-ed2/Chapter
_12/2.0.0/spark-ai-
apps/src/main/scala/org/textclassifier/PipelineComponentExample.
scala

How pipelines work

We run a sequence of algorithms to process and learn from a given dataset. For example, in text classification, we split each document into words and convert the words into a numerical feature vector. Finally, we learn a predictive model using this feature vector and labels.

Spark ML represents such a workflow as a pipeline, which consists of a sequence of PipelineStages (transformers and estimators) to be run in a particular order.

Each stage in *PipelineStages* is one of the components, either a transformer or an estimator. The stages are run in a particular order while the input DataFrame flows through the stages.

 The following images are taken from `https://spark.apache.org/docs/l atest/ml-pipeline.html#dataframe`.

In the following figure, the **dp**Text document pipeline demonstrates the document workflow where Tokenizer, Hashing, and Logistic Regression are the components of the pipeline. The `Pipeline.fit()` method shows how the raw text gets transformed through the pipeline:

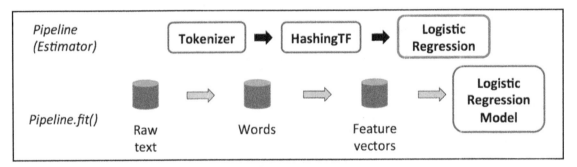

When the `Pipeline.fit()` method is called, at the first stage, the raw text is tokenized into words using the **Tokenizer** transformer, and in the second stage, words are converted to the feature vector using the term frequency transformer. In the final stage, the `fit()` method is called on the **Estimator Logistic Regression** to get the **Logistic Regression Model** (PipelineModel) over the feature vectors.

The Pipeline is an estimator, and after `fit()` is run it, produces a PipelineModel, which is a transformer:

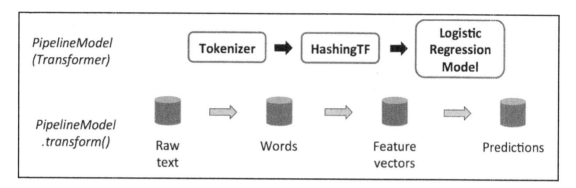

`PipelineModels.transform` method is called on test data and predictions are made as shown.

Pipelines can be linear that is, stages are specified as ordered array or non-linear where the data flow forms a **directed acyclic graph (DAG)**. Pipelines and PipelineModels instead perform runtime checking before actually running the pipeline.

The DAG pipeline example is shown here:

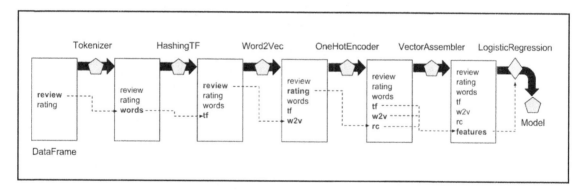

The following example `TextClassificationPipeline` introduces the concepts of transformers and estimators:

```
package org.textclassifier

import org.apache.spark.ml.{Pipeline, PipelineModel}
import org.apache.spark.ml.classification.LogisticRegression
import org.apache.spark.ml.feature.{HashingTF, Tokenizer}
import org.apache.spark.ml.linalg.Vector
import org.utils.StandaloneSpark


/**
 * Created by manpreet.singh on 12/02/17.
 */
object TextClassificationPipeline {

  def main(args: Array[String]): Unit = {
    val spark = StandaloneSpark.getSparkInstance()

  // Prepare training documents from a list of (id, text, label)
  // tuples.
  val training = spark.createDataFrame(Seq(
    (0L, "a b c d e spark", 1.0),
    (1L, "b d", 0.0),
    (2L, "spark f g h", 1.0),
    (3L, "hadoop mapreduce", 0.0)
  )).toDF("id", "text", "label")

  // Configure an ML pipeline, which consists of three stages:
  // tokenizer, hashingTF, and lr.
  val tokenizer = new Tokenizer()
    .setInputCol("text")
    .setOutputCol("words")
  val hashingTF = new HashingTF()
    .setNumFeatures(1000)
    .setInputCol(tokenizer.getOutputCol)
    .setOutputCol("features")
  val lr = new LogisticRegression()
    .setMaxIter(10)
    .setRegParam(0.001)
  val pipeline = new Pipeline()
    .setStages(Array(tokenizer, hashingTF, lr))

  // Fit the pipeline to training documents.
  val model = pipeline.fit(training)
```

```
// Now we can optionally save the fitted pipeline to disk
model.write.overwrite().save("/tmp/spark-logistic-regression-
  model")

// We can also save this unfit pipeline to disk
pipeline.write.overwrite().save("/tmp/unfit-lr-model")
// And load it back in during production
val sameModel = PipelineModel.load("/tmp/spark-logistic-
  regression-model")

// Prepare test documents, which are unlabeled (id, text) tuples.
val test = spark.createDataFrame(Seq(
  (4L, "spark i j k"),
  (5L, "l m n"),
  (6L, "spark hadoop spark"),
  (7L, "apache hadoop")
)).toDF("id", "text")

// Make predictions on test documents.
model.transform(test)
  .select("id", "text", "probability", "prediction")
  .collect()
  .foreach { case Row(id: Long, text: String, prob: Vector,
    prediction: Double) =>
    println(s"($id, $text) --> prob=$prob,
    prediction=$prediction")
  }
}
}
```

You will see the following output:

```
17/02/12 12:46:22 INFO Executor: Finished task 0.0 in stage
30.0
(TID
30). 1494 bytes result sent to driver
17/02/12 12:46:22 INFO TaskSetManager: Finished task 0.0 in stage
30.0 (TID 30) in 84 ms on localhost (1/1)
17/02/12 12:46:22 INFO TaskSchedulerImpl: Removed TaskSet 30.0,
whose tasks have all completed, from pool
17/02/12 12:46:22 INFO DAGScheduler: ResultStage 30 (head at
LogisticRegression.scala:683) finished in 0.084 s
17/02/12 12:46:22 INFO DAGScheduler: Job 29 finished: head at
LogisticRegression.scala:683, took 0.091814 s
17/02/12 12:46:22 INFO CodeGenerator: Code generated in 5.88911 ms
17/02/12 12:46:22 INFO CodeGenerator: Code generated in 8.320754 ms
17/02/12 12:46:22 INFO CodeGenerator: Code generated in 9.082379 ms
(4, spark i j k) -->
```

```
prob=[0.15964077387874084,0.8403592261212592],
prediction=1.0
(5, 1 m n) --> prob=[0.8378325685476612,0.16216743145233883],
prediction=0.0
(6, spark hadoop spark) --> prob=
[0.06926633132976247,0.9307336686702374], prediction=1.0
(7, apache hadoop) --> prob=
[0.9821575333444208,0.01784246665557917],
prediction=0.0
```

Code listing:
https://github.com/ml-resources/spark-ml/blob/branch-ed2/Chapter
_12/2.0.0/spark-ai-
apps/src/main/scala/org/textclassifier/TextClassificationPipelin
e.scala

Machine learning pipeline with an example

As discussed in the previous sections, one of the biggest features in the new ML library is the introduction of the pipeline. Pipelines provide a high-level abstraction of the machine learning flow and greatly simplify the complete workflow.

We will demonstrate the process of creating a pipeline in Spark using the StumbleUpon dataset.

The dataset used here can be downloaded from
http://www.kaggle.com/c/stumbleupon/data.
Download the training data (train.tsv)--you will need to accept the terms and conditions before downloading the dataset. You can find more information about the competition at
http://www.kaggle.com/c/stumbleupon.

Here is a glimpse of the `StumbleUpon` dataset stored as a temporary table using Spark SQLContext:

```
|           url|urlid|     boilerplate|alchemy_category|alchemy_category_score|avglinksize|commonlinkratio_1|commonlinkratio_2|commonlinkratio_3|commonlinkratio_4|
|http://www.conven...| 7018|{"url":"convenien...|               ?|                    ?|      119.0|      0.745454545|      0.581818182|      0.290909091|      0.018181818|
|http://www.inside...| 3402|{"url":"insidersh...|               ?|                    ?|1.883333333|       0.71969697|      0.265151515|      0.113636364|      0.015151515|
|http://www.valetm...|  477|{"title":"Valet T...|               ?|                    ?|0.471502591|      0.190721649|      0.036082474|              0.0|              0.0|
|http://www.howswe...| 6731|{"url":"howsweete...|               ?|                    ?| 2.41011236|      0.469325153|      0.101226994|      0.018404908|      0.003067485|
|http://www.thedai...| 1063|{"title":" ","bod...|               ?|                    ?|        0.0|              0.0|              0.0|              0.0|              0.0|
|http://www.manice...| 8945|{"title":"Origina...|               ?|                    ?|4.327655311|      0.978757515|      0.895791583|      0.669138277|      0.422044088|
|http://blogs.babb...| 2839|{"title":" ","bod...|               ?|                    ?|1.786407767|      0.552631579|      0.149122807|      0.052631579|      0.01754386|
|http://humor.cool...| 2949|{"title":"Supermo...|               ?|                    ?|3.417910448|      0.541176471|      0.270588235|      0.176470588|      0.117647059|
|http://sportsillu...| 4156|{"title":"Genevie...|               ?|                    ?|1.154761905|      0.504424779|      0.427728614|       0.02359882|              0.0|
|http://www.chican...| 8004|{"title":"Ten way...|               ?|                    ?|1.292682927|      0.421965318|      0.306358382|      0.011560694|              0.0|
|http://nerdsmagaz...| 3201|{"url":"nerdsmaga...|               ?|                    ?|1.888888889|          0.59375|         0.171875|           0.0625|         0.046875|
|http://bitten.blo...| 6704|{"title":"Microwa...|               ?|                    ?|2.618902439|      0.707317073|       0.33604336|      0.119241192|      0.051490515|
|http://www.peta.o...| 3561|{"title":"Creamy ...|               ?|                    ?|2.881944444|       0.54822335|       0.23857868|      0.106598985|      0.040609137|
|http://www.refine...| 8138|{"title":"Photo 1...|               ?|                    ?| 1.76969697|      0.381818182|      0.181818182|      0.048484848|      0.006060606|
|http://sportsillu...| 1754|{"title":"Alyssa ...|               ?|                    ?|1.158208955|       0.50591716|      0.428994083|      0.023668639|              0.0|
|http://twenty1f.com/| 4881|{"title":"Twenty1...|               ?|                    ?|2.133333333|      0.655737705|      0.213114754|      0.196721311|      0.196721311|
|http://allrecipes...| 5483|{"title":"Apple D...|               ?|                    ?|2.328502415|      0.427777778|      0.205555556|      0.061111111|      0.019444444|
|http://hypersapie...| 4781|{"url":"hypersapi...|               ?|                    ?| 2.85483871|      0.428571429|      0.103896104|      0.038961039|              0.0|
|http://www.phoeni...| 7053|{"title":" ","bod...|               ?|                    ?|2.278481013|      0.552419355|      0.266129032|      0.052419355|       0.02016129|
|http://www.comple...| 1033|{"title":"The 25 ...|               ?|                    ?|1.127516779|      0.636363636|      0.048484848|              0.0|              0.0|
only showing top 20 rows
```

Here is a visualization of the `StumbleUpon` dataset:

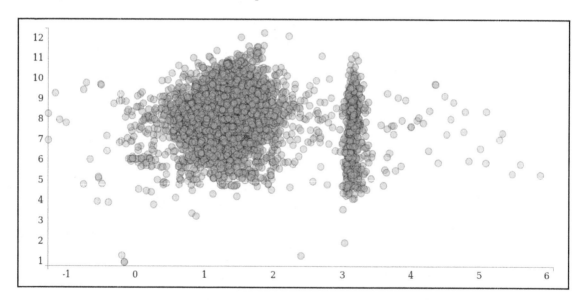

StumbleUponExecutor

The `StumbleUponExecutor` object can be used to choose and run the respective classification model, for example, to run `LogisiticRegression` and execute the logistic regression pipeline or set the program argument as `LR`. For other commands, refer to the following code snippet:

Before we proceed, a few words on the Logistic Regression estimator. Logistic Regression works for classification problems where classes are nearly linearly separable. It searches for a single linear decision boundary in the feature space. There are two types of logistic regression estimators available in Spark: binomial logistic regression estimators to predict a binary outcome, and multinomial logistic regression estimators to predict a multiclass outcome.

```
case "LR" =>
  LogisticRegressionPipeline.logisticRegressionPipeline(
  vectorAssembler, dataFrame)

case "DT" =>
  DecisionTreePipeline.decisionTreePipeline(vectorAssembler,
  dataFrame)

case "RF" =>
  RandomForestPipeline.randomForestPipeline(vectorAssembler,
  dataFrame)

case
  GradientBoostedTreePipeline.gradientBoostedTreePipeline
  (vectorAssembler, dataFrame)

case "NB" =>
  NaiveBayesPipeline.naiveBayesPipeline(vectorAssembler,
  dataFrame)

case "SVM" => SVMPipeline.svmPipeline(sparkContext)
```

Code listing:
https://github.com/ml-resources/spark-ml/blob/branch-ed2/Chapter
_12/2.0.0/spark-ai-
apps/src/main/scala/org/stumbleuponclassifier/StumbleUponExecuto
r.scala

Decision Tree Pipeline: Pipeline uses a decision tree estimator to classify the StumbleUpon dataset as part of the ML workflow.

A decision tree estimator in Spark essentially partitions the feature space into half-spaces using axis-aligned linear decision boundaries. The effect is that we have a non-linear decision boundary, possibly more than one:

```
package org.stumbleuponclassifier

import org.apache.log4j.Logger
import org.apache.spark.ml.classification.DecisionTreeClassifier
import org.apache.spark.ml.evaluation.MulticlassClassification
  Evaluator
import org.apache.spark.ml.feature.{StringIndexer,
  VectorAssembler}
import org.apache.spark.ml.{Pipeline, PipelineStage}
import org.apache.spark.sql.DataFrame
import scala.collection.mutable

/**
  * Created by manpreet.singh on 01/05/16.
  */
object DecisionTreePipeline {
  @transient lazy val logger = Logger.getLogger(getClass.getName)

  def decisionTreePipeline(vectorAssembler: VectorAssembler,
    dataFrame: DataFrame) = {
    val Array(training, test) = dataFrame.randomSplit(Array(0.9,
      0.1), seed = 12345)

    // Set up Pipeline
    val stages = new mutable.ArrayBuffer[PipelineStage]()

    val labelIndexer = new StringIndexer()
      .setInputCol("label")
      .setOutputCol("indexedLabel")
    stages += labelIndexer

    val dt = new DecisionTreeClassifier()
      .setFeaturesCol(vectorAssembler.getOutputCol)
      .setLabelCol("indexedLabel")
      .setMaxDepth(5)
      .setMaxBins(32)
      .setMinInstancesPerNode(1)
      .setMinInfoGain(0.0)
      .setCacheNodeIds(false)
      .setCheckpointInterval(10)
```

```
    stages += vectorAssembler
    stages += dt
    val pipeline = new Pipeline().setStages(stages.toArray)

    // Fit the Pipeline
    val startTime = System.nanoTime()
    //val model = pipeline.fit(training)
    val model = pipeline.fit(dataFrame)
    val elapsedTime = (System.nanoTime() - startTime) / 1e9
    println(s"Training time: $elapsedTime seconds")

    //val holdout =
    // model.transform(test).select("prediction","label")
    val holdout =
      model.transform(dataFrame).select("prediction","label")

    // Select (prediction, true label) and compute test error
    val evaluator = new MulticlassClassificationEvaluator()
      .setLabelCol("label")
      .setPredictionCol("prediction")
      .setMetricName("accuracy")
    val mAccuracy = evaluator.evaluate(holdout)
    println("Test set accuracy = " + mAccuracy)
  }
}
```

You will see the following output displayed:

Accuracy: 0.3786163522012579

Code listing:
https://github.com/ml-resources/spark-ml/blob/branch-ed2/Chapter
_12/2.0.0/spark-ai-
apps/src/main/scala/org/stumbleuponclassifier/DecisionTreePipeli
ne.scala

The visualization of predicted data in a 2-dimensional scatter plot is shown here:

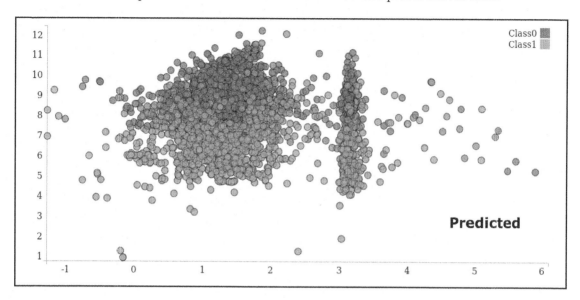

The visualization of the actual data in a 2 dimensional scatter plot is shown here:

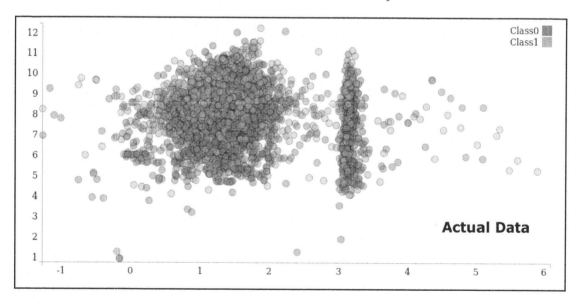

Naive Bayes Pipeline: Pipeline uses a naive bayes estimator to classify the StumbleUpon dataset as part of the ML workflow.

A Naive Bayes estimator considers the presence of a particular feature in a class to be unrelated to the presence of any other feature. The Naive Bayes model is simple to build and especially useful for very large data sets:

```scala
package org.stumbleuponclassifier

import org.apache.log4j.Logger
import org.apache.spark.ml.classification.NaiveBayes
import org.apache.spark.ml.evaluation.MulticlassClassification
  Evaluator
import org.apache.spark.ml.feature.{StringIndexer,
  VectorAssembler}
import org.apache.spark.ml.{Pipeline, PipelineStage}
import org.apache.spark.sql.DataFrame
import scala.collection.mutable

/**
  * Created by manpreet.singh on 01/05/16.
  */
object NaiveBayesPipeline {
  @transient lazy val logger =
  Logger.getLogger(getClass.getName)

  def naiveBayesPipeline(vectorAssembler: VectorAssembler,
    dataFrame: DataFrame) = {
    val Array(training, test) = dataFrame.randomSplit(Array(0.9,
      0.1), seed = 12345)

    // Set up Pipeline
    val stages = new mutable.ArrayBuffer[PipelineStage]()
    val labelIndexer = new StringIndexer()
      .setInputCol("label")
      .setOutputCol("indexedLabel")
    stages += labelIndexer

    val nb = new NaiveBayes()

    stages += vectorAssembler
    stages += nb
    val pipeline = new Pipeline().setStages(stages.toArray)

    // Fit the Pipeline
    val startTime = System.nanoTime()
    // val model = pipeline.fit(training)
    val model = pipeline.fit(dataFrame)
    val elapsedTime = (System.nanoTime() - startTime) / 1e9
    println(s"Training time: $elapsedTime seconds")
```

```
    // val holdout =
    // model.transform(test).select("prediction","label")
    val holdout =
      model.transform(dataFrame).select("prediction","label")

    // Select (prediction, true label) and compute test error
    val evaluator = new MulticlassClassificationEvaluator()
      .setLabelCol("label")
      .setPredictionCol("prediction")
      .setMetricName("accuracy")
    val mAccuracy = evaluator.evaluate(holdout)
    println("Test set accuracy = " + mAccuracy)
  }
}
```

You will see the following output displayed:

```
Training time: 2.114725642 seconds
Accuracy: 0.5660377358490566
```

Code listing:
https://github.com/ml-resources/spark-ml/blob/branch-ed2/Chapter
_12/2.0.0/spark-ai-
apps/src/main/scala/org/stumbleuponclassifier/NaiveBayesPipeline
.scala

A visualization of the predicted data in a 2-dimensional scatter plot is shown here:

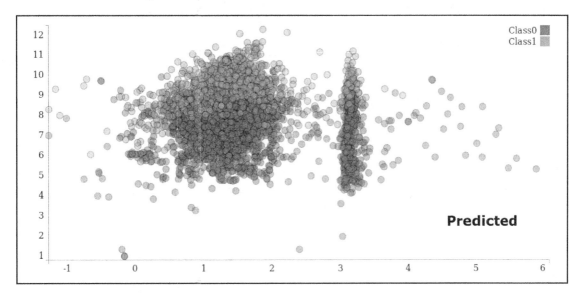

A visualization of the actual data in a 2 dimensional scatter plot is shown here:

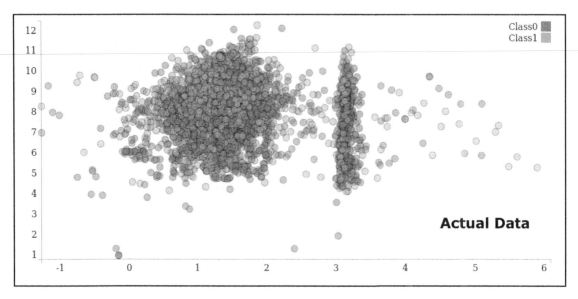

Gradient Boosted Pipeline : Pipeline uses Gradient Boosted Tree estimator to classify StumbleUpon dataset as part of ML workflow.

A Gradient Boosted Tree Estimator is a machine learning method for regression and classification problems. Both **Gradient-Boosted Trees** (**GBTs**) and Random Forests are algorithms for learning ensembles of trees. GBTs iteratively train decision trees to minimize a loss function. spark.mllib supports GBTs.

```scala
package org.stumbleuponclassifier

import org.apache.log4j.Logger
import org.apache.spark.ml.classification.GBTClassifier
import org.apache.spark.ml.feature.{StringIndexer,
    VectorAssembler}
import org.apache.spark.ml.{Pipeline, PipelineStage}
import org.apache.spark.mllib.evaluation.{MulticlassMetrics,
    RegressionMetrics}
import org.apache.spark.sql.DataFrame

import scala.collection.mutable

/**
  * Created by manpreet.singh on 01/05/16.
  */
```

```
object GradientBoostedTreePipeline {
  @transient lazy val logger =
    Logger.getLogger(getClass.getName)
    def gradientBoostedTreePipeline(vectorAssembler:
      VectorAssembler, dataFrame: DataFrame) = {
      val Array(training, test) = dataFrame.randomSplit(Array(0.9,
      0.1), seed = 12345)

    // Set up Pipeline
    val stages = new mutable.ArrayBuffer[PipelineStage]()

      val labelIndexer = new StringIndexer()
      .setInputCol("label")
      .setOutputCol("indexedLabel")
    stages += labelIndexer

    val gbt = new GBTClassifier()
      .setFeaturesCol(vectorAssembler.getOutputCol)
      .setLabelCol("indexedLabel")
      .setMaxIter(10)

    stages += vectorAssembler
    stages += gbt
    val pipeline = new Pipeline().setStages(stages.toArray)

    // Fit the Pipeline
    val startTime = System.nanoTime()
    //val model = pipeline.fit(training)
    val model = pipeline.fit(dataFrame)
    val elapsedTime = (System.nanoTime() - startTime) / 1e9
    println(s"Training time: $elapsedTime seconds")

    // val holdout =
    // model.transform(test).select("prediction","label")
    val holdout =
    model.transform(dataFrame).select("prediction","label")

    // have to do a type conversion for RegressionMetrics
    val rm = new RegressionMetrics(holdout.rdd.map(x =>
      (x(0).asInstanceOf[Double], x(1).asInstanceOf[Double])))

    logger.info("Test Metrics")
    logger.info("Test Explained Variance:")
    logger.info(rm.explainedVariance)
    logger.info("Test R^2 Coef:")
    logger.info(rm.r2)
    logger.info("Test MSE:")
    logger.info(rm.meanSquaredError)
```

```
    logger.info("Test RMSE:")
    logger.info(rm.rootMeanSquaredError)

    val predictions = model.transform(test).select("prediction")
    .rdd.map(_.getDouble(0))
    val labels = model.transform(test).select("label")
    .rdd.map(_.getDouble(0))
    val accuracy = new
      MulticlassMetrics(predictions.zip(labels)).precision
    println(s"  Accuracy : $accuracy")
  }

  def savePredictions(predictions:DataFrame, testRaw:DataFrame,
    regressionMetrics: RegressionMetrics, filePath:String) = {
    predictions
      .coalesce(1)
      .write.format("com.databricks.spark.csv")
      .option("header", "true")
      .save(filePath)
  }

}
```

You will see the following output displayed:

```
Accuracy: 0.3647
```

Code listing:
https://github.com/ml-resources/spark-ml/blob/branch-ed2/Chapter
_12/2.0.0/spark-ai-
apps/src/main/scala/org/stumbleuponclassifier/GradientBoostedTre
ePipeline.scala

Visualization of predictions in a 2-dimensional scatter plot is shown in the here:

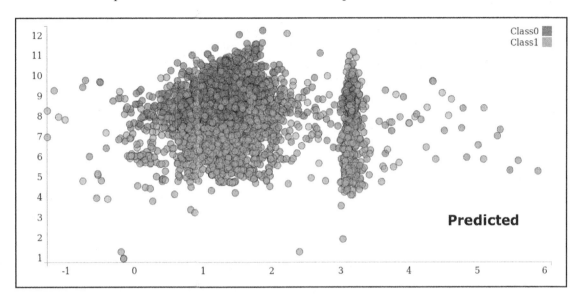

Visualization of actual data in 2 dimensional scatter plot is shown in the following:

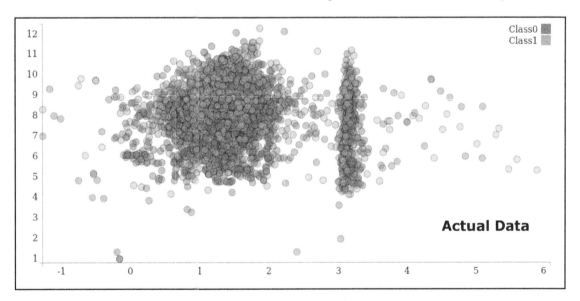

Summary

In this chapter, we covered the basics of Spark ML Pipeline and its components. We saw how to train models on input DataFrame and how to evaluate their performance using standard metrics and measures while running them through spark ML pipeline APIs. We explored how to apply some of the techniques like transformers and estimators. Finally, we investigated the pipeline API by applying different algorithms on the StumbleUpon dataset from Kaggle.

Machine Learning is the rising star in the industry. It has certainly addressed many business problems and use cases. We hope that our readers will find new and innovative ways to make these approaches more powerful and extend the journey to understand the principles that hold learning and intelligence. For further practice and reading on Machine Learning and Spark refer `https://www.kaggle.com` and `https://databricks.com/spark/` respectively.

Index

2

20 Newsgroups dataset
  about 415, 417
  and TF-IDF features, document similarity 432
  feature hashing 428
  raw features, comparing with processed TF-IDF
    features 438
  reference link 415
  stemming 427
  stop words, removing 422
  terms, excluding on frequency 425
  text classifier, training TF-IDF used 435
  TF-IDF features, extracting 415
  TF-IDF model, building 428
  TF-IDF weighting, examination 431
  tokenization 419
  tokenization, improving 420
  Word2Vec models, creating with Spark ML 443
  Word2Vec models, training with Spark MLlib 442

A

Abstract Window Toolkit (AWT) 392
accumulator
  about 23, 24
  reference link 24
accuracy, classifications model 257
additive smoothing
  reference link 278
Akaike information criterion (AIC)
  about 301
  reference link 301
Algorithmic Optimizations 121
algorithms supported
  classification 119
  clustering 120
  regression 120

ALS model 197
  evaluation 208
alternating least squares (ALS) 49, 184
Amazon EC2
  references 38
  Spark cluster, launching 38
  Spark, executing 37
Amazon Elastic Map Reduce
  reference link 43
  Spark, configuring 43
  Spark, executing 43
Apache Spark
  about 9
  data pipeline 115
association rules learning 54
AUC 260
average precision at K (APK) 212

B

backpropagation 251
bag-of-words model
  about 161, 412
  reference link 413
  stemming 162
  stop words removal 162
  tokenization 162
  vectorization 162
base form 427
batch interval 450
batch machine learning system
  versus real time machine learning system 114
bike sharing dataset
  features, extracting 289
  reference link 289, 294
  regression model, training 296
BikeSharingExecutor 295
binary classification 225

bisecting K-means
    about 51, 364
    iterations 372
    training 365
    WSSSE 372
Breeze
    vectors 72
broadcast variable
    about 23
    reference link 24
Broyden-Fletcher-Goldfarb-Shanno (BFGS) 55
built-in evaluation functions, MLlib
    MAP 218
    MSE 217
    RMSE 217
    using 217
business use cases
    customer segmentation 107
    for machine learning system 106
    personalization 106
    predictive analytics 108
    predictive modeling 108
    targeted marketing 107

C

caching
    with Spark Streaming 453
calculus
    about 65, 98
    differential calculus 98
    integral calculus 99
    Lagranges multipliers 99
categorical features 155, 156
classification 119
classification algorithm
    decision trees 52
classification models, types
    about 227
    decision trees 244
    ensemble method 247
    linear models 228
    Naive Bayes model 241
classification models
    about 108
    accuracy 257

AUC 260
    feature standardization 263
    performance, evaluating 257
    performance, improving 263
    precision 259
    prediction error 257
    prediction, generating for Kaggle 256
    prediction, generating for StumbleUpon 256
    recall 259
    ROC curve 260
    training 254
    training, on Kaggle 254
    training, on StumbleUpon 254
    tuning parameters 263
    using 256
Cloud Dataproc
    about 57
    Google Compute Engine, Spark cluster 57
    Hadoop versions 57
    job, submitting 61
    reference link 58
    Spark versions 57
cluster 337
cluster boundaries
    iterations, effect 379
cluster predictions
    movie clusters, interpreting 353, 355
clustering models, types
    about 338
    hierarchical clustering 345
    K-means, clustering 338
    mixture model 345
clustering models
    cluster predictions, interpreting on MovieLens
        dataset 353
    external evaluation metrics 360
    internal evaluation metrics 359
    performance metrics, computing on MovieLens
        dataset 360
    performance, improving 359
    training 350
    training, on MovieLens dataset 351
clustering
    about 50, 120
    as dimensionality reduction 386

GMM, used 376
collaborative filtering
  about 177
  Latent factor model (LFM) 179
  neighborhood methods 178
Comma-Separated-Value (CSV) file 26
Command Line
  Scala environment, setting up 69
complex numbers 70
components, machine learning system
  data cleansing 110
  data ingestion 109
  data pipeline, in Apache Spark 115
  data storage 109
  data transformation 110
  loop testing 112
  model deployment 112
  model feedback 113
  model integration 112
  model monitoring 113
  model training 112
computations 121
content-based filtering 177
convergence 339
corpus 412
cross-validation
  about 279
  reference link 280
customer lifetime value (CLTV) 283
customer segmentation 107

D

data cleansing 110
data ingestion 109
data pipeline
  in Apache Spark 115
data storage 109
data transformation 110
data
  exploring 129
  features, extracting 155, 190, 412
  missing data, filling 153
  movie dataset 141
  processing 152
  transforming 152

user dataset, exploring 131
  viewing 129
DataFrame 480
DataFrame, Spark
  about 25
  reference link 447
DataFrame, SparkR 35
dataset
  accessing publicly 126
  count bar chart, rating 147
  MovieLens 100k dataset 127
  number distribution, rating 149
  rating 145
Decision Tree Pipeline
  about 491
  reference link 492
decision trees
  about 276, 302
  depth 277, 329
  impurity 277
  maximum bins 330
  reference link 245, 246, 286, 306
degrees of freedom 301
derived features 158
differential calculus 98
dimensionality reduction model
  about 53, 383
  clustering as 386
  evaluating 405
  features, extracting from data 387
  matrix factorization, relationship with 386
  PCA 384
  PCA, and SVD relationship between 403
  PCA, executing on LWF dataset 398
  PCA, used for projecting on LFW dataset 402
  reference link 386
  singular values, evaluating on LFW dataset 406
  SVD 385
  training 398
  types 384
  using 402
directed acyclic graph (DAG) 485
discretized stream (DStream) 450
distributed vector representations 441
divisive clustering 346

document 412

E

Eigenfaces
  about 399
  reference link 400
eigenvectors 88
Elastic Cloud Compute (EC2) 10
ensemble method
  about 247, 306
  GBT 249, 309
  multilayer perceptron classifier 251
  random forests 247, 306
Estimator Logistic Regression 484
estimators 480
evaluation metrics algorithm 54
Expectation-Maximization (EM) 375
external evaluation metrics
  about 360
  reference link 360

F

facial images
  converting, to grayscale 392
  feature vectors, extracting 395
  loading 392
  resizing 392
false positive rate (FPR) 261
fault tolerance
  with Spark Streaming 453
feature hashing
  about 413
  reference link 414
feature mixing
  reference link 414
features, classification models
  about 267
  correct form of data, using 270
  cross-validation 279
  tuning model, parameters 271
features
  about 155
  categorical features 155, 156
  derived features 158
  extracting, from bike sharing dataset 289

extracting, from data 190, 253, 289, 346, 387, 412
extracting, from LFW dataset 387
extracting, from MovieLens 100k dataset 190
extracting, from MovieLens dataset 346
extracting, packages used 169
feature hashing 413
normalizing features 167
numerical features 155, 156
standard scalar 173
standardization 263
term weighting schemes 412
text features 156, 161
TF-IDF features, extracting from 20 Newsgroups
  dataset 415
fields
  about 70
  complex numbers 70
  hyperplanes 78
  real numbers 70
  vector operations 74
  vector spaces 71
  vector types 72
  vectors 71
  vectors, in Breeze 72
  vectors, in machine learning 78
  vectors, in Spark 73
FP-growth algorithm
  about 54, 219
  applying, to Movie Lens Data 222
  sample 219
frequent pattern (FP) 219
function
  constant function 94
  functional composition 94
  Gaussian function 94
  hypothesis 95
  identity function 93
  linear functions 92
  polynomial function 93
  probability distribution function 94
  types 92
fuzzy K-means 345

G

Gaussian Mixture Model (GMM)
  about 50, 375
  clustering, item data plotting 378
  clustering, user plotting 378
  used, for clustering 376
generalized linear models (GLMs) 53, 298
GloVe
  reference link 441
Google Cloud SDK
  reference link 57
Gradient Boosted Pipeline 496
gradient descent 96
Gradient-Boosted Tree (GBT)
  about 249, 309, 496
  iterations 332
  MaxBins 333
  reference link 251, 309, 498
GraphX
  about 122
  reference link 122

H

Hadoop Distributed File System (HDFS) 11
Hadoop
  version 57
hash collisions 414
Hessian 98
Hierarchical Cluster Analysis (HCA) 51
hierarchical clustering
  about 345
  reference link 346
hold-out set 280

I

impression 228
initialization method
  reference link 344
input source 450
integral calculus 99
IntelliJ
  Scala environment, setting up 67
internal evaluation metrics
  about 359

reference link 359
inverse document frequency (IDF) 170, 412
item data
  iterations, effect on cluster boundaries 379
item recommendations
  about 202
  inspecting 207
  movies, generating for MovieLens 100k dataset
    202
iterations
  effect, on WSSSE 361

J

Java Development Kit (JDK) 11
Java Runtime Environment (JRE) 11
Java Virtual Machine (JVM) 10
Java
  Spark program 29

K

K-fold cross-validation 280
K-means ++
  about 344
  reference link 344
K-means
  about 50
  cluster predictions, interpreting on MovieLens
    dataset 353
  clustering 338
  clustering models, performance evaluating 359
  initialization method 344
  reference link 339
  training 350
Kaggle
  about 127
  classification model, training 254
  predictions, generating 256
  reference link 127
KDnuggets
  about 127
  reference link 127

L

Labeled Faces in the Wild (LFW) dataset
  about 387

face data, exploring 388
face data, visualizing 390
facial images, extracting as vectors 391
features, extracting 387
normalization 396
PCA, executing 398
PCA, used for data projecting 402
references 387
singular value, evaluating for SVD 406
Lagranges multipliers 99
Latent Dirichlet Allocation (LDA) 51
Latent factor model (LFM) 179
Least Squares 120
least squares regression
  about 285
  reference link 285
likelihood 97
lineage 453
linear algebra
  about 65, 67
  fields 70
  function 91
  matrix 79
  Scala environment, setting in IntelliJ 67
  Scala environment, setting on Command Line 69
linear models
  about 228, 272
  intercept 326
  iterations 273, 322
  Kaggle, features extracting 233
  L1 regularization 325
  L2 regularization 325
  logistic regression 230
  multinomial logistic regression 231
  references 229
  regularization 275
  step size 274, 323
  StumbleUpon, dataset visualizing 232
  StumbleUpon, features extracting 233
  StumbleUponExecutor 235
  SVM 239
linear regression 296
link function 228
Logistic Regression Model 484
logistic regression

about 52, 229, 230
reference link 301
loop testing 112

M

machine learning algorithms
  ALS 49
  classification algorithm 52
  clustering 50
  FP-growth algorithm 54
  GMM 50
  HCA 51
  k-means 50
  LDA 51
  Limited-Memory BFGS (L-BFGS) 55
  Naive Bayes 52
  PIC 50
  random forest algorithm 53
  streaming k-means 51
  supported, by Spark 49
machine learning pipeline
  example 488
  StumbleUponExecutor object 490
machine learning system
  about 65, 104
  architecture 116
  business use cases 106
  components 109
  reinforcement learning 104
  supervised learning 104, 108
  types 108
  unsupervised learning 104, 108
matrix factorization
  about 179
  ALS 185
  basic model 184
  explicit matrix factorization 180
  implicit matrix factorization 183
  relationship with 386
matrix operations
  ceiling 86
  elementwise addition 84
  elementwise argmax 86
  elementwise comparison 85
  elementwise max 86

elementwise multiplication 85
elementwise sum 85
floor 87
inplace addition 85
matrix
  determinant 87
  distributed matrix, in spark 82
  eigenvalues 88
  eigenvectors 88
  in machine learning 90
  in Spark 80
  singular value decomposition 89
  types 79
Maven build tool
  about 30
  reference link 30
Maximum A Posteriori (MAP) 375
Mean Absolute Error (MAE) 287, 288
Mean Average Precision at K (MAPK) 208, 212
mean-squared error (MSE) 208, 210, 287, 473
Mesos 10
mini-batches 449
mixture model
  about 345
  reference link 345
MLlib version
  comparing 123
  Spark 1.6, to Spark 2.0 123
MLlib
  about 117
  algorithms supported, comparison 119
  developer APIs 120
  methods 120
  Spark Integration 122
  Spark ML, performance improvement over 117
  URL, for optimizing 121
  vision 122
model deployment 112
model feedback 113
model integration 112
model monitoring 113
model training 112
Movie Lens Data
  FP-Growth algorithm, applying 222
MovieLens 100k dataset

about 127
features, extracting 190
recommendation model, training 192
reference link 127
MovieLens dataset
  about 127
  cluster predictions, interpreting 353
  clustering models, training 351
  features, extracting 346
  performance metrics, computing 360
MovieStream 105
multilayer perceptron classifier
  reference link 253

N

Naive Bayes model
  about 52, 241
  reference link 52
  references 241, 243
Naive Bayes Pipeline
  about 493
  reference link 495
Natural Language Processing (NLP) 412
normalizing features
  about 167
  ML, used 168
numerical features 155, 156

O

online learning model
  evaluation 472
  performance, comparing with Spark Streaming 473
online learning
  about 114, 448
  streaming K-means 472
  streaming regression model 465
  streaming regression program 466
  with Spark Streaming 465
online machine learning
  reference link 448
optical character recognition (OCR) 104
overfitting
  reference link 276

P

packages
 IDF 170
 skip-gram model 171
 tf-idf 169
 used, for feature extraction 169
 Word2Vec tools 171
ParamGridBuilder
 reference link 236
Pearson correlation coefficients 179
personalization 106
Pipeline API 121
pipeline
 about 479
 components 480
 creating, in Spark 488
 DataFrame 480
 estimators 480
 reference link 483, 484
 transformers 480
 working 483
PLANET project
 reference link 121
plotting 100
positive class 225
posterior 97
Power Iteration Clustering (PIC) 50
precision-recall (PR) 260
precision
 about 259
 reference link 260
prediction error 257
predictive analytics 108
Predictive Model Markup Language (PMML)
 about 54
 references 121
predictive modeling 108
PrefixSpan algorithm 54
principal component analysis (PCA)
 about 53, 90, 120, 384
 Eigenfaces, interpreting 401
 Eigenfaces, visualizing 399
 executing, on LFW dataset 398
 reference link 386

SVD, relationship between 403
 used, for projecting data on LFW dataset 402
prior 97
probability classifier 52
producer application 455
public datasets, AWS
 about 126
 reference link 126
PySpark 33
Python
 Spark program 33

R

R-squared coefficient 289
R
 about 17
 Spark program 35
random forest algorithm 53
random forests
 about 247, 306
 reference link 248, 309
Read-Eval-Print-Loop (REPL) 15
real number 70
real time machine learning system
 versus batch machine learning 114
recall
 about 259
 reference link 260
recommendation engines
 about 175
 effective, scenarios 176
recommendation model, types
 about 176
 collaborative filtering 177
 content-based filtering 177
 matrix factorization 179
recommendation model
 ALS Model 197
 ALS model, evaluation 208
 MAPK 212
 MLlib's built-in evaluation functions, using 217
 MSE 210
 performance, evaluating 208
 training 192
 training, implicit feedback data used 195

training, on MovieLens 100k dataset 192
types 176
user recommendations 198
using 196
recommendations 107
Red, Blue, and Green (RGB) 391
regression 120
regression models, types
about 284
decision trees 286
least squares regression 285
regression models
BikeSharingExecutor 295
decision trees 302
ensemble method 306
generalized linear regression 298
linear regression 296
MAE 288
MSE 287
performance, evaluating 287
performance, improving 313
R-squared coefficient 289
RMSE 287
RMSLE 288
training 294
training, on bike sharing dataset 296
tuning parameters 313
using 294
regularization
references 275
reinforcement learning 104
Resilient Distributed Dataset (RDD)
about 18
caching 22
creating 19
reference link 23
Spark operations 19
ROC curve 260
Root Mean Squared Error (RMSE) 208, 287, 473
Root Mean Squared Log Error (RMSLE) 288

S

Scala Build Tool (SBT)
about 27
reference link 27

Scala chart
reference link 135
Scala environment
setting up, in IntelliJ 67
setting, Command Line 69
Scala
reference link 441
Spark program 26
SchemaRDD 25
scikit-learn
reference link 401
singular value decomposition (SVD)
about 53, 384, 385
PCA, relationship between 403
reference link 386
singular values 406
singular values, evaluating on LFW dataset 406
singular values 385
skip-gram model 171, 441
SORT benchmark
URL 56
Spark 1.6
to Spark 2.0 123
Spark 2.0
features 123
text classification 439
Spark cluster
about 12
creating 58
launching 38
on Cloud Dataproc, Google Compute Engine 57
references 13
Spark ecosystem
leveraging 122
Spark ML
performance, improvement over MLlib 117
using, benefits 55
Word2Vec models, creating on 20 Newsgroups
dataset 443
Spark MLlib
Word2Vec models, training on 20 Newsgroups
dataset 442
Spark program
in Java 29
in Python 33

in R 35
in Scala 26
reference link 33
Spark programming model
about 13
accumulator 23
broadcast variable 23
RDD 18
Spark shell 15
SparkConf 14
SparkContext 14
SparkSession 15
Spark shell 15
Spark Streaming application
creating 454, 458
Spark Streaming receivers 450
Spark Streaming
about 122, 449
actions 452
caching 453
fault tolerance 453
input source 450
online learning 465
online learning model, performance comparing
473
reference link 122
references 454
state, tracking 451
transformation 450, 451
window operators 452
Spark
configuring, on Amazon Elastic Map Reduce 43
DataFrame 25
executing, on Amazon EC2 37
executing, on Amazon Elastic Map Reduce 43
installing, locally 11
machine learning algorithms, supported 49
reference link 11
references 9, 22
setting up, locally 11
UI 47
vectors 73
version 57
SparkConf 14
SparkContext 14

SparkR
about 35
DataFrames 35
SparkSession 15
SQL operations
reference link 447
standard scalar 173
stateful streaming 463
stemming
about 162, 427
reference link 427
stochastic gradient descent (SGD) 184, 272, 448
stochastic subgradient descent (SGD) 54
stop words removal 162
stop words
about 422
reference link 424
stream processing
about 449
caching, with Spark Streaming 453
fault tolerance, with Spark Streaming 453
producer application 455
Spark Streaming 449
Spark Streaming application, creating 454
Spark streaming application, creating 458
stateful streaming 463
streaming analytics 461
streaming K-means
about 472
reference link 472
streaming regression model 465
streaming regression program
about 466
streaming data producer, creating 467
streaming regression model, creating 469
structured streaming 477
StumbleUpon
classification model, training 254
predictions, generating 256
references 231
StumbleUponExecutor
about 490
reference link 235, 491
supervised learning 104, 108
Support Vector Machine (SVM) 229

reference link 239

T

target variable
  log-transformed targets, training impacts 317
  training, created to evaluate parameters 321
  transforming 313
targeted marketing 107
Term Frequency 412
term frequency-inverse document frequency (tf-idf)
  about 169, 412
  features, and 20 Newsgroups dataset document
    similarity 432
  features, extracting from 20 Newsgroups dataset
    415
  processed features, comparing with raw features
    on 20 Newsgroups dataset 438
  reference link 413
  used, for training text classifier on 20 Newsgroups
    dataset 435
  using 432
term weighting schemes 412
test set 280
text classification
  with Spark 2.0 439
text classifier
  training, on 20 Newsgroups dataset tf-idf used
    435
text data
  features 411
text features
  about 156, 161
  extraction 162
  sparse vectors, from titles 165
text processing
  impact, evaluating 438
  raw features, comparing with processes TF-IDF
    features on 20 Newsgroups dataset 438
tokenization 162, 419
tokenizer 484
tokens 419
top-down clustering 346
training set 280
Trainvalidationsplit
  reference link 237

transformers 480
tree clustering 345
true positive rate (TPR) 260
tuning model
  decision tree, data splitting 321
  decision tree, parameter setting impact 328
  decision trees 276
  Gradient Boosted Trees, parameter setting
    impact 332
  linear models 272
  linear models, parameter setting impact 321
  Naive Bayes model 278
  parameters 320
  testing sets, creating to evaluate parameters 321
tuning parameters
  target variable, transforming 313

U

UCI Machine Learning Repository
  about 126
  reference link 126
unsupervised learning 104, 108, 337
user dataset
  exploring 131
  occupation, counting 137
User Interface (UI)
  in Spark 47
user recommendations
  about 198
  inspecting 200
  item recommendations 202
  movie, generating from MovieLens 100k dataset
    199

V

variance 286
Vector Assembler 294
Vector Indexer 294
vector operations
  about 74
  add operation 74
  comparing 77
  dot operation 75
  geometrical representation 77
  mean, finding 76

multiply operation 75
normalization 76
vector spaces 71
vectorization 162
vectors
  about 71
  in Breeze 72
  in Spark 73

W

windowing 452

within cluster sum of squared errors (WCSS) 339
word stem 427
Word2Vec models
  about 441
  creating, with Spark ML on 20 Newsgroups
    dataset 443
  reference link 441
  training, with Spark MLlib on 20 Newsgroups
    dataset 442
Word2Vec tools 171
WSSSE
  iterations, effect 361